Freedom and Law

Freedom and Law

A Jewish-Christian Apologetics

Randi Rashkover

FORDHAM UNIVERSITY PRESS
NEW YORK 2011

Copyright © 2011 Fordham University Press

All rights reserved. No part of this publication may be reproduced, stored in a retrieval system, or transmitted in any form or by any means—electronic, mechanical, photocopy, recording, or any other—except for brief quotations in printed reviews, without the prior permission of the publisher.

Fordham University Press has no responsibility for the persistence or accuracy of URLs for external or third-party Internet websites referred to in this publication and does not guarantee that any content on such websites is, or will remain, accurate or appropriate.

Fordham University Press also publishes its books in a variety of electronic formats. Some content that appears in print may not be available in electronic books.

Library of Congress Cataloging-in-Publication Data

Rashkover, Randi.
   Freedom and law : a Jewish-Christian apologetics / Randi Rashkover.
     p. cm.
   Includes bibliographical references and index.
   ISBN 978-0-8232-3452-3 (cloth : alk. paper)
   ISBN 978-0-8232-3453-0 (pbk. : alk. paper)
   ISBN 978-0-8232-3454-7 (epub)
    1. Liberty—Religious aspects. 2. Law—Biblical teaching. 3. Judaism—Relations—Christianity. 4. Christianity and other religions—Judaism. I. Title.
   BL65.L52R37   2011
   296.3′96—dc22

2011007166

Printed in the United States of America
13 12 11   5 4 3 2 1
First edition

*To my husband, Andy,
and my daughter, Anna*

CONTENTS

Introduction: Emancipating Law   1

PART I. THE LOGIC OF EXCEPTIONALISM

1. Sacrificing Election: Divine Freedom and Its Abuses   9
2. Monotheism and Exceptionalism   43
3. Modern Judaism, Law, and Exceptionalism   76

PART II. THE LOGIC OF THE LAW

4. The Biblical Theology of Abiding   101
5. The New Thinking and the Order of Wisdom   143

PART III. JUSTIFICATION IN THE LAW
AND JEWISH-CHRISTIAN APOLOGETICS

6. The Law of Freedom, the Freedom of the Law   187
7. Christianity and the Law: The Law as the Form of the Gospel   226

    Notes   275
    Bibliography   317
    Index   327

Freedom and Law

INTRODUCTION

Emancipating Law

> Said Rabbi Joshua the son of Levi: Every day, an echo resounds from Mount Horeb (Sinai) proclaiming and saying: . . . (Exodus 32:16): And the tablets are the work of G-d, and the writing is G-d's writing, engraved on the tablets; read not 'engraved' (*charut*) but 'liberty' (*chairut*). . . .
>
> —PIRKEI AVOT 6:2

Freedom and Law: A Jewish-Christian Apologetics is the result of unfinished business remaining after my account of Jewish and Christian witness in *Revelation and Theopolitics: Barth, Rosenzweig and the Politics of Praise*. Two issues emerged in particular:

- The question of whether Jews and Christians whose religious lives centered upon doxological praise of God could authentically care for nonbelievers without imposing their theological position upon them
- My own realization that *Revelation and Theopolitics* had only just begun to develop an account of the character and implications of the reality of divine freedom

This book is the fortunate by-product of my effort to expand the analysis of divine freedom and my discovery of how this more-developed account dramatically changed my picture of key Jewish and Christian ideas: most importantly, divine law and divine judgment on the one hand, and human freedom and human rest on the other hand. The reason I describe this book as a fortunate by-product is because while I studied the correlation between divine and human freedom, I stumbled upon a conception of how Jews and Christians can speak to persons outside their communities, which I had not recognized earlier as an element in the theology of praise.

Consequently, *Freedom and Law: A Jewish-Christian Apologetics* is a book about the paradigm-altering power of divine freedom. The volume showcases a third aspect in a triad of theological freedoms. In *Revelation and Theopolitics*, I outlined the character of divine freedom as radically other, and the freedom it afforded human persons to recognize God through a life of communal testimony. My purpose in editing *Liturgy, Time and the Politics of Redemption* was to describe the freedom of God to draw near us in our prayer and the reciprocal freedom of persons to petition God for what they and others need. This book illuminates the freedom of God to issue judgments or order wisely and the correlative human freedom to recognize others. The focus here is on how divine freedom expresses itself in divine law, and by extension, grounds the reality of human freedom as ordered within this law.

The primary goal of *Freedom and Law* is to unveil the transformation of ideas that arises from the identification of law with freedom: in particular, the new view of the relationship between the divine-human encounter and the reality of human desire, the production of knowledge, and the meaning of power. Beyond this, it is my hope that readers of this book will recognize how this presentation of the freedom of divine law and its emancipatory effects upon Jewish and Christian social engagement challenges a contemporary wave of scholarship that identifies Jewish law as the originary source of polemic between nations, and therefore as historically responsible for the exceptionalism that undergirds contemporary conflict in the work of such recent thinkers as Jacob Taubes, Giorgio Agamben, and Alain Badiou. *Freedom and Law* consists of three main sections: The Logic of Exceptionalism, The Logic of Law, and Justification in the Law and Jewish-Christian Apologetics.

Part I: The Logic of Exceptionalism

Part I analyzes the logic of exceptionalism. Exceptionalism characterizes a philosophical or theological account that arises from a polemical context and establishes an adversarial relation between peoples by portraying the adversary as false. The logic of exceptionalism is reductionist in so far as it evaluates all claims in view of a criterion of truth but as rooted in desire, is doomed to its own falsification because the desire for a truth-claim does not operate as a sufficient justification for truth. Exceptionalism, or what may alternatively be called the "logic of sacrifice," inevitably gives rise to feelings of guilt and anxiety on the part of persons subjected to these unyielding and narrow standards. This book maintains that the logic of exceptionalism permeates forms of philosophical and cultural thinking, but in particular, Jewish and Christian theology. In Chapter 1, "Sacrificing Election: Divine Freedom and Its Abuses," I discuss recent scholarship in political theology that identifies this logic with Jewish law, and in particular, the work of Giorgio Agamben. Despite Agamben's characterization of Jewish law as exceptionalist, I argue that a careful reading of Agamben's *The Time That Remains*—and in particular, what he refers to as the "messianic 'as not'"—displays a logic of exceptionalism within Agamben's own thinking and represents a strain of exceptionalism within Christian theology predicated upon a misunderstanding of the structure and logic of sovereignty.

In Chapter 2, "Monotheism and Exceptionalism," I take up the challenge presented in recent scholarship by Regina Schwartz that deepens antipathy toward Jewish law by rooting the so-called exceptionalism of Jewish law in the larger and more damaging context of Jewish monotheism. In my response to Schwartz, I enlist the aid of Moshe Halbertal's and Avishai Margalit's *Idolatry*, which systematically deconstructs overly generalized claims concerning the analytic link between monotheism and intolerance. Halbertal's and Margalit's book indicates that the greatest challenge to a successful apologetics resides in Jewish philosophical claims asserting the absolute "error" of idolatrous positions turning to Moses Maimonides' theology as their prime example. In the final section of the chapter, I examine the charge of exceptionalism launched against Maimonides' account of divine nature. I conclude that Maimonides' account of divine freedom is limited to his account of God's creation of the world, and therefore his theology exemplifies how a particular and absolutely asserted conception of God can perpetuate an exceptionalism over and against any reality, divine or otherwise outside itself.

In Chapter 3, "Modern Judaism, Law, and Exceptionalism," I examine the flip side of the dialectic of desire whereby desire is not dismissed in the name of a higher theological truth but rather is crowned superior to and unregulated in its relation to law. This chapter examines a renewed focus upon law within a strain of modern Jewish thought, beginning with the work of Baruch Spinoza and continuing into the work of Gillian Rose and David Novak. Each of these thinkers presents a nonrevealed and materialist conception of the law, by which I mean a notion of law in which human desire assumes a central role. Here, I argue that despite the significant headway made by these thinkers in rerouting philosophical analyses toward a focus upon the law, nonrevelatory law stands in perpetual tension with the nature of human desire, which it is designed to delimit.

Part I concludes that when desire remains unadjudicated within the production of knowledge, it produces strains of polemical thinking, whose effects appear not only in cultural, political, and philosophical thinking but most significantly for this volume, in theological accounts of the divine-human relationship in Judaism and Christianity. The problem of exceptionalist logic is that it assumes that election satisfies desire. *Freedom and Law* argues that election motors desire as desire and not as the pretense to its own *telos*. The impact of the dialectic of desire upon characterizations of monotheism and election in both traditions has rendered successful, nonpolemical Jewish-Christian relations near impossible.

Part II: The Logic of the Law

In Part II, I argue that one cannot invoke a doctrine of election without rigorous scrutiny of texts that portray an electing God and elected people. When we scrutinize these texts, the character of freedom and law shows itself to be different than that found in exceptionalist logics. More specifically, freedom and law show themselves to be reciprocal concepts: Neither divine freedom nor human freedom can be thought apart from the law of God's affirming difference from everything else—a law that is performed in and through the religious life and practices of persons who dwell within the affirming order of this difference.

Chapter 4, "The Biblical Theology of Abiding," explores the scriptural basis of the notion of divine freedom as law, and in particular, the relationship between this account of God and the character of rest and security that it affords persons as they operate within this law. Here, I also discuss how this focus on the rest and order of covenantal existence generates a new conception of the meaning of divine wisdom and judgment and the connection between this account of judgment and the nonteleological character of divine forgiveness.

Chapter 5, "The New Thinking and the Order of Wisdom," offers a philosophical presentation of the logic of law first through an examination of Franz Rosenzweig's New Thinking as an extension of F. W. J. Schelling's theology of divine freedom. Schelling's theology introduces philosophically the link between divine freedom and law earlier introduced in the Biblical analysis of the God. For Schelling, divine freedom expresses itself inevitably as the lawful affirmation of what is other than God. In this account, freedom and law are not diametrically opposed but reciprocal concepts so far as they emerge first from an act of divine freedom and subsequently infuse the performance of human freedom. Rosenzweig's essay, "The New Thinking," deepens the analysis of the nexus between divine freedom and divine law and articulates the impact of both upon the freedom of human action and knowledge of the world. Here, I show how the logic of the law introduces a paradigm shift in analyses of how human desire relates to power and the production of knowledge about the world—or what is history, politics, and philosophy—and compare this shift with Michel Foucault's notion of genealogy. Ultimately, I argue that while both knowledge within the law and Foucault's genealogy expose the dialectics of desire operative in knowledge production, only knowledge within the law affords new nonpolemical and nonreductionist approaches to intellectual history, politics, and philosophy insofar as still motivated by desire, lawful knowledge retains the right or freedom to issue truth claims when these claims are justified within the lawful order of the freedom of others to assert alternative claims.

Part III: Justification in the Law and Jewish-Christian Apologetics

Part III constitutes the centerpiece of my account of the logic of the law. In this part, I apply the logic of the law to the encounter between God and persons or "election" and examine the impact of the logic of the law on Jewish-Christian apologetics. Chapter 6, "The Law of Freedom, the Freedom of the Law," begins with an expanded account of Rosenzweig's phenomenology of revelation, where I argue that the event of revelation is the event of a divine, unconditional gift of love. As unconditional gift, divine love registers as divine command to receive or testify to this love. The inevitable link between unconditional love and command reflects, I argue, the nature of divine law as the free affirmation of the difference between God and persons. Divine command does not dialectically negate that which fails to conform to its standard. Rather, within the order of divine freedom, divine command mandates a recognition of a divine-human difference, which is the condition of the possibility of human freedom. If God were not other, we would not be free.

Beyond this, Chapter 6 analyzes the character of human freedom, which here emerges—and in particular, what it means to say that persons are justified in the law. Existentially, persons ordered by the law are free in their desire when human desire is, on the one hand, affirmed by divine love and differentiated from divine love, on the other hand, so far as it is no longer identified as the agency of its own teleological satisfaction. Desire remains desire, and persons may rest in the self-consciousness of who they are in the order of God. By extension, persons ordered by the law are emancipated from the moral guilt and anxiety that inevitably accrue from their failure to fully perform an ideal or an exceptionalist standard of truth when that standard conflicts with fundamental human needs.

With this focus upon the character of justification within the law, Chapter 6 moves into an account of the impact of the logic of the law for how we understand the meaning of religious truth. As recipients of divine revelation, persons are epistemologically justified in their religious assertions to the extent that they may admit the *possibility* of the truth of exterior positions. *Exterior claims* include claims made prior to or after by persons in their own tradition (i.e., historically exterior claims) along with claims made by persons outside their tradition.

Chapter 6 ends with a description of how this epistemological account installs a new post-polemical logic for Jewish-Christian relations. Historically speaking, apologetics required the defense of one's position to a nonbeliever. Alternatively, the logic of the law situates all epistemological defense or justification within the order or freedom of God. If the condition of the possibility of my claim is the reality of divine freedom, such freedom also justifies the possibility of another's claim. Consequently, the condition of the possibility of my claim is the possibility of the truth-value of another's claim and to defend my tradition means to recognize the possibility of truths exterior to my own. Here, I draw from Rosenzweig's essay, "Apologetic Thinking," where he identifies apologetic defense with my freedom to "admit the lie" that any one of my claims has universal applicability or truth. Apologetics is rerouted from a tug-of-war over competing truths into the exercise of exposure to the range of other possible claims, and Jewish-Christian relations acquire a basis for a curriculum of free learning within the law.

Finally, Chapter 7, "Christianity and the Law: The Law as the Form of the Gospel," examines Christianity's relation to the law and justifies the utility of an apologetics of the law for Christian theology through an analysis of Karl Barth's notion of the freedom of the law. Part III concludes with an interpretation of the nexus between law and wisdom in the Book of Job and demonstrates the overlap between my reading of Job and that provided by Barth in the *Church Dogmatics*.

PART ONE

The Logic of Exceptionalism

ONE

Sacrificing Election: Divine Freedom and Its Abuses

The epistolary correspondence between Franz Rosenzweig and Eugene Rosenstock-Huessy written in 1916 during the chaos and anxiety of WWI presents contemporary readers with one of the most perplexing accounts of Jewish-Christian relations to date. This conversation is often hailed as a pioneering example of the benefits of dialogical-thinking for Jewish-Christian relations, but it is no such thing.[1] Little work has been done to shed light on the challenges presented in these letters.[2] It is the central contention of this chapter that the letters expose two dramatically different approaches to Jewish-Christian relations—what I will refer to as a logic of law and a logic of sacrifice, the former seen in Rosenzweig's position and the latter in Rosenstock-Huessy's position. In this chapter, I will argue further that by exposing these two different logics, these letters educate contemporary readers to the long-standing dominance and danger of the logic of sacrifice. What is at stake in the logic of law will develop over the course of this entire book. This chapter aims to give a detailed exposition of the logic of sacrifice and the negative effects that it has produced as the dominant (and recently resurgent) approach to Christian attitudes toward Judaism and offers an introduction to the logic of the law as first presented by Rosenzweig in his responses to Rosenstock's correspondence.

The letters between Rosenzweig and Rosenstock-Huessy do presuppose some common ground: in particular, the shared influence of the work of F. W. J. Schelling. The chapter will discuss Schelling's theology of divine freedom as presented in his 1815 version of the *Weltalter*. More specifically, the chapter will argue that while Schelling's *Weltalter* presents a philosophical basis to the logic of law, only Rosenzweig's letters reflect this logic in contrast to Rosenstock-Huessy, who appropriated aspects of Schelling's theology—and in particular, his language of the Johannine age—but reinterpreted these features into a larger account of the unique and universal significance of Christ. Consequently, the chapter will show how this shared interest in Schelling's theology ultimately failed to alter what in the end is a bold display of the dangers of a logic of sacrifice when applied to Christian-Jewish relations.

The Logic of Sacrifice: Exceptional Thinking and the "Outbidding" of Jewish Election

ROSENSTOCK-HUESSY

Rosenstock-Huessy's correspondence with Rosenzweig offers contemporary readers a fascinating introduction to the body of work produced throughout his lifetime.[3] Influenced in part by F. W. J. Schelling, Rosenstock-Huessy's work (like Rosenzweig's) bore the marks of a thinker unwilling to succumb to the stalemate of idealism and its implicit nod at state power expressed through systems and cultures of "expertise." While I will explore this link between Rosenstock-Huessy's speech-thinking and Schelling's account of knowledge and existence herein, suffice it to say here that Rosenstock-Huessy's commitment to overcoming idealism and rehabilitating speech as the organon of thought is already at work in the letters with Rosenzweig.[4] Speech, Rosenstock-Huessy tells us, is the only recourse that we have to overcoming the cult of the ego as it dominates philosophy, the sciences, and even religion. Introducing themes he will discuss in much greater detail in his later works,[5] Rosenstock-Huessy's letter to Rosenzweig dated Oct. 28, 1916 offers a microcosmic account of his overarching critique of naturalism without revelation. Left to its own devices, human thought functions from fear. Faced with the prospect of their own deaths, persons and cultures develop static world views that try and fail to shield us from change.

Natural understanding, then, knows front and back, left and right and helps itself in this enclosure with a net of analogies . . . because secretly it is frightened of its own powerlessness, it has hardened into concepts, metaphors that have become sacrosanct. To these it withdraws as if to a concrete base in order to be able to maintain the impregnability of the natural mind.[6]

But static systems insistently held, Rosenstock-Huessy asserts, not only fail to diminish fear but fix boundaries of self-certainty that as intractable have significant and serious consequences. Naturalism in philosophy, science, and religion denies history. Fear mandates an unchanging world and denies humanity a living sense of time as past, present, and future. Furthermore, fear circles us into isolation, and the more afraid we are, the less we relate and link to one another. This, Rosenstock-Huessy calls the "culture of paganism."

Naturalism, therefore, should not stand alone. Naturalism needs revelation, and in particular, a revelation of Word or Logos. Unlike the myths and systems of paganism, the revelation of Jesus as the Logos "is redeemed from itself, from the curse of always only being able to correct itself by itself. It enters into relationship with the object of knowledge."[7] While, Rosenstock-Huessy says, "the word of man must always become a concept and thereby stagnant and degenerate, God speaks to us with the 'word become flesh,'"[8] and in this way, the revelation of Christ as the Word of God illuminates or reveals a word and its encounter with alterity (word and body). Words are not meaningful monologically but are products of and shaped by encounters or relationships. The revelation of Christ redeems or transforms our language from word to speech and opens a horizon of changeability, response, and time. The revelation of Christ breaks through the solipsism and dogmatism of paganism and over and against the meaningless effort to deny the reality of change, invites those who witness to it into a new life that openly admits the reality of human death as change but promises the future possibility of a human communion and unity with others that alone affords a higher meaning. Historical meaning is restored. Not only invited into a phenomenology of encounter with another through the precedent of the Word of Christ, humanity gains also a thick account of the meaning of time—interpreted through the meaning of the Word of Christ itself. As the Logos, Jesus orients time—or, as Rosenstock says, constitutes the "bond from heaven to earth. He is the "measure of all things,"[9] the source of the possibility of continuous and changing meaning. Jesus is the center of history. That he has come constitutes our true past. That we hear him and can respond to him constitutes our present, and that all will communicate in a unity through a universal speech constitutes our promised future.

If the letters between Rosenzweig and Rosenstock-Huessy revolved solely around their shared reactions to German idealism and interest in revelation,[10] they would present a benign account of two young German thinkers shedding the world views of their fathers. However, the premise of the conversation is not the conversation. The real conversation is about Judaism and Christianity, and when applied to this particular issue, Rosenstock-Huessy's anti-idealism becomes much less innocent. The heart of Rosenstock-Huessy's account of Judaism through the lens of Christianity appears in the three letters dated October 28 and 30 and November 2, 1916. In what follows, I will show how Rosenstock-Huessy's account of Christianity's relationship to Judaism hinges upon a certain presentation of Christ's sacrifice on the cross. Understood in the aforementioned context, Christological sacrifice ought to mean nothing other than the opportunity for new life in a universal human community available to all. However, as I will show, placed in the context of a conversation about Judaism, this account of sacrifice presents a more complicated logic.

Let me begin by pointing out that for Rosenstock-Huessy, revelation assumes the form of a sacrifice, where sacrifice is understood as an act of currency and division. On the one hand, a sacrifice is a kind of currency—an offering of something for the benefit of accruing "credit" for that offering. Moreover, as an attainment of worth or value, a sacrifice divides or distinguishes that and those who have worth (currency) from that and/or those who do not. It is an act whereby participants are divided and identified by whether they have or have not participated. For Rosenstock-Huessy, Christ sacrifices himself. He offers himself up and accrues the benefits of this currency or "credit" for all those who witness it. Beyond this, however, Rosenstock-Huessy points out that those who are sacrificed for or by Christ are also sacrificed in Christ because to be a Christian is to make Christ's story one's own. Consequently, sacrifice also divides participants from themselves so far as sharing in Christ's story means offering what is inessential (their "life" and their bodies) for what is essential—their soul—or their eternal spirit. Christians cast off their inessential selves as sinners accruing the benefit of essential redemption. Citing from Deuteronomy 7:6, Rosenstock-Huessy uses the language of election to describe this phenomenon of communal sacrifice. The "new humanity from universal need and sin that ever newly born *corpus christianum* of all men of good will [is] a *'being called out from all people'*. . . ."[11] Those whose sin is redeemed through this sacrifice constitute the newly elect. But of course, there would be no newly elect if there were not a formerly elect, and the implication is that this sacrifice marks the "difference" precisely between the formerly elect and the newly elect—between Jews and Christians.

That Rosenstock-Huessy's notion of the Christological sacrifice performs what Jacob Taubes calls an "outbidding"[12] of Jewish election is best evidenced in his discussion of the difference between the sacrifice of Christ and the sacrifice of Abraham. Abraham, Rosenstock-Huessy says, sacrificed only his son: his people. Christ, however, sacrificed himself. Although it may seem that Rosenstock-Huessy is simply *distinguishing* between Abraham's classically pagan concern for the well-being of his own people and Christ's sacrifice of self as the branding of a new mode of relationality, his rhetoric assumes the logic of outbidding. My election, my sacrifice, exceeds your sacrifice and excludes you. It circumcises me in a new covenant in relation to which you are cast out, left over and inessential. Under the guise of recovering the language of Jewish election, Rosenstock-Huessy misuses and misrepresents the meaning of election to suggest a cutting away of what is essential from what is inessential. If, as I will argue later in this volume, election means difference, it does not mean a separation of the essential from the inessential. Rosenstock-Huessy's misuse of sacrifice to outbid Jewish election goes so far as to accuse Jews of squandering their own elective promises with Christians legitimized as their official inheritors.

The Jews have the saying that one day all people will come to Jerusalem to pray, and

> [T]hey always crucify again the one who came to make the word true. In appearance they wait upon the word of the Lord, but they have grown through and through so far away from revelation that they do everything they can to hinder its reality. With all the power of their being they set themselves against their own promises. . . .[13]

Viewed from this context, Jews have held two positions in relation to Christianity. Prior to the destruction of the Temple in 70 CE, Rosenstock-Huessy suggests, the Jews' rejection of Jesus as Christ verified the truth of the Christian message. Having "crucified Jesus," they legitimized the new sacrifice through which they were rendered valueless. After 70 CE, the Jews lose this function, according to Rosenstock-Huessy. Post-destruction of the Temple Christianity encounters other expressions of paganism that will suffice to legitimize its judgment against all those who do not accept Christ. "Christ [he says] today has people enough to crucify him!"[14] Post-70 Judaism loses its prior negative function. Replaced by non-Christian culture, Jews remain only as a ghostly people—a people devoid of land and language—a people denied spiritual and cultural currency, doomed to borrow life from others until its inevitable dying off. "God preserves his signs for as long as our blindness needs them. But one must not rely on them, as if they were eternal petrifications; rather must one hasten to drink from the source, to drain it dry before it runs dry."[15] So presented, the sacrifice of Christ spins a frame of meaning that at once divides those who participate in it from those who do not. Judaism is understood only in this context, interpreted through the lens of the "truly elect," and from this position, rendered illegitimate and then discarded.

The negative effects of Rosenstock-Huessy's logic of sacrifice go beyond this denigrating account of Judaism. While Judaism constitutes the prime target of Christian outbidding, its interpretation and dismissal is not the only casualty. As represented here, the capriciousness of the divine election through Christ marks a distinction between Christians and everyone else. Rosenstock-Huessy's indebtedness to the division between Christianity and paganism drives his account of modernity in *The Christian Future* as it drives his account of history generally speaking. All nations are either taken up into or not taken up into the Christian meaning of history. There is no middle ground. Cultures maintain no meaning outside of the Christian narrative. Euphemistically, Rosenstock-Huessy appeals to a post-ecclesiastical vision of Christianity, or what he, drawing from Schelling, refers to as the "Johannine" blurring of boundaries between cultures and nations. "Today the task is to translate Christianity for the single isolated individual who can be anything: Jew, Christian, pagan"[16]—but to translate Christianity for this individual is to discredit him as anything but Christian. No spiritual transcendence over and against the war of the nations,[17] Rosenstock-Huessy's Johannine vision is the reign of Christianity—a new and improved Christendom. And yet, when all is said and done, even the Christian is not shielded from the logic of sacrifice, expected as she is to divorce herself from her own body and her own love of life for the sake of an end of days—a higher union or communion—a more meaningful future to come. The logic of division leaves no one unscathed. Anything in the past or the present unrelated to the Christological expectation is offered up, and the Johannine era empties out into the nihilism of self, body, and life. "[H]e that would save his life shall lose it, and he who loses his life for Christ's sake shall find it: death has paradoxically become the key to everlasting life."[18]

THE EXCEPTIONALIST WORLD VIEW: AGAMBEN, TAUBES, AND BEYOND

This logic of sacrifice is not unique to Rosenstock-Huessy but has a long history in Christian, Jewish, and secular thought. The purpose of this volume is to focus on the theological expressions of this logic of sacrifice, or what I will also refer to as "exceptionalism" in conversation with a logic of law that I will argue when applied to Christianity, offers an alternative to Christian exceptionalism's dismissal of Judaism. Moreover, in my account of law, I will demonstrate how any theology of the Word, Jewish or Christian, demands this correction, and to the extent that it incorporates an understanding of the law into its account of the Word presents a basis for apologetic relations in a way that is prohibited by the logic of sacrifice.

However, before identifying the appearance of this logic of sacrifice in thinkers prior to and after Rosenstock-Huessy, it is important to hone in more exactly on the content and ramifications of this logic. Since the turn of the new millennium, there has been a resurgence of interest in Paul's work by contemporary philosophers and political theorists, such as Slavoj Žižek, Jacob Taubes, and Giorgio Agamben. These re-readings of Paul's work are important because each in its own way attempts to tackle the question of Paul's relation to Judaism and Jewish law. The effort to read Paul in his historical context and prior to centuries old categorizations of either Judaism or Christianity is surely to be appreciated. Later in this chapter, I will discuss Taubes's *The Political Theology of Paul*. Here, I am interested in tackling Giorgio Agamben's *The Time That Remains*. More specifically, I will argue that Agamben's linguistic analyses aside, *The Time That Remains* does little real historical-critical work contributing minimally to biblical scholarship's efforts to situate Paul's work in his original setting. By utter contrast, *The Time That Remains* does present us with a glowing example of the logic of sacrifice read into Paul's letters. In what follows, I will examine critically Agamben's *The Time That Remains* as a prime example of the logic of sacrifice, and with the additional help of Jacob Taubes's *The Political Theology of Paul*, explore the range and depth of negative consequences that emerge from this overarching logic—most significantly, although not exclusively, with respect to its presentation of Judaism.

My critique of Agamben's messianism begins with his account of the messianic "as not." Agamben extracts this concept from his reading of Paul's I Corinthians 7:29–32, and when citing Paul, says

> "But this I say, brethren, time contracted itself, the rest is, that even those having wives may be as not [*hōs mē*] having, and those weeping as not weeping, and those rejoicing as not rejoicing. . . . For passing away is the figure of this world. But I wish you to be without care." *Hōs mē*, "as not": this is the formula concerning messianic life and is the ultimate meaning of *klēsis*. Vocation calls for nothing and to no place.[19]

16   *The Logic of Exceptionalism*

This fundamental concept generates the full-flowering of Agamben's messianism, its methodological and social implications.[20] As I proceed to examine the elements of Agamben's messianic exceptionalism as exposed within his rhetorical and then epistemological and sociological privileging of the category of the "as not," I will introduce alternative positions emergent from the logic of the law as it will be presented in this book. At this introductory level, I will only name the alternative positions possible through the logic of the law and develop each alternative option in subsequent chapters.

The Division of the Division

For Agamben, the "as not" operates as the key to a messianic emancipation. Nonetheless, it is my contention here that the "as not" introduces the logic of exceptionalism or sacrifice into Agamben's account. Agamben begins with a review of Paul's description of himself as both apostle and as *aphorismenos*. What, Agamben asks, does it mean when Paul identifies himself as *aphorismenos* (separated), or used as the verb *aphorizo*, as in "he who separated me from the womb of my mother and called me through his *grace* (emphasis mine)'" (Galatians 1:15)?[21] In Agamben's reading, Paul is one who is "separated" as "called." But this separation through *calling* is a separation from a prior separation as a Pharisee. *Aphorismenos*, Agamben reminds us, "is nothing more than the Greek translation of the Hebrew term *parush* . . . that is, 'Pharisee.'"[22] Agamben emphasizes the exclusionary character of the Pharisees as those who "distinguished [themselves] from other factions in Judaism and [for whom] the law [was] conceived as a 'dividing wall' or a 'fence' surrounding the Torah that prevents contact with any impurity."[23] Consequently, Agamben says that

> by defining himself as *aphōrismenos* . . . Paul thus alludes, in an ironic, albeit cruelly ironic fashion to his separation of times past, his separation as a Pharisee . . . and He refers to it and negates it in the name of another separation . . . a separation according to the messianic proclamation . . . so that *aphōrismenos* implies something like a separation to the second power, a separation, which . . . divides and traverses the divisions of Pharisaic laws.[24]

With this reading of *aphōrismenos*, Agamben introduces the notion of the messianic division of division or the *as not*. If the theory goes, "the principle of the law is . . . division," as Agamben argues, and Jewish law divides between Jews and non-Jews (circumcision/foreskin), the messianic division of division challenges the conceptual exhaustion represented by these two categories. Said otherwise, if "Jew and non-Jew" as the central division of the law is conceptually successful, it will technically leave no "remainder" of persons not classified. But, Agamben suggests, it is precisely this conceptual success that the messianic calls into question and divides. The messianic logic calls into question the wholeness of Jew plus non-Jew equals All. More foundationally, it calls into question the stability of each individual category: that is, Jews equal Jews, and non-Jews equal non-Jews. From the perspective of the messianic, neither individual category is "pure" because Paul subsequently distinguishes between the "Jew of the flesh and the Jew of the spirit," and Agamben says, "the same thing happens to the non-Jew (even if Paul does not explicitly say so) [namely that] the (true) Jew is not the apparent one and that (true) circumcision is not that of the flesh."[25] The Jew is separated from himself because the true Jew is not Jewish but Christian. The same, of course, goes for the non-Christian, who is really "Jew." In other words, under the "cut" of the messianic division, the Jew is separated from himself and the non-Jew separated from himself with both categories exposed and/or un/interpreted through a messianic division. Most significantly, this division of division leaves a remnant in its wake—the remainder that is neither Jew nor non-Jew but instead, what is left after each has been hollowed out or deconstructed. This Agamben refers to as the *as not* or the "complete loss of man"[26]—that which has not been destroyed in the destruction of the prior classification.

> The messianic vocation is not a right, nor does it furnish an identity rather it is a generic potentiality that can be used without ever being owned. To be messianic, to live in the Messiah signifies the expropriation of each and every juridical-factical property under the form of the as not. This expropriation does not however, found a new identity. . . .[27]

Agamben compares the social portrait of the messianic with Marx's vision of a classless society premised upon the critical identification by the proletariat of the nature of "estate" or *Stand*.[28] The proletariat's critical undressing of "estate" into class—that category, which unlike the category of "estate" or *Stand* does not attempt to veil the contingencies and character of life for individuals within separate *Ständ* (that is, the oppression of individuals in low estates) but exposes them—therefore undermines the classificatory system of the estate without elevating the proletariat to a new identity. To speak of the proletariat as a new class with "rights" is, Agamben says, one of the deadliest interpretations of Marx's thought. The vision of the messianic emergent from Paul, he argues, advances a community without "rights"—a community that has divided the juridical through the form of the "as not." Agamben's social vision of the "as not" offers a kind of Johannine vision of a post-identity community of persons.

However, Agamben's post-identity vision is disingenuous, and instead of earmarking a soteriological approach toward an eschatological all in all, it exposes Agamben's division of division as exceptionalism—a model of the logic of sacrifice. In his own estimation, the division of division suggests a division of "difference"—a society of persons and relations "absolutely irreducible to power relationships."[29] In fact, however, Agamben's logic of the division of the division leaves a remnant: an exclusionary remnant produced in the very sacrifice or excavation of prior content. Such a hollowing out or abandonment of that which is divided offers no basis for a communion beyond "rights" but just the opposite—a privileging of that which endures the hollowing out and still stands even after the messianic destruction has finished its work. If, on the one hand, Agamben's excavation of Jewish and non-Jewish division results in what he refers to as the "non–non-Jew," the characteristic feature, if you will, of the non–non-Jew ought to be its lack of identity, or the fact that as Agamben says it "cannot be defined. . . ."[30] To immediately, however, have recourse to the language of remnant such that the "that which cannot be defined" constitutes a remainder which *qua* remainder is separate and/or different from that which came before undermines the meaning that Agamben seeks to assign to the non–non-Jew. To make the point another way, I might suggest that Agamben's claim to exposing a division of a division relies upon a dehistoricized notion of Pharisee or a conflation of Pharisee with Sadducee: namely, those Jews who refused to recognize historical changeability and insisted upon steadfast literal distinctions between categories. By refusing to read "Pharisee" as a historicized notion, Agamben not only fails to expose a division of division but simply moves the dividing line that he claims to excavate. Herein, I will discuss how what here amounts to a flawed rhetorical privileging of the "remnant" results in a dangerous epistemological and social privileging when understood in the context of Agamben's analysis of sovereignty and law.

REDUCTIONISM

When enhanced by his account of sovereignty and law, Agamben's privileging of the remnant, or the "as not," will, in his estimation, constitute a universal point of privilege from which all else can be interpreted. A common feature of expressions of the logic of sacrifice is an exceptionalism premised upon an account of universalism beyond difference. Exceptionalist ideologies (both secular and theological) articulate a vision of universalism as election or election as universalism. Secular accounts of the logic of sacrifice assume the rhetoric of the wise over and against the foolish, the spiritual over the material, or the elite versus the masses. But the characteristic feature of the logic of sacrifice is not simply this distinction of the one over the other but the additional and inextricably linked claim to a universalism of this exception. Linked always to a "future" or deeper universalism, exceptionalism veils and/or legitimizes its divisiveness and its abandonment of the inessential with its claims toward the universal well-being of all humanity.

Consequently, one of the most pervasive features of the logic of sacrifice is its reductionism, or what I will refer to as a hermeneutics of analysis or expertise. Implicit in the operation of sacrifice or exceptionalism is not only a discarding of one part in its outbidding by another but a presumption that the discarding sheds the inessential for the essential or truth. Applied to the earlier discussion of the *as not*, we see Agamben privilege the reality of the "true Israel" or the "true remnant" as that which survives the sacrifice or transformation into the *as not*. This privileging of the remnant is the result of a conceptual reductionism whereby what is sacrificed is deemed inessential and destroyed, and what remains is profiled as the source of new life and future possibility. At work here is an intellectual reductionism whereby the operation of sacrifice or exception produces an authentic "reading" of truth. Agamben's appeal to Marxist *Ideologiekritik* offers another useful example. Only the proletariat properly interprets the reality of *Stand* as class. The reduction of *Stand* to class is not one of a myriad of ways of interpreting *Stand* but rather the correct reading of *Stand* such that any other rendering counts as ideological, repressive, or concealing. In this way, the logic of sacrifice funds a culture of expertise. Only those participants in the sacrificial logic acquire the interpretative lens that equips them to see truth and distinguish it from all other forms of misunderstanding and blindness. Earlier, I discussed Rosenstock-Huessy's reduction of Judaism and his reduction of history. If Jesus is the center of history, any other interpretation of history and culture registers as denial at best and actively productive of error and sinful at worst, deserving of the death that inevitably, in this schema, comes to all without the new life of the eschatological future.

The same assault on history arises from Agamben's messianism as it does from Rosenstock-Huessy's eschatological anticipation. Agamben insists that messianism is not apocalypticism. Note, he says, the "extraordinary interlacing of these two concepts, they are literally placed within each other. *Kairos* does not have another time at its disposal; in other words, what we take hold of when we seize *kairos* is not another time, but a contracted and abridged *chronos*."[31] The messianic is not an eschatological flight from reality. The power of the messianic seizes reality, seizes "history," and implicates itself within time: It does not nullify time. For Agamben, messianic time is the tense encounter between *chronos* (historical time) and *kairos*, which results in the making or operation of the end-time. Messianic time, as the time between the arrival of the Word and the fulfillment of the word, inserts itself to labor toward the end-time within history as we know it. *Chronos* is never the same after this inserted operation of making an end, and *kairos* is itself never free from its need to use, take, or "seize" history as the environment for its labor toward the end. Messianic time, he says, "is the time we need to make time end or *the time that is left to us* [emphasis, mine]."[32] Those of us without the lens of messianic time live, he says, as

> . . . impotent spectators [insofar as] our representation of chronological time as the time in which we are, separates us from ourselves and transforms us . . . into spectators who look at the time that flies without any time left, continually missing themselves, messianic time is an operational time in which we take hold of and achieve our representations of time, is the time *that* we ourselves are, and for this very reason, is the only real time, the only time we have.[33]

Regardless of Agamben's insistence upon the immanence of the messianic moment, the messianic account of time imposes a hermeneutics of history wherein the time that we live in unaccounted for by the messianic achieves value only as used. Unused, it is impotent and inessential. It is not "real time." Agamben appropriates history for and through the messianic inversion so that it is no longer "lived" but taken. But history, as the documentation of lived events, resists reductionist interpretation and demands a candid exposition of happenings even along with an acknowledgment that such an effort to produce a candid exposition will inevitably result in multiple accounts. Such a view stands in marked contrast to Agamben's celebration of what he claims is Paul's more typological approach to historical narration.

> Men appropriate their history, and what once happened to the Jews is recognized as a figure and reality for the messianic community. And just as the past becomes possible again through memory—that which was fulfilled becomes unfulfilled and the unfulfilled becomes fulfilled . . . and the recapitulation of the past is a summary judgement on it.[34]

History is dissolved by judgment and analysis. In contrast to this hermeneutical reductionism, the logic of law offers a system of mapped relations, which follows events as narrated and subject to multiple (endless) interpretations.

GRACE VERSUS LAW

Although the preceding discussion illuminates the symptoms of Agamben's exceptionalism, the key to accounting for this exceptionalism derives from Agamben's account of sovereignty and law. Moreover, an analysis of the link between Agamben's exceptionalism and his account of sovereignty and law will help explain how when applied to his understanding of Judaism, Agamben's exceptionalism has debilitating effects on Jewish-Christian relations.

Agamben approaches the category of sovereignty through an analysis of the nexus between law and sovereignty in Pauline messianism on the one hand, and in the work of the famous jurist Carl Schmitt on the other hand. The messianic, Agamben insists, is not a dialectical antithesis of the law. Paul did not posit faith over and against works or grace as the opposite of law. Rather, the messianic is an operation that takes place within the law just as messianic time is an operation that takes place within history. Here is where Agamben's reading of Paul's category of law differs from the juridical theory of legal exceptionalism or sovereignty found in Schmitt's work. If, according to Schmitt, the normativity of the law within a legal system is impotent in moments of crisis and relies therefore on the decision-making power of a sovereign outside of or exterior to the law, this means that the law needs the extra-legal for its own force. On the other hand, the extra-legal is inextricably bound to the law so far as it is the sovereign's decision making that grounds the possibility of any legal system. In this account, law and exception stand linked by the dialectic of each other's lack. But, Agamben asserts, this view is not "exceptional" enough; the messianic remnant is "an exception taken to its extreme."[35] If Schmitt's sovereign represents the force of the extra-legal or the exception to the legal upon the legal, still it remains dialectically linked to the legal and therefore limited in its exceptionalism. Agamben places Schmitt's analysis of the law next to Derrida's dialectical account of lack. Both constitute unfulfilled cries for a messianic completion, which one finds only with Paul's messianic "as not." For Agamben, Paul's account of faith as the "law of justice" presents a more far-reaching exceptionalism. What does Agamben mean here? If the "law of justice" is more exceptionalist than Schmitt's account, how can Agamben insist that the messianic is not antinomian?

For Agamben, the answer derives from his claim that the messianic as a law of justice constitutes the innermost meaning of "law." It is the suspension of the law *qua* normative and the fulfillment of the law *qua* grace. Agamben's claim that the messianic presents the innermost meaning of the law comes from his analysis of the concept of *pistis* (faith)—a promise or announcement that performs a trust between persons and thereby with this trust establishes a "guarantee" or a "credit" later. Agamben suggests that in this originary meaning, *pistis* links to a number of force-fields, including magic, law, and trust or faith. Oaths hold an almost magical power, and when broken, can unleash dramatic consequences. As expressions of trusting relationships, oaths function as contractual terms; and finally, oaths reflect and develop grounds of trust and/or credit between those involved. On this point, Agamben is rather specific insofar as there is a particular economy characteristic of faith. To have faith in or trust another demonstrates a willingness to invest in that other. Faith is like a pledge to the other which presupposes that the other has credit or is legitimate. Consequently, faith endows the other with an asymmetrical authority over the faithful. Agamben gives the example of a conquered city that "unconditionally surrenders themselves to the hands of the enemy, making the victor hold to a more benevolent conduct. In this instance the city could be saved and its inhabitants granted a personal freedom while not being completely free."[36] But, Agamben points out, this authority is not tyrannical. The authority of the one endowed with credit is legitimized by the faithful; consequently, this authority reacts benevolently to it by offering a kind *charis* (grace) or "favor" to the faithful. This sociopolitical model is important for Agamben because he will suggest that it is this character of faith and its economy that constitutes the "innermost" meaning of the law so that the normative value of the law loses its value as soon as its origins and essential meaning in "trust" are rediscovered.

The preceding point becomes clear when Agamben stretches his analysis by paralleling his interpretation of *pistis* with the Hebrew *emunah* (faith) to describe the personal loyalty operative in biblical *berit* (covenant). The element of loyalty and trust between the parties is, according to Agamben, so central to the covenantal pact that not only does it precede the Mosaic giving of the law chronologically, but the very relevance and normativity of any of the particular Mosaic laws derives singularly from this phenomenon of trust. Agamben reinvokes Schmitt's distinction between the extra-legal as the normative force of the legal here, suggesting that *emunah* constitutes the innermost meaning of the law. However, Agamben insists that Paul's messianic adaptation of the relationship between *pistis* and law exceeds a Schmittian tension between law and an extra-legal trust insofar as

> [M]essianism [hereby] appears as a struggle within the law, where the element of the pact and constituent power leans toward setting itself against and emancipating itself from the element of the *entolé*, the norm in the strict sense. . . . The

messianic is therefore the historical process whereby the archaic link between law and religion . . . reaches a crises and the element of *pistis* of faith . . . ends paradoxically to emancipate itself from any obligatory conduct and from positive law.[37]

Not only is faith or trust the innermost essential meaning of the law. Messianism is the operation wherein this pre-judicial, faith, or trust liberates itself from and deactivates the obligatory feature of the covenantal relationship. It is not, in Agamben's account, the particularity of the law from which faith emancipates itself but its normativity or obligatory character. Said otherwise, faith emancipates itself from the rights and duties structure of the law, hollowing out this inessential element, leaving in its wake the messianic remnant of the relationship between a sovereign and grace-giving God and the faithful servant. This relationship in Agamben's account represents the law of justice over and against the law of command. Given the narrative that Agamben provides, readers may applaud the messianic victory over normativity. It is important, however, to look more closely at this messianic lifting of the law out of it normativity because the subtraction of normativity from the covenant of grace presents enormous challenges to Jews and Christians both.

To begin with, Agamben's account of Paul's messianic faith performs just the sort of reductionism by exception previously described, and applied here, props up a supersessionist reading of Paul's "new covenant" language.

> The juridical or prejuridical origin of the notion of faith and the situation of faith in the caesura between faith and obligation paves the way for a correct understanding of the Pauline doctrine of the "new covenant." Mosaic law is preceded by the promise that was made to Abraham. This promise is hierarchically superior in as much as Mosaic law is powerless to render it inoperative. The Mosaic law of obligations and works, is defined in 2 Corinithians 3:14 as the "old covenant" and is rendered inoperative by the Messiah.[38]

If this sort of interpretation of Paul is the logical outcome of the effort to see him in his historical context, I, for one, would opt for an entirely ahistorical reading of Paul. That it is not a successful account of Paul's historical situatedness has been powerfully suggested by contemporary scholarship that challenges the implicit supersessionism in Paul's work by scholars such as Paul Gager and N. T. Wright.[39]

Second, Agamben's sacrifice of the normativity of the law at the altar of grace grounds a faulty and dangerous account of divine sovereignty. This mistaken account of the nature of divine sovereignty and the concomitant account of the meaning of justification, atonement, and faith that emerges

24   *The Logic of Exceptionalism*

from it functions as the very nucleus of the logic of sacrifice. It is the challenge of this book to not only identify the problems associated with exceptionalism's mistaken view of sovereignty, but more importantly, present a more philosophically and theologically rigorous account of the nature of divine freedom and its relationship to the central issues of justification, atonement, and truth.

Simply said, Agamben endorses a theology of divine sovereignty or grace (a theology of the freedom of the Word) devoid of a theology of the law. Moreover, Agamben's problematic conception of sovereignty will lead to a distortion in his account of other issues, including justification, atonement, and truth. While I will demonstrate on what grounds a theology of divine sovereignty devoid of law is philosophically amiss, the purpose of this discussion is to highlight the problems it causes for the previously stated issues.

Let us return then to Agamben's account of the relationship between the faithful and the sovereign in the covenantal pact before and outside the normativity of command. Earlier, I described the character of trust that the faithful has in the sovereign and the grace offered by the sovereign to the faithful. Agamben argues, "grace seems to even define a real 'sovereignty' (*autarkeia*) . . . God loves a cheerful giver and God is able to abound all grace in you. . . ."[40] The problems implicit in this relationship were foreshadowed earlier in my review of Rosenstock-Huessy's theology, and there are two that are most important. First, the absolute sovereignty of the God of the faithful reinforces the exceptionalism and exclusion characteristic of the logic of sacrifice. If it is the case that the loyalty from the faithful inspires the sovereign God to extend *charitas* or favor to them, this *charitas* is offered to none but them. The sovereign God has no obligation to others. His loyalty or protection cuts through and reflects the difference between those who are within the covenant and those who are without the covenant. Persons outside of the covenant have, in this account, no rights—no legitimate claim for protection of any kind. The God of the faithful is a God only for the faithful, and a life outside the covenant is legitimately left to the forces of contingency without regret or obligation. The sovereignty of trust exceeds a sovereignty of rights, and as we saw in Rosenstock-Huessy's account, the inevitable result of such an exclusionary sovereignty is the denigration and nullification of persons outside the bounds of the covenant.

There are quite significant epistemological implications to this application of the logic of sacrifice to the question of the rights of persons outside the covenant. There is a correlation between normativity and good reasons.

To the extent that Agamben's messianic sovereignty exceeds normativity, this means that even the faithful are without rights. According to Agamben, the law of justice is enough. The abundance of divine grace suffices to protect the faithful even if such sovereignty cannot be challenged or subject to any legal limits. Consequently, the faithful have no recourse to compel or oblige the sovereign to beneficence. Epistemologically speaking, this means that faithful witness consists only in a repetition of the goodness of the sovereign. One can quickly imagine the Jobian scenario wherein this same divine sovereignty unleashes less than beneficent behavior and still, the faithful witness has no recourse to ask why or demand a reason. God's sovereignty is self justifying. In the final chapter of the book, I will provide an analysis of the book of Job and address the character of divine sovereignty there and its relationship to the law. For here, it is important only to note that a sovereignty that exceeds command is a sovereignty that permits no rational questioning on the part of the faithful.

Agamben's account of sovereignty translates directly into his description of the nature and character of witness or proclamation. Reflecting on Paul's insights upon the nearness of the word—as Paul radically alters Deuteronomy's account of the nearness of the law (Deuteronomy 30:11–14), Agamben says that the messianic word is near to us in the "mouth and the heart."[41] Offered to us by grace, the grace above the law, the word that we ingest is the self-justifying word of the Lord. If it gains its self-justification and truth from the grace of God, it is nonetheless a word that "swears on itself [and] . . . becomes the fundamental fact"[42] when spoken by the faithful. Self-evident and generative of reality, the witness of the faithful expresses the absolute truth of the sovereign and is open to no contest, to no challenge, to no demand at justification. Inheriting the absolute truth of the sovereign power, the faithful are accountable to none, and their proclamation exceeds and excludes any who might question it. The logic of sacrifice inscribes a proclamation of truth beyond justification, beyond account.

As earlier suggested, Rosenstock-Huessy and/or Agamben might respond by suggesting that the covenant between God and the faithful is available for all who hear. No one need be left out of God's favor—only those who choose to deny or reject it. If their rejection results in punishment and suffering, it is no one's fault but his own. But, this argument for the universalism of the elected community suffers its own limitations, for even the "elect" are not spared the negative consequences of the power of a God whose freedom exceeds and denies normativity. On the one hand, as described, the life of the faithful is a life of the elect—a life of the exceptional remnant faithful to the God who blesses the faithful with his free and sovereign favor. As blessed, the faithful enjoy the luxury of their witness, accountable to none but the community of the faithful who share in the truth of their proclamation. On the other hand, however, the life of the faithful is also a life of fear and trembling. If the faithful are "justified" in their witness, it is only because the self-justifying God justifies them. They are not, as Luther so frequently pointed out, justified in themselves. Left to themselves, they are the unjustified sinners, deserving of the same punishment and wrath that they insist legitimately afflicts others outside the covenantal pledge. The life of the faithful is a life of anxiety—a life of uncertainty. If the Word of God is near, it nonetheless mystifies believers. Such a life of fear and trembling is the correlative to the account of divine sovereignty that exceeds normativity found in Agamben's reading of Paul.

The logic of sacrifice leaves no one immune to the self-alienation of the exception. While the exceptional have more reason to hope for a positive future than the unexceptional, even the exceptional undergo a self-erasure or an inner sacrifice, in Agamben's terms, a messianic sacrifice that cuts out parts of their existence, parts of their humanity for the sake of that innermost essence that alone sustains value. If by way of summary we may suggest that at the heart of Agamben's logic of sacrifice is not only a logic of division but, as importantly, a mistaken account of the nature of sovereignty, it will be the objective of this book to present a philosophically legitimate and biblically authentic account of divine freedom wherein sovereignty does not exceed the law but freely offers a law through which persons are justified existentially, morally, and epistemologically.

TAUBES AND EXCEPTIONALISM

The earlier criticism of Agamben's reading of Paul as exceptionalist gains credence when considered in light of Jacob Taubes's *The Political Theology of Paul*. Taubes's analysis of Paul as a Hellenistic Jew whose messianism had all to do with an internal polemic within and not outside his Judaism sounds, in certain respects, strikingly similar to Agamben's account of a messianism that seizes Judaism and its structures from within and not from the vantage point of a new religious tradition. Nonetheless, if both thinkers regard Paul's theology as inextricably linked to the Judaism of his day, only Taubes suggests the extent to which this indebtedness registers as exceptionalism or outbidding within Paul's theology of the cross itself. If, then, Taubes and Agamben offer similar readings of Paul's view of the law and faith, and yet Taubes identifies Pauline messianism as an expression of outbidding over and against the dominant legitimacy structures of the day (Jewish law and

Roman law), then Taubes's account of Paul helps illuminate the extent to which Agamben's messianism conforms to the logic of exceptionalism.

Like Agamben, Taubes's Paul presents a transvaluation of values across the Jewish board that includes the establishment of a new conception of people-hood, a new notion of love over law, a new view of salvation history, and a new approach to interpreting sacred text. Also like Agamben, Taubes points to Paul's insistence upon the true covenant and the true heirs of the covenant, the true "remnant." Where Taubes's analysis departs from Agamben's, however, is in his ability to identify this Pauline transvaluation of Jewish values as a product of the Pauline desire to consciously outbid or out-do the adversary, who in his own mind, cast him out from the community of first-century Roman and/or Jewish legitimacy. Taubes's account of outbidding showcases the paradox, or what I will also call the "dialectic of desire in its pursuit of truth." On the one hand, desire seeks truth. On the other hand, desire *qua* desire never achieves truth, and therefore gives rise to either a dogmatism that denies the reality of desire or a defeatism or anxiety over the failure to produce stable truth. In its effort to avoid either outcome, desire motors a heuristic of exceptionalism. In other words, it pursues the veracity of an unstable position through the logic of overriding an opposing position.

Taubes's analysis of Paul's letters illuminates the operations of this dialectic in Paul's claims regarding Jewish law. To the extent that it was Jewish law, in particular, that in Taubes's analysis legitimized Judaism within the legalism of the Roman Empire, it is Jewish law that bears the brunt of Paul's outbidding. "My thesis," Taubes says, is that "Paul understands himself as outbidding Moses,"[43] and much of the New Testament, he argues, includes evidence of this outbidding.

> [T]ake for example the Gospel of Matthew. In it, the Sermon on the Mount is a surpassing of the sermon at Sinai: "You have heard that it was said. . . . But I say to you. . . ." This is a strategy of outbidding. All of salvation history is an imitation: Jesus has to flee to Egypt, come from Egypt and so on. There the outbidding parallel between Moses and Christ is drawn.[44]

The link between Agamben's Paul and Taubes's Paul in conjunction with Taubes's exposition of the defensive exceptionalism at work in Paul's theology of the cross helps lend credence to my critique of Agamben's account as exceptionalist. Taubes's analysis of Paul illuminates the extent to which neither Agamben nor Rosenstock-Huessy recognizes the force of desire in their assertions. This does not mean that I also agree with Taubes's reading of the *Epistle to the Romans* anymore than I agree with Agamben's. And although in this book, I will not present a re-reading of Paul's Epistle to the Romans, I will provide a basis for a theology of the Cross that because it honors and does not cast out the lawfulness of the Word may provide inspiration for new readings of the meaning of the law within Paul's Romans.

This excursus into Agamben's work strove to more carefully identify features of a logic of sacrifice. In summary, I may say that a logic of sacrifice or exceptionalism characterizes a philosophical or theological account that consciously or not arises from a polemical context: a context motivated by desire and whose conceptual framework operates to outbid or falsify its adversary. The unique marks of this falsification include a logic of division or exception wherein the position of the pioneer of the new truth illuminates, cuts through, or sacrifices the falsehood of the earlier position and projects itself as the innermost essence of this prior position. Drawing its essential truth from the prior position, the new position legitimizes itself as the rightful inheritor of the claims made by the earlier position. Motivated by the desire to crown itself the new and exclusive truth, the logic of sacrifice is inevitably reductionist. That the logic of sacrifice permeates secular and theological thought and right-wing and left-wing ideologies as well is brilliantly displayed by what amounts to a genealogy of exceptionalism presented by Taubes in *The Political Theology of Paul*. There, in a later-written appendix, Taubes remarks upon the insignificance in the difference between the Frankfurt school and Carl Schmitt's work when viewed through the analysis of exceptionalism. After recounting his student days in support of left-wing causes, Taubes insists that "this left-right scheme doesn't hold and . . . in fact the old Frankfurt School stood in a very intimate relation to Schmitt. . . ."[45] Although he does not spell this out, Taubes identifies Habermas and the Frankfurt school with the exceptionalism in Schmitt's political thought because both systems presuppose a cutting way at a prior truth when that truth is viewed as itself a declaration of superiority over and against contrary positions. Both systems move from this assumption of the binary and exclusionary nature of truth to promote a higher (deeper) truth that alone provides authentic sight and interpretation. We can see this in Habermas's sociolinguistic hermeneutics of suspicion premised as it is on his transcendental conditions of normative discourse[46] and in Schmitt's theory of the sovereign and the decision of the exception as the true and yet formerly concealed condition of the possibility of legal normativity as described in his *Political Theology*.[47] One can even find a logic of exceptionalism in thinkers who have discovered it. Taubes draws attention to Nietzsche's pioneering work in unveiling the polemical character of Christian theology but notes Nietzsche's own investment in out-Pauling Paul. With Zarathrustra, Taubes says, Nietzsche sought "to build himself a counterfigure in the Dionysian, immanent world—that is to penetrate all the way into the secret of the Christian mystery . . . and [pit] Dionysus against the crucified one, Dionysus as the crucified one. That's Nietszche."[48]

Interestingly enough, Taubes's *Political Theology* speaks little about the impact of the logic of sacrifice upon Jewish philosophy. Nonetheless, the logic of sacrifice appears in the work of many Jewish philosophers, and two of them in particular will be discussed in this volume: Maimonides and Spinoza. More often than not, the logic of sacrifice presents itself in Jewish philosophers whose systems tout the exceptionalism of the wise or the rational as the innermost meaning of the law. Intentionally or otherwise, these accounts devalue the law that ultimately gets sacrificed as a means to the higher *telos* of knowledge. With regard to Jewish thought therefore, this book strives to present an alternative to these accounts of the dichotomy between law and wisdom.

Perhaps my greatest debt to Taubes consists in his ability to help me pursue a more careful and nuanced analysis of Christian reappropriations of the Jewish doctrine of election. Typically, Jewish theologians invested in Jewish-Christian relations gravitate toward Christian theologians whose thought identifies the Christian message with Jewish covenantal elements. There is and should be a Jewish interest in Calvin or in Barth given their placement of the Christian message within the biblical and covenantal relationship. It was this common identification of the character of the transcendence of the biblical God over and against the pretensions of modern humanism that drew together that most noteworthy collection of post-WWI theologians identified with the Patmos group, including Rosenzweig, Rosenstock-Huessy, Barth, and others. Recognition of the contours of a logic of sacrifice, however, foists a note of caution over this alliance around the sovereignty of God as it has come to be identified with Word of God theologies. If it is the case that a retrieval of the transcendence and freedom of the biblical God constitutes a powerful point of recognition by Jews and Christians, this shared recognition can easily deteriorate into powerful strains of anti-Judaism if not regulated against a logic of sacrifice. It is the central contention of this book that Christian appropriations of the sovereign and electing God of the Hebrew Scriptures will wax exceptionalist and produce not only a powerful anti-Judaism but an inevitable failure in the Christian apologetic effort to engage with non-Christian culture generally speaking unless they simultaneously identify this God as a God whose grace does not exceed the law but is expressed through the law as this law is freely offered by God to human persons. Within Christian theology, as I will show, this idea is best represented by Karl Barth's understanding of the "Law as the Form of the Gospel."

Beyond Sacrifice

My discussion so far, beginning as it did with the letters between Rosenzweig and Rosenstock-Huessy, has provided an analysis of Rosenstock-Huessy's position within the paradigm of exceptionalism. However, there are indications in the letters that Rosenstock-Huessy's position could have moved in another direction if he had taken up the points of commonality or premises that permitted the conversation to develop in the first place—and, in particular, Rosenzweig and Rosenstock-Huessy's shared indebtedness to the work of F. W. J. Schelling.

The dramatic difference between Rosenzweig's and Rosenstock-Huessy's positions in the letters is blatantly exposed in their characterizations of sacrifice. If Rosenstock-Huessy mines the sacrifice of Jesus on the cross for a plenitude of meaning, Rosenzweig focuses less on the "meaning" of Abraham's sacrifice and more on the paradoxical character of the event instead. "Abraham did not offer something, not 'a' child, but his only son, and what is more, the son of the promise, and sacrificed him to the God of this promise; the meaning of the promise according to human understanding becomes impossible through this sacrifice. . . ."[49] Why and how is the sacrifice meaningful only as a display of its own impossibility or meaninglessness? To begin, we might note Rosenzweig's rejection of any traditional notion of sacrifice as an offering of a currency within an economy. If, in fact, it is the promise that functions as the object of worth with the sacrifice of Isaac the currency required, it would seem odd if the currency undermined the object of worth. The sacrifice of Isaac (the potential sacrifice of Isaac) undermines the very economy of sacrifice as offering and its meaning begins here. The sacrifice of Isaac is not an offering but a ritual or performance of "return" that exposes a logic of abiding or dwelling. "Now," Rosenzweig says

> . . . to return to the subject: the two sacrifices, that on Moriah and that on Golgatha have this in common, then, as against all pagan sacrifices: that nothing was got out of them (since what was sacrificed is identical with what was given back), but the sacrifice itself becomes in effect the abiding object of faith, and thereby that which abides.[50]

It is important to recognize that Rosenzweig attributes this meaning of abiding to both the Abrahamic and the Christological sacrifice. In his view, both question an economy of offering and reinforce an economy of rest. In Rosenzweig's account, there is no cutting away or separation of wheat from chaff. There is no essential offering and inessential currency. There is an exercise of presenting what there is and what will be: that is, of what abides and is "given" but not given away. Sacrifice names or defines what is either given or received, but it does not perform an exchange or even a movement of elements. It marks a sabbatical of sorts that offers a candid exposition of what is and who owns. Rosenzweig's account of sacrifice provides a microcosm of the logic of law, and insofar as he uses the analysis of sacrifice to build a bridge between Judaism and Christianity, it is this alternative reading of sacrifice as abiding that marks the ultimate difference between his understanding of Jewish-Christian relations and Rosenstock-Huessy's.

Rosenzweig's correspondence with Rosenstock-Huessy is the first place where we see this logic of law in his body of work. This logic derives in part from Rosenzweig's reading of Schelling's *Weltalter*. However, Schelling's work influenced Rosenstock-Huessy just as much as it influenced Rosenzweig. It is, therefore, their shared inheritance of Schelling's account of revelation that constitutes one of the crucial premises of their correspondence and created the possibility of a stronger exchange between the two thinkers had Rosenstock-Huessy retained the influence of Schelling's account of revelation in his letters and later works. Rosenstock-Huessy never entirely shed Schelling's influence, but this influence was ultimately overshadowed by his emphasis on the centrality of meaning lodged within the one sacrifice of Christ over and against the authenticity of other parallel revelatory possibilities.

THE INFLUENCE OF SCHELLING

The logic of law that I endorse in this volume can be said to have both a philosophical and a biblical basis. Chapter 4 will discuss the logic of the law rooted in the biblical world view. Philosophically speaking, the logic of law can be traced back to Schelling's account of divine freedom in the *Weltalter* as this account is taken up and expanded by Rosenzweig into his New Thinking.

The key to Schelling's significance for Rosenzweig and Rosenstock-Huessy lies in his account of divine revelation.[51] Recall Rosenstock-Huessy's response to Rosenzweig's question regarding nature and revelation earlier. Rosenstock-Huessy distinguishes revelation from "natural understanding," which he argues presents neither a concept of the "Above" nor a concept of "that bond from heaven to earth which makes space stable, like a rock of bronze. . . ."[52] Natural understanding is self enclosed and self perpetuating, never exposed to an alterity that orients it to a larger context of order. Both Rosenzweig and Rosenstock-Huessy invest tremendous significance in the notion of revelation as an act by another, which as other simultaneously awakens the one who experiences it to something exterior to itself and orders this one into a new context of relation to this exterior. If for both Rosenzweig and Rosenstock-Huessy, revelation is a free act that as event installs an order of lawfulness upon that which it acts, it is from Schelling that both have received this understanding. Let us review Schelling's account of divine revelation.

Schelling's *Weltalter* is a philosophical portrait of divine life.[53] For my purposes, there are four aspects of the divine life illuminated by Schelling's account that are of central significance to the logic presented in this book.[54] They are the notion of the divine free act; the link between God's free act and divine existence (that is, revelation); the subsequent identification between God's act and existence *and* divine self-knowledge or self-revelation (wisdom); and finally, the crucial nexus between divine revelation, divine self-consciousness, and divine ordering or lawfulness (the structuring of what is other from God in the context of an "above and a below"). At the end of the day, Schelling's profile of divine life forges connections between divine life, revelation, wisdom, and law that are unprecedented philosophically and correspond to the unique character of the biblical God as that God, too, presents a thick relation between divine wisdom, divine law, and divine revelation.[55] That the Jewish philosophical tradition has long denied this link among revelation, wisdom, and law is the subject matter of Chapters 2 and 3 of this volume. For here, I will strive to articulate Schelling's repair of prior philosophical antinomies between a God who reveals and commands and a God of wisdom who knows God-self in eternity.

Divine Freedom and the *Actus Purus* Schelling's *Weltalter* presents a philosophical poetics of the nature of God's life and vitality. Philosophically speaking, the account of divine life begins with the presupposition that we live in a world where there is something rather than nothing. Schelling's account of God begins epistemologically (although not ontologically) with the recognition of the existence of the world. From the existence of the world, we may, Schelling argues, deduce a particular portrait of God: namely, a God of Being and non-Being. Said in other terms, the existence of the world permits us to deduce a God of a free act—a God who "acts" and a God who "is"—that is, a God with a determinate nature. What does this mean?

The reality of an existing world presupposes a free act by something other than that existing reality. Schelling reaches this conclusion by negating its opposite possibility. Necessity and existence are contradictory terms for Schelling. If something exists necessarily, it does not come into or out of existence. It simply "is." Necessity is the character of being, which remains self-same without time or change. Existence is a carving out from being—a differentiation of a unique life that is marked by a beginning and end presupposing change. To the extent that nature (our world) displays this coming into and out of existence, it is not governed strictly by the necessity of its own nature but must be affected by something other than this necessity, or what is a freedom that imparts a newness or a change. We might say that what exists is that which is affected by an event or act by something other than itself—something not of its own nature or being. Existence derives from an event or act of transcendent non-Being upon being.

However, Schelling's account of the created world as it exists also presupposes a God of nature and not only a God of pure free act. Why? The argument is this. "For without a nature, the freedom in God could not be separated from the deed and hence, would not be actual freedom."[56] If God were only free act and not also nature, then freedom would *de facto* constitute God's nature or necessity. But then freedom would no longer be freedom. Freedom is only freedom in contrast to a nature, and therefore, the God who acts freely *qua* non-Being is also a God for whom "there is a distinction between God and his Being."[57] If, however, from an existent world, we deduce a God in whom there is a distinction, what is the relationship in God-self between God's free acting and God's essential being or necessity?

In the *Weltalter*, Schelling refers to the classical post-Aristotelian portrait of the God of the philosophers who as perfect being is eternal and unchanging. "Everyone, he says, departs from the assumption that the Godhead is in itself an eternal stillness, totally engulfed in itself and wrapped up in itself, at least so far, they are speaking intelligible words."[58] However, Schelling also recognizes how difficult it is for these same philosophers to reconcile an eternal, unchanging God with the possibility of the creation of a world other than this self-same eternal God.

> For how ... what is first purely and fully wrapped up in itself can, in a subsequent moment or act (for it cannot be though otherwise), emerge out of itself without

ground or occasioning cause, or how it could by itself sublimate or interrupt its eternal unity and stillness: this simply cannot be rendered intelligible with any kind of thought.[59]

And yet Schelling began, as we all do, with the reality of a created world.[60] Consequently, Schelling understands that creation is the central problem in philosophical theology, and to the extent that we can offer an exposition of how creation is possible, we will stumble upon a plausible account of the God who creates. In view, however, of the gap between an eternal God whose only action preserves that God's own unity and the created order that is ontologically different, it would seem that eternal necessity cannot exhaust the character of a God who creates.

There are in Schelling's analysis two essential problems with the portrait of the eternal God of necessity in view of the issue of creation. First, as we know, in addition to maintaining an eternal nature, God must also exist as a God who acts; otherwise, there would be no creation. Second, God's essential being is not a unity. Not only is God related to God-self as an act beyond Being, but more fundamentally, God *qua* nature does not (as many philosophers prior insisted) consist of a unity of essential Being. According to Schelling, divine Being functions as a tense and restless polarity within God's Being itself. How do we know this? Let me explain.

If it is the case that the God of the created order is a God who is both Being and beyond Being, this suggests that the God of Being does not exhaust what Schelling refers to as the *Godhead*. "Being" is neither stable nor sufficient as a characterization of the God of the created world. To speak, however, of an insufficiency or lack in God's nature is to suggest that God's essential nature is not a full or complete unity but rather a dynamic internal movement of unstable parts, or what Schelling refers to as *potencies*. If God's eternal being were stable and complete, there would be little reason for God to create a world other than his own Being. Maimonides, for one, has difficulty with this issue, as I will discuss in Chapter 2. Given Maimonides' account of the absolute unity of God, he cannot explain why or how God could create a world that is either not identical to and thereby indistinguishable from God, and therefore, not in fact a world; *or* explain how the world that is "different" from God can be a product of a stable and perfect ontological unity. If, however, God's Being does not consist in a stable unity, a space opens up for the possibility of a "difference" within God-self—for a something more or other within God to appear that could *qua* extra-divine Being, somehow account for the existence of a reality other than that of divine nature. In Schelling's account, this is the case with respect to God's own nature. God's essential nature is not a strict and pure unity. Rather, it consists of a perpetual engagement by two potencies, what he calls *necessity* [nature] on the one hand and *freedom* or *spirit* on the other. Neither has, in his view, a monopoly on Being, and each vies to exhaust or define the divine nature. Consequently, neither achieves being, but both exist in the cycle of a tireless and eternal campaign for Being within the divine nature. Schelling refers to the reality of this endless cycle as a third potency—the reflection of a constant drive—and he describes a

> . . . life that eternally circulates within itself. . . . Hence now one, now the other is that which has being. Taking turns, one prevails while the other yields. . . . There is only an unremitting wheel, a rotator movement that never comes to a standstill and in which there is no differentiation. . . . There are the forces of that inner life that incessantly gives birth to itself and again consumes itself eternally commencing, eternally becoming, always devouring itself and always again giving birth to itself.[61]

It is, therefore, the eternal and restless cycle of this internal polemic that constitutes the nature of divine necessity. Divine necessity from this vantage point is not a by-product of a perfect ontology but a product of an ontological stalemate the result of the inadequacy of either potency to constitute ontological completion or rest.

Having explained the polemic and restlessness of divine necessity, we have still not explained how this necessity reconciles with the reality of the created order. Schelling's answer is that God creates the world through an act of self-revelation and or coming into existence. If divine necessity commits God to an eternal seclusion of internal restlessness, revelation is the free act by which God externalizes God's own nature into a stable reality as nature and spirit. Revelation is the event or happening through which God *qua* nature is acted upon by God *qua* Other. Through this event, God achieves life or comes into existence from the seclusion of his restless eternity. God's life is a result of an internal event of self-relationality or self-othering. Existence, even in the case of God, is relational and temporal. It is an event that happens. This coming into life or existence is what Schelling also refers to as *creation*. The distinction, in other words, between God and the created order derives from the very difference between God's being and God's act within God-self.

How does the divine act of freedom upon the divine nature give rise to a divine revelation—an exposure of God's nature to another? In the *Weltalter*, Schelling argues that the God beyond Being relates to the divine nature as both a "yes" and a "no." On the one hand, as we have seen, the pure act of

God, which is inevitably Beyond Being, must issue a "no" or draw a distinction between itself and the nature of divine being. If divine freedom were only an affirmation of divine nature or necessity, there would be no divine freedom at all. The creation of the world is premised upon this difference within God, and this difference is described as the divine "no" over and against the divine nature or Being. On the other hand, divine freedom would not be freedom unless it could possibly affirm divine nature without however identifying with or standing affected by its [nature's] limitations. Divine freedom as an act not only therefore distinguishes itself from divine nature but affirms divine nature as an act of "love"—that mode of affirmation that sustains difference. If, as we recall, divine nature—driven by the polemic between nature and spirit within itself—could not transform either nature or spirit into stable reality, it is nonetheless through the affirmation of the free divine will that both nature and spirit within God's essence achieve a fullness of reality. Devoid of the fullness of being themselves, God *qua* Being beyond Being inserts a newness or a change upon both potencies. A freedom Beyond Being, the *actus purus*, Schelling argues, acts without desire. Its action is a pure act—all rest, no desire—it is that rest which "the eternal nature desires." It is "not a being and does not have being, although it is also not the opposite. . . . Rather it is eternal freedom, the pure will, but not the will to something such as the will to reveal itself, but rather the pure will without obsession and craving, the will insofar as it actually does not will."[62] As affirmation, therefore, of God's own nature, as the will that acts upon something and not nothing (otherwise as we suggested there would be no world), this affirmation offers the reality of rest and stability to God's very own nature and hereby gifts God's existence through this act. Reality as we know it, nature and spirit are hereby brought into existence as nothing other than God's bringing God-self into existence. God exists and reveals God-self in our world as this is gifted by the freedom of God's own act upon God-self.

With this event of God *qua* Other acting upon God *qua* nature and thereby bringing God as nature into existence (that is, manifesting God *qua* nature as this nature is "exposed" before another, the other of God as Beyond Being), a new and different notion of "All" arises that differs dramatically from a dialectical conception of "All." Prior to the act of divine freedom upon divine nature, divine nature produced no real All but only the perpetual exchange and irresolution of the potencies of nature and spirit. With the affirmation (love) of divine freedom upon itself as object or nature, however, nature participates in the freedom from desire of the God beyond Being. Divine nature as nature and spirit gets taken up into the rest of pure activity, and nature and spirit achieve a stability or a position.

> In view of eternal freedom, the summit of nature is also elevated to freedom and with it all the other forces simultaneously come to continuance and being in that each force enters into its appropriate place. . . . If the first ground of nature is known in that first potency by virtue of which the necessary being locked itself up within itself . . . and if the spirit world is known in the second potency which stands opposed to the first potency then . . . the third potency . . . is that universal soul by which the cosmos is ensouled. . . . It is the eternal link between nature and the spirit world as well as between the world and God. It is the immediate tool through which alone God is active in nature and the spiritual world.[63]

Nature and spirit, the two poles of divine nature, are stabilized as acted upon and ordered. Not only do they achieve existence by virtue of the affirmation of divine freedom: They achieve an existence each unto themselves—no longer contingent upon the battle for being with the other, no longer seeking to reduce one to the other. In the reception of the divine act of freedom, each achieves an existence within an order of separate entities. This is not the dialectical assertion of a claim, the negation of a claim, and the arrival at a synthesis representative of the highest or innermost truth advanced in each of the earlier negations—a dialectic that we recognized in the logic of sacrifice. Rather, the act of divine freedom names and gifts each into an ordered and defined position through which they may rest in their irreducibility.

At this point, we can see Schelling's account of the link between divine freedom and divine existence as this existence constitutes God's revelation through the created order. Divine revelation in this account is, therefore, synonymous with divine existence and self-othering. God exists only as God reveals and is revealed. As well, divine existence or revelation—what is the very act of God's ensouling or gifting God to God-self, is as also inextricable from an act of divine self-ordering. Divine love, in Schelling's account, does not love unless it orders. To love, "ensoul," or "gift" in any other way is to love without freedom. To give freely is to give each what it needs to be what it is that is, to distinguish each thing from another. It is not to establish a lack between one thing and another. Things are not distinguished through an order of privation but through an order of the fullness and restfulness of what they are. Divine love or freedom is an act of free ordering and lawfulness.

Divine Wisdom If, however, divine revelation means the coming into existence of the divine nature as the recipient of a free act by the God beyond being, and if this coming into existence means the coming into an order of being as this order derives from a free act of divine love, then it is also the case that revelation produces or gives rise to a self-consciousness or divine wisdom. Divine revelation produces the opportunity for divine wisdom (and, by extension, human wisdom as the recognition of what I am as exposed in this order or in this context). Divine wisdom is the divine self-consciousness made possible when God has posited God-self as an object and a subject. If God *qua* freedom is God as subject, on the one hand, this God achieves self-consciousness in God's act of freedom and distinction from God *qua* nature. In this respect, divine wisdom is the same as the eternal act of "distinction" from God's nature: what Schelling refers to as an "eternal act of the dawning of consciousness."[64] From the perspective of the divine subject, divine wisdom presupposes the objectification of God's nature as "past" and distinct from God's freedom. On the other hand, and more significant for the analysis here, divine wisdom also emerges when God *qua* nature is exposed or manifest when acted upon or brought into existence through the act of divine freedom. Knowledge in this account means the awareness of having been acted upon and/or brought into existence through the activity and freedom of the other. Knowledge, then, is the account or the narration of what has happened to make "me" (here, God) into a defined, ordered, and separate element. God achieves knowledge as exposed relationally by God-self as Other. Divine wisdom is the knowledge of God's ordering of God's own nature and/or God's recognition as ordered into the lawful relations of nature and spirit, neither of which is reducible to each other.

It is this model of divine self-knowledge as the self-identification of one who is ordered by another that funds both Rosenzweig and Rosenstock-Huessy's epistemological departures from the tradition of modern philosophy from Descartes to Hegel. As applied to human knowledge, human persons as created, participate in God's self-knowledge. Like the created order, generally speaking, human persons are acted upon by a free act that is dramatically other and concomitantly affirming. Moreover, acted upon by this other, human persons are positioned into an order of relations, and knowledge or wisdom means an awareness of this placement—of who and what I am in this context. A product of a divine act of freedom without desire, I am self conscious or wise in the rest or repose of my self-definition. I am self conscious as I am named although I am not named by myself and do not need to name myself in order to know myself. Self-consciousness, therefore, does not imply sovereignty of awareness, nor does it imply the humiliation of sin or failure to know or be free. Rather, it implies the recognition of my place in the order and the character of my existence as relational and subject to the alterations by what and who act upon me.

SACRIFICING AND ABIDING

It is very important to contrast Schelling's portrait of knowledge against the knowledge asserted in the logic of sacrifice. Recall that a logic of sacrifice is premised upon the paradox of the desire for truth. To desire truth is not to possess it. And yet, the logic of sacrifice pretends to present a truth that it possesses in contradistinction to the falsehood of its adversary. Motivated by her desire, the practitioner identifies an essential truth that falsifies or cuts away at the claim of the adversary and hails herself the owner of the justified and true position. As we have seen, this move results in the reduction of all claims in light of their relation to the determined truth. That the logic of sacrifice is mired in paradox, however, results in the ironic application of this reductionism on to the practitioner herself. Given her inability to possess truth (by virtue of her desire), the truth she claims is innermost is never fully hers, and all that she is and all that she knows otherwise is itself sacrificed in the name of that truth, even if that truth's reality lies in a far distant future. The logic of sacrifice results in the two evils of intolerance and anxiety.

Schelling's account of divine life and human knowledge leads to a dramatically different result. Truth in Schelling's account (knowledge or wisdom) does not mean the falsification of another's claim. Truth or knowledge is not represented by the claim that still stands after the process of falsifying a prior claim is completed. Truth or knowledge is a result of an event or an encounter between one thing and another. Even divine self-consciousness presupposes a having been acted upon by God-self as Other. Knowledge is never self certain, and knowledge is not a process of determining truth by falsification. Knowledge arises from an event and can be narrated only by the one who is affected. This is what Rosenzweig means when in the letters with Rosenstock-Huessy, he says

> I believe that there are in the life of each living thing moments, when it speaks the truth. . . . It may well be then that we need say nothing at all about a living thing but need do no more than watch for the moment when this living thing expresses itself. The dialogue which these monologues form between one another I consider to be the whole truth. That they make a dialogue with one another is the great secret of the world, the revealing and revealed secret, yes, the meaning of revelation.[65]

The Logic of Exceptionalism

Of course, we see this understanding of "knowledge as response" in Rosenstock-Huessy, too, and he identifies it as the central message of the Christian revelation. This, he argues, is what Jesus teaches as the Word which became flesh: namely, that "the logos is redeemed from the curse of always only being able to correct itself by itself. . . ."[66] If truth is response, then truth is always changing; and consequently, speech-thinking is never reductionist and cannot give rise to a hermeneutics of analysis or a hermeneutics of history characteristic of the logic of sacrifice.

Finally, Schelling's account of God's life and the nature of divine and human knowledge not only guards against reductionism, but it also funds a knowledge of rest or repose within an order of law. It funds, as Rosenzweig's account of sacrifice so clearly exposes, a wisdom of abiding. According to both Rosenzweig and Rosenstock-Huessy, speech-thinking implies that knowledge is historical. However, Rosenstock-Huessy indentifies Christological truth with a stable source of historical response and changeability. Earmarking this singular location of meaning inevitably alters any recognition of historicity emergent from the structure of speech-thinking. Exceptionalism overrides historicity. Alternatively, Rosenzweig's notion of abiding exposes history and permits a documentation of events or happenings as they occur.

Still, knowledge in Schelling's account is not simply the perpetual documentation of change within the drama of encounter. Knowledge is also the self-consciousness of the "who" I am within the order. All the while that I respond, all the while that I change, I remain the one ordered by the transcendent—by the difference between God's act beyond being and my existence as both commanded and loved in and through this act. If, as Schelling indicates, nature and spirit emerge as distinct from God and as loved or gifted by God, they therefore emerge and exist in the affirmation and definition of the fullness of their being as ordered by the God who ensouls them. Applied to persons, therefore, knowledge or wisdom is also a composition of our responses to a changing world on the one hand and the self-consciousness of the irreducibility of our position as human and therefore complete and different from world and God on the other hand. If truth in the logic of sacrifice commits one to self-alienation or self-sacrifice, knowledge in the context of revelation presupposes the fullness of my humanity within the lawfulness of the divine order. Revelation resolves the apparent antinomy between a recognition of historical truth and its dissolution into relativism. Rosenzweig's position on revelation introduced in the letters reflects the two-fold character of knowledge as historical and knowledge as ordered. As both Rosenzweig and Rosenstock-Huessy attest, revelation is orientation.[67] It is grace ordered in law. It is this awareness that Abraham, according to Rosenzweig, performs in the sacrifice of Isaac. Abraham can perform the sacrifice and know that he will not have to sacrifice at all. He abides and Isaac abides in their irreducibility as exposed in the revelation of the God who acts in freedom: that is to say, commands (in difference from) and loves (as affirmation of) and positions them according to the structure of the divine order.

Ultimately, it is Rosenzweig's steadfast assumption of Schelling's account of the nexus between divine existence, divine revelation, divine wisdom, and divine law that permits him to articulate an alternative to Rosenstock-Huessy's troublesome account of Jewish-Christian relations. As this volume will indicate, the account of law and its relation to apologetics is fully developed by Rosenzweig only in later works: most importantly, his essay, "Apologetic Thinking." Nonetheless, the basis for this essay already appears in Rosenzweig's letters. Earlier, I noted how Rosenzweig proposed the same interpretation for the Abrahamic and Christological sacrifice.

> The two sacrifices, that on Moriah and that on Golgatha have this in common . . . nothing was got out of them (since what was sacrificed is identical with what was given back) but the sacrifice itself becomes in effect the abiding object of faith, and thereby that which abides. *That which abides is different* [emphasis, mine] on the one hand, an external community, and on the other an external man and the consequences of this make mutual understanding so difficult that the one side is always being seduced into classifying the other with those that know of nothing abiding.[68]

This quote presents the basis for a Jewish-Christian apologetics rooted in the logic of the law. Both Judaism and Christianity identify revelation as the nexus of gift and order, but this understanding of revelation affords them a unique position for a defense of their faith to the other. Who is the Jew or the Christian in this context? She is the one for whom God's revelation or encounter takes on a certain documentation—a certain narration in a certain context. No doubt, Rosenzweig avers, the Jew and the Christian differ with respect to "what" abides, "who" is affected, the description of how they are affected and what it means. All this is the stuff of our traditions, our textual and liturgical accounts of revelation, creation, and redemption. That we abide, however, means that each of us abides as ordered and affected by God. Such an order does not reduce us nor alienate us from our humanity. Rather, it endows us with what we are out of the freedom of the God whose law does not emerge from desire but from affirmation. Still, as we are, we are limited. We are not the other. We cannot consume the other nor reduce the other to our perspective. Standing in the law, our self-consciousness offers us what Rosenzweig will later refer to as a "candid exposition"[69] of the self—a snapshot of our position within the divine order.

What are the consequences of this self-consciousness for apologetics? If apologetics is a defense of the faith to another, the lawfulness of our position requires that we defend our position only so far as we also identify the limits of our position. We are, in other words, justified only in and through the law. It is precisely this position that Rosenstock-Huessy ignores. Rosenstock-Huessy honors the grace of God but not the law. Such an oversight guarantees the triumphalism of the Christian perspective, and ultimately, reduces the wisdom of revelation to a human account of the meaning of Christ as the "center of history." Alternatively, Rosenzweig's position suggests that any claims we may make concerning revelation are justified to the extent that we understand them within the larger context of our indebtedness to the God who acts. Such a position permits a religious community to verify a position through time without permitting it to absolutely falsify another's claim. Defense of the faith is tantamount to a presentation of the conditions of the possibility of the justifiability of my claim. Does such a defense require an openness to the other's claim? Not necessarily. It does, however, permit the possibility of such an openness if reasons to engage in this openness are presented. The possibility of this openness is, of course, premised upon the sober and candid recognition of the nature of the other's claim as a series of narrated responses to changing history as registered or narrated by the other community and defined within the context of the divine order. Rosenzweig's reference to the tendency by Jews and Christians to write off one another's claims as false (non-abiding) is part-and-parcel of his appreciation of how difficult it is for Jews and Christians to distinguish between their right to verify or document their knowledge of God and world and their desire to link this verification with a concomitant falsification of each other's position. Implicit in Rosenzweig's comment is his claim that lawfulness is necessary to regulate the desire for truth. Said otherwise, Rosenzweig's recognition of the temptation to permit our desires to script our histories and declare them truth is his recognition of the seduction of the logic of sacrifice. His alternative to this logic and his response to Rosenstock-Huessy in particular as he introduces it here in the letters is the recognition that although we are free to relay our histories, our histories are the product of and structured by the infusion of divine grace and law. It is the central task of this book to detail this logic of the law and expose its paradigm-altering affect upon Jewish-Christian relations.

TWO

Monotheism and Exceptionalism

The central argument of Chapter 1 discussed how Jewish-Christian relations have been paralyzed by Christian accusations of Jewish exceptionalism that fail to identify the logic of exceptionalism operating within Christian theology's unbridled account of divine sovereignty and concomitant antipathy toward Jewish law. Recent scholarship by Regina Schwartz and Martin Jaffee among others has deepened this Christian antipathy toward Jewish law by rooting the so-called "exceptionalism" of Jewish law in the larger and more damaging context of Jewish monotheism. Not only do these scholars suggest, like Agamben, that Jewish law is divisive, but they also argue that the divisive character of Jewish law emerges from an intractable and often violent intolerance characteristic of biblical and then later developed forms of Jewish monotheism. If the central objective of this volume is to demonstrate the apologetic capacity of a revelatory account of Jewish law, it is crucial to contend with arguments that attempt to link Jewish monotheism with clear and certain intolerance toward other. Chapters 4, 5, and 6 will present the logic of law that constitutes the heart of a theology of revelation and offers a philosophically and theologically rigorous basis for a Jewish (and Christian) apologetic, but it is the goal of this chapter to challenge recent assaults against Jewish monotheism.

The chapter will proceed in three parts. First, I will review and critique Regina Schwartz's *The Curse of Cain*, which represents the most vitriolic and rhetorically damaging presentation of biblical monotheism's fundamental intolerance. From here, I will turn to an analysis of Moshe Halbertal's and Avishai Margalit's *Idolatry*. Halbertal's and Margalit's work systematically deconstructs overly generalized claims concerning the analytic link between monotheism and intolerance. Halbertal's and Margalit's book illuminates the difference between metaphysically grounded and nonmetaphysically grounded claims against idolatry. In my estimation, Halbertal's and Margalit's work indicates that the greatest challenge to a Jewish apologetics resides in Jewish philosophical claims asserting the absolute "error" of idolatrous positions. Margalit and Halbertal earmark Moses Maimonides' work as the greatest example of a philosophically rooted anti-idolatrous position. My effort to establish a basis for a revelatory apologetics must contend with the charge of exceptionalism as launched against Maimonides' account of divine nature.

Therefore, the third part of the chapter will analyze the extent to which Maimonides' account of monotheism waxes exceptionalist or not—and if exceptionalist, precisely how and/or in what ways. Here, I will consider Margalit's and Halbertal's suggestion that the divine exceptionalism in Maimonides' *The Guide of the Perplexed* derives from the Greek elements in his thought and is countered by the classically Jewish aspects of his program. Ultimately, I will disagree with this assessment because to argue that Maimonides is not an exceptionalist when and only when one considers the Jewish aspects of his thought over and against the Greek aspects of his thought only repeats the logic of exceptionalism within this evaluation itself. To be non-exceptionalist, Maimonides' portrait of monotheism must render both the so-called Greek and Jewish elements of his theological account valid and irreducible to the other. In what follows, therefore, I will argue that although Maimonides' theology of monotheism retains a tension between a portrait of divine being as inviolate and transcendent on the one hand and a profile of a divine freedom capable of acting on behalf of that which is other than God on the other hand, Maimonides' recognition of the possibility of divine freedom anticipates an account of monotheism that retains an emphasis upon both the transcendence of divine nature and the divine capacity to extend toward that which is other than God. In this way, Maimonides' work points to a theology of divine freedom and law, which

I will argue can be found in the Hebrew Scriptures along with the later philosophical and theological work of Franz Rosenzweig and paves the way for a non-exceptionalist, philosophico-theological account of monotheism.

Monotheism and Exceptionalism: The Curse of Cain?

Since the 1990s, the field of religious studies has entered a new phase of self-consciousness attempting to chip away at long-standing, western assumptions concerning religion. Topping the list of problematic presuppositions stands the unexamined bias toward monotheism in analyses of world religions. As a result of this methodological self-consciousness, few persons today doubt the monotheistic biases plaguing the fathers of religious studies starting with Otto, continuing with Hume, and reinforced in Durkheim and Weber. Unfortunately, this effort to call into question monotheistic biases in the study of religion has swelled beyond the reinforcement of a self-critical stance in scholarship and has devolved into frontal attacks against biblical and Judaic monotheism as antagonistic toward and intolerant of nonmonotheistic positions. Regina Schwartz's *The Curse of Cain* is, in my estimation, largely responsible for the rhetorical shift away from a careful critique of ideological assumptions to an attack on biblical monotheism in particular.[1] Given the significance of the biblical texts for any Jewish account of revelation and law, it is important to contend with Schwartz's critique of biblical monotheism before presenting my account of the apologetic potential of a Jewish logic of revelatory law.

According to her introduction, Schwartz's book is an effort to "trace the notion of identity born in violence to the Bible . . ."[2] and to the concept of the monotheistic God of the biblical text in particular. Throughout Chapters 1 and 2, Schwartz offers interpretations of biblical texts to illuminate and support her fundamental claim. By Chapter 3, however, this approach breaks down when she shifts her central claim and says

> [I]t should be apparent by now that what I have been exploring here is not a single view of the Other that is somehow "in the bible," but instead pursuing a strategy of reading the Bible that makes any single consistent ideological viewpoint difficult to defend. Such a strategy makes it difficult to use the Bible as a political club.[3]

There are, therefore, two ways to tackle Schwartz's project. The first, which I will pursue in Chapter 4, is to explore biblical texts and interpretations that offset her identification of monotheism and intolerance. Here, however, I will offer an internal critique of her book and argue that the book employs two different and contradictory logics and cannot successfully support its central claim linking monotheism and intolerance.

Schwartz's *The Curse of Cain* begins with the following assertion, "monotheism is a myth that grounds particular identity in universal transcendence. And monotheism is a myth that forges identity antithetically against the Other."[4] The first part of Schwartz's book discusses the biblical basis of this link between a divine exceptionalism and human identitarianism. Schwartz pays particular attention to the notion of covenant, which first offered by God to Abraham, and then to the Jewish people at Sinai, "cuts" through Abraham and his descendants by dividing the descendants into the class of those who are obedient and accepted and those who are disobedient and excepted. As Schwartz puts it, "the Hebrew phrase for 'he made a covenant,' *karat berit* is literally 'he cut a covenant,' and the violence of that ostensibly dead metaphor is dramatized in each of the biblical ceremonies of the covenant."[5] Schwartz chooses to ignore that the covenants are premised upon unconditional promises of love, land, and future. In Genesis 17, it says

> And I will establish My covenant between Me and thee and thy seed after thee throughout their generations for an *everlasting* [italics, mine] covenant, to be a God unto thee and to thy seed after thee. And I will give unto thee, and to thy seed after thee, the land of thy sojournings, all the land of Canaan, for an *everlasting* [italics, mine] possession; and I will be their God.[6]

Still, Schwartz argues that just as the covenant cuts and divides Jewish identity, it also cuts and divides Jews from non-Jews: that is, all persons who stand outside of the covenantal structure. Predicated upon the pledge of absolute obedience to the sovereign God, covenantal exceptionalism is exponential, cutting internally first and then externally as well.

Ultimately, Schwartz roots this chain of exceptionalism in what she calls "the metaphysics of scarcity afflicting the God of the Hebrew Scriptures himself." Only a God, she argues, without enough would insist upon an absolute, unwavering loyalty as a strategy for retaining the little that he has. Consequently, the God who does not have enough issues strict laws that delimit the freedom of those who are commanded in the name of securing their exclusive allegiance. Biblical law, Schwartz contends, derives from a conflict of desire within God himself and stimulates an internal conflict for those who are delimited by it and against those who fail to adhere to it.

> Most systems of ethics are predicated upon the assumption of scarcity, the notion that there is not enough to go around . . . it is the combination of scarcity and its

stepchild greed that gives rise to the ethical dilemmas of which life is made. . . . The law assumes that we cannot have what we want and so we will covet, steal or even kill our neighbor to get it. . . . I wonder (as much as Paul does in Romans) if the laws protecting men from violence against one another are not the corollary of conceiving identity in violence in the first place. It seems that defining ourselves against the Other sets in motion a cycle of violence that no legislation can hold.[7]

In Chapter 2, Schwartz extends the link between monotheism, covenantal identity, and identity with the land. According to Schwartz, the God who (in her own account) seeks to secure his people's allegiance promises them a land to inherit if and when they obey him. Again, Schwartz's reading of the biblical text is premised upon a far-reaching neglect of the nature of God's promise as unconditional. The promise of the land is part and parcel of God's "everlasting" covenant with the Jewish people regardless of their obedience.[8] Nonetheless, Schwartz argues that "their existence is subject to a contract: their God demands loyalty from them and in return promises them, numerous descendants, almighty nation, and land."[9] Slavishly identitarian, the Israelites lap up the exclusive relationship God offers them and use this identity to violently distinguish themselves from others all the while they live in the silent fear of losing this identity and being excepted or exiled from the land their faith has evidently earned them. In the language of the previous chapter, Schwartz translates a logic of law into a logic of sacrifice, accessorized with all the elements of currency, payment, and perpetual fear of loss.

Later, Schwartz takes matters further when she describes the Israelites as a conquered people who pathologically respond to their plight by morphing into conquerors themselves. If Schwartz suggests that exile is the spatial expression of the existential condition of exception built into the relationship with the monotheistic God who demands exclusive loyalty for himself, it is also, she argues, the justification for conquest, and she says, "Narratives of conquest and exile are the logical elaborations of a doctrine of land possession."[10] Taken as a whole, monotheism produces conquerors whose desperate desire to reclaim the land they once possessed gives them the false sense of justification to dishonorably and violently assume possession of someone else's land.

It is worth noting that Schwartz's characterization of the Israelites as conquerors contradicts the logic in her prior interpretation of the text. If the semantic-logical nexus between exile and conquest is predicated upon land ownership, then this logic does not apply to the Israelites. By her own account, the Israelites inherit the land from God. God owns and possesses the land, and the biblical text indicates this time and again as I will detail in Chapter 4 on the Sabbatical.[11] If, as Schwartz asserts, landedness is conditioned upon obedience to God, return to the land is equally premised upon obedience to God and not a matter of autonomous conquest. We can see the fault lines in her logic when toward the end of her chapter, she reiterates her earlier position and says

> [T]he nexus of exodus, conquest, monotheism and possession and the intractable logic that binds them together are set in stark relief—a people are possessed, they are delivered from oppression, they are conferred a land, and all are a ringing endorsement of monotheistic omnipotence.[12]

Here, Schwartz is right. The coming into the land is a testament to monotheistic omnipotence (among other things, monotheistic love and care as well) and not a testament to the unlimited right of the Israelites to inhabit autonomously and possess the land that God's promise alone guarantees.

The logical gaffe at the end of Chapter 2 is only one example of the logical flaws in Schwartz's argument. If the objective of Chapters 1 and 2 is to offer a basis for the assertion that monotheism results in intolerance, the remainder of the book offers a demonstration of how the surplus of semantic possibilities afforded by the biblical text undoes efforts to defend absolute propositions as final interpretations of the biblical text. The more she engages in the text, the more Schwartz sees how the text interrogates its own apparently self-certain conclusions. This recognition in hand, Schwartz must qualify or alter her insistence upon the textual link between monotheism and intolerance. Try as she may, the biblical text will not support the claim that monotheism antagonistically and violently rejects the other.

Perhaps the best example of Schwartz's logical conundrum emerges in her analysis of the character of kinship. Given her commitment to showing the linking of monotheism, identity, and intolerance to others, one would expect Schwartz to use the kinship texts to identify hard and fast distinctions concerning kin and non-kin. But Schwartz's walk through the biblical material suggests otherwise, as seen in her discussion of the book of Ezra. Insistent upon her thesis, she argues that

> Ezra wants to erect a virtual fence or a wall around Israel, to deem everything inside holy and everything outside polluted. The demand that those who have intermarried must put away their foreign wives is framed as his effort to purify Israel of its abomination. . . . This recourse to the Levitical category of purity is

the most xenophobic utterance the Bible will make about drawing the borders of Israel by kinship. . . .[13]

Schwartz connects Ezra's intolerance toward others to Ezra's monotheism. The "virulent particularism in Ezra's order . . . springs from that special kind of particularism, zeal for monotheism. . . ."[14] But Schwartz's reading of Ezra hits a wall shortly thereafter when she notes that the book of Ezra problematizes the possibility of defining the foreigner. And she says

> [T]he land is unclean with the impurity of the people, but who are "these people of the lands". . . . When the "peoples of the lands" become a generic Other . . . this renders Ezra's project of purifying Israel of foreigners impossible. Apparently, being intent on rejecting the foreigner does not simplify the task of defining and not being able to define him makes him difficult to reject. Like kinship, purity is an impossible project.[15]

Schwartz is a careful enough reader to recognize the text's ability to problematize itself, but she does not seem to understand how this feature undermines the intent of her larger project.

Schwartz's reading stumbles on other occasions when the biblical text problematizes her sought-after interpretation. For example, by the end of her chapter on nationalism, she finds herself concluding that "a bible that suggests that identity is a question rather than an answer, provisional and not reified, fails to underwrite nationalism, imperialism and persecution of the Other, in part because it fails to make any clear claims about who the Other is."[16] Taken together, each of these examples compromises her ability to defend her original claim linking monotheism and intolerance, and readers are left unconvinced of its textual basis.

Describing Intolerance

If Regina Schwartz's *The Curse of Cain* offers a striking example of how difficult it is to use the biblical text as evidence of an incontrovertible link between monotheism and intolerance, Halbertal's and Margalit's *Idolatry* demonstrates the absence of a monolithic account of monotheism within the biblical and post-biblical Jewish tradition. Moreover, Halbertal's and Margalit's book helps distinguish between nonmetaphysically grounded bases for anti-idolatrous assertions and metaphysically grounded bases for anti-idolatrous assertions within the Jewish tradition. Only metaphysically grounded claims can support intolerance because they claim to be absolute.

ANTI-IDOLATRY IN THE JEWISH TRADITION: NONMETAPHYSICALLY
ROOTED CLAIMS

One half of Halbertal's and Margalit's book documents and analyzes several different, nonmetaphysically grounded sources of anti-idolatrous tendencies within Judaism. My argument here is that because these sources of anti-idolatrous positions are both indeterminate and not rooted in metaphysical claims, they cannot be used to support assertions of an absolute and necessary link between monotheism and intolerance.

Halbertal and Margalit offer an extensive survey of anti-idolatrous positions within the Judaic textual tradition. They consider the biblical antipathy for idolatrous worship, biblical and rabbinic prohibitions upon idolatrous representations, and Jewish claims regarding the link between myth and paganism. Of particular note are their analyses of the biblical antipathy for idolatrous worship and the biblical and rabbinic prohibition on idolatrous representations.

According to Halbertal and Margalit, the bible uses metaphorical language to describe the sin of idolatry. The bible does not present a philosophical rejection of idolatry but expresses its disdain for idolatry by comparing it with the community's moral disdain for its metaphor of marital betrayal. For example, Hosea 1:2, 2:9–11, 14–15:

> And she did not consider this: It was I who bestowed on her the new grain and wine and oil. . . . Assuredly, I will take back My new grain and in its time and My new wine . . . thus I will punish her for the days of the B'alim, on which she brought them offerings . . . she would go after her lovers, forgetting me—declares the Lord.[17]

Still, Halbertal and Margalit argue, regardless of how many similar examples one can find, metaphorical expressions of anti-idolatrous sentiment do not present absolute claims against idolatry. From my perspective, this means that they cannot be enlisted as evidence to support a link between biblical monotheism and absolute intolerance toward idolatry. Why? Because just as often as the biblical text enlists the metaphor of the adulterous wife to express disdain for idolatry, equally as often it destabilizes that same metaphor and shows God forgiving the Israelites. As the authors suggest, "[t]he metaphor of the relationship between husband and wife is extended to the reconciliation stage but here the metaphor is liable to become inappropriate."[18] If Israel and God were really husband and wife, reconciliation would be impossible. But God is not a husband. God is not delimited by his emotions, but has the capacity to rise above them and forgive the Israelite nation and reestablish his vow for an everlasting covenant, as in Ezekiel 16:60: "nevertheless, I will remember the covenant I made with you in the days of your youth and I will establish it with you as an everlasting covenant."[19] And Hosea 11:9 says, "What I wrote was 'a man' but it has already been written, 'For I am God, not man.'"[20] The precariousness of the metaphor destabilizes its prior anti-idolatrous use.

Habertal and Margalit also evaluate the status and meaning of biblical and rabbinic prohibitions against potentially idolatrous representations. First, Halbertal and Margalit exemplify the extensive range of representations permitted by the biblical and rabbinic texts, thereby dislodging claims that Judaism forbids and is intolerant of any sort of representation of the divine.[21] Second, the authors argue that one must distinguish between metaphysically based representational prohibitions and biblical and rabbinic prohibitions rooted in the appropriateness of the representation. For an example, the authors look at Mekhilta of R. Ishmael va-Yehi, a derash on the Exodus 13:21 verse, "The Lord went before them in a pillar of cloud by day." Philosophers, the authors argue, would undoubtedly challenge the truth-status of the text's representation of God as passing in a pillar of cloud. The rabbis, on the other hand, were concerned only with the appropriateness of the representation. This biblical and rabbinic standard of appropriate representation, the authors argue, licenses many representations and makes it impossible to argue absolutely against any particular image as idolatrous. These texts offer no absolute standard because what is deemed appropriate is a matter of on-going decision and is not premised upon a single account of the truth of reality.

ANTI-IDOLATRY: METAPHYSICALLY ROOTED CLAIMS

Idolatry as Error The second half of Halbertal's and Margalit's book explores a second kind of anti-idolatry claim rooted in metaphysical positions, or what the authors refer to as "idolatry as error." Notably, Maimonides is the only Jewish thinker whose work the authors use to exemplify this sort of intolerance. If, as I have suggested, nonmetaphysically rooted expressions of anti-idolatry cannot be used to defend the identification of monotheism as intolerance, the same cannot immediately be said for metaphysically based claims. Metaphysically rooted assertions against the falsehood of idolatry may generate absolutist claims against idolatry, and if woven into the Jewish tradition, could bolster a critique of the link between Jewish monotheism and intolerance. Consequently, it is important to digest Halbertal's and Margalit's survey of these philosophically charged claims, and in particular, their place in the work of Moses Maimonides, commonly recognized as the most significant philosopher in the Jewish tradition. Halbertal's and Margalit's discussion of metaphysically rooted strains of anti-idolatry can be divided into two categories: incorrect ideas about God, and incorrect actions rooted in incorrect conceptions of teleological focus. I will discuss each in turn.

Throughout their book, Halbertal and Margalit identify Maimonides' thought with a philosophical strain of anti-idolatrous intolerance. In their view, Maimonides' philosophy promotes an absolute intolerance toward idolatry on the grounds of its unique portrait of divine nature as unified and simple. More specifically, the authors argue that Maimonides' insistence upon the character of divine unity and simplicity prohibits attributing any character of corporeality to God, and Maimonides' insistence upon simplicity renders any account of divine multiplicity and/or change also illegitimate.

For Maimonides, the belief in the oneness of God meant not merely denial of polytheism, which is obvious, but, more important, denial of the perception of God himself as a complex being. The description of God as one, according to Maimonides, refers mainly to his own "simple unity." "Multiplicity" is therefore not only the belief in many gods, but it is also an error that concerns God himself, which may be called "internal polytheism." The strict demand on unity implies a rejection of corporeality, which assumes that God is divisible like any body and which excludes more subtle violations of unity, such as linguistic predication, in general.[22]

Halbertal and Margalit spell out the implications of this restricted account of divine nature for the issue of divine representations and conclude that for Maimonides, neither pictorial nor linguistic representations count as legitimate monotheistic expressions. Pictorial images anthropomorphize God, and linguistic representations divide God's nature into definable terms. Halbertal and Margalit note that Maimonides' strict adherence to the limits of divine nature renders his thought antagonistic to so-called idolatrous positions outside the bounds of the Jewish tradition as well as pit his position against the Jewish textual tradition at large—biblical, rabbinic, and mystical, which (as discussed earlier) does not abide by the same philosophical requirements of the Jewish God. In fact, at the end of their book, Margalit and Halbertal go so far as to suggest that the heavy-handed metaphysical commitment to a doctrine of the unity of God derives from the Greek influence in Maimonides' work; and this explains, therefore, the tension between Maimonides' philosophy and significant pieces of the Jewish theological tradition. Maimonides, they say

[E]quates worshiping other gods with having a wrong concept of God in the mind while worshiping. The main mistake about God is the anthropomorphic conception of God, the very conception that made sense of idolatry in the biblical approach. . . . Uprooting idolatry is chaining the imaginative faculty, and eradicating its role in the formation of the metaphysical picture of the world and its impact on the political behaviour of the multitudes. The influence of Greek philosophical culture is crucial in the formation of this Mamonidean concept of idolatry. The Aristotelian vision of God as a non-anthropomorphic being, detached from the fluctuating life of the emotions and the finitude of the body, portrays the false god as the anthropomorphic god, the product of the imagination. It is an interesting dialectical move in which a conception of God which originated outside the Jewish tradition and was assimilated into the tradition, at least by Maimonides, redefines the boundaries of the tradition, leaving outside some of elements that had been within it.[23]

With this argument, Margalit and Halbertal attempt to distance Maimonides' philosophical intolerance from their larger account of the Jewish tradition. Later, I will take up Margalit's and Halbertal's claim and argue against it on their own terms: namely, that a Jewish perspective (theology) that dismisses the possible validity of the Aristotelian model waxes just as exceptionalist as an Aristotelianism that denies the possibility of a more anthropomorphic account of God. Nonetheless, my disagreement with their interpretation of the metaphysical intolerance in Maimonides' theology does not mean that their analysis of the wide range of anti-idolatrous expressions in the biblical and rabbinic tradition cannot contribute to my overall effort to dislodge absolute identifications of monotheism with intolerance. It simply means that more will have to be done to articulate the terms for a "non-intolerant" Jewish philosophical and theological position. It is the task of the third main section of this chapter to offer a more detailed examination of the tension in Maimonides' theology between divine nature and divine freedom to install the basis for such a position.

Wrong Actions The second sort of philosophical error identified by Halbertal and Margalit is an error in actions. By "wrong actions," Halbertal and Margalit mean actions that go against a foundational principle or a major premise of any given world view. A good example of a major premise in the monotheistic traditions is the assumption of divine purpose or teleology as a basis for human action. They explain, "a great error in this framework is thus a mistake that someone makes with respect to his ultimate purpose. . . . This occurs when [a person] does not understand what [his humanity] obligates him to do in the management of his life."[24] Within a teleological system, a wrong action is an action that does not promote the purpose that constitutes the premise of the teleological world view. Once again, Halbertal and Margalit hold up Maimonides' philosophy as a case study for a philosophically rooted teleological system that excludes others on the grounds of their failure to perform in ways that verify the fundamental metaphysical purpose.

> The connection between error and teleology is even stronger in a view that regards man's purpose as reaching knowledge of truths about God, knowledge with a propositional nature. This seems . . . to be Maimonides' view . . . man's purpose does not follow a formal plan. It is achieved not only with the intellect but also through the supreme cognitions and truths about divine matters that this unique ability gives us. Living according to the intellect is thus a necessary formal condition for achieving the ultimate human purpose . . . .[25]

Although Halbertal and Margalit do not distinguish between them, one's teleological world view can derive from either a philosophical or revelatory basis. It is my contention that the possibilities for propping up intolerant beliefs arise only from philosophically rooted teleological systems and not from revelatory accounts.

To investigate this difference, I will also reference Martin Jaffee's article, "One God, One Revelation, One People: On the Symbolic Structure of Elective Monotheism." In his article, Jaffee presents an analysis of Jewish, Christian, and Islamic monotheism that bears striking resemblance to the analysis of "right and wrong action" presented by Margalit and Halbertal. There is, Jaffee argues, a common symbolic structure to each of the three monotheistic traditions, which he labels "elective monotheism." Jaffee distinguishes elective monotheism from philosophical monotheism and argues that only elective monotheism illuminates the unique relationship between the one God and the one community. Within this relationship, Jaffee asserts, communities are endowed with a *telos* or purpose—the pursuit of which pits them against all others who have not been privy to that *telos* and who in much of the way Halbertal and Margalit describe, constitute falsifications of this essential objective. Elective monotheism privileges a single community and renders it unique in its pursuit of the divine purpose. Whereas metaphysical monotheism, Jaffee says, "is . . . primarily about God as he is in himself or in relationship to the created order . . . [elective monotheism] is much more about God as he is in relationship to historical human communities—a relationship characterized by the position of love and hate."[26] Echoing ideas that we heard in Schwartz's work, Jaffee continues, "elective monotheism is driven by the assumption that the God who loves does not do so indiscriminately; rather, the divine love is a scarce commodity.... The possession of divine love is itself the warrant for ontological hatred of the very existence of the Other...."[27]

Jaffee's identification of wrong action with revelation forces us to ask whether there is a difference between a teleological commitment to a philosophically rooted world view and a similar commitment to a revelatory one. Halbertal and Margalit do not distinguish between the two types of claims: philosophical and revelatory. Their failure to do so leaves readers vulnerable to accounts like that offered by Jaffee, which insist upon a specific link between revelatory-based accounts of teleology and anti-idolatrous intolerance. In fact, Jaffee goes farther than Halbertal and Margalit, who note the philosophical rejection of wrong actions by persons committed to a particular metaphysical teleology. According to Jaffee, a revelatory-based teleological system licenses its adherents to a potentially violent intolerance toward others whose wrong actions violate the essential premise of the divine purpose. Is Jaffee right? Does a revelatory source of communal *telos* promote more intolerance than a philosophical monotheism on account of the unique relationship between God and the "elective" community? A clear review of the meaning of revelation in the Jewish tradition evidences the very opposite: namely, that a philosophically rooted account of human *telos* has a much greater potential for exceptionalism than a revelatory one because it presupposes the possibility of an absolute human grasp of truth in a way that I will suggest revelatory accounts do not.[28]

Although it is the goal of this volume as a whole to support this thesis, a few points in defense of the claim may be offered here. Jaffee's emphasis upon the tendency by elective monotheisms to pit themselves with certainty against others who do not act on behalf of the same teleological program neglects a fundamental feature characteristic of revelatory positions: namely, the difference between God as the source of the teleological position and persons as its recipients. As I will argue throughout the volume, the difference between the divine and the human displays a lawfulness characteristic of Jewish and Christian revelation. The assumption of this law of "difference" prohibits recipients of the contents of a divine revelation from asserting these contents as absolute claims. Persons who receive these truths to do not possess them and cannot assert the absolute falsehood of others who do not. The obligation to adhere to these truths is not tantamount to the license to proclaim them with certainty. The testimony of a divine truth does not correlate with the philosophical assertion of another's falsehood. By neglecting this feature of revelation, Jaffee mistakenly confuses revelation with metaphysical hubris.

The earlier distinction between philosophically and revelatory-based wrong actions in hand, it would seem that with the help of Margalit's and Halbertal's work, we can now assert that much of the Jewish tradition cannot be used to justify blanket intolerance toward idolatry. We can also narrow the scope of our concern to metaphysical bases of intolerance with a particular focus on the work of Maimonides, whose work, it seems, retains an intolerance toward both wrong ideas and wrong actions. It is to the discussion of the exceptionalism in Maimonides theology to which I now turn.

The Metaphysics of Exceptionalism

Thus far, I have offered alternative responses to Schwartz's reading of biblical monotheism as well as Jaffee's account of the logical structure of monotheism, generally speaking. Before presenting a detailed theology of revelation that offers a viable basis for a Jewish and Christian apologetics, it is worth examining the work of Maimonides because Halbertal and Margalit identify his work as the prime example of a metaphysically based source of anti-idolatrous exceptionalism within the Jewish tradition.

In what follows, I use an examination of Maimonides' doctrine of the creation of the world to demonstrate the tension in Maimonides' theology between a philosophical commitment to an account of God's transcendent nature on the one hand and a philosophico-theological account of God's free engagement with the created order on the other hand. Drawing from the tendency in scholarship to insist upon one or the other reading of Maimonides, I will suggest that Maimonides' inability to reconcile these two elements within his theology indicates an implicit exceptionalism in his work. If Halbertal and Margalit want to suggest that any exceptionalism toward "wrong ideas" regarding monotheism has more to do with the Greek rather than the Jewish elements in his thought, I will challenge this argument by asserting that it is Maimonides' failure to sustain the validity of both aspects of the divine self (aspects that are not strictly Jewish or Greek), which signifies the strict exceptionalism or internal polemic against "wrong" views of the monotheistic God in his work. Said in the language of the previous chapter, Maimonides' monotheism perpetuates a logic of sacrifice with regard to its failure to admit an element of alterity or difference within its conception of God. Before leaving this discussion, however, I will identify mechanisms in Maimonides' theology that, if further developed, could provide a basis for a nonpolemically driven, apologetically useful philosophico-theological account of the monotheistic God, an account which I will detail in the remainder of this volume.

Maimonides' theology expresses a tension between two different concerns. On the one hand, he works hard to retain the purity and transcendence of a certain account of divine nature. On the other hand, his theology seeks to meet the conditions required to render certain aspects of Jewish life understandable: Jewish law, in particular. Perhaps the greatest evidence of this tension can be found in the classic divide in scholarship regarding Maimonides' doctrine of the creation of the world. There are two dominant, opposing accounts of Maimonides' explanation of the creation of the world: scholars who assert that Maimonides holds to a doctrine of creation *ex nihilo*, and scholars who insist that Maimonides holds one or another version of the creation of the world from divine necessity (that is, either the Aristotelian "the world is eternal" argument or the Platonic "creation *de novo*" argument).[29]

In this discussion, the first position is represented in the work of Kenneth Seeskin, and the second position represented in the work of Shlomo Pines. I will argue that either position by itself renders Maimonides' monotheism exceptionalist to the extent to which it precludes the viability of the other position: in the one case, a divine necessity that precludes the possibility of a divine free self-othering; and in the other case, a divine self-othering that remains incommensurate with an account of the necessity and wisdom of divine Being. The root of Maimonides' exceptionalism cannot be identified strictly with the so-called "Greek" elements within his theology but reflects Maimonides' inability to reconcile the God of Being with the God beyond Being. Nonetheless, I will also suggest that Maimonides' thought contains mechanisms within itself for altering this internal tension, mechanisms that reflect a theology of divine freedom and law.

In offering this argument, I first turn to an analysis of Seeskin's *Maimonides and the Origin of the World*. Against the tide of esoteric readings of the *Guide*,[30] Seeskin argues that Maimonides said what he meant and meant what he said regarding the doctrine of creation *ex nihilo*. Seeskin's argument centers upon two points: According to Maimonides, a doctrine of the creation of the world by a spontaneous act of God is a necessary pillar of Jewish law; and, such a doctrine is at least possible (if not certain) on the grounds that neither Aristotle's account of the eternal existence of the world nor Plato's account of creation *de novo* successfully explain the reality of existence and therefore cannot theoretically be used to undermine the possibility of creation *ex nihilo*. As Seeskin explains elsewhere, the doctrine of creation *ex nihilo* refers to the notion that God alone constitutes sufficient cause for the existence of everything that is not God; and furthermore, that "the entire universe is brought into being by an act of divine will."[31] By contrast, creation *de novo*, the position Maimonides identifies with Plato's view, asserts that God creates the world like a potter creates a pot by giving the preexisting clay a form it did not formerly have. Although both creation *ex nihilo* and creation *de novo* take for granted that creation involves a free divine act, and both differ from the classic Aristotelian position, according to which God creates by virtue of what God is rather than what God does,[32] this does not mean, according to Seeskin, that Maimonides opted in favor of it. As we will see, Seeskin maintains that in Maimonides' estimation, creation *de novo* cannot adequately account for the existence of a contingent world, and consequently, he rejects it as the best explanation of the origin of the world.

For my purposes, the most significant feature of Seeskin's analysis is his claim that Maimonides' rejection of the Aristotelian and Platonic accounts is tied up with what he calls the essentialism of their accounts of "being" or their refusal to recognize the possibility of a God who acts freely as part and parcel of or somehow related to the reality of his Being. Maimonides' polemic against the Platonic and Aristotelian models does not, however, in Seeskin's account reflect an antinomy within Maimonides' own thought. Seeskin does not think that Maimonides' support for a doctrine of creation *ex nihilo* stands in conflict with his emphasis upon the stability, necessity, and changelessness of divine Being. Nonetheless, as our discussion of Shlomo Pines's position will indicate, other scholars do regard a Maimonidean embrace of creation *ex nihilo* as contradictory to his concern with the stability and changelessness of divine Being such that Seeskin's position inadvertently points to an exceptionalism within the creation *ex nihilo* position.

CREATION AS THE PILLAR OF THE LAW

In *The Guide of the Perplexed*, Maimonides writes

> [T]he belief in eternity the way Aristotle sees it—that is, the belief according to which the world exists in virtue of necessity, that no nature changes at all, and that the customary course of events cannot be modified with regard to anything—destroys the Law in its principle, necessarily gives the law to every miracle and reduces to insanity all the hopes and threats that the Law has held out. . . .[33]

According to Seeskin, Maimonides understood the necessary contradiction between an Aristotelian conception of the eternity of the world and the necessary theological preconditions of Jewish law. Seeskin unpacks the implications of Maimonides' claim as follows: The existence of the law presupposes that the world is not governed by necessity. Rather, Jewish law presupposes that reality is subject to change. But to say that reality is subject to change is to say that things (and people) can come in and out of existence—something may or may not be. Consequently, Seeskin continues, Maimonides understands that Jewish law reflects a fundamental difference between essence and existence and rejects a Platonic identification of existence with essence whereby existence constitutes an "accident" of essence. In Maimonides' view, essence means the reality of the thing that "remains the same whether or not [it] is instantiated."[34] Therefore, essence, Seeskin says, "remains neutral with regard to existence."[35] The existence of a thing is not an accident of the essence of a thing but an accident or feature of the concrete individual reality in which an essence is embodied.

There are two important implications of Maimonides' insistence upon the difference between existence and essence. The first, as Seeskin indicates, is that essence cannot be the cause of existence. The existence or embodiment of an essence in a concrete individual thing is of no significance to the reality of its essence because essence "remains the same whether or not it is instantiated"[36]. The essence of a thing cannot explain why it does or does not exist. "Because the reason for the existence of a finite thing must be sought in something other than the essence, eventually all talk of existence must culminate in a God who exists necessarily and confers existence on other things."[37] Second, the contingency of an existent thing demands an explanation of its origin. That existence is not reducible to essence results in the inevitable query, "Why is there something rather than nothing—or why does this thing exist or not exist?" And if the reality of existence cannot be explained by recourse to the eternality of essence or being, then it can be explained only by recourse to a reality that can give rise to something other than itself through a free act "beyond" what we conceive of as its essence or being. Only a Being capable of acting freely can account for why there is something and not nothing. This is what Seeskin means when he says, "I suggest therefore, that according to Maimonides, *bereshit* has to imply temporal as well as causal priority. God is not just the principle that underlies the world (causal priority) but the agent that brought the world into existence."[38]

Seeskin's reading attributes to Maimonides a position that we have already seen laid out in Schelling's *Ages of the World*: namely, that the reality of an existing world requires the possibility of a God who acts as an agent in a manner that differs from any possible effect of essence alone, as we apprehend it. And he says

Maimonides called attention to a fundamental feature of human existence: the world does not present itself to us as the effect of an eternal process that can only culminate in one result but as the object of a free and benevolent will. Thus the world is contingent in the sense that God could have created a different world or no world at all . . . in a word, existence is a gift.[39]

GREEK EXCEPTIONALISM AND THE FAILURE TO GRASP CONTINGENCY

Plato The second of aspect of Seeskin's argument attempts to show that although not absolutely certain, a doctrine of creation *ex nihilo* is possible insofar as neither of the two dominant Greek accounts adequately explain the origin or fact of existence.[40] In one way or another, both the Aristotelian and the Platonic accounts remain limited by a philosophical *essentialism*, wherein a set definition of the fundamental reality of divine nature as necessary and eternal prohibits the possibility of the creation of a world that exists and is different from God's own eternal necessity.

Of the three possible theories of the origin of the world announced in *The Guide of the Perplexed*—namely, the Aristotelian, the Mosaic, and the Platonic—Maimonides discusses the Platonic least of all. Nonetheless, Seeskin argues that Maimonides rejects the Platonic account.[41] Maimonides discusses Plato's view in 2.13 of the *Guide*. There, he emphasizes that

> They [the followers of Plato] believe that there exists a certain matter that is eternal as the deity is eternal and that He does not exist without it, nor does it exist without Him. They do not believe that is he is the same rank in what exists as He . . . but that He is the cause of its existence; and that it has the same relation toward Him as, for instance, clay has toward a potter or iron toward a smith; and that He creates in it whatever He wishes. Thus He sometimes forms out of it a heaven and an earth, and sometimes He forms out of it something else.[42]

Why according to Seeskin does Maimonides reject the Platonic view? As Seeskin sees it, Maimonides rejects the Platonic view because it does not adequately explain the existence of a contingent world from a noncontingent God. Although Maimonides thinks, Seeskin says that

> [The Platonic view] is compatible with free will in God and can be supported by passages where the Demiurge is said to deliberate, make judgments and promise not to destroy the heavens . . . [nonetheless] a God with free will is more than a first cause of the world but a God who can give the gift of existence, issue commandments, and promise redemption."[43]

Matter in Plato's account is eternal, and the mere fact that the deity imposes order upon it does not mean that this God can create a contingent world.

In Seeskin's estimation, Plato's thought waxes far too essentialist for Maimonides. By essentialist, Seeskin means that for Plato, perfection means limit or essence—"to be one thing rather than another."[44] From this point of view, an "infinite" God is "not a mark of perfection" because infinity suggests that which exceeds limits and essence. Plato's Demiurge is, therefore, bound by the perfection of its essence and cannot and will not violate this structure. But, Seeskin suggests, Maimonides cannot explain the reality of contingent existences from the vantage point of the limits of this essence. The *Guide*, Seeskin indicates, argues differently and says that "[God] has no discernible essence . . . He . . . has no causes anterior to Him that are the cause of His existence and by which, in consequence, He is defined. For this reason it is well known among all people engaged in speculation . . . that God cannot be defined."[45]

Aristotle Seeskins's discussion of Maimonides' position on the Aristotelian view deepens this claim that Maimonides' commitment to the theological presuppositions of the law distances him from classic Greek accounts given their refusal to assert a God capable of acting beyond the limits of a defined nature. According to Seeskin, Maimonides rejects Aristotle's account and declares it the opposite of the Mosaic position because Aristotle's position presupposes a correlation and ontological identity implicit in the causal relationship between God and world—an identity that in Maimonides' view is incompatible with the account of the world implicit within the law. In the *Guide* (2.14), Maimonides discusses Aristotle's arguments for the eternity of the world as it derives from his analysis of the world on the one hand and from his account of the nature of God on the other hand. For my purposes here, I am interested only in Maimonides' review of Aristotle's arguments from the nature of God.

The premise of these arguments is the correlation between God's nature and the reality of the world: a premise that, as mentioned, Maimonides will reject as incompatible with the demands of the law. The main thrust of these arguments is that creation *ex nihilo* defies the nature of God and therefore must be impossible. Divine nature is inviolate, and the nature of the world must correspond to and reflect this nature. In particular, three of the five arguments posit a gulf between God's nature and wisdom and any assertion of a divine will that incurs change in this nature. For example:

1. If God created the world *de novo*, this would mean that prior to this act, God had the potential but not the enacted ability to create such that creation entails divine change. But God's nature is such that God does not change; therefore; he cannot create a new world.

2. Or, if an agent acts now but not before, this must be because there was something keeping it from acting before.
3. Or, finally, if God acts to will a new thing at a given point in time, then we must wonder what God was doing before that time, and if the answer is "nothing," this reflects the absurdity of the question.

As Seeskin indicates, Maimonides presents two different kinds of responses to these Aristotelian (and/or neo-Aristotelian)[46] arguments from the nature of God. The first set of responses takes for granted the Aristotelian notion of divine nature and attempts to demonstrate how the creation of the world from nothing can comport with it. The best example of this sort of argument presented in Seeskin's account is the argument from "delayed effect." If the Aristotelian challenge suggests that God cannot act to create something new without changing from one disposition or status to another, the argument from delayed effect retorts that God can will out of necessity. In other words, God can will from out of the perfect intent of his wisdom. As reflective of this perfect intent, God's will does not undergo any change just because the object willed is temporal. The important distinction is between willing change and changing one's will. "I can," Seeskin says, "will today something that will not be accomplished until tomorrow and something completely different the next day without interference from outside factors."[47] Just because something in the world (or in this instance, the "world itself") changes does not mean that this change is not willed from out of the set directive of the divine wisdom or nature. God's will is always active. It does not move from potency to actuality even though it can will something that is by virtue of this will, moved from potency to actuality in time.

In the second sort of response, Maimonides changes his strategy, according to Seeskin, and challenges the essentialism in these arguments or what is their insistence upon the limits of the divine nature or wisdom. We see an example of this essentialism in the third argument reviewed by Maimonides: namely, that God is perfect, and therefore, whatever is a product of this perfection is itself "the most perfect existent that is" and *qua* perfect "does not serve an end beyond it."[48] Said otherwise, existence is perfect as it is, and therefore should exist perpetually as it is, and is therefore eternal. Of course, as Seeskin elucidates, the argument rests upon the assumption that we know the character of divine wisdom and its limits, and therefore, if this wisdom is perfect, anything emergent from this perfection would be the same. What if, Maimonides asks, we do not fully apprehend the nature of divine wisdom? What if we do not have a complete definition of the divine nature? Then, we could not establish the correlation between God's nature and the nature of the world. Thus, Seeskin says, Maimonides replies, "The world is consequent upon His perpetual and immutable wisdom. But we are completely ignorant of the rule of that wisdom and of the decision made by it."[49] In Seeskin's view, Maimonides challenges the essentialism in Aristotle's argument by recourse to negative theology. God is incomparable to all else, and therefore, the reality of God negates the theological meaning of anything positive (or negative) that we might say or predicate about the divine nature.

While Maimonides—as Seeskin and others have made clear—distances himself from the radical position of the Mutakallimūn, a group of Islamic theologians who argue that the world is a product and reflection of the divine will free from a discernible nature,[50] Maimonides does suggest that Aristotle's account of the limits of divine nature too rashly dismisses the transcendence and possible freedom of a perfect God: a freedom of God to act both within the limits and outside of the limits of what we deem his nature. In Maimonides' estimation, the divine nature is perfect, but its perfection renders it beyond our full apprehension. God's perfection is not reducible to the essentialist definition of the divine being and its concomitant claims regarding its inviolate structure but exceeds the limits of this structure and sustains an unknowability derived from the uniqueness of its very perfection itself. Who are we to say that God cannot create a world that is different from himself without betraying his own nature? As Seeskin states, there are for Maimonides "no grounds for asserting a resemblance between an act of will and the object willed in the act . . . the categories of cause and change do not apply to the will."[51] Unlike the Mutakallimūn, we can, the argument goes, ascribe wisdom to God because if we did not, "God's actions would be futile or frivolous because they would not accomplish anything. . . ."[52] This does not mean that we apprehend the divine wisdom, and in 2.19, Maimonides argues that "the world is consequent upon His perpetual and immutable wisdom. But we are completely ignorant of the result of that wisdom and of the decision made by it."[53]

By arguing that Maimonides uses negative theology to challenge an Aristotelian essentialism, Seeskin does not mean to suggest that Maimonides' support for the doctrine of creation *ex nihilo* conflicts with his own emphasis upon divine unchangability, unity, and necessity. While Seeskin holds that Maimonides rejects the former, this does not mean that he rejects the commensurability between divine freedom (will) and divine nature (wisdom) but only that we cannot know how the two are commensurate. Seeskin does admit that Maimonides offers conflicting accounts of the relationship between will and wisdom, but he attributes these changing positions to varying rhetorical contexts: When speaking about the Mutakallimūn, Maimonides emphasizes "wisdom"; when speaking against Aristotle, he emphasizes "will," and sometimes he even conflates the two, suggesting that the difference between them is unimportant.[54] Nonetheless, Seeskin insists that we not "read these passages as evidence of relaxed standards of rigor"[55] but see them as invocations of a negative theology that ought to discourage us from speculating about God's nature and will at all. In Seeskin's account, it is Maimonides' invocation of negative theology that saves the day from one of two troubling positions either: a devolution into a Greek essentialism, which denies the possibility of the creation of the world as the free gift of the free God whose will and wisdom both exceed our apprehension; or the contradiction between divine will and divine wisdom (between the God "beyond Being" and the God of "Being").

Seeskin's interpretation of Maimonides' position is helpful because it demonstrates the essentialism and the exceptionalism in the Aristotelian and Platonic accounts when used to negate the possibility of the freedom of God to act "beyond" a discernible essence.[56] As presentations of God's being, which prohibit the possibility of a free divine act, they not only "except" or dismiss the reality and value of anything that is "not" identical or self-same with divine nature, but they also "except" any aspect of God's own self that does not constitute a repetition of this delimited essence as well. Greek essentialism becomes Greek exceptionalism when "being" is "inviolate" and cannot reach beyond or validate anything beyond itself.

Still, the question remains whether Seeskin's reading of Maimonides' support for the doctrine of creation *ex nihilo* waxes exceptionalist as well. Seeskin attempts to show how God's free act of gifting existence does not conflict with God's Being. But is he right? Does Maimonides' support for the doctrine of creation *ex nihilo* conflict with his own claims concerning divine nature—and if so, does not this mire Maimonides' support for the freedom of God in a reverse exceptionalism whereby assertions of divine being are precluded by this account?

Pines Seeskin's interpretation of Maimonides is challenged by a number of Maimonidean scholars. Not only is there scholarship that disagrees with Seeskin's interpretation of Maimonides' support for creation *ex nihilo*, but many of these scholars would also contest his suggestion that a Maimonidean support for creation *ex nihilo* does not conflict with Maimonides' account of divine nature.

Shlomo Pines's work is a good example. Pines's central argument states that creation *ex nihilo* conflicts with Maimonides' theology of divine nature, and therefore, it is not Maimonides' philosophical position. Pines does not attempt to reconcile the two readings of Maimonides' account of monotheism. In his "Introduction to the Guide," Pines identifies the link between Maimonides' theology of divine free will and that of the famous Mutakallimūn scholar Al-Gahazli, whose own account of the freedom of God was designed to demonstrate the difference between the God of religion and the God of the philosophers. In particular, Pines says that

[W]e may entertain the supposition that the antithesis established by
Maimonides between the God of religion who possess a free will, in the exercise of which He is not bound to act in accordance with the order of nature, and the God of the Aristotelian philosophers, who is hamstrung by the immutability of this order, owes a great deal to al-Gahazli.[57]

Pines goes on to point how this antithesis shows up in 2.22 of the *Guide*, where Maimonides indicates the opposition between the view of religion in favor of a God of free will and the view of the philosophers: namely, "that the deity whom everyone who is intelligent recognizes to be perfect in every kind of perfection, could, as far as all the beings are concerned, produce nothing new in any of them. . . ."[58]

Nonetheless, although Pines—like Seeskin—recognizes Maimonides' strict divide between the God of religion and the God of the [Greek] philosophers, Pines disagrees with Seeskin's reading of Maimonides' own position and argues that just because Maimonides realized the "true issue between philosophy and religion, or religious Law, does not necessarily mean that in the final analysis he, like al-Ghazali . . . chose religion."[59] Maimonides, in Pines's reading, does invoke negative theology to support the view of religion over the view of the philosophers (2.25), but nonetheless, Pines maintains that a Maimonidean endorsement of this view would inevitably mire him in a "welter of inconsistencies" and contradict his position on "fundamental issues"[60]—in particular, his account of the commensurability between the eternality and necessity of divine wisdom and the eternality and necessity (and not the "freedom") of the divine will. "Negative theology," Pines says, "may not hold up to close scrutiny: Maimonides makes it clear that God is an intellect, with which the human intellect has at least an analogy; and he also affirms (although, taken literally, this statement contradicts his doctrine of the divine attributes) that in God will follows wisdom.[61] From Al-Ghazali's point of view, the last statement is tantamount to a negation of the nature of will."[62] From Pines's perspective, the free will of creation *ex nihilo* conflicts with the will that follows wisdom. In other words, any will that follows wisdom is not really a will at all, and at the end of the day, there is an incontrovertible contradiction between the free will of the God of creation and the wisdom of the God of Being. Although in Pines's view, Maimonides may have supported the religious position for political utility, it remained intellectually undesirable and in conflict with Maimonides' own philosophical position, and he says

> [I]t seems plausible to believe that, while for practical reasons, out of public spirit, Maimonides chose to aid and abet the faithful adherents of religion through the act of will referred to above, he belonged as far as his overriding intellectual convictions were concerned to the opposite camp.[63]

Undoubtedly, Pines's view gains support from Maimonides' regular insistence upon the character of divine perfection coupled with Maimonides' frequent insistence that the purpose of human life is to gain knowledge of and participate in the perfection of divine wisdom. In his discussion of the "Book of Job," Maimonides concludes, for example, that "true happiness, which is the knowledge of the deity, is guaranteed to all who know Him and a human being cannot be troubled in it by any of all the misfortunes in question. . . ."[64] Knowledge and intellectual union with God override human need and material life. Of course, Maimonides frequently suggests that knowledge of an object is tantamount to identity with the object.[65] Applied to knowledge of God, we might say that knowledge of God means a participation in the divine identity, which excepts or sacrifices human difference to the fundamental and exclusive reality of God.[66]

In an essay "Maimonides on the Eternity of the World,"[67] Haim Kreisel supports Pines's position and offers a direct response to Seeskin's view. Like Pines, Kriesel argues that Maimonides frequently asserts that will follows wisdom, and that because wisdom is necessary, will is also necessary and therefore not free. Kriesel also points to the *Guide* 2.22 where Maimonides presents both points of view in contradiction to each other, but according to Kreisel's reading, opts for the Aristotelian position. It is important to note that the Aristotelian position that Kreisel argues Maimonides favors is one of the arguments, which according to Seeskin, Maimonides refuted. If Kreisel is correct in this instance and if Seeskin is also correct that elsewhere Maimonides voices support for the "Mosaic" view, then the disagreement between the two scholars points to an unresolved tension in Maimonides' own position wherein both positions seem to be unhinged by each other.

In the *Guide* 2.22, Kriesel points out that Maimonides begins by criticizing the Aristoteliean conclusion that, "it would follow that the deity, whom everyone who is intelligent recognizes to be perfect in every kind of perfection, could, as far as all the beings are concerned, produce nothing new in any of them; if He wished to lengthen a fly's wing or to shorten a worm's foot, He would not be able to do it."[68] And Kreisel also points out that not long after Maimonides seems to negate his own view, "But Aristotle will say that He would not wish it and that it is impossible for Him to will something different from what is; that it would not add to his perfection but would perhaps from a certain point of view be a deficiency."[69] According to the second claim, the notion of divine freedom operative in creation *ex nihilo* not only does not "add" to the divine perfection but could possibly tarnish this divine perfection. If, in other words, in Maimonides' estimation, negative theology is only legitimate when it admits possibilities that do not contradict with what we know about God's perfection, then any extension of negative theology to include a doctrine of divine freedom falls directly into the category of claims that (could) contradict divine perfection. What matters for Kreisel is that Maimonides seems to endorse the latter position, and Kreisel says, "Maimonides does not proceed to rebut Aristotle's counterargument as we would expect him to do but allows Aristotle to have the last word on this matter, thereby signaling his agreement with Aristotle's position."[70]

Later, Kriesel summarizes the common ground between his and Pines's position and asks, "if [we assume that] divine choice for Maimonides is a product of wisdom (*Guide*, 2.18) could God ever act differently?"[71] If divine will follows divine wisdom, then divine will has no freedom. In other words, in Maimonides' account, there is no such thing as an arbitrary will. "Maimonides appears to treat all divine decisions as reflecting purpose, and I interpret the notion of 'purpose' in Maimonides' thought as combining wisdom and will. . . . In 3.25 he treats all of God's actions as good and excellent. . . .",[72] but then, Kreisel argues that a will that is nothing other than the purpose of a necessary God is not a free will. In this instance, a non-arbitrary freedom is no freedom at all.

What can we conclude about the import of Pines's and Kreisel's response to Seeskin's argument? Their positions challenge Seeskin's assessment of the commensurability between God's free will and God's nature in Maimonides' account and thereby demonstrate the exclusivity or polemical character of a Maimonidean account of creation *ex nihilo*. To the extent to which Maimonides' support for creation *ex nihilo* cannot be reconciled with an account of the Being of God, then the charge of intolerance can be launched not only against essentialist or "Greek" elements in his thought but against the more "Jewish" account as well. From this perspective, support for creation *ex nihilo* sacrifices Maimonides' own concept of divine being for the sake of asserting the possibility of a free God who acts beyond a nature that we can apprehend. If we read Maimonides charitably, the most we can argue is that it is *possible* that Maimonides' account of the God of freedom does not stand in conflict with the God of being. Still, from this vantage point, the doubts about this commensurability raised by Pines and Kreisel at the very least require that we admit that Maimonides has not explicitly resolved these issues. If Maimonides' theology has the potential to sustain the validity of both the God beyond "Being" and the God of "Being" in a way that undoes either position's exclusivity and/or exceptionalism against "wrong" ideas of God—that is, the possibility that the God of eternal necessity could also operate as a free God capable of an act of free grace in the creation of the world—then this potential must be made more explicit than Maimonides has done.

In the last section, I would like to pursue the latter possibility by deepening Maimonides' account of negative theology such that we see a way forward toward the recognition of both a God of Being and a God beyond Being as the cornerstone of a philosophico-theological account of monotheism. It is the central aim of this book to offer a philosophico-theological account of monotheism that does not promote exceptionalism but grounds the possibility for a healthy apologetic exchange between Jews and Christians and between both traditions and wider culture. In this final section, I will suggest that although Maimonides' theology of God cannot by itself present a non-exceptionalist account of monotheism, Maimonides' turn toward the category of divine freedom anticipates a theology of divine freedom and law that does not promote a logic of sacrifice but adjudicates polemical positions and can provide a viable basis for a successful Jewish and Christian apologetics.

The Unity of God and the God Beyond Being

In *The Guide of the Perplexed*, Maimonides emphasizes the unity of God as the centerpiece of his theological account. "His essence is . . . one and simple."[73] For Maimonides, the notion of God's oneness derives from the notion of God's uniqueness or incomparability with anything else. If God is unique, then God is the only thing that is incomparable to anything else. As such, this God cannot be made of various accidents or characteristics because an attribute is either, he says, the same as the essence—in which case, any discussion of accident is tautological—or an accident constitutes something "superadded" to that thing—in which case, the thing superadded is not necessary to God and could therefore also participate in the reality of another (different) thing, compromising the incomparability of God.[74]

As we have seen, however, the reality of contingent existence challenges Maimonides' conception of the unity of God. On the one hand, the reality of the world suggests a God of free will capable of creating something that is both new and different from God. On the other hand, the notion of the uniqueness of God suggests that God cannot create freely and/or relate to that which is different from or other than God without compromising the absolute uniqueness [wisdom] of God from all else. At the very least, we can say with some confidence that Maimonides does not explicitly explain how the apparent tension between these two aspects of God might be resolved. We might state it this way: The reality of the contingent world seems to suggest a difference between God's nature and Godself that alone compromises the absolutism of either of these theological positions. To say that there is a difference between God's nature and Godself is not to say necessarily that there is a contradiction between these two features. It is, however, to admit that Maimonides' account of the oneness of God runs into difficulty with the admission of the reality of the world.

At this point, I would like to revisit Seeskin's suggestion that the method of negative theology holds the key to resolving the apparent tension. However, I would like to suggest that Maimonides' account of negative theology did not go far enough, and that if it had, he would have found a plausible way to reconcile the apparent split between the God of wisdom and the God of will such that neither could assert itself absolutely, and neither could legitimize an absolute intolerance toward varying accounts of the reality of God [in this case, each other]. What do I mean?

To explain what a more developed approach to negative theology might entail, I will refer to the model of negative theology used in Schelling's *Weltalter* as described in Chapter 1. Like *The Guide of the Perplexed*, the *Weltalter* is concerned to explain the character of the monotheistic God. Also like the *Guide*, the theology of the *Weltalter* begins with the recognition of the existence of the world—an existence that, for reasons very similar to Maimonides' account of creation *ex nihilo*, requires the assumption of a God who acts freely. The world consists of existences that *qua* contingent, come in and out of being and are not self perpetuating. As contingent, their existence presupposes having been affected by an event or act by something other than themselves. Existence presupposes something that as beyond any being we can apprehend, we can know nothing rational about. From this point, theology can only ask about the God whom we do not know.

So, who, according to Schelling, is the God we do not know? As we learned in Chapter 1, the God whom we do not know is both: the God beyond Being whose free act creates the world of existence, along with the God of Being whose nature is differentiated from God's own free act. There are two ways to explain this claim. One way, as discussed in Chapter 1, is to understand Schelling's claim that "without a nature, the freedom in God could not be separated from the deed and hence, would not be actual freedom."[75] That is, if God were only free act and not also nature, then freedom would constitute God's nature or necessity. But a freedom that constitutes nature is no longer freedom. Freedom then always stands as differentiated from and related to nature.

A second way to understand Schelling's identification of both the God beyond Being and a God of Being is to see it as the result of a negative theological deduction. Said simply, the application of the negative to a God whom we do not know produces two different sorts of negative claims. On the one hand, the God whom we cannot know is a God whom we cannot know because this God exceeds being or cannot be accounted for through our knowledge of being. On the other hand, we might also say that the God whom we do not know is a God whose being or nature simply exceeds our apprehension. Later in our discussion of Rosenzweig's *The Star of Redemption*, we will see these two modes of negation identified as a negative negation (the God whose nature negates anything, including nature) and the positive negation (the God whose very nature is more than any nature we have ever apprehended).

By recognizing how a negative theological deduction produces both the prospect of a God beyond Being along with the possibility of the God of superlative Being, Schelling permits the reality of the existence of the world to generate the possibility of both aspects of theology in contrast to Maimonides, who frequently positioned each aspect in contradiction to the other (*Guide* 2.22). From Schelling's account, we learn that there is possibly a God who is both beyond Being and of the highest Being and within whom there is a difference between these aspects. Such a difference, however, does not imply a contradiction because both apparently constitute the God that we do not know. Such a position clearly resembles Seeskin's analysis of the relationship between free will and wisdom in God, but as we have seen earlier, the surety of Seeskin's reading is placed in doubt by scholars for whom Maimonides' emphasis upon divine wisdom over and against divine will at the very best, dissolves the latter into the former.

The way forward, therefore, clearly presupposes an acknowledgment of the reality of both aspects of theology and to the extent to which Seeskin's reading is correct, Maimonides' work points in the right direction, just not explicitly enough. However, there is more to Schelling's theological deduction than the recognition of the positive difference and reality of both God's free act and God's transcendent, eternal, and necessary being. If, following Schelling (and Seeskin even), we begin by recognizing the reality of both aspects of God, we also reach the conclusion, quite obvious but quite significant: that the God of Being here deduced is not exhaustive of who God is or complete in itself. Said otherwise, any divine Being that together with a free act beyond Being constitutes the reality of God, is not determinative of God by itself. Seen from this perspective, we can say that divine Being or divine nature is not stable. If it were stable (sufficient), there would be no room, no cause for a divine activity that freely generates that which is other than the divine nature. On the one hand, Schelling says, "Everyone . . . departs from [starts from] the assumption that the Godhead is in itself an eternal stillness, totally engulfed in itself and wrapped up in itself. . . ."[76] On the other hand, however, these same philosophers, he says, acknowledge that they also cannot understand how a God that is "first purely and fully wrapped up in itself can, in a subsequent moment or act, emerge out of itself without ground or occasioning cause, or how it could by itself sublimate or interrupt its eternal unity and stillness. . . ."[77] That they cannot understand this points to two conclusions: The God of eternal stillness cannot, it would be seem, freely step outside of itself and in a moment or act, "sublimate or interrupt its eternal stillness"; and to the extent to which there is a created world of existence, some other aspect of God must therefore be operative in this deed. Divine Being is not exhaustive, and divine Being is not, in this sense, absolute. It points to or intends divine will. In the *Weltalter*, Schelling describes the internal restlessness of divine nature as a microcosmic reflection of the difference between being and will played out above—here, played out between the two potencies of God's Being, what Schelling refers to as divine nature and divine spirit (freedom). Neither exhausts the divine nature, and both compete to do so. The result, as discussed in Chapter 1, is a tireless campaign for Being, which produces only a stalemate from the failure of both. Any indication of divine necessity, therefore, is in Schelling's account less a reflection of the perfection of a stable divine Being and more the reflection of the mutual cancellation performed by the two warring potencies within the divine nature itself.

Out of this announcement of the reality of both the God of Being and the God beyond Being emerges a theology of divine difference, whereby the restlessness of divine nature points to the need for a divine activity from which it is different. We might, if moving ahead from Seeskin's account, suggest that Maimonides' thought anticipates this development. Or, we might, if following along with Pines and Kreisel, recognize that such a development constitutes the opposite of Maimonides' intention so far as a full deduction of the reality of both the God beyond Being and the God of being reflects a difference that emerges in God's very nature itself—a difference that stands in blatant opposition to Maimonides' emphatic identification of the oneness of the divine essence. It is important to keep in mind here, however, that to the extent to which the latter reading is the correct reading of Maimonides' work—namely, that one way or another, will and wisdom stand in conflict—Maimonides' thought displays an exceptionalism that renders one of the two positions illegitimate. By contrast, as we will see, the development of Maimonides' thought from a more complete account of the negative theological deduction will permit the retention of the validity of both the reality of divine Being and the reality of God's free act beyond Being [or what we might say constitutes the condition of the possibility of the validity of Seeskin's position]. And while we have played out how Schelling's negative theological deduction permits the reconciliation of both elements in chapter one, it is worth revisiting this movement here in conversation with our analysis of Maimonides' theology.

If at this juncture, we understand how one deduces the notion of divine freedom and how any account of the divine nature and necessity is inevitably altered by the reality of divine freedom, we still do not understand the nature of the relationship between divine freedom and divine nature/necessity. In fact, we have already stumbled upon the answer to this question earlier. Recall that according to Schelling, the deduction of the God of a free act from the reality of existing things, intuitively or otherwise, also presupposed the reality of the nature or being of God. Freedom, we indicated, is only freedom both in difference from and also in relation to being. With this recognition, Schelling introduces the key to resolving the tension within Maimonides' theology along with the philosophical lynchpin of this volume: namely, the double-character of divine freedom as gift/law and law/gift.

In Schelling's own language, divine freedom relates to divine nature as both a "yes" and a "no." On the one hand, God's will is free from and/or other than divine "being." God's freedom is not God's essence or is not constrained by God's essence. The will is not a constitutive element in the campaign for divine being. The will extends beyond divine Being and freely creates that which is other than God's Being or the existence of things. The God who creates what is other is a God who is other than its own nature.

On the other hand, to be truly free, divine freedom must not only differentiate itself from divine nature but must also affirm divine nature at the same time. Divine freedom would not be freedom unless it could affirm divine nature without, however, identifying with or standing affected by its [nature's] limitations. In short, divine freedom both differentiates itself from and affirms that which is other. Moreover, divine freedom affirms divine nature generally speaking, and in particular, affirms both aspects of the divine nature that formerly vied but failed to achieve stability of being. Affirmed, or as Schelling says, "loved" through God's free act, both achieve the stability of their own identification and no longer vie to reduce the other to themselves. The verification of the positive difference between God's Being and God's nature is also reflected in the verification of the positive difference between the two aspects of God's Being.

Of course, what we see here is the fact that God's free will loves through order and/or that order or lawfulness constitute the mode or manner whereby God enacts his free love or grace. And in the *Weltalter*, Schelling says, "Before this, there was no space and the three [the two potencies and the failed and restless totality] principles were not apart from each other. Now, since they sacrifice being one and the same, space comes to be and there emerges a true 'over' and a true 'under'. . . ."[78] Law organizes difference by affirming each thing in its own space.

> But this Godhead, which to or in itself neither has being nor does not have being, comes to have being on account of the life that stands subordinate to it and in relationship with it. Now, the Godhead is supported by eternal nature and keeps over it not unlike the sun over the earth or the bird over its brood. Whoever should find this simile ignoble, need only compare the expressive word at Genesis 1:2, in accordance with its fundamental meaning. Now, the Godhead recognizes in nature its own eternal nature and is from now on, albeit free with respect to nature and neither bound to it nor growing into it, nonetheless inseparable from it.[79]

Schelling describes divine freedom as the *actus purus*, or the will that has no desire. Such a position breaks the antinomy between will and wisdom suggested by Pines's and Kreisel's interpretation of Maimonides. To say as Schelling does that divine freedom manifests a pure will or a will without desire sounds similar to Maimonides' effort to speak of a will that intends only what is perfect. In fact, it is a quite different claim that describes a will that does not intend what is only perfect but does not intend at all. The *actus purus* is a will without *telos* and not a will that always already fulfills its *telos*. To speak of the latter is, as we have seen, to render the notion of will superfluous. To speak of the former is to describe a will—what in this instance is a freedom to make that which is other than oneself, or a gift which *qua* gift is offered without intent or design. In this sense, divine will possesses the unique ability to give only what the other needs and not what it itself desires. The free God gives freely from out of the lawful difference between itself and the other.

Consequently, we can say that the free God gives not only as the God beyond his own Being, but as the God whose Being transcends all other being. The free God gives freely in wisdom. If Maimonides' account cannot successfully preserve a genuine portrait of divine will, Schelling's account not only preserves the portrait of divine will as extensive, but does so without negating the reality of divine wisdom as well. Divine being is retained in the affirmation of the free act of God, and the retention of divine nature or wisdom secures the freedom of God from overreaching into the humanity of the desires and needs it meets. The unique capacity of the free God to love freely and wisely ultimately registers as the opportunity for a marriage between need and rest in that toward which God extends Godself. If frequently, Maimonides' work suggests the repose that comes to persons who achieve union with the intellectual wisdom of God in the sacrifice of their physical selves,[80] Schelling's account presents the possibility for repose without the sacrifice of one's physical self and the needs that constitute the difference between persons and God. The lawful difference between God and what God creates balances the needs of the other with the wisdom and stability of divine being. A full repose does not require the nullification of need, and the satisfaction of need does override the value of rest.[81]

What can we conclude has happened to Maimonides' concern for the oneness of God? Have we had to discard his doctrine of the oneness of God in order to work against an exceptionalism in his thinking? Does the retention of the oneness of God force readers to choose between his emphasis upon the freedom of God and his insistence upon the necessity of God? Yes and no. If by oneness, Maimonides means that God's will and God's wisdom are always the same, then the only way to liberate Maimonides from exceptionalism is by dismantling the assumption about divine oneness. If, however, by oneness, Maimonides means a union between wisdom and will that we cannot define but that retains both within the lawful difference of the freedom of God, we might suggest that Maimonides' reflections upon the freedom of God lay the groundwork for the identification of the relationship between freedom and law that constitutes the central idea of this volume and that offers an alternative philosophical account of monotheism that guards against exceptionalism in general and the exceptionalism against idolatry in particular and that can ultimately offer a basis for a vital Jewish and Christian apologetics. With regard to the specific issue of anti-idolatrous intolerance, at the very least, the preceding discussion demonstrates the sorts of conditions required for theology to legitimize more than one account of the reality of God, which are the link between divine freedom and divine lawfulness. As I will show in Chapters 5 and 6, when fully developed, a theology of divine freedom and law can not only admit the possibility of alternative accounts and representations of the divine but can also admit the possibility of secular or a-theological accounts as well, but I will reserve that analysis for these later chapters.

THREE

Modern Judaism, Law, and Exceptionalism

The logic of sacrifice presents itself theologically in one or two expressions. Either it presents a profile of divine sovereignty that as unadjudicated excepts any notion of alterity within or exterior to Godself, or it presents a notion of the unbridled sovereignty of human desire over and against any theological or social limit. In the prior chapter, I illuminated an example of how and when a particular and absolutely asserted conception of God can perpetuate an exceptionalism over and against any reality, divine or otherwise, outside this affirmation. In this chapter, I want to examine the flip side of the dialectic of desire, whereby desire is not dismissed in the name of a higher theological truth but rather is crowned superior to and unregulated in its relation to law.

More specifically, this chapter examines a renewed focus upon law within a strain of modern Jewish thought, beginning with the work of Baruch Spinoza and continuing into the work of Gillian Rose and David Novak. Each of these thinkers presents a nonrevealed and materialist conception of the law.[1] By materialist, I mean a notion of law in which human desire assumes a central role in the development and maintenance of law.

This chapter argues that despite the significant headway here made in rerouting philosophical analyses toward a materialist conception of the law, a materialist conception of the law, which is nonrevelatory, stands in perpetual tension with the nature of human desire that it is designed to delimit. Consequently, nonrevelatory law, materialist or otherwise, is not free, nor is it freely performed by persons whose desire and/or interests are hereby constrained by it. Law that does not stand in a reciprocal relationship with divine freedom remains coercive and cannot engender an authentic Jewish-Christian apologetics.

Spinoza's Biblical Judaism

All too often, Spinoza's work is interpreted as a precursor to German Jewish liberalism.[2] This tendency to read Spinoza through the lens of German idealism limits a full appreciation of his ethics and his account of Jewish law and material existence.[3] Spinoza's attention to the central role of human desire in the development and maintenance of law helps reclaim the significance of "carnal Israel," a point not frequently recognized in scholarship on Spinoza's work.[4] However, what Spinoza gains by pointing to a covenantal account of human need in conjunction with Jewish law, he loses in his refusal to entertain a theology of a revelatory God. In particular, Spinoza's neglect for a theology of revelation renders his account incapable of linking an embodied Jewish particularity to a positive relationship with the wider world. Even the Mosaic Judaism favored by Spinoza could, in his own account, offer no stronger mandate to love the neighbor or even engage in rational discourse with non-Jews than any other normal democratic nation. Lacking a theology of revelation that can acknowledge human desire without diagnosing either moral defeat or the divinization of this desire, Spinoza's thought wrinkles efforts to appreciate a link between a tradition's historical self-consciousness and its commitment to communicate with and make sense to other historically justified traditions. In what follows, first I will detail Spinoza's anthropology of human desire and its relation to law in the state as exemplified in Spinoza's profile of biblical Judaism; and second, I will address the limits of this analysis with regard to apologetic discourse.

GOD, NATURE, AND HUMAN BEINGS

For Spinoza, laws of justice (human or divine) emerge from society with the state as the primary structure of human social life. Standards of justice and injustice are not endemic to nature or God but arise only with the structuring of human social organization as human beings participate in God and/or nature. Society is not, according to Spinoza, rooted in nature. Rather, society is a tool that human beings use to adjudicate between their participation in the infinite substance of divine reality and their finite existence and will to self-preservation. In Spinoza's account, there remains a problematic divide between the anti-teleological nature of divine substance and the will for self-preservation characteristic of human life. This tension shapes the drama of human existence whereby persons seek to guarantee their own existence over and against external forces of nature that proceed without regard for it, and yet also strive to participate directly in the eternal reality of divine substance through the achievement of a higher (rational) understanding of these forces and laws of nature. Consequently, societal laws designed to service the aims of collective self-preservation inevitably position their societies against other societies on the one hand and also against the patterns and outcomes of the unchanging laws of external nature on the other hand.

Part I of the *Ethics* gives a careful presentation of Spinoza's view of God without which we cannot understand his account of society and law. This God cannot be described as a God of revelation if by revelation, we mean a God who communicates with and relates to humankind and who reveals himself transactionally.[5] Still, Spinoza's God is not the typical God of the philosophers, either, for neither is he a source of nor identifiable with ethical standards of justice or injustice. Spinoza begins his account of God with an analysis of the category of "substance" or that which "must be in itself and be conceived through itself."[6] As things that are in and conceived through themselves, substances are the bases for their own attributes that characterize the "what" of any substance. In Spinoza's account, however, reality is exhausted by one and only one substance. If there were two substances, these two would have to consist of different attributes or attributes that bear nothing in common with one another. But, Spinoza reasons, substances with nothing in common cannot cause each other (something cannot give rise to something that it neither participates in nor can conceive of) and, therefore, a substance can only cause itself. Therefore, it follows that there is only one substance that causes itself—and, by extension, existence constitutes one of the attributes of substance. The identification of substance with God becomes clearer with Spinoza's identification of substance as infinite. Substance is infinite because there is only one substance, and to be finite would mean that this one substance would be limited by another substance of the same nature; but, any other substance of the same nature would, of course, be the same as this one substance. Therefore, substance is infinite and not limited.

As infinite, substance has infinite attributes. An attribute is "that which the intellect perceives of substance as constituting its essence"[7]—the "what" of "substance." But, Spinoza reasons, an infinite substance must then presuppose an infinite character or "attributes" because "the more reality or being [a substance] has, the more . . . its attributes . . . express."[8] There are, in other words, an infinite number of ways for substance to 'be' or express itself in reality. As infinite and constituted by an infinite number of attributes, substance or God not only necessarily exists but is therefore eternal. If God necessarily exists, as noted earlier, then he or it exists always.[9] But, of course, this also means that because God's existence and his essence are one and the same, then all of God's attributes are also eternal. Nothing, therefore, Spinoza argues, in nature is contingent. All nature is necessary and therefore, "from the necessity of the divine nature determined to exist and to act in a definite way."[10] But, of course, if nature is not contingent, then there is no gap between how reality is and how it ought to be. Divine necessity generates natural or divine laws, but these laws are only descriptive and not prescriptive because reality is necessarily determined. This is why Spinoza argues that there is no difference between the divine intellect and divine volition. God thinks what is, and what is is conceived in and through God.

What about the existence of particular things that appear to change and go in and out of existence? There is a difference, Spinoza explains, between *natura naturans* and *natura naturata*. *Natura naturans* includes God and God's infinite essences and refers to "what is in itself and conceived through itself"—that is, what creates and/or causes. *Natura naturata* consists of modalities or "affects." If God has infinite attributes, these attributes are expressed in infinite numbers of ways, and these infinite ways can produce or include realities that are, of course, particular, changing and/or in and out of existence as expressions of reality and not, in effect, reality itself. Modalities are what follow from nature's self-causation. *Natura naturata* are things that are caused by and conceived in something else, and are, therefore, finite in that their existence depends upon the attributes by which they are defined and conceived. This distinction explains the appearance of things coming in and out of existence, but it does not add an ethical dimension to Spinoza's ontology of God and nature. Nature, Spinoza tells us "has no fixed goal and . . . all things in nature proceed from all eternal necessity and with supreme perfection."[11]

What about human beings? In the *Theologico-Political Treatise*, Spinoza says, "the state of nature must by no means be confounded with a state of religion but must be conceived as without either religion or law and consequently without sin or wrong."[12]

Why then do people enter into social relationships and constitute ethical standards? In the *Ethics*, Spinoza argues that "the essence of man is constituted by definite modifications of the attributes of God."[13] In particular, human beings are modalities of two divine attributes: thought and extension. On the one hand, the human mind is a modality of divine thought or one of the ways divine thought thinks. In particular, it is divine thought thinking the "the idea of an actually existing thing."[14] But of course, all "ideas" have corresponding objects because God's essence is always existence. Therefore, the "idea of the human mind" has an object, and that object is "the actually existing thing" or the body. Therefore, Spinoza says that "whatever happens in the object of the idea of the human mind will necessarily be in the mind . . . (or rather) the idea of that thing will be in the mind."[15] The human mind is the sum total of ideas of the affections of what the body feels. Because, therefore, human beings are modalities of divine thought and divine extension, and because divine thought and extension necessarily follow the same order of existence,[16] human beings consist of a unity of mind and body whereby the mind's ideas are constituted by the body's affects.

The unique nexus between mind and body determines the range of human knowledge. The human mind has ideas of the affects of the human body, and this constitutes the limit of the basis of its knowledge. There are, in Spinoza's account, three levels of knowledge. First, there is what he refers to as "causal knowledge"—the knowledge that arises from the ideas immediately influenced by the body's affects. Sensory knowledge generates memory and imagination because over time, the mind habitually links sensations with ideas and can conjure them at any time. Rooted in the reactions of the body, causal knowledge produces contingent accounts of reality not necessarily linked to how things are but only to how things feel to the body.

Second, there is the knowledge that emerges from what Spinoza calls the "common notions" or reason. Common notions are true or adequate ideas that arise from the fact that there are certain things common to all bodies, and so perceived, their ubiquity raises them above the level of image to an idea that is said to reflect the nature of reality even though they derive from affects of the body.

Intuition, the knowledge of God's thought and extension, is the highest form of knowledge. This knowledge helps persons overcome the limitations of their bodies but only because it presupposes the eternal mind as separate from the body. Intuition is the key to human tranquility in nature and the antidote to the perpetual limits of the human body and mind within a world of external forces it cannot know and control.

However, human life is more challenging than the preceding account would suggest because as persons, we do not experience the affects of the body neutrally but experience our world as either painful or pleasurable. Pain or pleasure is related to our fundamental drive for self-preservation. "Each thing," Spinoza argues, "insofar as it is in itself, endeavors to persist in its own being."[17] We know this, Spinoza says, because no thing can be destroyed except by something external to it. Granted that this is the case, no thing destroys itself, but things persist in their being unless affected by something else. This drive to persist—*conatus*—divides reality into powers, each attempting to persist against the power of other things. "No thing can have in itself anything by which it can be destroyed that is, which can annul its existence. On the contrary, it opposes everything that can annul its existence; and thus, as far as it can and as far as it is in itself, it endeavors to persist in its own being."[18] Human beings, like all things in nature, are defined by this desire to preserve themselves over and against other powers in nature. Consequently, human beings do not experience their world neutrally but react positively (pleasure) to affects that help preserve their being and negatively (pain) to affects that work to destroy it.

There are three emotions: pleasure, pain, and desire (the yearning for more pleasure). As well, there are what Spinoza refers to as "passive" emotions and "active" emotions. Passive emotions are images or ideas of experiences of either pleasure or pain that arise from the circumstances of nature: that is, emotions that depend upon external causes and/or objects. We may come to desire objects of pleasure (or love) and seek to avoid emotions generated by objects that cause us pain or that we "hate," but our ability to successfully control these emotions is significantly limited because we experience these emotions without reason: without, in other words, knowledge of objects and their causes such that we can understand when they will affect us in a particular way and when they will not. In fact, we will always be bound to certain passive emotions because our knowledge of reality is always limited by our bodies. This, of course, is troubling in view of our desire for self-preservation. If we cannot control our emotions, we cannot control the extent to which we are positively or negatively affected by external objects in our world: that is, we cannot have full control over our own self-preservation. This gives rise to feelings of fear and hope. Equally troubling is the fact that passive emotions pit persons against one another.

Because what counts as circumstantially pleasing or hateful to one person differs from the identification of pain or pleasure for another, persons will inevitably produce varying motives for behavior that more often than not conflict with the motives and behaviors of others. The basic principle is that we love whatever loves what we love, and we hate whatever hates what we hate.[19] Still, men like themselves praised, "[t]he more a man imagines he is praised by others, the more this pleasure is fostered . . . and . . . therefore, everybody will most enjoy regarding himself when he regards in himself something that he denies of others . . . it is therefore clear that men are prone to hatred and envy."[20]

There are active emotions, too, but there is no such thing as a painful active emotion. All active emotions are pleasurable. An active emotion is a feeling of pleasure that persons get when the mind produces an adequate idea: that is, when persons reason. Reasoning produces pleasure because when the mind reasons, it conceives of itself as reasoning, and this self-awareness acts as an expression of self-affirmation or preservation. Active emotions, therefore, refer to "strength of mind" and produce emotions such as "courage" and nobility or generosity. To the extent that the mind is aware of its own power, it gains in courage. To the extent that the mind is aware of the laws of nature, it is ennobled and generous toward others who share in this human nature rather than set against them as is the case when persons understand themselves only in terms of their immediate and passive emotions.

Clearly, Spinoza recognizes the challenges that people face living in nature. Our passive emotions are very powerful and take our attention away from common notions or ideas of objects rationally known but not immediately present. "An emotion cannot be checked or destroyed except by a contrary emotion which is stronger than the emotion which is to be checked."[21] Passive emotions are also powerful because they arise in response to aspects of nature that even the most rational among us cannot understand (devoid as we all are of eternal minds separate from bodies). "It is impossible for a man . . . not to undergo changes other than those which can be understood solely through his own nature and of which he is the adequate cause . . . man is necessarily always subject to passive emotions."[22]

We do have some tools for accommodation. We have active emotions that strengthen us in our efforts to preserve ourselves. Active emotions empower us in relation to nature by helping us understand nature causally and not reactively. As well, active emotions are synonymous with the use of our reason, and as we reason, we enjoy the self-awareness of ourselves as active minds. Moreover, reason identifies an additional resource for empowerment: namely, the commonality of human nature. "Man is God to man," says Spinoza, and by this he means that there is nothing more advantageous to a person than another rational person. Reason is the faculty that discovers points of commonality among all persons. Once discovered, all persons can pursue these shared interests, increasing the likelihood that any single person will acquire the object of their interest. Collective effort is more effective than individual effort. Therefore, reason concludes that rationally organized social existence constitutes a key mode of accommodation to nature. This in turn produces friendships and piety or charity because I will want to help others achieve the same goals that I pursue because I know that collective action benefits us all. Reason, therefore, offers a clear justification for social existence or the "state."

THE STATE AND CARNAL ISRAEL

We have now reached the most important aspect of Spinoza's work as it relates to the central questions of this chapter: How does Spinoza understand law and what is its relationship to human desire? How does this view of law inform his understanding of Jewish life? The answers lie in Spinoza's description of the state. Earlier, I indicated how the *Ethics* envisions a rational basis for the state. In the *Theologico-Political Treatise*, Spinoza makes matters more complex when he says

> [I]f all men could be easily led by reason alone and could recognize what is best and most useful for a state, there would be no one who would not forswear deceit for everyone would keep most religiously to their compact in their desire for the chief good, namely the preservation of the state.... However, it is far from being the case that all men can always be easily led by reason alone; everyone is drawn away by his pleasure, while avarice, ambition, envy hatred and the like so engross the mind that reason has no place therein.[23]

Nonetheless, Spinoza argues, it is apparent to all—those guided by reason and those guided by [passive] emotion—that we are still better off when we help one another than when we do not. Driven by the desire for self-preservation, persons are drawn to pursue that which offers them hope for survival and to avoid that which they fear will destroy them. But, Spinoza reasons, life alone promises more harm of injury than life together, and because "no-one ever neglects anything which he judges to be good, except with the hope of gaining a greater good, or from the fear of a greater evil; ... no-one can honestly promise to forego the right which he has over all things ... unless the fear of a greater evil or the hope of a greater good."[24] But, of course, this is exactly what happens with respect to the option to live collectively in a state. Without life in the state, persons, as we have seen, legislate themselves and choose whatever helps preserve them in the face of nature. The state, by contrast, offers persons the possibility of security but only insofar as they cede their "natural" right to self-legislation: that is, their natural right to act on the basis of their own individual desire. In joining a state, persons (in theory) choose to live according to laws that determine the groups' actions. This simultaneously decreases the chances that individuals will harm each other and increases the chances that individuals will discover common interests that they can more effectively meet when working together. In Spinoza's language, persons entering this pact cede their natural power to self-legislate to the "sovereign." The sovereign can be either an individual (monarchy) or the collective itself (democracy).

Sometimes in Spinoza's account, it appears that the sovereign wields too much power. ("The state must be preserved and directed by the sole authority of the sovereign. . . ."[25]) This is not the case, however. Any authority is only as powerful as the source of its legitimacy, and in the case of the sovereign, this means that this power presupposes and is contingent upon the willingness of those who cede their natural rights to it. Sovereignty is lodged in the power of the *conatus*, the human will to self-preservation. "No-one can ever so utterly transfer to another all his power and his rights as to cease to be a man."[26] Moreover, persons who cede their natural rights do so, more often than not, from a calculus of benefit over harm. Sovereigns must appeal specifically to the localized accounts of what constitutes benefits and/or harms in the view of those legislated. Sovereigns are accountable to the particular interests and demands of the particular people that they rule, and the laws they create must work to the advantage of those whose support they require. In this way, state laws become a lens through which one can read the desires of a particular group at a particular time in history.

> It will always be vain to order a subject to hate what he believes brings him advantage, or to love what brings him loss or not to be offended at insults, or not to wish to be free from fear . . . for men have never so far ceded their power as to cease to be an object of fear to the rulers who received such power and right. . . .[27]

Therefore, Spinoza says, "laws should in every government be so arranged that people should be kept in bounds by the hope of some greatly desired good, rather than by fear, for everyone will do his duty willingly."[28]

Social existence constitutes the basis for ethics in Spinoza's account. Outside the state, there are no standards of justice or injustice. Within the state, justice and injustice are linked directly to compliance and/or noncompliance to the laws of the sovereign. Consequently, a person from another state can be only either an ally or an enemy. An ally is a citizen of another state with whom the citizen has found some advantage in relating. Alliances are formed only when the relationship serves, and therefore correlates with the laws and needs of the state to which one belongs. "No-one enters into an engagement, or is bound to stand by his compacts unless there be a hope of some accruing good, or fear of some evil; if this basis be removed the compact thereby becomes void. . . ."[29] Alliances are historically contingent. An enemy, on the other hand "is one who lives apart from the state and does not recognize its authority either as a subject or as an ally."[30]

In both instances, the status of relationships is predicated upon the acceptability of these relationships within the terms established by the particular states involved. It is important to note, therefore, that all states will retain some enemies. If alliances are premised upon overlaps in state interests, and if state interests reflect the localized and particular interests of citizens, then state interests tend to be historically and culturally particular and frequently idiosyncratic, and this decreases the opportunity for alliances. On the other hand, one might argue that all nations share certain interests in natural resources for example, and therefore they ought to be able to establish alliances to protect their own economic interests. Clearly, this happens sometimes, but frequently it does not. From a Spinozistic perspective, this would be a result of the fact that either one party has greater access to the resource that both want, and consequently, the party without access would hate the party with access because the latter's access works against the self-preservation of the former; or the (idiosyncratic) cultural and historical differences between nations already generate so much enmity (we tend, Spinoza says, to like others that like what we like and hate others that hate what we like) that it makes any alliance a significant challenge. The odds that nations' differences will make it impossible to locate productive similarities loom large in Spinoza's account.

What about religion? Doesn't Spinoza argue that religion and the study of sacred scriptures in particular is a successful practical tool for encouraging love of the neighbor—and if so, would not this offer a check against the tendency to think of citizens of other states as enemies? Scripture does, in Spinoza's account, promote obedience to God—and by extension, charity and justice to the neighbor and not only to the citizen. Religion has great practical value. Nonetheless, religion (prophecy, scripture, and so on) has little or no theoretical value: that is to say, religion is not philosophically accurate. To view religion this way is to encourage superstition, or what is tantamount to stoking the fires of hope and fear over and against reason's more efficient mode of accommodating persons to the challenges of nature. Religion is useful so far as its philosophical pretensions are held in check. This is the job of the sovereign, Spinoza argues. Religion is great for the state, and its purpose is to serve the state. Its mandate to love the neighbor enhances the stability of the state. The laws of religion (ceremonies) are and ought to be governed by the state and therefore cannot be used to critique the state and/or its laws.

> [M]any persons deny that the right of deciding religious questions belongs to the sovereign power and they accordingly assume full license to accuse and arraign it . . . however . . . religion acquires its force as law solely from the decrees of the sovereign. God has no special kingdom among men except insofar as He reigns through temporal rulers. Moreover the rites of religion and the outward observances of piety should be in accordance with the public peace and well-being, and should therefore be determined by the sovereign power alone.[31]

The religious call to love the neighbor cannot dismantle the economy of ally and enemy established by the power of the sovereign and the laws of the state.

Law, therefore, correlates directly to human desire in Spinoza's account. Spinoza understands that a standard of justice that persons can and will comply with is more effective at sustaining a society than so-called *a priori* norms that are unachievable for individuals at any given time. Laws are achievable in Spinoza's account because persons want to comply. Compliance serves their interests as these interests are historically expressed.

SPINOZA'S COVENANTAL JUDAISM

A lot of ink has been spilled over Spinoza's views on Judaism. For many years, Spinoza scholars emphasized Spinoza's departure from traditional Judaism, but more recent work has both downplayed the significance of his excommunication[32] and focused attention on Jewish elements in Spinoza's thought.[33] In this context, I want to pay particular attention to Spinoza's account of biblical theocracy as an important reflection on the structure of covenant. More specifically, I want to highlight how Spinoza's account of the relationship between law and desire permits him to offer a meaningful account of the Mosaic covenant that underscores the theological and political significance of Jewish materiality.

According to Spinoza, we can find an excellent example of a thriving state by examining biblical Israelite society. In his account, Spinoza argues that coming from slavery, knowing little or nothing about rational law-making, the Israelites nonetheless entered into a pact with God via Moses whereby they ceded their individual rights for self-legislation to a divine sovereign who promised them security and prosperity. "Being then in a state of nature, they followed Moses in whom they chiefly trusted and decided to transfer their right to no human being but only to God."[34]

The key to appreciating Spinoza's account of Judaism is in his identification of God as sovereign over an essentially democratic polity. Theocracy and democracy are directly linked. Although led by Moses out of Egypt, the Jews of the Mosaic covenant pledged their natural rights to God. They did so, according to Spinoza, not on rational grounds but rather because the God who redeemed them from slavery demonstrated a concern with their security and welfare and promised to aid them as a material society now and in the future.

> This promise or transference of right to God was effected in the same manner as we have conceived it to have been in ordinary societies . . . in order that this covenant might be ratified and settled, and might be free from all suspicion of deceit, God did not enter into it till the Jews had had experience of His wonderful power by which alone they had been, or could be, preserved in a state of prosperity.[35]

The role of divine aid and promise is reflected as well in Spinoza's account of the nature of biblical law. A theological sovereign focused on encouraging obedience by way of issuing material aid also legislates laws that serve the same function. Here, Spinoza's description of the Mosaic covenant resonates with traditional Jewish accounts of the covenant. In Deuteronomy, we read, "And now, what does YHWH your God demand of you? Only this to hold Yhwh your God in awe, to walk in all his paths, to love him . . . to observe YHWH's commandments and his laws, which I enjoin upon you this day, for your own benefit. . . ."[36] This Deuteronomic text reannounces the classic biblical account of the Sinaitic covenant. God issues unconditional promises and love, and in return, the Jews perform lawfully out of love for the God who has redeemed them. In his now classic *Sinai and Zion*, Jon Levenson highlights the covenantal structure implicit in this text and explains:

> On God's side lies an obligation to fulfill the oath he swore to the Patriarchs, to grant their descendants the promised land, to be their God. Israel, for her part is to realize her love in the form of observance of her master's stipulations . . . for they are the words of the language of love. . . . It is not a question of law or love but law conceived in love, love expressed in law.[37]

The law, in other words, is not a burden as stressed in Deuteronomy:

> For this commandment which I command thee this day, it is not too hard for thee, neither is it far off. It is not in heaven, that thou shouldest say: "Who shall go up for us to heaven, and bring it unto us, and make us to hear it, that we may do it?"
>
> Neither is it beyond the sea, that thou shouldest say: "Who shall go over the sea for us, and bring it unto us, and make us to hear it, that we may do it?" But the word is very nigh unto thee, in thy mouth, and in thy heart, that thou mayest do it.[38]

Performed in the context of this covenantal relationship of care and obligation, Jewish normative life thrives.

However, not only does Spinoza's account of biblical society reflect the covenantal structure maintained in traditional Judaism, but Spinoza also recognizes a link between biblical theocracy and a democratic polity, and in so doing, he draws a very promising portrait of the relationship between the Jewish community's material and historical needs and their ethical life. In Spinoza's account, successful states can be either monarchical or democratic with the difference having to do with who has the power to interpret the validity and/or relevancy of the law. In monarchy, this power is limited to the king. As discussed earlier, however, this does not mean that a king need not be concerned with the interests of his subjects because his power ultimately resides with them. By contrast, a democracy offers participants access to channels of legal interpretation. Technically, they cannot change the law themselves, but they can interpret it so that it can more directly meet their needs; and/or they can, after having interpreted it, consult with the sovereign and request changes. By pledging themselves to God rather than a human sovereign, the Jews of biblical society secured themselves the right to have equal access to interpreting divine law according to their needs without privileging any one person's needs over any other. They all, Spinoza says, "were equally bound by the covenant and . . . all had an equal right to consult the Deity, to accept and to interpret His laws, so that all had an exactly equal share in the government. . . ."[39]

Spinoza's account of Jewish life and law is appealing. Obedience to God and the commitment to a lawful society need not require the de-materialization and/or de-historicization of the Jewish people. Covenantal life offers a theo-political model whereby localized and historically changing needs are negotiated together with the promise of divine aid and thereby help to produce a healthy motivation for a lawful and materially secure body politic. Certainly, there are a number of problems with Spinoza's account of Judaism. First, he holds that the events described in the biblical narrative are imaginative in nature and not necessarily true philosophically speaking. Second, Spinoza asserts that diasporic Judaism is apolitical in nature and therefore meaningless. To continue to perform Jewish law without a Jewish state is just superstitious. In point of fact, however, Spinoza's dismissal of diasporic Judaism is not the most significant flaw in his system. If one wanted to, one could think imaginatively about how to reignite the political character of Jewish law even in the diaspora.[40] Of greater concern is the inability of Spinoza's model to justify a positive engagement between Judaism and other cultures, particularly in a pluralistic environment.

From Enmity to Apologetics: The Limits of a Nonrevelatory Account of Law

THE PROBLEM OF PARTICULARITY

One way to identify the problem is to ask whether granted Spinoza's positive conception of law and its relation to collective desire, this account allows desire so much influence over law that a people's law amounts to nothing more than the institutionalization of their own parochial desires. To the extent that law reads desire without limiting it, Spinoza's account of the state in particular and Judaism in general will produce a conflict between the notion of a historical collectivity and the ability for nations to communicate with and recognize each other's validity. How dominant is desire's influence upon law, and to what extent does its influence preclude the possibility of a free and lawfully motivated apologetics with respect to Judaism in particular?

At face value, Spinoza's Judaism and Jewish law function in the service of the desires of the Jewish people, individually and collectively. All law in Spinoza's account is delimited by the desires of individual persons insofar as it is individuals who cede their natural rights, as discussed earlier. As well, however, once ceded to the nation or sovereign, members of the state still collectively maintain power to critique the sovereign or state law when that state law fails to meet their interests. This applies to biblical Judaism as well. Although Spinoza's position permits law-givers sole authority to author the law, their choices are always subject to the acceptance or rejection by subjects, and therefore the possibility of noncompliance and/or revolt function as expressions of legislative power premised upon desire.

Moreover, not only do the desires of the community inform legal interpretation, but they also inform the character of Jewish interest in and/or relationship with non-Jewish culture. Earlier, I indicated how in Spinoza's account, nations will engage in positive relationships with other nations only to serve the interests of their own people. The Jewish nation is no less particularistic, no more universally inclined than any other nation. Carnal Israel is devoted to its sovereign insofar as that sovereign contributes to its localized needs and consequently, Jews will clearly defend their law and their state as superior to others. To judge other cultures, however, by the standards of one's own desires leaves little chance for authentic dialog with other cultures and can, in the worst case scenario, breed enmity and jealousy between nations and cultures. Is there any limit on this desire? Is there any possibility for the critique of a nation's collective interests? If so, what is the source of this critique—and more importantly, can it provide a positive motivation for an authentic recognition of the validity of another culture's law and historical interests? It is one thing for a nation to be able to critique itself and another for a nation or culture or tradition to be able to acknowledge the validity of another tradition.

REASON, THE PHILOSOPHER, AND THE POSSIBILITY OF A JEWISH APOLOGETICS

Theoretically speaking, Spinoza's political model does permit the possibility of the critique of a nation and its collective desires as these have been instantiated in law. According to both the *Tractatus* and the *Ethics*, states and their laws are not ends in themselves but are developed for the purposes of establishing universal social commitments between persons. Man is not God to man only in cases of shared citizenship. Rather, "man is God to man" is a rational principle that grounds Spinoza's ethics of universal charity and justice. Historical collectivities ought to promote good citizens and good neighbors. But for whom? Well, for those who understand the purposes of the state: that is, for philosophers or rationally educated citizens. Let us then look at the point of view of the philosopher-citizen and see whether she can open a critique of the nation that also encourages citizens to engage rationally with noncitizens.

The philosopher in Spinoza's state will be able to offer citizens a bird's-eye view of their national interests and thereby establish a position of sobriety and understanding of what drives national interests, generally speaking. Theoretically, this ought to enable the philosopher-citizen to encourage understanding of other cultures similarly motivated in their national interests. Depending on one's reading of Spinoza's *Tractatus*, the philosopher will give one of three possible explanations of the drive for national interest. Each explanation could point to a connection between the desire for self-preservation and broader universal interest in others. This, however, does not mean that philosophers who offer these explanations will be able to persuade any body politic (and in this case, the Jews) that they will want to engage in a successful apologetic defense or rational communication with different cultures because the recourse to reason in each instance stands in conflict with the realities of human existence. The philosopher alone may be able to critique his own society, but neither will he want to engage in further apologetic efforts, nor will he be able to persuade others to do likewise. Let us look at the three possible bases for rational critique and apologetics.

One: The state and its laws are in the service of the *conatus*: that is, of each individual's desire for self-preservation. More particularly, the state and its laws are a testament to reason's awareness that we serve our own self-interests more effectively when we identify features that we have in common and act collectively on these shared needs. The state, in this account, is the best attempt to create the conditions for not only love of the citizen, but love of the neighbor—a universal ethics of justice and charity. Seen from this vantage point, other states' particular interests are only expressions of their own efforts to identify commonalities among persons—a step along the path of creating a more universal human collective—and therefore although we need not agree with their particular nexus of interests and laws, we can surely understand their motivations and these can offer a basis for conversation.

Reason's account here does potentially delimit the power of collective national desire as it is expressed through law. Desire and law are valuable here not in and of themselves but only insofar as they function as an important stepping stone toward the higher goal of justice and charity. Nonetheless, this does not mean that either the philosopher or the nonphilosopher citizen will engage freely in this critique for the sake of generating a rational understanding of noncitizens. This is because while reason appears to be able to delimit collective national desires, it cannot delimit the individual desire for self-preservation that funds the state from the start. What does this mean? It means that depending on how one reads Spinoza, one may conclude that in his account, human nature (the *conatus*) and human reason are not identical, and in fact, are in some degree of conflict with each other.[41] Nature, in this reading, has priority over reason. As the effort to establish a state in the service of the love of the neighbor, reason is not an end in itself but credible only so far as it furthers the interests of the *conatus*, only so far as it can persuade persons that they can more effectively preserve themselves when working collectively. Reason must prove its worth before the bar of nature. This, however, is not easy, and persons will not freely agree to take on the rational perspective. Persons, Spinoza argues, forfeit their freedom for the sake of participation in the state, but they do not do so freely but only with great incentive. This explains why Spinoza suggests that alliances will be established between nations less on rational grounds and more on grounds of mutual interest. We are not rational by nature, and to be rational presupposes a forfeiture of freedom that many persons, the philosopher included, may not want to incur for the sake of understanding another culture beyond their own.

Two: Reason, qua the state, is the best and most natural extension of our *conatus*. Persons who opt to enter the collective on the calculation of self-interest via collective action do engage in a kind of rational deliberation such that entrance into the state incurs no real forfeiture of freedom only the logical extension of natural interests. The calculus of power is a form of reason, and reason is always an expression of the calculus of power. If, therefore, the rational justification for the state is that collective interests are more effective than individual pursuits in guaranteeing human self-preservation, then the national collective is only a step toward a more universal community whereby persons benefit from the efforts of all persons and not only those of their own nation. Read this way, the life of the citizen (on the one hand) and the love of the neighbor (on the other) are both natural expressions of our natural drive for self-preservation. Human nature fulfills itself in and through a universal culture of justice and charity. From this perspective, persons should, the philosopher could argue, attempt to understand noncitizens not only for the sake of acquiring benefits for their own national interests but also for the higher purpose of establishing universal points of common interest that effectively strengthen all toward self-preservation. As before, reason's labor generates a position from which the philosopher-citizen can critique national solipsism. Nonetheless, this philosopher can no more easily advocate a free and positively pursued apologetics than our first philosopher. As noted earlier, the problem concerns a tension surrounding rational activity as described in Spinoza's account. Although in this scenario, reason does not have to do battle with human nature as above, it does stand in conflict with divine nature. In this conflict, apologetic discourse leads to the de-moralization of reason's own effort. Why?

According to Spinoza's own account, no matter how rational we are, and no matter how many of us are rational, we will never be as powerful as nature. We are, in effect, a speck in the larger orbit of bigger, competing powers. Human reason's reach will, in this context, always be made a mockery of in relation to the inevitable limits of its power before other elements in nature and nature's own power herself. "The force whereby a man persists in existing is limited, and infinitely surpassed by the power of external causes."[42] At the end of Book IV of the *Ethics*, Spinoza says, "[H]uman power is very limited and is infinitely surpassed by the power of external causes, and so we do not have absolute power to adapt to our purposes things external to us. However, we shall patiently bear whatever happens to us that is contrary to what is required by consideration of our own advantage...."[43] This sounds easier than it is. In fact, the philosopher who encourages persons to love their neighbors and/or at least pursue rational discourse with them will get laughed out of town by both nonphilosopher citizens who know little of reason's arguments as well as by philosophers who by contrast know precisely reason's arguments and know the realities of the human position of inevitable disempowerment within nature. It's one thing to tell folks to patiently endure their powerlessness. It's another to ask them to continuously fight against it when defeat is inevitable.

Third: The philosopher might pull out all the stops and argue that the ultimate position of blessedness or love of God solves the aforementioned problems. Blessedness, the philosopher can say, offers the highest level of human reason and this reason, so far as it participates in the divine reason, accrues the benefits of divine knowledge: that is, power and eternality. To the extent that an apologetic effort toward rational discourse across nations functions as a stepping stone toward this level of perfection and divine intuition, citizens (rational and irrational) may develop an interest in it. Everyone wants eternal life. But, even here, the philosopher will have a hard argument to sell. After people read the small print, they will realize that blessedness of the kind that affords absolute freedom from the powers of nature is available only for the eternal mind without, and not with the body. So far as we have bodies, Spinoza says, we are always enslaved to the limits of our passive emotions because our knowledge is always limited to the affects of the body and cannot reach into nature beyond this basis. The philosopher's promise of eternal life through knowledge happens only when the mind lives on past the death of the body. This, of course, flies in the face of person's drive toward self-preservation linked as it is to continuation of bodily existence. "Nobody, unless he is overcome by external causes contrary to his own nature, neglects to seek his own advantage, that is, to preserve his own being."[44] Reason and/or apologetics, in this instance, are attractive only when we assume the ultimate dichotomization of mind and body. Applied to Judaism, it is no longer the physical members of the Jewish body politic who will achieve this freedom. Rather, persons who achieve blessedness identify with God so wholly that their human *conatus* is no longer a factor. Yes, the logical slippage between human nature and nature writ large is erased but only at the expense of the loss of material life, and

94 *The Logic of Exceptionalism*

along with it, the divinization of divine desire or conatus. Either, therefore, peace is achieved when human desire is destroyed, or human desire is satisfied in the transformation into divine desire. In either event, the two poles of human desire and free discourse and/or understanding of others cannot be reconciled. If I am a desiring person, I will not want to engage in apologetic discourse; and if I am blessed and saved, I will no longer be able to.

In conclusion, Spinoza's account of Judaism, rooted as it is in a vibrant account of the relationship between human desire and law, affords a more historically authentic and covenantally accurate account of Jewish life than is often realized. Nonetheless, Spinoza's attempt to link law and desire in Judaism cannot explain how Judaism's material and historical life not only links to law but beyond to its ability to understand and communicate with non-Jewish culture. Missing from Spinoza's account is a revelatory context for the relationship between law and desire. Only this context will resolve the tension between material particularity and need and cross-cultural communication—what here I will refer to as a "free apologetics."

Materiality Becomes the Law

GILLIAN ROSE'S DIALECTICS OF DESIRE

The second materialist account of law I want to examine is that presented by Gillian Rose in *Mourning Becomes the Law*. In this work, Rose sought to reclaim the philosophical significance of law as the lens of desire. Like Spinoza, Rose offers a materialist conception of law that is motivated by, represents, and responds to the claims of human desire.[45] The five short essays in this book elegantly and poignantly expose how any ethics beyond the law leaves persons bereft of the tools for how to live in our politicized, urbanized, and embattled world. How do we mourn; where might we find grace; how could we be willing to live with others when we have to deal with our own economic, political ,and familial challenges? We work at the law. Close to the ground, within earshot of the chorus of individual need and conflict, Rose's account of law arises from what she calls the "comedy of Absolute Spirit."

According to Rose, law is the limit on desire that emerges from the misrecognition of self in other. Persons, Rose assumes, project themselves on to the world and on to other persons. By nature, we seek to find ourselves and our desires affirmed by our surroundings. Still, intersubjectivity challenges our self-conception and understanding of the world. Rather than result in the desired recognition of self, encounters with others produce a mis-recognition of oneself and other. On the one hand, I mis-recognize you because of your relation to your self (I expected you to be like me); and on the other hand, I mis-recognize myself because I failed to take your self-relation into consideration in my understanding of the world. "My relation to myself is mediated by what I recognize or refuse to recognize in your relation to yourself; while your self-relation depends on what you recognize of my relation to myself."[46] The outcome that Rose calls the "broken middle, the third term which arises out of misrecognition of desire, of work and of my and your self-relation mediated by the self-relation of the other."[47] "Law" is another term for the content of the broken middle. Law is the content of new information generated by the exposure of the one to the other. This content educates persons on the path toward authentic mutual recognition. The more they mis-recognize themselves, the more they learn how to relate to another. Socially produced knowledge adjudicates social relations. As the reflection of mutual mis-recognition, law represents the limit on individual desires that militate against the movement toward mutual recognition.

Rose's account is definitely a step in the right direction. Law is generated from the ground up and not imposed on persons from an exteriorly invested source of power. Law is a social and not a political by-product. Moreover, unlike Kantian law, the law of the broken middle is in touch with the reality on the ground. It legislates real persons in real encounters, taking up and adjudicating the manifold sorts of claims persons make on each other instead of legislating abstractly over and against the range of real desires, real conflicts, and real patterns of reconciliation.

However, there are a number of problems with Rose's law of inter-subjectivity. If tyrannical forms of law are troubling because they are untouchable, unchangeable, and impervious to critique, it is also true that Rose's version of inter-subjective law is overly unstable: the precarious outcome of perpetual battles of desire. In other words, law happens *despite* the interests of those involved, and the rise of legislative efforts toward mutual recognition breeds a perpetual resentment on the part of those involved that works against the move toward mutual understanding and not in favor of it. In this view, law is always one battle away from dissolution. It is hard won and not easily sustained. It is, Rose says, through law that "self-consciousness comes to learn of its investment in denying the actuality of itself in another."[48] Selves are invested in denying the law because it caps their desires.

"[T]he falling towards or away from mutual recognition,"[49] the law that limits desire is also limited and threatened by desire. Slavishly, it follows the battles between persons swinging in and out of existence with the periodic bursts of "mis" and then mutual recognition. Unlike Spinoza's sovereign ruled directly by desire, Rose's law fights the good fight against desire—working hard to achieve a mutual recognition that authentically overcomes the raging investments of individual players. In the end, however, Rose's inter-subjectively generated law is just as vulnerable to the hegemony of desire as Spinoza's sovereign. Always embattled and resented law weakly attempts to adjudicate a truce between persons whose "investment in denying the actuality of itself in another" always surfaces to sabotage the road toward mutual recognition. To succeed, law must not only adjudicate between persons: It must represent fully the persons whom it orders. It cannot order despite those it governs: It has to order on behalf of them.

That Rose understood the limits of her own account of law shows up in oblique references to a notion of "grace" in her work.[50] Taking the lead over and against the law, unmet desire often declares the law unjust. Still, Rose argues, even those afflicted by unjust applications of the law, must return to the law. But why? Why should the one who has lost because of the law return to the law? Mourning must become the law, she says. "The mourner returns to negotiate and challenge the changing inner and outer boundaries of the soul and of the city; she returns to their perennial anxiety."[51] To return to the law is to move out of loss and into anxiety. But why would this help? One might think that the return to anxiety is the return to the drive of the self toward mis-recognition—a restoration of the self in the comedy of social life. But if this is what Rose means, it's not what she says. Instead, she says that we return to the law because the "law is abundant and abounding: it is not the contrary of grace. . . ."[52] The implication is that law is the site of human social anxiety *and* points to the reality of a divine grace that hears and acknowledges the needs and desires of others without perpetuating a battle of mutual neglect. Rose never tells us directly how or why these two might link through law. Indirectly, however, Rose's identification of the two sides of law—anxiety and grace suggests what David Novak would refer to as "natural law"—or what I would refer to as "theological desire."

DAVID NOVAK: NATURAL LAW AND NATURAL DESIRE

David Novak's analysis of natural law constitutes the third and final example of a nonrevelatory law. The two prior accounts of law and its relationship to desire suffer from a crucial debilitating flaw. Both place law in the service of desire rather than the reverse. But to say that law is in the service of desire is to say that desire behaves as if it can reach fulfillment with or without the law. It acts, in other words, without a self-consciousness of its nature as desire. By definition, desire is the longing for something missing. To forge ahead with force over and against temporary limits is inauthentic—a denial or form of self-alienation of its own that, like all concerted exercises in self-alienation, results in despair for the denier. We have not yet discovered an account of the free law that rises above desire, and in so doing, not only limits but judges or offers a "candid exposition" of the desire that it limits. Only a "free law" will permit desire its authentic role as longing and liberate it from the burdensome pursuit of its own fulfillment.

How does Novak's natural law fit into this analysis? Natural law is the law that indicates that human efforts toward mutual recognition are always unsatisfactory to participants. As the preceding review of Rose's phenomenology of the broken middle shows, socially generated law leaves participants feeling ill at ease—or, in Novak's language, not at home in the world of social relations. Why? For two reasons:

> The social world is a world in which I don't recognize myself because I do not feel recognized by the other: that is, a world where I do not feel at home.
> The social world reminds me of the limits of my freedom or my finitude and causes me, therefore, to wonder, "What is 'my' purpose here?" Natural law is nothing more than the fact of this situation. It is the law of our finitude and the law of the limit of society's ability to make this world a home where we feel we have a purpose.

Clearly attuned to the order or natural law of the world he lives in Abraham, Novak says, nonetheless asks

> What is my place in the world? That question lies at the heart of Abraham's desire for God's presence. . . . This question arises from our experience of the phenomenal order of things. . . . What we soon learn from this order is our own mortal vulnerability, our superfluity in the world . . . we discover the immanence of our own death. . . . As a result of this existential predicament, the transcendent desire that goes beyond immanent need arises.[53]

From a legal perspective, natural law translates into a limit on all forms of idolatry, both individual and social. Manifest socially, natural law is an aspect of human experience. Still, it does not offer a pool of positive prescriptions but only a universal limit on the pretensions of any human political or legislative system to satisfy human need and create community. "[N]atural law is the province of philosophy and not theology precisely because it is not directly derived from the words of revelation but, rather, from reflection on the limits or ends of the human condition itself."[54] From an existential perspective, natural law is an expression of theological desire. Premised upon the failure of persons to recognize each other as the basis of a true community, natural law points to a nonhuman, transcendent source of recognition and community. But natural law can do no more than point to the need for this transcendent source or revelation. It cannot identify that source itself.

How does natural law hold up in terms of our analysis of nonrevelatory law? Compared with Spinoza and Rose, Novak's natural law comes closest to achieving the sort of freedom reserved for revelatory law. On the one hand, natural law limits desire. Certainly, more than Spinoza's sovereign whose success rises or falls with the desires of those he legislates, and even more than Rose's law of social limit, Novak's natural law limits the pretensions of human desire to achieve its own fulfillment. Natural law reflects and therefore exposes the limits of human desire as it seeks to fulfill itself in the reflection in another or others. Nonetheless, natural law remains bound to the desire it limits. Novak says that natural law is a "*Grenzbegriff*—a boundary concept"[55]. It arises out of and yet is parasitic upon that which it limits. Consequently, while natural law points to the need for transcendence, it affords no access to a trans-human exteriority. It cannot initiate its own order but asserts an order contingent upon the dictates of the desire it limits and is, therefore, not free. Natural law cannot judge desire. It simply indicates its end-limit.

Like the accounts of nonrevelatory law in Spinoza and Rose, the advances made by Novak's more materialist account of natural law are overshadowed by the inability of Novak's natural law to present both a positive recognition of human desire and the need for its delimitation. If, then, each of these three thinkers offer important changes to our philosophical conception of law, their thought remains mired within the dialectic of desire characteristic of exceptionalist thinking and cannot offer a basis for a peaceful recognition of the validity of one's own desires and the rights of others.

PART TWO

The Logic of the Law

FOUR

The Biblical Theology of Abiding

In Part I of this book, I sought to identify the limits of a theological or an anthropological account of freedom devoid of normative limitation. Chapter 1 introduced the social and philosophical exclusion or exceptionalism that results from an effort to dichotomize between freedom and law and, in particular, the negative consequences for Jewish-Christian relations. Chapter 2 focused on the link between divine power and intolerance when divine power is understood outside a more complete analysis of divine nature as self-sustaining power together with relationality. Chapter 3 attended to the dialectics of human desire, or what are the negative effects of the pursuit of human desire unregulated by a self-consciousness of the limits of desire. The purpose of Part II of the volume is to offer a biblical and theo-philosophical account of a theology of law and freedom and demonstrate the paradigm shift that this theology affords for understanding the nature of human freedom, human knowledge, and human social relations. In Part III, I will demonstrate the positive effects of a theology of law and freedom for the work of Jewish-Christian apologetic engagement.

It is the central contention of this chapter that a theology of law and freedom has a firm foundation within the Hebrew Scriptures and supports a notion of human life as an abiding within this order. Here, I hearken to the account of Abrahamic "remaining" earlier pointed to by Franz Rosenzweig in his discussion of the meaning of the sacrifice of Isaac in Genesis 22. As we recall, sacrifice, according to Rosenzweig, is not an offering but a ritual or performance of "return" that exposes a logic of abiding or dwelling.[1] In this chapter, I not only recognize this account of "remaining" elsewhere within the scriptures but pursue how this notion contributes to a larger network of categories deriving from the nexus between law and freedom within the divine nature and extending all the way into biblical presentations of the meaning of human justification, *halakha*, wisdom, history, and atonement/restoration. This is not the same as saying that the Hebrew Scriptures exclusively present a theology of law and freedom. It is to argue that such a logic operates extensively and repeatedly throughout a large variety of biblical texts.

The chapter will begin with an analysis of the link between the theology of divine creation described in the Hebrew Scriptures in Genesis 1, Deutero-Isaiah and psalms, and a theology of redemption characteristic of the account of divine theophany at Sinai in Exodus and the Deuteronomistic accounts of divine redemption. The second section will identify the theology of law within the paradigmatic account of the Abrahamic covenant. My discussion will amplify the prior discussion of the biblical theology of creation and also elucidate the significance of the frequent invocations of the Abrahamic covenant in the presentation of Sinaitic material. This section will focus particularly upon the implications of a theology of law and freedom for the meaning of Abrahamic justification. The third section will demarcate the theology of law and freedom within accounts of the Sinaitic covenant and focus upon the meaning of *halakha* in this context. Particular attention will be placed upon the semiotic significance of *halakha* in general and the signifying function of the law of the Sabbatical and Jubilee year in particular. As "signs" of the covenant, both the Sabbatical and Jubilee year verify the theology of law and freedom. Moreover, the semiotic function of the Sabbatical and Jubilee year suggests a crucial connection between the capacity of persons to abide freely within the divine order and a concomitant notion of wisdom as the self-awareness of one's place within this order. Consequently, my discussion of the Sabbatical and Jubilee year will forge an important connection between a life within the law and the wisdom emergent from the law. Finally, in the fourth part, my analysis of the Jubilee will connect the theology of law and freedom to the meaning of atonement and the nature of divine forgiveness. By extension, this discussion will introduce a corresponding conception of history by way of an analysis of the reference to the concept of the Jubilee year within Isaiah 61.

Creation and Abiding

According to G. Von Rad, biblical scholarship has far too long attempted to earmark a unique and foundational theology of the created order. Despite rigorous debates regarding the compositional dating of Genesis, scholars have permitted their theological hermeneutics to remain overly influenced by the canonical positioning of the Genesis text, concluding from this that the "creation of natural order by God [operates] as a motive for faith either in the prophets or the psalms,"[2] laying the groundwork for a subsequent theology of redemption. From Von Rad's point of view, good biblical scholarship shows that if anything, the order of theological primacy is reversed, as he states, "the Yahwistic faith of the Old Testament is based on the notion of election and therefore primarily concerned with redemption."[3] Manifold examples of the biblical discussion of creation reveal the ideological overlay of a theology of redemption, references to God's gracious election of Israel, and his continued promise to her. Undoubtedly, Von Rad's position has merit from within the world of biblical scholarship. Nonetheless, my interest in his position has less to do with this polemic and more to do with the theology of the biblical text that Von Rad inadvertently or otherwise exposes. In his *From Genesis to Chronicles*, Von Rad presents a detailed account of his argument. Analyzing a range of texts—including Deutero-Isaiah (43:1, 44:21, 44:24); Psalms 74; and finally, Genesis 1—we are, Von Rad, argues "struck by the ease by which two doctrines often thought to be very different are in effect brought together."[4]

Von Rad begins by citing examples of the connection between Israel's notion of land and nature and her own experience of God's saving action (for example, Leviticus 25:23). Still, Von Rad argues, the biblical text offers many examples of the connection between God's act of redemption and God's work in creation that speak about the created order and nature more generally and not strictly about the land of Israel itself. Von Rad cites Isaiah 44:24: "Thus has Yahweh said, your Redeemer and the One who formed you from the womb. . . . It is as if for Deutero-Isaiah, the creation of the world and the redemption of Israel both exemplify the same divine dispensation."[5] We can, he suggests, find a similar nexus between God's creative acts and divine redemption throughout the psalms, citing Psalm 74 in particular, "Yet my God is from old, working salvation in the midst of the earth." And Von Rad argues further "there is no theological cleavage between the priestly writer and Psalm 89 or 74."[6] Genesis 1, he argues, operates as a classic priestly text and efficiently and effectively uses a theology of divine creation to justify a theology of divine salvation. Genesis 1, he argues

> ... is not an independent theological essay ... the writer naturally takes his own theological stand ... representing the redemptive relationship between Yahweh and Israel. In order to justify this relationship theologically, he starts from the creation of the world and shows how at each stage in the course of history, new statutes and ordinances are revealed, which increasingly guarantee the redemption of the people of God. Thus, here, too, the creation of the world by Yahweh is not being considered for its own sake. ... P's presentation of it, is wholly motivated by considerations of divine redemption.[7]

Von Rad's scholarship is premised upon the shock value of this nexus between the God who orders nature and the God who redeems Israel, but it is the central claim of this chapter that theologically speaking, the connection between divine order and divine grace is not surprising. In fact, Von Rad's text analysis supports my effort to identify a biblical picture of the character of divine nature as the freedom *qua* power to create and present the lawful difference between God as creator and that which is created on the one hand and the character of divine nature as the freedom to care for and be present with that which God has created in this lawful difference on the other hand.

First, the divine act of creation exposes the character of divine freedom *qua* sovereignty. In creation, God exercises the freedom to establish a lawful difference between Godself and that which God creates. The point is echoed all throughout the psalms, "Before the mountains were born and land and world formed, throughout all time you are God" (Psalms 90:2), and in Jeremiah, we read, "Indeed lord God, surely you have made heaven and earth by your great power and outstretched arm, nothing is too difficult for you" (Jeremiah 32:17).

Still, the creator God, as Von Rad reminds us, exercises a divine dispensation. Divine sovereignty is not, even in the Genesis 1 account, limited to this expression of alterity but enacts a reaching out toward the other it has created such that the initial ordering of the difference between itself and its creation operates as a framing affirmation of this creation. A famous midrash asks, "Why was the world created with a beth? ... Because it connotes blessing. And why not with an alef? Because it connotes cursing. . . . Hence the Holy One, blessed He, said 'Lo I will create it with the language of blessing and would that it may stand!' "[8] The blueprint presented in Genesis 1 portrays this divine blessing as manifest in an order of mutual dependency and care. Undoubtedly, God creates a world and persons as agents through whom God may realize his purpose, but as well, God provides and cares for what he has created. The natural world is to be guarded over by persons, and persons flourish by virtue of the provisions afforded by the natural order. That both reflect the divine interest in his creation is reflected upon even by Maimonides, who identifies divine mercy as a primary attribute of action and says

> [W]henever one of His actions is apprehended, the attribute from which this action proceeds is predicated of Him, may He be exalted, and the name deriving from that action is applied to Him. For instance, one apprehends the kindness of His governance in the production of the embryos of living beings, the bringing of various faculties to existence in them and in those who rear them after birth— faculties that preserve them from destruction and annihilation and protect them against harm and are useful to them in all the doings that are necessary to them. Now actions of this kind proceed from us only after we feel a certain affection and compassion, and this is the meaning of mercy. God, may He be exalted, is said to be merciful, just as it is said, Like as a father is merciful to his children. . . .[9]

Affirmation of the irreducible value of human life extends beyond the physiological order of human birth and growth. God's freedom as care offers the basis for a full affirmation of human need and desire. Creation, we might say, is already redeemed, and consequently, a theology of divine freedom as law and grace precipitates an identity between ontology and teleology. If, according to Genesis 1:28, persons are created to service the divine will, it is also the case that the conditions by means of which they are to exercise this responsibility presuppose the full affirmation of their humanity, their physical needs (Genesis 1:29), and social needs (Genesis 1:27).

Fulfillment of the divine will is tantamount to the fulfillment of human irreducibility. Logically speaking, once in place, it is the reality of this human irreducibility that constitutes one of the necessary conditions for the structure of a divine-human relationship or covenant (the other being the irreducibility of the divine already established in the reality of divine freedom). What is an authentic relationship if it does not involve both, the willingness to acknowledge the reality of the other all the while retaining the irreducibility of oneself? It is for this reason that David Novak insightfully interprets the meaning of the image of God as the capacity for a relationship to God. "The image of God is the active mutuality possible only between God and humans. . . . The world we make by our action together is for the sake of each other."[10] Ontologically speaking, persons are nothing other than that irreducible reality that constitutes one pole in the relationship with God (and world), and they need not aspire to be anything else. This does not mean that persons relate to God devoid of need. Rather, affirmed in the law of difference between themselves and God, persons abide in their need.

We might juxtapose this against two other commonly held positions: Persons are affirmed in their capacity to fulfill their needs; and persons are affirmed by virtue of their ability to override their needs. Both accounts of human nature presuppose a divinization of persons that results in the sacrifice of their humanity. The first instance appears in variant expressions of humanism, whereby overconfident assessments of the capacity of human nature to satisfy the needs of persons result either in the divinization of communities, which insofar as they insist upon their capacity to fulfill individual need ultimately deny persons the freedom to admit the reality of unfulfilled need (that is, eliminate the validity of the need to pray); or in the creation of a privileged class of a few deemed uniquely capable of funding the needs of the many, set up as the objects of petition or idolatry. We can find both instances in Marxism: the first in Marx's early work,[11] and the second in Leninist adaptations of Marx's thought.[12]

In the second commonly held formulation, human nature is affirmed rationally and identified with the acquisition of knowledge or access to truth, theoretical or practical. As we have seen in both Maimonidean and Spinozistic accounts, this sort of ontological determinism inevitably generates teleological pursuits that *qua* rational alone neglect human embodiment. Although both Maimonides and Spinoza acknowledge the demands of embodied life, both understand these demands as secondary and subordinate to the intellectual apprehension of God. If, in the first case, teleology was linked with persons' ability to fulfill their desires, here it is linked with the freedom to rise above them. In either instance, the reality of human need and the time it takes historically to pursue that need is excised on behalf of a higher *telos*. All too frequently, teleology functions as a disguise for the slippage between human reality and a superimposed account of human essence. Within the biblical context, however, persons are affirmed as what they are delimited to be: desiring, temporally conditioned agents who rightfully pursue these needs and desires but whose end or purpose is neither the final fulfillment nor ultimate negation of them.

Textually, it is the biblical notion of the Sabbath (Genesis 2:1–2) that most poignantly characterizes this paradigm of rest and affirmation within the order. According to Von Rad

> [T]he declarations about a Sabbath at creation contain one of the most remarkable and daring testimonies in the entire Priestly document. In reading these statements, which move, to be sure, at that extreme limit of the protological, one must once again remember especially that they too derive completely from Israel's position before God as it was constituted by the covenantal relation.[13]

Beyond calling attention to the covenantal character of the priestly announcement of the Sabbath, Von Rad goes on to highlight how the character of Sabbath rest operates as a commentary upon the logical structure of the created order, and he says

> The Babylonian creation epic also contains a concluding act following the work of creation; it is the public glorification of the god Marduk. . . . How different, how much more profound, is the impressive rest of Israel's God! This rest is in every respect a new thing along with the process of creation; it is anything but an appendix.[14]

But what kind of a new thing is this divine rest—what marks its unique character? On the one hand, Von Rad suggests that Sabbath rest connotes a "rest that existed before man and still exists without man's perceiving it. . . ."[15] In the context of my argument of a theology of law and freedom, this protological character of divine rest is reflective and constitutive of the nature of the divine itself, which in its freedom is constrained neither by the demands of its power nor the extensivity of its reach but operates actively in both capacities fully and without a scarcity that would promote an instrumentalism in its engagement with what is other than itself. However, Von Rad also notes that the Sabbath rest reflects the character of what emerges from the divine freedom—the products of God's free law. If, as the argument suggests, the biblical God rests as balanced between his own freedom as law and freedom as extensivity, so can the world and the persons made by this God rest, created as they exist within the context of this same balance of order and affirmation.

> The declaration mounts, as it were, to the place of God himself and testifies that with the living God there is rest. . . . This word about rest is not at all speculative; it speaks of one fact of God which is turned to the world . . . the world is no longer in the process of being created. It was not and is not incomplete but it has been completed by God. . . . . Even more, that God has "blessed," "sanctified" ("to sanctify" means to separate exclusively for God), this rest, means that P does not consider it as something for God alone but as a concern of the world, almost as a third something that exists between God and the world. The way is . . . prepared, therefore, for an exalted, saving good.[16]

That Von Rad identifies the priestly influence over this text and suggests that "these statements received their final form at the time of the exile, a time when Israel perceived in the Sabbath (and in circumcision) the real sign of the covenant. . . ."[17] only further supports my interpretation of the Genesis text as providing the theology of law and freedom, which structures both the Abrahamic and Sinaitic covenants as I will discuss here.

Justified in the Law: The Abrahamic Covenant

In Deuteronomy 7:8, we read "The LORD did not set His love upon you, nor choose you, because ye were more in number than any people—for ye were the fewest of all peoples—but because the LORD loved you, and because He would keep the oath which He swore unto your fathers;"[18] and in Deuteronomy 4, we are reminded, "And because He loved thy fathers, and chose their seed after them, and brought thee out with His presence, with His great power, out of Egypt, to drive out nations from before thee greater and mightier than thou, to bring thee in, to give thee their land for an inheritance, as it is this day; know this day, and lay it to thy heart, that the LORD, He is God in heaven above and upon the earth beneath; there is none else."[19] In view of the central objective of this chapter—to trace the presence of the logic of the law as it runs throughout scriptural texts and demonstrate the give and take between these texts as they express this logic—the immediate goal of this discussion is to identify the contribution made by texts detailing the Abrahamic covenant and, in particular, Genesis 12–19. The aforementioned link between the Sinai covenant and the Abrahamic covenant referred to in Deuteronomy can be found throughout the Hebrew Scriptures and rabbinic materials, the heart of which I will suggest is the notion of Abraham's justification in the law.

By using the language of justification within the law, I do not mean to reinvoke the centuries-old apparent dichotomy between faith and works. In point of fact, it is my central contention that the theology of abiding presented in Genesis 12–19 offers a refreshing and yet highly neglected alternative to this so-called polemic. We may, I believe, credit Martin Luther with the identification of this apparent divide. In *On Christian Liberty*, Luther argues that justification or acceptance of persons by God is through faith alone. By this, Luther means, as is well known, that persons are not justified by their own acts or merit. For the purposes of this discussion, I would like to highlight the implications of such a view for a divine command theology. If the preceding argument suggests that justification has no relation to our actions, then it would seem to follow that justification is not linked to our active response to divine command. If actions have no bearing at all on matters of justification, then divine command, which presupposes human actions, plays no role in justification either. That such a conclusion follows from Luther's justification through faith is apparent in his discussion of the relation between commandments and promises in the Old Testament. "The entire scriptures," he says, "is divided into two parts: commandments and promises. Although the commandments teach things that are good, the things taught are not done as soon as they are taught."[20] Commandments do not operate to stimulate good action. On the contrary, they remind persons of their disobedience—their inevitable failure to do what is good—and offer nothing other than a sign of God's rightful judgment and punishment. In direct contrast are the divine promises, offered by God through Christ Jesus "who suffered and rose." By promises, Luther means the gifts of "grace, righteousness, peace, liberty . . ." here presented through this Word in which one need only believe or have faith in order to be justified. "He who believes . . . will be saved. . . ."[21]

It is hard to imagine any clearer articulation of the divide between command and promise than the preceding account of the justification through faith. Citing Paul, Luther concludes that "God has consigned all men to disobedience, that he may have mercy upon all."[22] The Old Testament, he argues, tells the story of the former event, and the New Testament announces the latter. Later, Luther does address the life of righteousness, suggesting that as justified, persons can do the law—or rather that as justified, God fulfills the law "for them." Still, this subsequent nod to righteousness through Christ does little to offset two most damaging implications of Luther's justification through faith: the invocation of the inevitable link between divine command and the warrant for Israelite judgment or punishment; and the de-normatization of the covenantal structure.

To understand how Jewish-Christian relations have been almost irreparably marred by the Christian invocation of the divine punishment of Israel, one only needs to read Richard Rubenstein's *After Auschwitz*, where he demonstrates how a commitment to an unqualified theology of reward and punishment leaves Christians with little theological choice than to read the Holocaust as a consequence or reflection of divine wrath.[23] Arguably, Luther's insistence upon the divide between divine command and divine promise provides a viable theological rationale for such a position.

Equally damaging to Jewish-Christian relations is the impact of Luther's justification through faith on Christian interpretations of the theological

110   *The Logic of the Law*

significance of covenant. By excising the significance of divine command from the covenantal logic, Luther paves the way for the complete prioritization of grace over law so characteristic of much of the New Paul theology. As discussed in Chapter 1, Giorgio Agamben's antinomian interpretation of the covenant of Abraham along with his prioritization of the reception of the Word of God as near in the believer's faith has already exemplified the dangers of Luther's account. As I argued, the de-normatization of covenantal theology funds an exceptionalism whereby "justification" or "rights" rest solely upon a non-normatively regulated expression of divine grace. Such an approach not only wreaks havoc upon Jewish-Christian relations, reducing Judaism to a refusal to recognize the priority of God's singularly redeeming grace, but it also fails to provide a lens through which we may understand certain central covenantal texts in the scriptures—most noteworthy, Genesis 19, which portrays Abraham's challenge to God's plan to punish Sodom and Gomorrah. A better understanding of Genesis 19 is possible from the vantage point of a theology of justification in the law when by this, we mean that Abraham is justified in and by the divine command not in contradistinction to the divine promise, but as the agency of it. To see how such a theology emerges from the text, let us now turn to a discussion of Genesis 12–19.

JUSTIFICATION IN THE LAW: *L'ECH L'CHA*

According to biblical scholars, Genesis 12–25 constitutes a scriptural unit.[24] Although theology and source criticism do not always overlap, in this case, I believe that they do; and in what follows, I will offer a reading of Genesis 18 and 19 as contextualized by an interpretation of Genesis 12–17. More specifically, I will suggest that Genesis 12–17 introduces the critical nexus between divine command and divine favor characteristic of covenantal theology, with Genesis 18–19 offering a detailed commentary or "derash" on this particular formulation.

Genesis 12:1 offers an explicit articulation of the correlation between divine command and divine freedom. "Hashem said to Abram, 'Go for yourself from your land, from your relatives, and from your father's house to the land that I will show you. And I will make of you a great nation; I will bless you, and make your name great, and you shall be a blessing'" (Genesis 12:1). A careful look at the Hebrew of these two verses suggests that their meaning can be understood by a proper translation of the first two words that God directs to Abram: "לֶךְ-לְךָ."

Why, we might ask, does the text use the formulation לֶךְ-לְךָ when לְךָ alone would suffice to convey God's imperative that Abram and Sarai leave their home? לְךָ-לְךָ means not only "go" but go "for yourselves." The command does not stand alone but is inseparable from the supplement that going is for their benefit, and this addition alters the meaning of the imperative so that Abram and Sarai are commanded not only to "go" but more specifically "to receive." The imperative is transformed into a gift. Still, one might ask the opposite question regarding the relevance of the initial לְךָ. Why does the text include this as an imperative and not merely indicate God's granting a gift to this couple? A simple statement of grant alone does not reveal the dynamic of the divine gift whereby in so offering the gifts here promised, God stands asymmetrically related to Abram and Sarai. His freedom to grant what will be of benefit for them points to an authority or an alterity, which implies a sovereignty unique to God in this position as the one who gives. Only the imperative "go" or "receive" captures this irreducible difference between the two sets of participants.

With לְךָ-לְךָ, we see the logic of the law built into the very narrative of Abram's and Sarai's covenantal curriculum. Here, divine command points to the ordered difference between the divine and the human along with the benefit of this command for the commanded. The command does not ensnare them in error. If the Hebrew Scriptures presents a theology of order, it also presents a theology of justification. In this Sidrah, Abram and Sarai are invited to abide within this order, their obedience to God's command nothing more and nothing less than their reception of this invitation to dwell in their humanity together with the covenantal God. Promise and command, the two features of divine freedom as sovereignty and favor, are inextricable from each other and set in place an analogous nexus between human obedience and reception of grace. Covenant is normative in its very structure, and human obedience to God is coterminously acknowledgement of the divine and the grounding of human right.

The remainder of Genesis 12–17 details the features or elements of this covenantal dwelling, and they are land, nation (or children), and blessing. Genesis 17 requires specific attention for while scholars are in general agreement that the covenant affirmed here constitutes a basic repetition of the terms stated in Genesis 12,[25] Genesis 17 introduces two new elements into the structure of covenant beyond the formulation in Genesis 12: the unconditional character of the covenantal relationship; and the presentation of a particular law (*halakha*), circumcision.

For quite some time, biblical scholars have suggested a categorical divide between the Abrahamic covenant and the Davidic covenant on the one hand, and the Sinaitic covenant on the other, identifying the first two as "promissory" covenants and the latter as an "obligatory" covenant.[26] Part of the goal of this chapter is to offer a theological account of the promissory covenant. In the process, my argument runs up against this historical-critical division. Characteristic of the promissory type—or what is otherwise referred to as the Royal Grant model—is the presentation of "gracious promises by YHWH not subject to any conditions."[27] The defining element of the Royal Grant model is, therefore, its unconditionality and the emphasis upon the rights of the vassal. Theologically speaking, the unconditionality of the Abrahamic covenant presented in Genesis 17:13 acts as the essential plank in the logic of law. Already, Genesis 12 structures a divine-human relationship rooted in the unique character of divine freedom as sovereign command and gracious favor. Genesis 17:13 extends God's gracious favor into unconditionality, and the Abrahamic covenant represents God's everlasting commitment to the protection and welfare of Israel. Undoubtedly, the unconditional character of the divine favor has not been lost on Jewish theologians,[28] but few Jewish thinkers have discerned the implications of the unconditional character of the covenant for a Jewish theology of atonement, and even fewer have unpacked the implications of this unconditionality for Jewish apologetics generally speaking and Jewish-Christian relations in particular.

I will offer a more detailed analysis of the implications of divine unconditionality for a Jewish theology of atonement. For now, we can say that the theological implications are best summed up in the rabbinic dictum "although she has sinned, Israel is still Israel."[29] Such a view stands at odds with Luther's command-disobedience paradigm. Israel, the covenantal logic suggests is established and sustained by the covenantal invitation for all time. That such a view will also challenge Christian theological attempts to apply a reward-punishment schema in order to justify claims of the anachronicity of Israel and its covenant is clear, and will be examined in greater detail.

As well, it is the central contention of this book as a whole that the precise balance between covenantal normativity and unconditional favor presents unusually positive conditions for Israel, non-Israel or Jewish, non-Jewish relations. As will become clearer both in my interpretation of Genesis 18 along with the more philosophically driven analysis in Chapter 6, the affirmation of Israel's identity in the everlasting commitment of the Abrahamic promise permits Israel the freedom to engage with others without the identitarian investment characteristic of nontheologically grounded social and cultural relations. However, before turning to a detailed discussion of Genesis 18 and the two-fold demonstration of Abraham's free and positive engagement with those outside the covenantal frame, it is important to attend to the second of the new elements presented in Genesis 17: the law of circumcision.

One of the most significant implications of a theology of divine freedom and order concerns the meaning of *halakha* or Jewish law. Genesis 17 marks the first presentation of *halakha* for the Abrahamic community, beginning with the law that "This is My covenant, which ye shall keep, between Me and you and thy seed after thee: every male among you shall be circumcised."[30] Chapter 2's discussion of Regina Schwartz's *The Curse of Cain* has already set the stage for the import of such an analysis. In Schwartz's view, the performance of biblical law (and by extension, rabbinic law) operates as a mode of violence management. The product of a capricious and demanding God, law functions as a tool to offset divine wrath. As such, obedience to divine law in Schwartz's account presupposes the perpetual attendance to the divine over and against communal and individual interest. Law is sacrificial in nature, if by sacrificial, we mean the participation in a currency of debt and payment used to mollify the irrational demands of the monotheistic God. In her own words

> Yes, Israel's identity is instituted by transcendent omnipotence, but that omnipotence threatens to destroy the very identity it is called upon to establish. God is both the guarantor and the threat to Israel. What was once the fragility of identity has become outright violence, a violence made explicable, perhaps even bearable, as the will of an omnipotent sovereign whose wrath could be managed through obedience.[31]

Schwartz's description echoes Luther's narrative of the wrath of God to the Israelites and the desperate and futile attempt by them to control this wrath through obedience.

The performance of *halakha* by the Israelites means something altogether different when we take into account the nexus between divine command and divine freedom as unconditional care established over and again in the biblical text. Undoubtedly, the performance of *halakha* sustains multiple meanings within the Hebrew Scriptures and the rabbinic texts. Later, I will draw attention to some of these accounts, which will include *halakha* as language to express communal need, *halakha* as a vehicle for the imitation of divine justice, and *halakha* as an expression of the community's desire or love for God. Here, however, I want to introduce one of the most significant functions of *halakha* for the purposes of my analysis: its role as a "sign" of the covenant.

In Genesis 17, we read, "This is My covenant which you shall keep between Me and you and your descendants after you: Every male among you shall be circumcised. You shall circumcise the flesh of your foreskin, and that shall be the sign of the covenant between Me and you."[32] That circumcision does not operate as a mode of violence management is evident in view of the unconditionality of the covenant. The text is clear that the function of the law is semiotic. The law signifies, points to, or teaches the "covenant." Of course, by covenant, we mean the order of affirmation emergent from the nexus between law and freedom in the biblical God. By extension, therefore, *halakha* exposes and constitutes a repetition of the revelation of this order. Over the past 25 years, biblical scholars have begun to acknowledge the powerful connection between *halakha* and wisdom within the Hebrew Scriptures[33]—a connection that dramatically alters perceptions of the meaning of biblical wisdom. No longer regarded as merely a practical set of claims universally held by communities in the ancient Near East,[34] wisdom in the Hebrew Scriptures is now often identified directly with Torah law. Understood within the context of a theology of law and freedom, the wisdom of *halakha* presents a significant paradigm shift regarding the meaning of knowledge/truth and the justification of claims. I will take up this connection between covenantal theology, *halakha*, and the wisdom tradition in the Hebrew Scriptures; and in Chapters 5 and 6, I explore the philosophical implications of it for the meaning of Jewish theology.

Genesis 17's identification between circumcision as a "sign" offers a first glimpse of this powerful connection between law and wisdom. Theologically speaking, it is not surprising to find a link between *halakha* and wisdom in the central account of the Abrahamic covenant. As indicated earlier, the structure of the Abrahamic covenant affords Abraham and his descendants an affirmation or a capacity to abide in their relationship to God and in their relationship to others. To be justified in the law or affirmed in the order of the free God is to abide within an existential security or rest. However, security presupposes order, and we abide, therefore, in the particularity of our humanity, not in the dissolution of our difference from God. In this way, the acceptance of divine favor goes hand in hand with the awareness of our delimitation within the order or what is the self-consciousness of our human irreducibility. As a "sign," law announces and repeats this order offering a liturgical occasion for reflection upon it.

If circumcision is a sign of the covenant, what are the elements within this order? What does this law teach about the order of Abrahamic abiding? In what follows, I would like to suggest that we read Genesis 18 as a commentary on the wisdom implied in the law of circumcision.

GENESIS 18: THE SEMIOTICS OF CIRCUMCISION

Genesis 18 constitutes a new Torah portion: *Vayera*, or "Hashem appeared." At first glance, the "revelation of God" at Mamre seems to mark an altogether new narrative. What does circumcision have to do with an appearance of the divine and a subsequent visitation of three strangers? Rabbinic opinion posits a number of possible readings. According to one midrashic tradition, God appeared to Abraham precisely because he wanted to visit him after he had undergone the trial and tribulation of circumcision.[35] What about the possibility that God appeared to Abraham as a reward for his willingness to perform the law? Has Abraham earned God's presence? In what follows, I will argue instead that the divine act of appearance functions as an acknowledgement (sign) of Abraham's earlier reply to the law of circumcision. God's revelatory nearness constitutes one response in a dialog of mutual acknowledgment and gracious reception.

The Dialog of Gift/The Dialog of Prayer Earlier, I suggested that Abraham's compliance with the divine command to circumcision constituted a recognition or acknowledgement of the covenant. Here, I would like to suggest that not only might this acknowledgement or sign refer to the covenant generally speaking, but that it constitutes in particular, a performative acknowledgement of the promises or gifts implicit within it. Seen from this perspective, the performance of the law operates as an expression of one's reception of the divine gift or recognition of God's grace. But how do Abraham and his descendants receive divine grace? Ever since Derrida's work, it has become popular to assert the impossibility of authentically receiving a gift. We can never, Derrida argued, accept a gift without sacrificing ourselves.[36] The alterity of a gift is so powerful that any acknowledgement of it registers as a response to a divine command, which requires the forfeiture of the individual person in order to demonstrate proper awareness of the giver's alterity. Such a view is challenged by the justification in the law characteristic of the Abrahamic covenant. As justified within the command, Abraham's acknowledgement of the divine gift—what is his obedience to it and recognition of it—does not require the sacrifice of self but sustains the affirmation of the originary gift. We may look to Genesis 18 for additional support for this view.

First, God's visitation with Abraham demonstrates the sufficiency of Abraham's semiotic gesture and the coterminous affirmation of Abraham in his humanity in the enactment of it. Abraham's successful reception of the divine promise is indicated by the choreography of the scene: Abraham, the text says, "was sitting at the entrance of the tent in the heat of the day."[37] According to a famous midrash, Abraham "wished to rise but God said to him, 'Sit, and thou art a token to thy children: as thou sittest while the Shechinah is standing, so will the children sit and the Shechinah stand,' as it 'says God standeth (nizzab) in the congregation of God.'"[38] Abraham should sit. Compliance with the law should not require an exertion of self, particularly under the circumstances when as the rabbis indicate, he is particularly weak. We are, as Eliot Wolfson remarks, upon the same verse, "justified in assuming that the Jewish people are thus portrayed on account of their capacity to receive the providential presence of God."[39] If the Derridean model requires a forfeiture of self unto death, the divine-human exchange within a theology of the freedom of the law registers as the sufficiency of our efforts to communicate, to receive hospitality or gift and respond appropriately. That the rabbis also identify a connection between the divine visitation here in Genesis 18 and the divine visitation occasioned by the building of the temple and subsequent cultic sacrifice[40] points to the impact of the theology of law and freedom upon the meaning of sacrifice as well. In both, the divine presence represents the sufficiency or the housing of law and sacrifice within an order of justification such that obedience always suffices to warrant the divine presence when this divine presence is already presupposed by the institution of law or sacrifice as free response.

Second, not only does the divine appearance indicate that Abraham's obedience to the command fully meets the requirements of authentic acknowledgement without a forfeiture unto death, but the divine drawing near also points to the free sign or acknowledgement coming *from* God, which Abraham's own act precipitates. Here, in particular, we can benefit from the reflections of the seventeenth century Talmudist, Or HaChaim, who explains that "when people carry out great deeds, God shows himself to them as a token of tribute. . . ."[41] It is hard to overlook Or HaChaim's notion of the divine action as a token of acknowledgment and not see in it a reference back to the notion of circumcision as a "sign." Interpreted this way, the divine appearance at Mamre signifies God's own participation in a free dialog of mutual acknowledgement and reception. As I have argued, it is the structure of covenant as the expression of the nexus between God's freedom as command and God's freedom as promise that funds the freedom of this semiotic chain of reception. If Abraham's gesture of obedience is housed in the prior affirmation of God's providential care, God's subsequent demonstration of care presupposes the same originary act of grace. *All* divine activity described in the Hebrew Scriptures presupposes this covenantal structure. As a result, all demonstrations of divine care reflect the nature of this freedom and do not (necessarily) signify contingent responses to human action.[42]

The Dialog of Doubt   What more does the law of circumcision teach us about what it means to abide within the divine order? Earlier, we learned that performance of the law expresses an authentic reception of divine care. Reading the account of Abraham's hospitality to the three strangers and his conversation with God regarding the impending punishment of Sodom and Gomorrah, we learn how abiding within the freedom of God's order also permits the free pursuit of justice for the rights of persons. With this analysis, we return to my earlier effort to distinguish a divine command theology of law and freedom from any de-normativized account of covenantal structure. The nexus between divine sovereignty as command and divine freedom as care provides a theological grounding for the rights of persons, rights that Abraham acts upon in his hospitality toward the visiting strangers and his defense of the (potentially) innocent persons within Sodom and Gomorrah.

Theologically speaking, the basis of human rights results from the particular dynamic between God's freedom as sovereignty and God's freedom as care for persons.[43] Each facet of freedom delimits the other. In the case before us, it is divine care that delimits divine sovereignty such that God's freedom to command cannot exceed or overwhelm the divine drive to care for what he has created. Taken together, the two aspects of freedom infuse the divine nature within an interior limit or normativity from which persons directly benefit.[44] The two examples in Genesis 18 teach us how justification within the covenantal scheme operates as a basis for the acknowledgement of the rights of others. Abraham's hospitality to the visiting strangers demonstrates his understanding of the theological basis of his own justification and his rightful application of that same theological grounding for the strangers. That neither the visiting strangers nor the population of Sodom and Gomorrah whom Abraham subsequently defends stand within the community of Abraham does not mean that they are excluded from this theological basis for human rights. Although Abraham's encounters with God grant him a direct experience with a revealing God, both the rabbis and a long list of Jewish philosophers attribute to Abraham a knowledge of the theological source of all reality prior to these revelatory encounters.[45] Abraham's direct encounters with God afford him a more directly existential experience of the creator God, which works to expand his knowledge of the creator God who commands and cares for all that he has made. As David Novak says, "Revelation brings the truth of being elected to conscious mutual relationality. [Still] the creation of humans in the imago Dei is also election;

hence the Torah is the 'book of human history (toldo ha'adam)' (Genesis 5:1, Nahmanides) . . . It brings the meaning of being created in the image of God to human awareness and action."[46]

In a Talmudic exegesis of Genesis 18:3, "And he said 'My Lord, if I find favor in Your eyes, please pass not away from your servant'," the rabbis bring into relief how as an expression or imitation of the divine freedom to care for persons, attention to the rights and needs of others functions as a normative delimitation upon the freedom of God's commanding power. Assuming that *adonoi* refers here to God, Abraham, the rabbis indicate, opts to leave God in order to care for the strangers; and as the rabbis says, Abraham's action shows that "hospitality to wayfarers is greater than receiving the Divine Presence."[47] We might in this light read Abraham's request to God as an argument premised upon the claim "if I find favor in your eyes," then it follows that I should freely attend to others who also "find favor in your eyes." Abraham's right to attend to the needs of others flows directly from the theo-logic or interior normativity of the divine nature itself.

The same theme appears in Abraham's challenge to God's justice in verses 20–23. Here, Abraham exercises an even greater freedom of right and application of right than he did prior. Calling into question God's righteousness, he challenges God to defend Godself and asks, "Will You also stamp out the righteous along with the wicked? . . . It would be sacrilege to You to do such a thing. . . . Shall the Judge of all the earth not do justice?"[48] Justified within the command of the covenantal God, Abraham is fully within his own rights to demand an account from God of his impending actions. The reality of God's own freedom to care for who and what he creates legitimizes Abraham's demands, and in his own response, God affirms Abraham's theological expectation permitting his mercy to delimit his demand for justice. "And Hashem said, 'If I find in Sodom fifty righteous people in the midst of the city, then I would spare the entire place on their account'" (Genesis 18:26). The interior normativity of the divine nature translates into a dynamic divine-human relationality where both parties sustain the rights of their irreducibility and the freedom to act upon the other.

Undoubtedly, Abraham's dialog with God in Genesis 18 brings to mind Job's challenge to God in the Book of Job. In Chapter 7, "The Law as the Form of the Gospel," I suggest that the Book of Job profiles the logic of the law. However, I do not locate evidence of the logic of the law in Job's challenge to God's justice but rather in the world view presented by the whirlwind speeches at the end of the book. If so, why recognize Abraham's challenge as reflective of the normativity implicit within the covenantal structure and Job's as outside it? Simply said, Abraham's assertion of rights operates within his recognition of divine authority. Abraham understands that he is justified within and not without the divine command. Job disregards the covenantal order—that very order reaffirmed in God's proclamation of sovereignty reflected in the whirlwind speech where he asks

> Where wast thou when I laid the foundations of the earth? Declare, if thou hast the understanding. Who determined the measures thereof, if thou knowest? Or who stretched the line upon it? Whereupon were the foundations thereof fastened? Or who laid the corner-stone thereof, When the morning stars sang together, and all the sons of God shouted for joy? Or who shut up the sea with doors, when it broke forth, and issued out of the womb; When I made the cloud the garment thereof, and thick darkness a swaddling band for it, And prescribed for it My decree. . . .[49]

Abraham's awareness of the divine condition of the possibility of his own freedom (and the freedom/rights of others) is apparent in a number of examples in the Genesis 18 text. The two most notable are first, Abraham's humble announcement of God in his request to leave his presence and care for the strangers, "'My lord, if now I have found favour in thy sight, pass not away, I pray thee, from thy servant. . . .'"[50] The second appears in the dialog regarding Sodom and Gomorrah, where Abraham renders his own place within the logic of the law explicit and says, "Behold, now, I desired to speak to my Lord although I am but dust and ash."[51] That Abraham's recognition of the contingency of his existence goes hand in hand with his status as affirmed in this same humanity is evidenced by his immediate return to his challenge of God, "What if the fifty righteous people should lack five? Would You destroy the entire city because of the five?"[52]

The Sinaitic Covenant and the Normativity of Grace

Our analysis of the Abrahamic covenant complete, we can now pursue the overlap in theological orientation between the Abrahamic and Sinaitic covenants. In addition to the two Deuteronomy texts cited earlier (Deuteronomy 7:7–8 and Deuteronomy 4:37), there are many other examples of references to the Abrahamic covenant and the unconditional character of its promises within presentations of the Sinaitic covenant. Deuteronomy 10:12–15 says

> And now, Israel, what doth the LORD thy God require of thee, but to fear the LORD thy God, to walk in all His ways, and to love Him, and to serve the

LORD thy God with all thy heart and with all thy soul; to keep for thy good the commandments of the LORD, and His statutes, which I command thee this day? Behold, unto the LORD thy God belongeth the heaven, and the heaven of heavens, the earth, with all that therein is. Only the LORD had a delight in thy fathers to love them, and He chose their seed after them, even you, above all peoples, as it is this day.[53]

Each of these instances tears away at efforts to dichotomize the two covenants as promissory (Abrahamic) and obligatory (Sinaitic). Jon Levenson's work has arguably done the most to dispel this apparent divide. In his well-known *Sinai and Zion*, Levenson boldly announces the reality and role of divine grace within the biblical presentations of the Sinai covenant. Analyzing the covenant structure in comparison to the suzereignty formulary, Levenson identifies the presentation of God's redemption of the Israelites from Egypt with the formulary's historical prologue. Important for us is Levenson's recognition of the historical prologue as signifying God's historical act of grace toward the Israelites. "History is recited so as to elicit a consciousness of obligation, a response to unmerited benevolence and an awareness of the reliability of the would-be suzerain."[54] That the rabbis also recognized the reality of God's grace over and against either raw divine coercion or the calculation of reward/punishment is evident in the Talmudic exegesis of Exodus 19:17:

> And they took their places at the foot of the mountain; (Exodu. 19:17): Rabbi Avdimi b. Hama b. Hasa said, this teaches that the Holy One held the mountain over them like an [overturned] tub and told them; "If you accept the Torah—well and fine; otherwise, you will be buried right there." Rav Aha b. Jacob said: This furnishes a powerful disclaimer regarding the [acceptance of the] Torah.[55]

Still, Levenson's challenge of commonly held assumptions within biblical scholarship extends beyond this insistence upon the element of unmerited love within the covenant structure of Sinai. Motivating the analysis in *Sinai and Zion* is the tackling of a second assumption driving biblical scholarship, what is the tendency to overemphasize the historicity of the Sinaitic covenant at the expense of the significance of law as a response to this event. For my purposes, Levenson's engagement with this interpretation exposes a view of the meaning of the law that correlates directly with the theology of law and freedom above outlined and helps understand how *halakhic* life operates within this context.

If, the argument moves, we begin with the recognition of the element of divine grace within the Sinai account ("see how I bore you on eagle's wings" Exodus: 19:4) and its concomitant correlation with Israel's obedience to

The Biblical Theology of Abiding 121

divine stipulations, we must nonetheless ask about the logical relationship between these two covenantal elements. Which constitutes the hermeneutical key for the other? Is the performance of the law strictly responsive and thereby subordinate to the event of God's gracious act in history, or is God's gracious act in history for the purpose of grounding a relationship of mutual obligation? According to Levenson, the former view is represented in G. Ernest Wright's work, *The Old Testament against its Environment*. There, Wright correctly draws attention to the historical specificity of the Exodus and the revelation at Sinai as described throughout the biblical text. Nonetheless, Levenson argues that "in his [Wright's] thinking, the religion of Israel was a religion of recital, in which the highest spiritual level consisted of narrating the mighty acts of God. The key term is event."[56] Within this context, the meaning of *halakha* is determined by its role as a response to this event. Law is secondary, and its meaning historically contingent. Law might operate as a positive response to this particular event, but any alteration in divine activity could offset this value and substitute the law with other more appropriate responses. Brewing beneath Levenson's critique is his identification of the hidden antinomian perspective, fueling this interpretation of the legal theology of the Exodus and Sinai accounts. More pointedly

> [T]he idea that the recitation of sacred history is the essence of Israelite religion and that the *mitsvot* are subordinate to history is but a secularization of the Christian concept of an "economy of salvation" which enables one to inherit the status of Israel without the obligation to fulfill the Mosaic law. . . . Once the total plan has been made known, the law, good in its own time, becomes obsolete and even a hindrance to appreciation of the new revelatory event.[57]

The revelation of Christ supersedes the revelation at Sinai, and faith supersedes the law as the authentic response.

But, Levenson asks, is this reading supported by the biblical text? If as Levenson and others acknowledge, the covenantal material found in Exodus and Joshua in particular bear some resemblance structurally to the suzereignty formulary used by kings to their vassals, then it would seem to follow that the role of the historical prologue within the biblical texts would also logically or hermeneutically reflect the structure of those treaties as well. According to biblical scholars, the suzereignty treaties present a series of steps the first being the "preamble" where the king identifies himself; the second, the historical prologue or antecedent history, which Levenson says

> . . . is a statement of the past relationship of the parties. Sometimes, the suzerain stresses his benefactions towards the vassal . . . this seems to have been one of

the central purposes of the historical prologue . . . to encourage a feeling of gratitude in the vassal so as to establish firmly the claim of the suzerain upon him . . . [that is], a sense of obligation.[58]

The same logic applies to the covenant. God announces his identity and, specifically, his redemption of Israel from Egypt. He does so, Levenson avers, to encourage a sense of obligation on the part of the Israelites—to help ground the primary relationship of obligation between king and community. "The historical prologue is only the prologue. It ceases to be at the point when the covenant takes effect. From that moment on, what is critical is not the past, but the observance of the stipulations in the present and the sort of life that such observance brings about."[59] This is further borne out, Levenson suggests, by the text's reference to the collective dimension of memory, "Your own eyes have seen what I did to the Egyptians. . . ." (v. 7). In this way, Levenson says, the text "obliges you . . . for you, by hearing this story and responding affirmatively become Israel."[60] The historical past is for the purpose of the community's covenantal present (and future) and not the covenantal observance of law for the purpose of paying heed to or perpetually signifying this singular moment in history.

The preceding reading presents a dramatically different account of the value of *halakhic* life from that presented in Wright's interpretation. If history serves the covenantal life of *halakhic* obligation rather than the other way around, then the meaning of law is no longer contingent upon historical events, divine or otherwise. The meaning of the law endures within the context of the covenantal relationship established between the God and the Israelites; only the backdrop is historically specific. To say that *halakhic* life is not contingent upon divine acts in history is not to say that divine grace is not a significant element within the motivating structure of Jewish life. It is to say, however, that it is not the only motivating element in *halakhic* life. Levenson's reading echoes the primary analysis of this volume as a whole, which recognizes the correlation between grace and normativity within the covenantal structure, a correlation that derives from a theology of divine freedom. Standing alone, a theology of divine grace like that presented in G. Wright's reading of Exodus 19 privileges the reality of divine freedom within history leaving persons vulnerable to alterations in these actions. As discussed elsewhere in this volume, although the God who redeems Israel from Egypt may appear committed to the welfare of the Israelites, the freedom to act in history alone cannot guarantee this faithfulness. Covenantal structure presupposes a normative limit upon the freedom of God to act graciously or otherwise, and in this way, offers a basis for the rights of persons to expect divine consistency or faithfulness. In Levenson's own language, "the sovereignty of God is larger than his suzereignty."[61] On what grounds can Levenson and I maintain this view?

Perhaps the most persuasive evidence emerges from the texts describing the nature of the covenantal relationship between God and the Israelites. As Levenson says, the covenant between God and the Israelites is a "mutual relationship between unequals. . . ."[62] Despite the asymmetry in status of the participants, neither participant is absorbed into the reality of the other, but each remains distinct. Implicit within this distinction is a law of difference between the two participants, an order of difference that constitutes the condition of the possibility of the relationship. Consequently, it is this law or order of difference that operates as an infusion of normative delimitation upon both the divine and the human in their historically fluid interactions. If history serves covenant, and if covenant presupposes a normative difference between the divine and the human, then even divine acts in history cannot rightfully destroy this difference without persons having a justifiable right to demand an account. Within this context, therefore, persons perform the law neither from fear of divine punishment nor from the hope of divine reward but rather out of the sense of calm or rest rooted in the confidence in God's perpetual faithfulness toward Israel. As we have seen, the structure of difference between the divine and the human within the covenant reflects the reality of God's freedom *qua* sovereign to create a reality that is other than God whereby the difference between creator and created is installed. Consequently, the covenantal delimitation upon God's freedom to act in history reflects only the internal stability or rest within the divine self discussed earlier in my analysis of the theology of creation.

Viewed from this perspective, *halakhic* life operates as both a response to divine infusions of grace as well as constitutes a sign of the more extensive reality of divine faithfulness secured by the law of difference between God and all that God creates. Such a view helps to explain why according to the prophet Hosea "all creation joins in the wedding ceremony."[63] The God of Sinai, Levenson says, is a God of "cosmic harmony:"[64] a God whose faithfulness is structured into the very order of his creation through the normative difference between the divine and all else that God affirms as irreducibly other than himself. History is inscribed and housed in this order, and "the vision is one of redemption through covenant, and the assumption seems to be that, where God mediates and thus guarantees covenant, the stipulations will be fulfilled as a matter of course."[65] *Halakha* is not a means to affect divine redemption. Rather, it is a testament to or

124   *The Logic of the Law*

a sign of an order already redeemed. It is the performative manifestation of the identification between what is and what ought to be as it abides within the freedom of the divine order.

In the article, "The Theologies of Commandment in Biblical Israel," Levenson reflects further upon this account of the enduring meaning of *halakha* as a sign of the "cosmic harmony" instituted by God and reflected in the Sinaitic covenant. Here, Levenson notes what he refers to as the "cosmological" account of the meaning of the *halakha* whereby

> [O]ne sees biblical law in its totality as of the same order as the laws of nature, the inner mechanism of creation. In this theology, the commandments appear not as the yield of a historical event, or at least not exclusively so, but as the extension into human society of cosmic order, divinely ordained and sustained. . . .[66]

Levenson points to Psalm 119 to evidence this connection between the motivation to perform the law and the faithfulness of God demonstrated in the ordering of nature.

> You are eternal, YHWH: Your word is positioned in the heavens. Your faithfulness is for all generations; You have established the earth and it stands. According to your ruling, day stands. For all are your servants. If your Torah had not been my delight, I would have perished in my affliction. Never will I neglect your precepts, for through them you have preserved my life.[67]

Halakha is a delight. It is an exercise in the sense of being sheltered and protected in an order premised upon both the transcendent alterity of God's creative sovereignty and the dramatic freedom of God's loving grace to affirm what is other than Godself. If my discussion of the biblical theology of creation highlighted the redeeming nature of God as creator, so in this discussion, we recognize the ordering sovereignty characteristic of the God of redemption. About Psalm 119, Levenson remarks

> The interesting point is that the laws the created order observes are here associated with the Torah whose precepts the psalmist practices. In other words, the stability and security which observance of the commandments has brought into his life is of exactly the same order as the regularity of the heavenly bodies . . . which he considers divine "rulings or judgments." In this theology, law is most closely associated not with the sudden and terrifying theophany on Sinai (in which the psalmist certainly also believed), but with the predictable and reassuring self-revelation of creation.[68]

Undoubtedly, both the biblical text and the Jewish tradition recognize a range of motivations governing *halakhic* performance. A thorough analysis of halakhic performance would point to the influence of human desire and human negotiation through history characteristic of *halakhic* reasoning and change.⁶⁹ God, the rabbis said, spoke to persons in human language, and *halakha* is lived and interpreted by Jewish communities whose application of it is influenced by communities' rightful pursuit of need and desire through time. The current analysis demonstrates on what grounds *halakha* operates as the lens through which the community may express and represent and adjudicate its needs. It is precisely *halakha's* role as a semiotic reminder of the freedom of the divine order that positions it to act as an agent of the affirmed needs of the community of persons who live by it.

The Semiotics of the Sabbatical Year: From Rest to Wisdom

In what follows, I would like to draw attention to the particular law of the Sabbatical year (and, by extension, the law of the Jubilee year) insofar as this commandment exemplifies the function of *halakha* as "sign," which refers explicitly to the theology of law and freedom.

THE SABBATICAL YEAR: A SIGN OF THE ORDER

The law of the Sabbatical year is first described in the book of Exodus where it states, "For six years you may sow your land and gather its produce; but in the seventh year you shall let it lie fallow and leave it alone."⁷⁰ In Leviticus 25, we read

> When ye come into the land which I give you, then shall the land keep a sabbath unto the LORD. Six years thou shalt sow thy field, and six years thou shalt prune thy vineyard, and gather in the produce thereof. But in the seventh year shall be a sabbath of solemn rest for the land, a sabbath unto the LORD; thou shalt neither sow thy field, nor prune thy vineyard. That which groweth of itself of thy harvest thou shalt not reap, and the grapes of thy undressed vine thou shalt not gather; it shall be a year of solemn rest for the land.⁷¹

According to Maimonides, the purpose of the Sabbatical year is to protect the land.⁷² Still, neither the biblical text nor a significant strain of the rabbinic tradition agrees with Maimonides on this point. Leviticus 25:2 stresses that the sabbatical operates as a Sabbath "unto the Lord," its main focus the honor of God as the ultimate owner of the land rather than the land itself. Rashi's commentary on Leviticus 25 echoes this theological interpretation, and he says

> "*A Sabbath to the Lord*": For the sake of the Lord, just as is stated of the Sabbath of Creation (see Exod. 20:10) [i.e., just as every seventh day is a holy Sabbath day, acclaiming that God Himself rested on the seventh day and thus acclaiming that God is the Supreme Creator of all existence, likewise, man must rest from working the land on the seventh year, for the sake of God, not for the sake of the land, so that it should gain fertility by lying fallow for a year]. (Sifthei Chachamim; Torath Kohanim 25:7)[73]

The primary function of the Sabbatical year is to allow the land to rest as an acknowledgment of the reality of God's unique freedom as the creator and owner of the land.

The rationale for the Sabbatical year, as presented in the Babylonian Talmud in the name of Rabbi Abbahu, is well known:

> A disciple came and said [to Rabbi Abbahu], what is the rationale behind the commandment of the sabbatical year? He answered . . . the Holy One, blessed be He, told the Israelites to sow six years, but rest on the seventh so that they shall know that the land belongs to the Lord; but they did not do so, but sinned and were exiled.[74]

According to this text, the rationale behind the commandment of *shemittah* is to bring home the message that human beings are not the owners of the land in their possession; rather, God is the Lord of the land.

At the same time, however, the Sabbatical year also demonstrates the dual character of God's freedom insofar as recognition of this freedom is not at the expense of human welfare. There are few more explicit suggestions of the nature of God's freedom as care than the reality of abundant provisions promised by God to those who observe the Sabbatical year. Leviticus 25:6–7 states, "And the sabbath-produce of the land shall be for food for you: for thee, and for thy servant . . . and for thy or the beasts that are in thy land, shall all the increase thereof be for food."[75] Once again, Rashi's commentary highlights our point:

> "*And [the produce of] the Sabbath of the land, shall be [yours to eat]*": Although I have prohibited the produce [of the Shemittah year] to you, I did not prohibit you to eat it or to derive benefit from it, only that you should not treat it as if you were its owner. Rather, everyone is deemed equal [regarding the use of the Shemittah year's produce]—you, [your slaves,] and your hired worker and resident. "*Yours to eat*": You may eat from what you treated as ownerless (הֶפְקֵר), but from that [produce] which is stored away, you shall not eat. (Torath Kohanim 25:10)[76]

Logically speaking, important consequences emerge from the correlation between the announcement of divine sovereignty and the recognition of divine care and interest in the welfare of persons represented in this portrait of the Sabbatical year. First and foremost is a logic of abundance. Recall for a moment Regina Schwartz's insistence upon the emptiness of the biblical God and its effects. Theological scarcity, she argues, leads to divine wrath. Divine wrath produces fear on the part of those who confront God and in turn lends itself to communal self-protection and enmity toward others. However, the Sabbatical law presents a very different picture. Not only does it point to a theology of power and abundance, but it also introduces a unique economy of care for the poor. In Deuteronomy 15, it states

> At the end of every seventh year you shall make a remission of debts. This is how the remission shall be made: everyone who holds a pledge shall remit the pledge of anyone indebted to him. He shall not press a fellow-countryman for repayment, for the LORD's year of remission has been declared.[77]

Evidently written at a later time and in the context of an urban rather than strictly agricultural society,[78] this additional provision focuses attention on elevating the economic status of the poor. The identification of this ethic for the poor after the originary announcement of the Sabbatical year, and within the context of the correlation between divine sovereignty and divine care grounds the unique character of the biblical ethic such that one is commanded to care for but not valorize the poor. The notion that a community can care for the poor only when it denounces materialism altogether is frequently identified with the ethics of the gospels: the Gospel of Luke, in particular.[79] Here, it is important to note the difference between an ideology around the poor and the economics of material comfort biblically presented. If as I am arguing a theology of law and freedom offers an alternative to exceptionalism, the concept of the Sabbatical year extends this alternative into the sphere of economics. Care for the poor emerges from and together with one's own sense of covenantally grounded material security. Rashi's commentary elaborates on this:

> "*for you, for your male and female slaves*": Since Scripture says [regarding Shemittah], "and the poor of your people shall eat [it]" (Exod. 23:11), one might think that it [the produce of the Shemittah year] is prohibited to be eaten by wealthy people. Scripture, therefore, says here, "for you, for your male and female slaves,"—we see that the [wealthy] owners and the male and female slaves are included here [to permit them also to eat of the Shemittah year produce]. (Torath Kohanim 25:12, and see Sefer Hazikkaron) . . . "*and for your hired worker and resident [who live with you]*": Even non-Jews. (Torath Kohanim 25:14). [Hired worker is one hired by the day. Resident is one hired by the year. (Bechor Shor)][80]

The effort to redistribute wealth does not require a valorization of the poor—only an effort to end their poverty.

THE SABBATICAL YEAR AS LITURGICAL TEACHING

As a sign of the order of God's freedom, the Sabbatical operates as a vehicle of communal learning. Most importantly, the Sabbatical year schools the community in the theological backdrop and covenantal context of the performance of the commandments. Like the law of circumcision and the Sabbath, the Sabbatical year provides a liturgical occasion for reflection upon the order of divine freedom within which communal life participates. If, as I will discuss, later interpreters will eschatologize the meaning of the Sabbatical—and by extension, the Jubilee year—excising them from their annual context and employing them as counterpoints to the *halakhic* system that they are said to critique and correct, an interpretation of the Sabbatical as a sign of the theology of divine freedom identifies the intimate connection between the Sabbatical and the *halakhic* system whose meaning and context it directly illuminates. This helps explain the link between the Sabbatical year and the public reading of the Torah specified by Moses in Deuteronomy 31:8:

> And the LORD, He it is that doth go before thee; He will be with thee, He will not fail thee, neither forsake thee; fear not, neither be dismayed. And Moses wrote this law, and delivered it unto the priests the sons of Levi, that bore the ark of the covenant of the LORD, and unto all the elders of Israel. And Moses commanded them, saying: 'At the end of every seven years, in the set time of the year of release, in the feast of tabernacles, when all Israel is come to appear before the LORD thy God in the place which He shall choose, thou shalt read this law before all Israel in their hearing. Assemble the people, the men and the women and the little ones, and thy stranger that is within thy gates, that they may hear, and that they may learn, and fear the LORD your God, and observe to do all the words of this law; and that their children, who have not known, may hear, and learn to fear the LORD your God, as long as ye live in the land whither ye go over the Jordan to possess it.'[81]

In this way and like the concept of the Sabbath, the Sabbatical year connects the concepts of abiding and rest and reflection or self-consciousness. By pointing to the divine order within which communal life abides, all three *halakhic* "signs"—circumcision, Sabbath, and Sabbatical—offer a mode of communal knowledge. To be aware that one is ordered is to be aware of what one is within this order. It is to be "defined" both as delimited and affirmed—that is, to be determined with regard to "what one is not" and "what one is" or "what place one has" within the order. Undoubtedly, human wisdom is predicated upon divine wisdom, or what we might refer to as "divine judgment" if by judgment, we mean the divine discernment—the divine self-awareness of the order of God's own freedom. The self-awareness that we acquire derives from the revelation of the order afforded by God through the laws of circumcision, Sabbath, and Sabbatical. Beyond this, however, both the Sabbath and the Sabbatical present the direct link between a liturgical occasion of rest and the opportunity for and/or the command to reflect upon, read, and interpret the meaning of the law and its theo-anthropological context.

In his article, "Theologies of Commandment in Biblical Israel," Levenson also asserts this link between *halakha* and wisdom. Speaking about the function of *halakha* as a "sign" that points to the reality of divine faithfulness, Levenson describes the direct connection between Wisdom and "covenant" articulated in Deuteronomy, Psalms, and the extra-canonical Ben Sira. He begins with Deuteronomy's identification law and wisdom, "See I have given you laws and judgments. . . . Observe them faithfully because this is your wisdom and discernment in the eyes of the peoples, who, on hearing all these laws, will say, 'Surely, this great nation is a wise and discerning people!'"[82] But what is the character of wisdom accrued in the performance of law? My argument is that law educates persons in the wisdom of their knowledge of God's faithfulness on the one hand, and their own historicity, delimitation, and humanity on the other hand. Levenson's textual analysis points in the same direction, and he argues that the "the connection between Deuteronomistic theology and the 'Wisdom Psalms' is stronger than is generally recognized."[83] Specifically, he turns to Psalm 119: "teach me good sense and knowledge . . . for in your commandments I have trusted," which he argues "sees biblical law in its totality as of the same order as the laws of nature, the inner mechanism of creation. In this theology, the commandments appear not as the yield of a historical event, or at least not exclusively so, but as the extension into human society of cosmic order, divinely ordained and sustained. . . .

> 'You are eternal YHWH, your word is positioned in the heavens, Your faithfulness is for all generations; You have established the earth and it stands. According to your ruling, day stands, For all are your servants. If your Torah had not been my delight, I would have perished in my affliction. Never will I neglect your precepts, For through them you have preserved my life.'"[84]

That this same structure infuses divine *halakha* means that the life of this law funds a wisdom and a self-awareness of this order and sponsors in persons the freedom afforded by this self-consciousness.

130 *The Logic of the Law*

There are numerous examples of this theology of wisdom throughout the Hebrew Scriptures. In the article, "Deuteronomy and Psalms: Evoking Biblical Conversation," biblical scholar Patrick Miller discusses what scholars refer to as the "Torah psalms" and describes the "meditative culture" presented by them:

> Since as far back as Ibn Ezra the negative forms of the verbs "walk", "stand" and "sit" in Psalm 1:1 have been associated with the positive instruction of Deuteronomy 6:7 to recite or repeat, that is to meditate upon, the words of the law "when you 'sit' at home, when you 'walk' on the way, when you lay down and when you arise." . . . In all three Torah Psalms, meditation plays a significant part. In Psalm 1, it is meditation on the Torah. In Psalm 19, the meditation of the psalmist at the end looks back on the law and the glories of God's handiwork. The meditation of the Psalmist in 119 is on the law as precepts (vv. 15, 78), torah (v. 97), decrees (vv. 99), statutes (vv. 23, 45) and promise but also on your wondrous works, (v.27). These psalms, together with others, lift upon what George Fischer and Norberth Lohfink have called the "meditative culture" of ancient Israel. In this way, the Psalter and Deuteronomy nurture . . . the regular rehearsal of the law in communal ritual and family life . . . as a way of instilling within each generation a vivid awareness of the community as a covenant people.[85]

Interest in the meditative or wisdom culture of Torah law is clearly growing among biblical scholars. Few theologians, however, have reflected upon this association. I will discuss the epistemological and social implications of a wisdom emerging from the freedom of God in detail in Chapter 6, but here it is important to introduce the basic features of this knowledge or enlightenment. Both Levenson and Phillips recognize how Torah wisdom offers a curriculum in the security offered by the transcendent and caring God. The consequences of the nexus between wisdom and rest or wisdom and security are significant for the ability of a covenantal community to engage in conversation and exchange with other cultures. A wisdom that teaches stability and rest is a wisdom that enables the community to freely engage with others without calculation or the need to see the other as the agency of the fulfillment of the community's desires or needs. Certainly a covenantal community may pursue separate or shared needs with other communities but need not do so with the expectation of the complete fulfillment of these needs such that the other community is reduced to a vehicle for the covenantal community's own teleological completion. Moreover, beyond the *theological* awareness emergent from Torah-wisdom, a *halakha* that points to the character of the divine order also points to the place of persons and communities within this order: their historicity and finitude.

This self-consciousness, together with the awareness of the freedom of God, presents unique conditions for what is the justification of the community's truth-claims within the limits of the law.

FROM JUDGMENT TO JUDGMENT: ISRAEL AND THE PROBLEM OF SIN

In my earlier discussion around the law of the Sabbatical, I suggested a new account of the meaning of divine judgment as discernment or reflection. I introduce this semantic innovation to support the over-arching argument of the book that states that all aspects of human finitude or need—for example, existential, physical, and/or moral—are included among those aspects of human life affirmed by the correlation between divine order and divine care. In my discussion of the Sabbatical year, and of human creation generally speaking, I demonstrated how a theology of law and freedom houses an anthropology of abiding within this need. A semantic alteration in the meaning of divine judgment as divine discernment or reflection upon God's own free order lays the groundwork for assessing the impact of the theology of law and freedom upon matters of moral finitude or failure and the character of divine judgment or response to this human limit. The questions before us, therefore are, what is the character of human moral failing as discussed biblically? And what effect does divine judgment have upon persons in this limit? Does divine judgment constitute a break with a theology of law and freedom if a God who judges sin punishes those whom he judges? Does the problem of sin institute an exceptionalism of divine punishment into the logic of law and freedom and thereby recalibrate the meaning of history within this context as the ebb and flow of punishment and/or reward contingent upon the correlation between the community's obedience and divine favor? As mentioned earlier, the application of a theology of reward and punishment to the history of Israel has had devastating effects upon Christian attitudes toward the evil of the Shoah, and no one has done a better job of articulating the fatal flaws with this logic than Richard Rubenstein. Of course, the greatest limitation in Rubenstein's account consists in his failure to identify an alternative theological strand within the biblical text—one that, as this book argues, not only does not commit Jews to a history of sacrifice before a punishing God and the enmity toward others that such a dialectic of favor-punishment with God would suggest, but in fact predisposes Jews to stand freely before both the covenantal God and noncovenantal communities.

I might begin to offer a defense of this position by referencing the connection between the announcement of the Jubilee year and Yom Kippur as stated in the biblical text. In Leviticus 25:8–13, it says

> Count off seven Sabbaths of years—seven times seven years—so that the seven Sabbaths of years amount to a period of forty-nine years. Then have the trumpet sounded everywhere on the tenth day of the seventh month; on the Day of Atonement sound the trumpet throughout your land. Consecrate the fiftieth year and proclaim liberty throughout the land to all its inhabitants. It shall be a jubilee for you; each one of you is to return to his family property and each to his own clan. The fiftieth year shall be a jubilee for you; do not sow and do not reap what grows of itself or harvest the untended vines. For it is a jubilee and is to be holy for you; eat only what is taken directly from the fields. In this Year of Jubilee everyone is to return to his own property.[86]

According to the biblical tradition, the Jubilee year is announced on "the tenth day of the seventh month, on the day of Atonement . . ." with a blast of the shofar. According to Rashi, the name *Yovel* is derived from the shofar, blowing which marks the fiftieth year. The Jubilee is announced with a blast that awakens the community to the order that it exposes. But why is it announced on Yom Kippur? More specifically, why does the Jubilee begin during and then follow after the ten days of repentance? Undoubtedly, the clearest connection between *Yovel* and Yom Kippur derives from both occasions' links to the Sabbath. The tradition refers to Yom Kippur as the Sabbath of Sabbaths. *Yovel* is rooted in the notion of the Sabbatical. Each observance precipitates a rest and a reflection characteristic of the theology of law and freedom. Leviticus 23 emphasizes and repeats the connection between the Day of Atonement and rest, and says

> On the tenth day of this month it is the Day of Atonement; there shall be a holy convocation for you. . . . You shall not do any work on this very day. . . . You shall not do any work; it is an eternal decree throughout your generations. . . . It is a day of complete rest for you . . . from evening to evening . . . shall you rest on your rest day.[87]

But the Day of Atonement is the day of reviewing and atoning for sin. Even then, we are commanded to "rest" and reflect. In both biblical and rabbinic texts, atonement refers to a reordering of or reflection upon proper order. The biblical text is concerned with a reordering of purity within the sanctuary, and the rabbis are concerned with a spiritual reordering or "return" to who we are in our relationship with God.[88] Such a return is not ontologically driven. In fact, the very notion of *teshuvah* suggests that we are what we ought to be, if only we would recognize this.

As the pinnacle of the Sabbatical, *Yovel* also reiterates the character of the divine order. On the one hand, laws of the *Yovel* indicate that we must return all property to its "inhabitants." The land is originally and essentially

God's, and we do not have the right to claim ownership of it and permanently sell it. According to the ArtScroll commentary, "The Jubilee laws bring home to people that the land and freedom are Divine gifts and that ownership reverts to those to whom He wills it.... There is a Supreme Owner."[89] On the other hand, the *Yovel* reaffirms how the divine law of difference affirms or "redeems" human flourishing because lawful acknowledgement of the divine ownership of the land is concomitant with the availability of the land to those who inhabit it. *Yovel* is the liturgical repetition of divine redemption—a redemption, in this case, of land, which repeats the legal structure's own institution of land redemption (Leviticus 25:24).

It is worth noting that the redemption of *Yovel* is not limited to those whose land is to be redeemed or those who have been enslaved and are now freed. Just as the Sabbatical promised care to all persons within Israelite society, so the Jubilee extends freedom to all inhabitants. This is not to say that the theology of the Jubilee guarantees material wealth. It does, however, guarantee material security because the Jubilee—like the Sabbatical—is accompanied by the divine promise that those who keep these laws will be blessed by God with security (v. 18) and an adequate harvest (v. 19; also Leviticus 26:3–13 and Deuteronomy 28:1–14). Neither Sabbatical nor *Yovel* stratify Israelite society socioeconomically but reorder the whole into a security within the order of God's land ownership and lawful authority. "You shall sanctify the fiftieth year and proclaim freedom throughout the land for *all* (emphasis, mine) its inhabitants."[90]

Time and again, the biblical text sponsors this self-consciousness of our place within the covenantal order. The link between the Yom Kippur and the *Yovel* reflects the ever-present character of the Sabbath and its assertion of rest within the order. However, beyond this, the connection between Yom Kippur and *Yovel* also exposes the link between a theology of law and freedom and an abiding within our moral finitude or frailty.

Although traditionally identified as the Day of Judgment, Yom Kippur marks the end of the period of divine judgment inaugurated by Rosh Hashanah, which the rabbis officially refer to as *Yom Ha Din*. On Rosh Hashanah, God decides "who will live and who will die, who will have a good life and who will have a bad life" for the next year. Similarly, the Sabbatical and *Yovel* invoke the prospect of divine punishment. In *Pirkei Avot*, we are told that failure to observe the Sabbatical year will result in exile.[91] Certainly, the biblical text includes many references to the correlation between Israel's sin and divine punishment.[92] Do these invocations of divine punishment present a notion of divine judgment that undermines the overriding context of divine freedom? Is Jewish history what Rubenstein suggests: the narrative dialectic between God's exceptional favor for "his" people and God's punitive destruction of this people? Certainly the logic of both moments would seem to presuppose the ontological supremacy of God over the people, an ontological supremacy that undermines the irreducibility of both participants within the covenantal structure. In either scenario, reward or punishment, the people are absorbed into the divine interest. They are rewarded so far as their will bends entirely to the divine interest. They are destroyed so far as it fails to.

It is my contention that the link between Yom Kippur and *Yovel* demonstrates how references to divine judgment are bookended by the theology of freedom and law. If in other words, we are "already redeemed," we are also "already forgiven." The logic of the law means that we are already cared for within the limits in which we exist as persons, but this extends to our moral need as well. Divine care does not discriminate against but houses our moral frailty and provides a context within which we are poised to consistently improve our moral condition—not, we should note, in order that we achieve moral perfection, but only so that we continue to aspire to moral correction. The biblical text does not essentialize sin so that it constitutes a diminution of the divine. If persons are neither affirmed nor rejected by virtue of their participation in a divine essence but affirmed only in the irreducibility that constitutes the condition of the possibility of their relating to God, then sin is tantamount to a failure to recognize one's place within the order and can be responded to by repositioning ourselves within this order. David Novak puts this well:

> In order to be worthy . . . humans do not have to have lived perfect lives. . . . "For there is no one (adam) so righteous on earth who has only done good and not sinned" (Eccl. 7:20). What is required of them is that they return to God and regret having offended him by their sins. "Return [at least] one day before the day of your death". . . . This regular return is a regular part of the liturgy . . . it is something we do together in community. It is not the herculean effort of moral and spiritual virtuosi.[93]

This is not to deny that moral failing might be met with divine punishment. It is to suggest, however, that neither sin nor punishment have the final word within the theology of law and freedom but operate along with and are contextualized by a subsequent restoration or rebirth, here symbolized by the connection between Yom Kippur as the final day of divine judgment and the announcement of the Jubilee redemption and restoration. Once again, Novak expresses this point, and says

> God's promise of the permanence of his covenant with Israel is the basis of her extraordinary claim on God that God not allow her to die as a people, that God

grant her perpetual life even in this world. "I shall not die but live, for I shall declare the works of the Lord".... (Psalms 118:17). This Jewish claim on God for survival is even more extraordinary in that it is not contingent on the virtue of the Jews. Israel's right to life ... is to be exercised even when she has turned against God. "Although she has sinned, Israel is still Israel".... Thus, even when Israel is rightfully punished by God for her sins, that punishment is never to be permanent.... "The Lord has certainly punished me, but he did not turn me over to death" (Psalms 118:18).[94]

That sin and punishment are both circumscribed by the conditions of divine freedom reflects the normativity implicit within the covenantal structure this freedom supports. The law of freedom guards against the absorption of persons into divine grace on the one hand and also restricts the extent to which persons can be dissolved into the divine will through punishment on the other hand. Both the finitude of the human power to sin and the freedom of God to assert his will are delimited by the divine freedom to affirm that which is other than God.

Finally, it is worth noting the implications of this account for a biblical theology of history. Understood as one among many moments within the overarching time of God's freedom, the negotiation between Israelite sin and divine punishment constitutes no more significant moment within Israelite history than any other moment of community need and striving. Neither is it the key to the continuation of Israelite history—nor, more significantly, a marker of its end. Within a theology of law and freedom, history means the repetition of the condition of the possibility of the covenantal relationship between the Jewish people and God as this relationship houses the range of contingencies that accompany such an existence. All moments are equally meaningful within this context of everlasting temporality. In Chapter 5, I will explore the implications of this biblical theology of history for intellectual history within and outside of the Jewish tradition. Ultimately, I will focus upon the import of this alternative account of history for Jewish-Christian relations. To conclude this chapter, I will introduce what is at stake for a Christian conception of Jewish history by examining Isaiah 61 and its invocation of the Levitical notion of the Jubilee.

ISAIAH 61: JUBILEE AND THE RESTORATION OF ISRAEL

In this final section of the chapter, I want to examine two different scholarly analyses of Isaiah 61:1–2: the first by Bradford Gregory, and the second by Paul Hanson. The point of the exercise is to expose how a dislocation of Isaiah 61, from both its Levitical context and from the preceding reading of the Jubilee, can support a Christian anti-Judaism. By contrast, a reading of Isaiah 61, which acknowledges its overlap with the theology of the Jubilee described earlier, opens up possibilities for a Christianity that comes to terms with the lawfulness of God, the normativity of covenant, and recognizes the perpetual reality of the Jewish covenantal community. The stakes connected with this possibility are high, given the citation of Isaiah 61 in Luke 4. My analysis is not meant to call for an adjustment within biblical scholarship in favor of a positive account of Israel or Judaism. Rather, I am suggesting that Christian theologians gain an awareness of how they read the biblical text and ask whether Christianity might recognize this strain of a theology of law for itself—and if so, how such a theology would impact upon Christianity's apologetic logic generally speaking, and with specific regard to its relation to Judaism. I will leave an extended analysis of the relationship between gospel and law within Christian theology for Chapter 7. Here, I want only to present the possibility of a hermeneutical repair of the Christian narrative of Jewish history as lost favoritism and the emergence of the church remnant as the new, "true Israel."

Isaiah 61:1–2 states, "The spirit of the Lord GOD is upon me; because the LORD hath anointed me to bring good tidings unto the humble; He hath sent me to bind up the broken-hearted, to proclaim liberty to the captives, and the opening of the eyes to them that are bound; To proclaim the year of the LORD'S good pleasure. . . ."[95] In an essay entitled, "The Postexilic Exile in Third Isaiah: Isaiah 61:1–3 in Light of Second Temple Hermeneutics," Bradford Gregory presents a reading of Isaiah 61 as a postexilic text that retains and develops the point of view and theology of exile. According to Gregory,

> Isaiah 61 provides one of the earliest attestations of the idea of a theological exile that extends beyond the temporal and geographical bounds of the Babylonian captivity. Furthermore, the subsequent appropriation of the text by later authors of the Trito-Isaianic corpus and its redaction into the canonical form of Third Isaiah and the book of Isaiah as a whole reveal a development of this concept of the ongoing exile that would flourish in later Second Temple writings. Thus, Isaiah 61 plays an important and pivotal role in the development of theological motifs and hermeneutical methods during the postexilic period.[96]

Gregory's argument consists of two main elements. First, he identifies what he refers to as a *typological* appropriation of Leviticus 25 in the Isaiah 61 text. Second, Gregory offers an interpretation of the theological meaning of this typological appropriation.

There are, Gregory asserts, good reasons for identifying an allusion to Leviticus 25 and its discussion of the Jubilee year in the Isaiah text. Gregory

The Biblical Theology of Abiding   137

points out the similarity in language between the two texts. "The correlation is made because of the similarity in phrasing between the two texts for example: Lev 25:10, 'You shall proclaim liberty in the land to all its inhabitants.' [and] Isa 61:1 . . . 'to proclaim liberty to the captives.'"[97]

Beyond this, Bradford argues in favor of the reference to the Jubilee by virtue of the theological account of debt-exile pervading Deutero-Isaiah to which this invocation of the Jubilee speaks in particular. If Deutero-Isaiah extends the meaning of the individual poor to the whole Israelite community in exile, the Isaiah 61 reference to the Jubilee constitutes a typological extension of the legal notion of individual property redemption to a symbolic redemption for the community as a whole or its restoration after exile. According to Bradford, Isaiah 61

> adopts the exile–restoration program of Second Isaiah for the situation of the postexilic community and secures the allusion to the jubilee release in Leviticus 25. For, as Benjamin Sommer notes, this emphasis on a return to ancestral land at the end of a period of servitude is absent from the broader ancient Near Eastern idea of the royal release (e.g., durâru). The end result is that what was prescribed for individual Israelites in Leviticus 25 has been developed typologically in reference to the entire community.[98]

At this juncture, Bradford has done little more than link Isaiah 61 to Deutero-Isaiah's theology of exile and restoration and demonstrate the typological extension of the poor and the redeemed from Leviticus 25. Nonetheless, Bradford argues that the allusions to the theology of exile and restoration in Deutero-Isaiah do not exhaust the meaning of this typological account. Isaiah 61, he argues, situates this typological extension of Leviticus 25 into a theology of exile, which the author of Trito-Isaiah establishes by references to Egypt first, Babylonia second, and his own post-exilic situation within Palestine, third.

> The prophetic voice in Isaiah 61 has conceived of himself, his community, and his mission in terms that are drawn from Second Isaiah. Yet to say that he has simply transferred prophecies concerning the release from exile to the righting of a non-ideal socioeconomic situation in the postexilic period is only partially correct. More likely, Third Isaiah has perceived a theological continuity between Israel's situation in exile and his own situation, one facilitated by the dual consideration that postexilic Israel was practicing the same kinds of sins that led them into exile in the first place (cf. Isaiah 5) and the fact that the metaphor for exile in Deutero-Isaiah, debt-slavery, was a concrete problem in his own day. Moreover, by alluding to Second Isaiah and pentateuchal traditions, Third Isaiah demonstrates that he sees a typological relationship between his situation and the setting of previous Hebrew texts. First, just as Second Isaiah understood the

138   *The Logic of the Law*

Babylonian exile as the antitype of the Egyptian captivity, so Third Isaiah has placed his own situation in typological relationship to the other two. The result is a threefold historical typology, moving from Egypt to Babylon to postexilic Palestine.[99]

By a theology of exile, Bradford means an analysis of the situation of Israel as dichotomized between either exile or redemption with the current moment and the forseeable future defined exilically and the end of this history or eschaton identified with redemption. According to Bradford, the writer of Isaiah 61 has not only typologized Leviticus 25, but he has essentialized its conception of poverty as sin and has eschatologized its notion of legal redemption.

> In reading Third Isaiah one gets the impression that the author does not see the situation in postexilic Palestine as appreciably better than the situation in Babylon. In both cases Israel remains "shackled" because of sin, and in both Israel awaits deliverance by Yhwh. Second, the prescriptions for the jubilee year have been eschatologized. By employing a typological relationship between the individual Israelite of Leviticus 25 and the entire postexilic community, Third Isaiah has moved the concept of the jubilee from a legal prescription to a prophetic-theological concept whereby the jubilee is indicative of eschatological deliverance. . . . .[100]

If Bradford is correct, Isaiah 61 marks a significant departure from the earlier account of the Jubilee within a theology of law and freedom. History or temporality in this account is severed from redemption. The excision of the one from the other is rooted in the sin of the community, the only antidote to which is a final deliverance from God at some deferred eschatological moment. According to Bradford, the notion of exile continuing beyond the return of Israelites in the sixth century "was exceedingly common in the later Second Temple period, both in apocalypses (e.g., Daniel 9; 1 Enoch; Testament of Levi 16–17; Assumption of Moses 3) and in other genres (e.g., Jub. 1:7–18; Tobit 13–14; CD 1:5–11). This view also pervades the NT."[101]

It is, however, worth noting that a notion of the continuation of the exile into the return in the land is not the same as a notion of a permanent historical exile, which resolves only in an eschatological future. Bradford cites Ezra-Nehemiah as texts conveying an analogous account of the continuation of exile. Undoubtedly, Ezra invokes a reward-punishment scheme (Ezra 7). Nonetheless, there is no eschatological deferment suggested in Ezra or Nehemiah. If anything, there is the mandate to restore the covenantal community and its legal core in the current moment. Ezra 9:9 points to the restoration of the covenant community, its laws and sanctuary in the land, "For we are bondmen; yet our God hath not forsaken us in our bondage, but hath extended mercy unto us in the sight of the kings of Persia, to give us a reviving, to set up the house of our God, and to repair the ruins thereof, and to give us a fence in Judah and in Jerusalem."[102]

Bradford does suggest that Isaiah 61 includes a mandate for obedience over disobedience as a necessary prerequisite for deliverance. "In the development of the Trito-Isaianic corpus the identity of the servants (i.e. the heirs of the Deutero-Isaianic Servant) becomes restricted to those who are obedient to Yhwh's commands."[103] Nonetheless, Bradford argues that Isaiah 61 identifies lawful obedience only with an eschatological restoration in contradistinction to the restoration of the here and now sought after by Ezra and Nehemiah in their efforts to reconstitute covenantal community. "The eschatological promises of chapters 60–62, therefore, become the exclusive inheritance of the faithful servants, while those who are unfaithful will be put to shame (66:13–16)."[104] Bradford even suggests that this reference to the faithful servants evokes the notion of the remnant—the true Israel singularly rewarded for eschatological deliverance over and against sinful Israel, punished and forgotten.

Thus, in the canonical shaping of the book of Isaiah, the picture of restoration in Chapters 60–62 has been swept up into an eschatological-cosmological framework that includes the

> vindication of Zion and the exaltation of the obedient remnant. The original understanding of the exile as a theological state has now been adopted as the paradigm of Israel's existence until the end of days, when Yhwh will set all things right.[105]

Bradford's essay is a skillful and scholarly analysis of Isaiah 61. However, as I have suggested before, theology and biblical scholarship do not always overlap in their interests and as theologians; it is important to recognize the implications of one reading of a biblical text over another. Theological interpretations of biblical texts adhere to a different set of criteria than biblical analyses. To the extent to which Christian theologians seek to avoid anti-Jewish readings of biblical material, it is important to identify, at the very least, a range of readings of any given text and recognize how certain interpretations may be damaging to Jewish-Christian relations. In the case before us, Bradford's scholarly reading of Isaiah 61 inadvertently helps contribute to anti-Jewish interpretations of the Isaiah text.

In her classic work on the origins of Christian anti-Judaism, *Faith and Fratricide*, Rosemary Ruether identifies the two potencies of prophetic and messianic sectarianism as the groundwork for subsequent Christian anti-Judaism. Although Ruether tends toward sweeping claims regarding biblical material, her identification of the intellectual elements leading up to Christian anti-Judaism are enormously helpful. By prophetic and messianic sectarianism, Ruether means the tendency within some prophetic material, and in later second temple sectarian claims to identify a "true Israel" whose "obedience qualifies it to be the recipient of that divine favor which the rest of Israel has lost through its apostasy"—that is, the "remnant . . . [which] God will make . . . into the root from which the nation will be reborn in a new and purified form"[106] coupled with an apocalyptic dualism that consigns fallen Israel to a darkened, sinful history and true Israel to an eschatological future of favor. According to Ruether, messianic sectarianism of this sort took hold within early Christianity as a Jewish sect, and together with later Christian Christological developments, establishes the basis for a logic of Christian anti-Judaism. And she says,

> We might say the essential characteristics of the sectarian viewpoint are an antithetical distinction between the true and apostate Israel; a definition of the true Israel as a spiritual, voluntarist community of personal conversion, rather than a tribal community; and a vilification of official Judaism and its rank-and-file members as apostate. Official Judaism is to be regarded no longer as part of the covenant and finally . . . to be seen as satanic in character. . . . It was in this milieu of Jewish messianic sectarianism that Christianity was originally born in Palestine.[107]

Ruether contrasts the preceding with what she refers to as a "Pharisaic inclusivity," according to which

> [E]very Jew is called to be a religious Jew. Yet the Jew who declines to accept the religious consciousness of Israel remains within the people and its covenant until such time as he definitively puts himself outside of it by adopting an antithetical identity. Becoming a Christian was the adoption of such an antithetical identity. Yet even here the medieval Rabbis insisted on regarding the Christian convert as a son of the covenant. . . . A Jewish Christianity which did not define itself as a new covenant, superseding the historical covenant of Abraham and Moses, but as a renewal standing within the one covenant, adding only the belief that it will be Jesus who will return as the Christ, might have remained as a form of Judaism. . . . Such a Jewish Christianity might have coexisted with Pharisaic Judaism . . . even as Essenic Judaism coexisted with Pharisaic Judaism. . . .[108]

Nonetheless, Ruether maintains, asserting a "new principle of salvation,"[109] early Christianity further developed its tendencies toward prophetic and messianic sectarianism, severing itself from the Jewish fabric from which it emerged.

It is not difficult to call into question Ruether's distinction between the Pharisaic notion of "all Israel" and the prophetic focus upon a remnant. A theology of law and freedom pervades prophetic material. Nonetheless, Ruether's identification of the marriage between sectarianism and apocalyptic dualism strikes at the heart of this volume's effort to distinguish between a logic of law and freedom and a logic of exceptionalism. Here, I want to draw attention to the coherence between Gregory's interpretation of Isaiah 61 and Ruether's account of apocalyptic sectarianism. According to Gregory, Isaiah 61 foreshadows a strand of Second Temple literature, which focuses upon the link between Israel, exile, and divine punishment and forecasts the redemption of an obedient remnant of this sinful community in a not-yet-but-anticipated eschatological end of history. With a troublesome degree of blindness, Gregory closes his article by remarking upon the association between his interpretation of Isaiah 61's and Luke 4's invocation of this same text. "The eschatological use of Isaiah 61 that is found . . . in Luke 4 is not . . . far removed from the literal sense . . . of Isaiah 61."[110] I am not suggesting that Gregory's reading of Isaiah 61 funds an inevitable anti-Judaism. I think Ruether is correct to argue that sectarianism alone only generates reformist groups within a single account of covenantal life. Nonetheless, the assertion of a division of Israel into true and apostate and the severing of Jewish history from the promises of divine redemption certainly places the Isaiah 61 text outside a theology of law and freedom and lays the groundwork for a more fully developed presentation of replacement theology. In closing, I would like to make use of an alternative account from biblical scholarship to present a pragmatically more productive reading of Isaiah 61 for Christian theologians to advance.

In *The Dawn of the Apocalyptic: The Historical and Sociological Roots of Jewish Apocalyptic Eschatology*, Paul Hanson demonstrates how one may read Isaiah 60–62 as a repetition of a theology of law rather than an introduction of a new theological paradigm of post-exilic thought. In particular, Hanson argues that Isaiah 60–62 draws upon and repeats the themes of Deutero-Isaiah, the central message of which is the "pure promise of restoration to the whole nation (62:10–12, 40:8–11, 52:7–10) based on the theme of pardon (60:10b, 40:1–2, 44:22, 54:7–8)."[111] Contrary to Gregory's post-exilic exilic mentality, the writers of Isaiah 60–62, Hanson avers sought to announce a "glorious picture of shalom,"[112] one which offers no mention at all of the preceding period of exile. "The people are . . . in Zion,"[113] Hanson argues. Their focus is upon rebuilding the sanctuary but, he continues, the authors focus not at all upon a remnant of the community but rather see themselves as the "priests of YHWH . . . whose needs . . . would be secured by an everlasting covenant and sealed by the fulfillment of ancient patriarchal promises."[114] In summary, Hanson explicitly links the theology of Isaiah 61 with the theology of abiding and says, "In Isaiah 60–62 the sealed gates [Ezek. 44:1ff] are cast open, for all people will be righteous and holy. . . . And this whole glorious restoration is to take place not because of any priestly effort to regulate the holy, but because 'your light has come, the glory of YWHW has risen upon you'" (60:1).[115]

The theological differences between Hanson's and Gregory's accounts are significant, particularly when one considers the reference to Isaiah 60–62 in the Gospel of Luke, Chapter 4. Gregory's assertion that there is a close connection between his reading of Isaiah 60–62 and the meaning of Jesus' reference to this text in Luke 4 not only sets the stage for an anti-Jewish perspective from within the Lukan text but forecloses new ways of reading Luke 4 in view of Leviticus 25, possibilities supported conversely by Hanson's retention of the theology of abiding and restoration within the late Isaiah text. The earlier analysis of the theology of abiding invites Christian theologians to consider the implications of their reading of Luke 4 and its reference to the Jubilee in Isaiah as a vehicle for repairing their understanding of Israel and Judaism. Current New Testament scholarship on the Nazareth periscope is extensive, and an appraisal of it could offer Christian theologians an opportunity to recognize a theology of law from within the Lukan gospel.[116] A consideration of these scholarly possibilities is beyond the scope of this chapter. However, together with an inquiry into how Christian theology may recognize a theology of law within its own understanding of the Word of God (which I will provide in Chapter 7), Christian theologians may avail themselves of a biblically based opportunity to repair Christian-Jewish relations.

FIVE

The New Thinking and the Order of Wisdom

A review of the terrain traversed in the book reveals two strands of thought labeled as the logic of law and the logic of sacrifice. In Chapters 1 and 2, I told parts of a story about a logic of law that presupposes a conception of divine freedom of love and order implicit in Rosenzweig's reconceptualization of the meaning of Abraham's sacrifice of Isaac and Maimonides' account of the relation between divine freedom and the creation of the world as other than God in *The Guide of the Perplexed*. Chapter 4 contextualized these two conceptions of divine freedom and divine law in an analysis of a biblical theology of abiding.

The second of the two strands has described the logic of sacrifice and its dialectic of desire. By dialectic of desire, I mean the character of the relationship between desire and divine sovereignty as it has been dealt with in a particular philosophical configuration. The dialectic of desire refers to the conception of divine sovereignty as unbridled freedom—the freedom that *qua* grace translates as an expression of love but *qua* divine power translates as the absence of the normative rights or legitimate needs of persons affected by this power. Rosenstock-Huessy's conception of Jesus as the meaning of history and Agamben's account of the messianic transformation of the law offered examples. My account of this mode of freedom devoid of lawful normativity spilled over into an account of a theological knowledge and testimony privileged by the reception of this unique freedom or grace. Consequently, I showed the link between an unregulated divine sovereignty and the free reign of desire on the part of those who claim privilege from the benefits of this free grace. Such unregulated divine freedom, I suggested, breeds a hermeneutics of expertise and essentialism shielded from critique. A God without law gives rise to a hubristic desire free to interpret truth and cut out falsehood.

On the other hand, I have also exposed the dialectic of desire from the other side of the relation, or what happens to human desire when it faces a God whose sovereignty is limited to the perpetuation of that God's unity and perfection. I traced this line of the dialectic of desire from the elements of exceptionalism within Maimonides' thought to the schism between the reality of God as an ideal and the correlative gap between persons and this ideal in Spinoza. Characteristic of this side of the dialectic of desire is a thorough-going anxiety in persons who strive to comport with a transcendent and ultimately inaccessible divine ideal but whose efforts inevitably come up short and produce a perpetual sense of inextirpable guilt or failure. God's inability to act freely for us is reflected in our inability to be freed from anxiety and guilt. Once again, desire reigns supreme, but here, it imprisons persons to a life of despair rather than propping up unjustified assertions. Even so, I have also argued that triumphalist claims that refuse justification are, when more deeply analyzed, cover-ups used to suppress deeply felt and unmet desires. As we saw in Chapter 1, the more loudly and actively that Rosenstock-Huessy's self-certain believer and Agamben's messianic revolutionary proclaim their truth, the more we recognize the precariousness of their proclamation. A hermeneutics of expertise siphons off those with truth from those without truth, but even those with truth are siphoned off within themselves—excepting elements of themselves and their needs and desires that do not register as significant in the meaning of things—whose proclamations then swing back and forth between false assertion and the inner anxiety and guilt over their own inability to fully identify with the truth or meaning asserted.

The purpose of this chapter is to offer a philosophical account of the logic of law, which I have already suggested can be identified in the Hebrew bible and appears in a truncated form in Maimonides' theology. That this biblically based and now philosophically presented logic of law offers the possibility for a new account of how Jews and Christians can speak and learn with one another has everything to do with the overall paradigm shift that plays out in new conceptions of how human desire relates to power as well as the ways that this relationship affects how Jews and Christians tell and hold their proclamations about God. Consequently, this chapter will expose the philosophical structures of the logic of the law and their power to reshape conceptions of history, power, and knowledge; Chapter 6 will examine the application of the logic of the law to the particular issue of Jewish-Christian relations.

Philosophically speaking, this chapter follows Rosenzweig's extension of Schelling's account of divine freedom, limited as it is (that is, Schelling's account) to an analysis of this freedom in the context of a negative theological deduction. In many respects, Rosenzweig saw his approach to philosophy—or what he referred to as the New Thinking—as the continuation and completion of Schelling's *Weltalter* into the picture of a living philosophy that emerges from a theology of divine freedom as law and love.[1] Consequently, I will argue that Rosenzweig's work presents a comprehensive account of the logic of law. In this chapter, I will offer a reading of several key essays in Rosenzweig's corpus along with portions of *The Star of Redemption* to draw out what it means to be "found in the order of the free God" and showcase the general paradigm shift for understanding knowledge and power possible with this logic.

In the first part of this chapter, I will examine the origins of the paradigm shift toward a logic of the law found in Rosenzweig's essay, "Atheistic Theology." In the second part, I will present a more developed account of the logic of law as it operates in the world and thereby affects knowledge of the world through an examination of Rosenzweig's essay, "The New Thinking."

Revelation as Orientation and the Law of Atheism

What is it like to be found in the order of God's freedom? Schelling's work does not answer this question,[2] but it receives close attention in Rosenzweig's thought. Although we do not find a full-blown landscape of a world ordered in divine revelation until Rosenzweig's later work in *The Star of Redemption* and his central essay, "The New Thinking," the seeds of this paradigm shift are present in an early essay, "Atheistic Theology."

Already by 1914, Rosenzweig had begun to play out a philosophical account of divine action, or what I already identified in Chapter 1 as the central notion of "revelation as orientation." On one level, "Atheistic Theology" extends Schelling's notion of divine freedom acting upon God-self as "nature and freedom" to an account of divine freedom acting upon persons in the world. Consequently, Rosenzweig's portrait of divine action on human life produces a snapshot of the "difference" between God and human beings so far as God acts, and we receive and respond. Said otherwise, Rosenzweig's "Atheistic Theology" introduces readers of Rosenzweig to his account of the irreducibility of God and persons characteristic of the logic of the law. On another level, "Atheistic Theology" charts new territory in an analysis of the logic of sacrifice and its dialectic of desire. In this vein, I would like to draw attention to three particular tasks performed by the essay:

> The essay exposes the natural and self-inflicted undoing of the logic of sacrifice. It offers, in other words, a deconstruction of the dialectics of desire and of the concomitant notion of power that accompanies it.
> The essay employs this exposure to introduce a new genealogy of intellectual history, what Rosenzweig and others spoke of as the meaning of "1800" and its relation to the meaning of "1900." The impact of Rosenzweig's conception of revelation as orientation upon how he understands the meaning of history will have to wait until the fuller account offered in "The New Thinking," but "Atheistic Theology" already lays the groundwork for a *novum* in intellectual history, and in particular, the story of the relationship between Greek philosophy and the development of German philosophy first in Hegel and then in Feuerbach.
> Finally, the essay attends to what remains of the concept of revelation as orientation after the work of both of these analyses. Here, illuminated through the notion of revelation as order, is a new conception of power or freedom rooted in act and response that is the correlation between divine freedom and human freedom.

UNRAVELING SACRIFICE

"Atheistic Theology" was in part prompted by Rosenzweig's concern about Martin Buber's "Three Addresses concerning Judaism," published in 1911. In these essays, Buber advances his (then) account of the eternal character of the Jewish blood community.[3] In Rosenzweig's perspective, Buber's theology of the Jewish people bore striking resemblance to other examples of chosen-people theology, including Hermann Cohen's account of the Jews as the exemplar of the "ideal community of mankind"[4] along with Jewish neo-Hegelian efforts (weak as they were) to redeem the chosen people's significance on the grounds of their contribution to the historical march of

Geist. In Buber, this chosen-people theology centered around the claim of the eternal-natural existence of the Jewish people—or, as Rosenzweig described, it the claim that

> [T]he people obtain the right to exist simply from their existence, independently of their factual achievements . . . [that is] it has the right to its existence in its own character, in the rushing of its "blood". . . . [Now, Rosenzweig says] an "Atheistic Theology" could be arrived at on the Jewish side.[5]

"Atheistic Theology" introduces the notion of revelation as order or law by a logical ground-clearing of the conceptual tendencies of Hegelian and Feuerbachian idealism or what amounts to an anticipation of the conceptual cancellation of ontological thinking and the dialectic of desire operative in both of these models.[6] Although only Hegel is mentioned directly, in the process of defining what it calls "Jewish people theology," the essay charts a conceptual dynamic that begins with the Hegelian notion of a people's, or *Volk's*, significance in relation to the "transnational" purposes or Ideas that it generates and moves into the adaptation of that notion in a "Jewish people theology," which argues instead that

> [A] people obtain the right to existence simply from their existence. . . . The people . . . that no longer lives and dies for the sake of transnational purposes has its right to existence in its own character . . . it is no longer said of a people that in it the world renewing Idea is carried to maturity, after which, an empty shell, it [the people] may then lie abandoned, but rather it is now grasped in such a way that through its "essence," the world will recover.[7]

Despite appearances, the move to a "Jewish people theology" is not altogether other than the Hegelian account. Rather, it is an inversion of it, which keeps all the elements of the conceptual account intact. If in the Hegelian account, a historical people are a location for the instantiation of the universal, transhistorical, absolute spirit, in the "Jewish people theology," then

> [T]he "essence" the constant character of the people acquires tremendous significance. . . . Instead of trying . . . to show the human under the might of the divine, one tries . . . to understand the divine as the self-projection of the human into the heaven of myth.[8]

The essay then proceeds to demonstrate the mutual need of each of these models for the other, the extent to which they constitute mirror images of a self-same conceptual move within the adoption of the "Jewish people theology" itself. My argument here is that Rosenzweig's mapping of the conceptual "identity" of the Hegelian and the Feuerbachian within Jewish people theology illuminates the dialectic of desire operative in the position itself—a position that permits itself to swing back and forth between two unsustainable positions by the sheer power of a will or a desire to maintain one of the two at any moment over and against the other. Let us look at the example more carefully.

Rosenzweig calls "Jewish people theology" an example of "atheistic theology," by which he means the reduction of God into things human. Rosenzweig also refers to "atheistic theology" as myth and says, "it is the superhuman grasped as the offspring of the human . . . it is the highest triumph of a theology hostile to revelation to sublate it entirely in favor of its first terms to show revelation to be mythology."[9] In the particular case in hand, chosen-people theology mythologizes the natural existence of the Jewish people in such a way that the "human actuality . . . recommends itself as a content of faith. . . ."[10] Mythologization of this sort hypostasizes an historical actuality and excises the revelatory origin or past out of which it is authentically funded. Here, we see the Feuerbachian inversion of the Hegelian *Volk* wherein God is accounted for as the "offspring" of persons. Self-certain in its account of self-origin, mythologization denies historical actuality's indebtedness to a cause in the past—outside itself. Yet, Rosenzweig says, "something of it remains."[11]

With this claim that "something of it remains," Rosenzweig identifies the failure of "Jewish people theology" to complete the "exceptionalism" operative in its exclusion of the divine and its collapse into the human: an effort motored by sheer human will alone, despite its failure to succeed. Consequently, Rosenzweig notes that the effort to squeeze an account of choseness into a hypostasized natural existent results in a restless polarity within the character of choseness itself—a restlessness that betrays the sufficiency of the stable account of its eternal self-origin. As we have seen many times before, truths sustained in desire are precariously held and unstable given the epistemological reality that desiring a truth does not constitute sufficient justification for the stability of a claim.

In this particular instance, the collapse of the divine into the eternality of the people burdens the concept of peoplehood with an internal self-divide between its own historicity and its transhistoricity. Said otherwise, to sustain itself, Jewish people theology opts into Hegelianism. It inverts into its conceptual mirror image to salvage itself. The ontological failure of the first claim demands the turn to another ontological claim, neither of which, of course, will remain stable as claims because both are driven by interest, and the interest at play is neither recognized nor adjudicated (ordered). The move into Hegelianism inevitably destroys the claim for the particular existence of the Jewish people, of course, and in this form of "Jewish people theology," Rosenzweig suggests that what in traditional Judaism constitutes an authentic difference between the actuality of the people and the kingdom of God, Jewish people theology strains to collapse into an identification of the "is" and the "ought" of Jewish future. Jewish people theology attempts to bridge this difference between historical actuality and eternal essence with a rhetoric around the will to unity: A "unified" historical people can or will assume eternal essence. And yet, the slippage between the actuality of the people and this teleological drive betrays the self-sufficiency of the character of Jewish peoplehood at any given moment in time, giving the lie to the program of collapsing the eternal into this historical via the mythological move. Pressed deeper into its own contradiction, the myth of the chosen people presents itself as the dogmatic identification between the eternality and the actuality of the Jewish people, and here collapses into fanaticism. In other words, in the wake of the instability of the Hegelian-informed move, the proponent of the original claim then asserts an identity between this so called "eternal" people and God: that is, she moves from the "atheism" of the existence of the people to the fanaticism of its theistic identity. In this case, atheism and theism are identified as different pieces in a shared conceptual orbit wherein each cancels the other in its effort to assert ontological stability.

With this account of the conceptual play within "Jewish people theology," Rosenzweig anticipates the critique of ontology offered in *The Star of Redemption* and "The New Thinking." As well, he anticipates the identification of the play of desire as it operates without adjudication in these modes of thought. The ultimate identity of the Feuerbachian, Hegelian, and then dogmatist positions refers, of course, to the common denominator of each: the unregulated and disordered performance of desire in the assertion of each of these positions. Moreover, with this commentary on "Atheistic Theology," we also see the implicit ramifications of this cancellation for an understanding of the meaning of power. Supporting one or the other claim, desire pretends to display a kind of power or force in its labor against other claims. The cancellation of each claim in regard to the other, however, exposes this display as nothing more than an exercise in coercion devoid of strength. Bereft of the real freedom required to act, desire displays no real power here, its coercive efforts a guise for the weakness of the position.

INTERPRETING 1800

Rosenzweig's "Atheistic Theology" introduces more than just an exposure of the precariousness of idealist ontology. It also presents the possibility of a new narrative of intellectual history. As a student, Rosenzweig participated in a twentieth-century revival of Hegelianism and its dialectical account of the history of ideas. "Nineteen-hundred" was read as a new and improved chapter in the triumph of the Hegelian account of the manifestation of the absolute in and through the "ethical and political mission of the German state."[12] In the context of a Hegelian dialectic, a Feuerbachian inversion of the relationship between the Absolute and the human would constitute a moment of antithesis waiting to be resolved in and through the account of a twentieth-century appropriation of the manifestation of the Absolute and transhistorical significance of the German state. Feuerbach's essential atheism would, in Taubes's language, be outbidden by Hegel's theistic account. What happens to this narrative when the dialectic of desire that funds it is exposed? According to Michael Morgan and Paul Franks, Rosenzweig's turn to revelation meant "an overcoming of the idea of 1800 . . . since Rosenzweig already thought of religion as the way to overcome the generation of 1800's deification of history."[13] Soon after making this claim, however, the writers admit that to speak of a "struggling against the 1800 divinization of history does not necessarily constitute a move beyond Hegelianism. . . ."[14] by which the writers recognize their error in characterizing Rosenzweig's turn to revelation as an overcoming or "move beyond" 1800. In fact, Rosenzweig's turn to revelation—the "something that remains" after the dialectic of desire is unveiled turns aside from the logic of outbidding and works instead to reinstate the reality of moments previously narrated in the dialectical account of history. Even before considering the impact of the "something that remains," or what is the intrusion of the divine into the human, the reciprocal cancellation of atheism by theism and theism by atheism renders absurd any dialectical account of intellectual epochs as it progressively erases each epoch in the next. If "something did not remain," there would be nothing to narrate, or perhaps there would be only one thing to narrate: the mantra of human desire in its unbridled attempt to assert its governing view of the world.

To recognize Rosenzweig's alternative genealogy of intellectual history requires recourse to a fuller account of revelation as orientation because this concept funds an account of action as "what happens" in time from which Rosenzweig develops his notion of history. We will see this development in the remaining discussion of "Atheistic Theology" and "The New Thinking." We can, however, use this opportunity to appreciate the significance of the ground-clearing that has already been performed in "Atheistic Theology" by comparing the possibilities it presents with the genealogy of outbidding presented by Jacob Taubes's *The Political Theology of Paul*.

In Chapter 1, I invoked Taubes's genealogy of outbidding to lay the groundwork for understanding the character of Agamben's messianic account of the law. Perhaps the greatest contribution of Taubes's *The Political Theology of Paul* is his recognition of the extent to which the logic of outbidding has dominated narratives of western intellectual history. Although he first identifies this logic in Paul's effort to legitimize the early Christian community as the true Israel, the true people of God, the true bearers of the covenant, Taubes finds a similar narrative in a whole range of theorists from Habermas to Schmitt to Nietzsche. By showcasing this dynamic, Taubes implicitly opens the possibility of a nonexceptionalist account of intellectual history, one that does not prohibit recognition of multiple world views and their attendant claims.

Although Taubes did not address the exceptionalism in the narrative around Athens and Jerusalem, one can see the logic of sacrifice operative here as well. Therefore, although Rosenzweig's "Atheistic Theology" directly reorients only the small intellectual epoch of German idealism, it is nonetheless possible to understand how the ontological cancellation that reorients this chapter in intellectual history can also be applied to reorient other chapters and thematizations of intellectual history as well: for example, the classic narrative of divide between Athens and Jerusalem.[15] The long-standing tug of war between Greek rationality and Hebraic Biblicism wherein when one is dominant and the other inadmissible goes by the wayside after the ontological ground-clearing performed in "Atheistic Theology." In this way, Rosenzweig's "Atheistic Theology" anticipates Rosenzweig's subsequent alternative to the Athens-Jerusalem divide found in his New Thinking, which relates theology and philosophy as separate and mutually instructive approaches to the discernment of truth. That we found the retention of this tension between Athens and Jerusalem in the scholarly reviews of Maimonides' work has as much to do with the inability of these scholars to identify a different narrative of intellectual history as it did with Maimonides' own inability to identify an alternative narrative.

Another example of an account of intellectual history reframed by the logic of "Atheistic Theology" is the story of the rise of secularization in the wake of the demise of Christendom. After the ontological cancellation, we can no longer assume the victory of secularism in the west over and against the theism of medieval Christendom. The fact that scholars of secularization can now distinguish between secularism as ideology and secularism as history[16] only shows how the ground-clearing that Rosenzweig performs in this essay resonates with a general shift in how we understand the movement of ideas in history. Rosenzweig's own account of the Johannine age as described in his later *The Star of Redemption* demonstrates how after his crucial turn toward the impact of revelation upon accounts of history, an account of the future of the relationship between church and religion would result in a hybrid notion of the Johannine age wherein church is impacted by secularity and secularity impacted by church with neither dominating the other.[17] Rosenzweig, a formerly self-identified Hegelian, recognized that history is not simply the struggle to coerce beliefs. Still, Rosenzweig remained concerned not to reduce history to a story devoid of stakes—a relativism wherein the interest for truth dissolves. He would find the key, of course, in his notion of revelation as orientation, the seeds of which are already implicit within his account of the divine and the human in "Atheistic Theology."[18]

REVEALING EXISTENCE

"Atheistic Theology" is not only an essay about revelation: It is an essay that performs a revelation, and in so doing, performs the conceptual alternative to exceptionalism or outbidding earlier described. If Morgan and Franks were right in their initial instinct that Rosenzweig's conception of revelation overcame his earlier Hegelianism, the article would easily inhabit a twentieth-century genealogy of post-Hegelian existentialism. But as noted, Morgan and Franks rescind their first instinct because they then admit that Rosenzweig's turn to revelation "does not constitute a move beyond Hegelianism." How so? To understand the meaning of Rosenzweig's turn to revelation requires a look back at his narrative of ontological cancellation.

On the one hand, the drama between Hegelian *Geist* and Feuerbachian humanity staged the mutual cancellation of the one by the other. On the other hand, this account of the narrative is not quite complete because our ability to recognize the varying moves by the first claim and then the second and then potentially back and forth again *ad infinitum* suggests the residual existence of each. What is nullified in their mutual cancellation is any pretense to ontological stability—a stability that would *qua* "being" permit the one reality to absorb or fully interpret the other reality away. This does not mean, however, that one cannot speak of humanity or God. It means that neither refers to an absolute conception of reality that orients or defines and names the essential reality of the other. Within the restless polarity between the two, "something remains," and that something is both the divine and the human as something other than essential being. Despite or rather, precisely because of the ontological cancellation, each of the two realities are revealed not as "what they are" but rather as how or what happens to them in their mutual interaction. We know this by a process of intellectual elimination. If both elements remain such that we may refer to them but yet neither is self sustaining, we must conclude that they exist by virtue of something other than themselves. If, however, that "something" is not and cannot be a "something" or an essence because if it were, it would nullify or interpret this reality away, the something must be a deed or an event—an action by another rather than an essence from another.

Of course, here we see the Schelling's theosophical logic now applied to an account of lived philosophy. Recall that for Schelling, God's act of freedom (*actus purus*) both differentiated the God beyond being from God *qua* nature and God *qua* spirit/freedom; and in this differentiation, or "no," also enacted a "yes," or gracious affirmation of God *qua* nature on the one hand and God *qua* spirit/freedom on the other: The resultant reality, of course, was the coming into existence of God or divine revelation [that is to say, the "revelation" of God] as nature and spirit are acted upon by God in his freedom. That both divine nature and divine spirit are affirmed and retained though fully differentiated from each other and from the God beyond being illustrates the lawfulness and order characteristic of the generative freedom enacted by God in this exercise of self-revelation.

Applied here, the existence of God and person implies the activity of each upon the other. The tension in the existence between God *qua Geist* and man as humanity refers to and presupposes that the humanity that continues to exist sustains this existence as acted upon by a divine intrusion.

> The distinctness of God and man, this frightful scandal for all new and old paganism, seems to be removed; the offensive thought of revelation, this plunging of a higher content into an unworthy vessel, is brought to silence. Yet something of it remains and must remain.... The human is broken through, the superhuman threatens to intrude through the breach into the arena of "Atheistic Theology."[19]

God acts and acts upon human beings. And therefore, just as the divine nature of God comes into existence as the recipient of the act of the God beyond being, so human being comes into existence as the recipient of divine freedom as well—something happens to it. Both theism and atheism are retained: God is without us (theism), and we are without God (atheism). Human beings are found in this event and found as both different from and irreducible to God. Already in this early essay, Rosenzweig illuminates some of his central philosophical elements drawn largely from Schelling's *Weltalter*:

> To be revealed—that is, to be brought into a revelation—is to exist, and to exist is to be ordered.
>
> Self-consciousness or self-knowledge is the consciousness of being ordered in an event of divine freedom: We acquire wisdom through the law.

At this point, I introduce these elements of what I call a "logic of law," but I will expand upon each of them in due course as we discover their perimeters in Rosenzweig's later works.

Furthermore, as expected, we can now recognize the new conception of history emerging from this notion of revelation as orientation. If existence is a being acted upon, history is the narration of this existence. It is the documentation of the act of another and my response to it. Of course, in this capacity, history is a documentation of power, but the power that it records is the power of an action and the correlative reaction of at least two irreducible actors. As a documentation of power, histories will vary with different actors but not because the documentation absorbs the reality of another into an essentialist account—but only because the perspective of the actor and the recipient of an action are obviously different. Unlike an exceptionalist account, each perspective retains worth on the grounds of its irreducibility. Each retains stability in the order of difference and affirmation of what it is. Aristotelianism, Biblicism, Hegelianism, and/or Feuerbachianism each reappear with their own account, but this multiplicity of accounts does not produce a relativism of meaningless claims. *This* multiplicity derives from the varying perspectives and interests of multiple players whose interests are always adjudicated in the order of irreducibility upon which the actions and reactions of players are strung.

In this way, "Atheistic Theology" even anticipates the central notion of testimony as the response by persons to the event of divine freedom. Yes, persons witness to a prior free act of the God of and beyond being. However, even this testimony is ordered by and in the founding by God. In another early essay, "'Urzelle' (Germ Cell) to *The Star of Redemption*," Rosenzweig links the intrusion of the divine act into human existence to the notion of command, a notion that takes on great significance in the *Star* and later writings. God's act is an act of command, and our response is a response to this command, but both transpire within and presuppose the order of difference between the actors—the lawfulness that sustains the existence and revelation of both. "God's command is an order . . . no law is given *to* the pious, for he stands *under* an 'order.'"[20] Of course, God is not the only actor. Just as we receive God's action, so God receives ours as well, and in "Atheistic Theology," Rosenzweig reminds us of the "key phrase of the master of the Kabbalah: God speaks: 'if you do not bear witness to me, then I am not' . . . God himself, not human presumption makes Himself dependent upon the testimony of man."[21] Of course, persons and God interact with a world in which they live as well—what in the *Star* and elsewhere constitutes the dynamic of redemption, but an analysis of this relation has to wait until a review of later texts.

Action, Power, and the Freedom of the Law

Like "Atheistic Theology," Rosenzweig's later essay, "The New Thinking" is a text that not only displays the meaning of revelation as orientation or law but actually performs a revelation of concepts. Methodologically, "The New Thinking" proceeds logically like "Atheistic Theology" from a deconstruction of ontology and its reductionism to an exposure of the kind of reality and thinking that remains in its wake. What "The New Thinking" essay adds to "Atheistic Theology" is its role as commentary upon the larger and later *The Star of Redemption*. Written in 1925 after the *Star* had already been published, Rosenzweig wrote, "The New Thinking" to clarify the intent of the *Star* as a philosophical book. Important for us is the fact that this essay presupposes the content of the *Star*, and in particular, the account of the deduction of the negative elements of God, world, and persons along with an account of the event of their existence and/or revelation, generally speaking. Consequently, "The New Thinking" offers a more extensive review of the effect of divine freedom as both grace and law upon the order and existence of the lived world. If we might say that "Atheistic Theology" offers a post-modern "Exodus" with God as liberated and the philosopher as liberator, "The New Thinking" provides a post-modern Wisdom text illuminating the lawfulness of existence, the meaning of providence and the nature of wisdom or knowledge appropriate to this order. That this essay speaks of "revelation" in terms of "existence," generally speaking, and focuses less on the particular account of revelation as the specific relationship between God and a people or a person in history only deepens the analogy to the world view that we find in Wisdom literature accounts, such as in Proverbs or even Ecclesiastes. We can, however, consult "The New Thinking" essay to begin to identify the link between Rosenzweig's account of revelation as existence, generally speaking, and the particular account of Jewish and Christian revelation that we will analyze in the next chapter. In short, the goal of this review of "The New Thinking" is to examine the text as a central presentation of the logic of law by

Illuminating the role of divine freedom as grace and law presupposed by "The New Thinking."

Identifying the connection between divine freedom in the creation of the world and the meaning of providence in this account: that is, describe what it means for the world to be "found in the order" of God's freedom.

Presenting the alternative account of knowledge or what we might refer to as "wisdom" so far as it documents the work of providence on the one hand and anticipates the actions of creaturely and human response on the other hand.

If by way of analysis, we surmise that Rosenzweig's "The New Thinking" offers a post-modern Wisdom account, this discussion will, like the "Atheistic Theology," imply an understanding of the relationship between knowledge and power, which opens the door to a new understanding of not only intellectual history as discussed earlier but sets the stage for a new account of the relationship between Judaism and Christianity as narratives of what it means to be found in the power and order of God.

"THE NEW THINKING": CLEARING THE GROUND

Most readers of Rosenzweig think of the now famous Book II of *The Star of Redemption* when considering his account of revelation. However, in "The New Thinking," the divine revelation narrated in Book II is linked to a more fundamental account of revelation as existence. Here, Rosenzweig places a discussion of the concept of revelation squarely in the middle of a philosophical distinction between a philosophy of essentialism and an epistemology of existence.[22] Essentialism, Rosenzweig argues, is an epistemological dead-end. "All philosophy asked about 'essence.'"[23] However, this quest for ontological knowledge is absurdly reductionist. To say that "'x' is" hinges the reality of something on something else. There is, obviously, no point in saying that "x" is "x." Still, the obsession with the language of being forces propositional claims, such as "x" is "y." But to say that "x" is "y" is no longer to speak of "x" but rather of "y." We have, in the very exercise of identifying "x," lost "x." Ontological knowledge nullifies the reality it claims to know. If, however, ontological knowledge leads to reduction, then reality must presuppose a not-knowing that preserves the irreducibility of the three elements we seek to know: human being, world, and God. According to Rosenzweig, this in turn means that where philosophy ends, experience begins. Why? Because speaking in positive terms, God, world, and man each constitutes a "being in itself," which does not lend itself to being perceived or known by another. That we acknowledge intuitively the *de facto* difference between God, world, and human being is presupposed in our very effort to reduce them one to the other. Nonetheless, as demonstrated earlier, ontological efforts "x-out" the intuited premises about which knowledge is said to be gained. All that remains always is the intuited God, world, and human being. "To the question of essence there are only tautological answers"[24]—and, therefore, the question becomes absurd. Where do we find these intuitions of a "god who is not the true God, a world which is not the vital world and humans who are not the actual humans . . . ?"[25] They function as the silent presuppositions of our experience of them. Experience, Rosenzweig says, does not experience the things that we claim to know, but rather what it experiences "it experiences in these matters of fact"[26]—these irreducibilities.

What then are we left with after the old philosophy has been thrown away? We are left with the New Thinking, which appreciates that the "healthy human understanding [is the guide] into a method of scientific thinking."[27] It is the fundamental argument of this reading that the "healthy human understanding" presupposes the work of divine freedom as grace and law. Whereas the sick human understanding insists on the "*idée fixe*"[28]—healthy human understanding waits—narrates and cognizes with "time." To know or wait is as well to welcome an effect—to allow something to happen—it is to wait in relation—and to "know" means to know what has happened in relation. "To know God, world, and man means to know what in the tenses of actuality they do or what happens to them, what they do to each other and what occurs by one another. . . ."[29] But here we already see the influence of the work of divine freedom as delimitation of difference and affirmation just as it operated in God's own encounter with God-self as other in Schelling's *Weltalter*. The existence of each of the three elements in relation with the other presupposes a logic of differentiation and affirmation that accompanies their irreducibility. On the one hand, "the separation of their 'being' is here presupposed for if they were not separated they could not interact. . . ."[30]—they are differentiated from the other [law]. On the other hand, it is only by interacting in time that they "open themselves up,"[31] lending themselves to the one and the other as contributors to the events of time: That is to say, within this delimitation and order, they are affirmed and recognized by each other, they are exposed or seen [grace].

Each of these two features of post-ontological existence (difference and affirmation) refer to the logic of divine freedom; and according to Rosenzweig, all three existences—God, world, and persons—are positioned or oriented in this setting from a prior act of divine freedom that founds them there. A review of the impact of divine freedom upon God-self, world, and person will illuminate how the reality of each of the three elements as existence presupposes divine freedom and the logic of law. While in the *Weltalter*, Schelling offers an account of God's acting upon God-self in the freedom of law and grace, following *The Star of Redemption*, "The New Thinking" extends the analysis of the effect of God's freedom on to God, world, and person. This is because Rosenzweig's "The New Thinking" goes farther than Schelling's work in shattering the idealist world-view.[32] Presupposed by "The New Thinking" essay but detailed in *The Star of Redemption* is the emergence into existence of the world as created and persons as named and loved. To the extent that both world and persons are acted upon by God's freedom, both are found within the order or God's love. Both, therefore, also constitute signs of divine power. This, however, is not to say that world and persons are only signs of divine power. Each stands in an active relationship with God and even with each other, and the nexus of relationships forged in the order or law of God's freedom constitutes the environment for redemption with each of the dynamics available for narration.

At this juncture, we are already familiar with the three primary elements of the divine action upon God-self derived from Schelling's account that apply to Rosenzweig's account of God, world, and person. These are:

To exist is to be revealed by or acted upon by divine freedom.
To be acted upon by the free God is to be delimited as different from God and affirmed in this difference.
To have knowledge is to know or narrate the having been acted upon in law and love. Knowledge is, in this sense, the wisdom of being affirmed and exposed or revealed in an order.

We can identify each of these features of divine freedom in its encounter with God, world, and persons in Rosenzweig's account in *The Star of Redemption*.

ORDERING AND AFFIRMING GOD AS OTHER

As both "Atheistic Theology" and "The New Thinking" show, the reality of God remains after the ontological house cleaning. But if God remains after ontology, this must mean that God is a something that exists. Still, as we have seen before, without the language of essentialism, we can no longer say that the God we find is a God who sustains God's own reality through an eternal stable being. To suggest this is not only to fall back into the language of ontology, but it is to reduce the God that remains to absolute

Being, a result that as we have seen all too clearly in the analysis of Maimonides' account in *The Guide for the Perplexed*, inevitably excepts God from God-self—in particular, excepts the God who "exists" with us and "for us" from the "true" God of Being. Consequently, if God remains after ontology, God remains because of something other than the God we find, and something other than Being. This something other, of course, is God beyond Being as act or event, and in this instance, the God who acts upon God-self and brings God-self into existence—or into "revelation." In Book I of the *Star*, Rosenzweig describes this process wherein God *qua* free acts upon God-self as "being," and in so doing, emerges in existence as one who creates the world. Most significantly for our purposes is the dual character of God's freedom as affirmation and distinction from God-self, or what I prefer to refer to as grace and lawfulness.

Rosenzweig's account of the God who experiences or exists begins by speculating upon who God would have to be given that God is unavailable to ontological knowledge. Who is the God that we do not know? Such an approach lands Rosenzweig in an account that mirrors Schelling's when he speculates that a negative deduction produces two different sorts of negatives: first, a positive negative—namely, a deduction of a positive divine nature that exceeds our apprehension; and second, a negative negative, if you will—namely, a deduction of a God whose nature always negates anything at all.[33] Rosenzweig, like Schelling, labels the first aspect as "nature" and the second as "freedom" with the God we do not know, consisting of a restless polarity between each of these characteristics. This "free Nay, shooting forth out of the negation of his Nought, is not in itself essence, for it contains no Yea; it is and remains pure Nay. It is not a 'thus' but only a 'not otherwise.'"[34] Of course, Rosenzweig clarifies that the freedom here spoken of is not the "freedom" of God but rather the freedom "in" God; and within God, as herein deduced, this energy of negation can only act against the divine essence or nature itself. "Caprice seems able to fall upon essence without being summoned or dragged in."[35] Nonetheless, so active upon the divine essence, this freedom, Rosenzweig says, sounding much like Schelling, "ends up in the magic circle of its inert being. This being does not emit any force toward caprice, and yet the latter feels its own force ebbing."[36] Inevitably, this movement culminates in the combination of freedom and nature into an "infinite" or active inertia. "For at that point the infinite power of the divine act so to speak enters the magnetic field of the divine essence, and while this power is still predominant over the inertia of that essence, it is already constrained by it."[37] And the result of this infinite inertia is a silence or solipsism in the exchange between the polarities: a

160   *The Logic of the Law*

God, in other words, that we cannot know. Here is the God who in "The New Thinking," Rosenzweig says, we silently intuit—the God represented by the formalism of Greek mythology or what Rosenzweig refers to as the "pagan God." How then does this God become the God who experiences, the God who exists?

For this, we must consult the account of God as creator in the *Star*. "A certain unrest," Rosenzweig says,

> . . . had overtaken the mythically directed theology of antiquity. It pressed for progress beyond the self-satisfied sphere of myth and thus appeared to demand that reversal of the merely living into the life-giving. . . . Antiquity arrived at monism, but no more. World and man have to become God's nature, have to submit to apotheosis, but God never lowers himself to them. He does not give of himself, does not love, does not have to love.[38]

Still, any emergence from the solipsism of the unknown God would require a prompting from outside this unity. To come into existence requires the impact of an exterior power. In this case, it is God who provides this act Himself because God acts outside his own being with a freedom that both distinguishes itself from this being and affirms this being as well. Rosenzweig says,

> [I]n the beginning . . . God's vitality, which seemed the end, transforms itself into a beginning. . . . This transformation . . . can find expression only as interchange of the two first arch-words. What merged as Yea emerges as Nay and vice versa, much like the contents of a travelers' trunk, which are unpacked in the opposite order from that in which they were inserted. . . . For those acts into which the birth out of the ground is divided do not grow dialectically forth one out of the other . . . the contrast between the dialectical method and that employed here is enormously important.[39]

According to Rosenzweig, the emergence of God as creator is the result of the impact of God's act of freedom upon both aspects of God's silent being. Like Schelling, Rosenzweig describes an event wherein God's act is both a negation or a delimitation of God's being (that is, divine freedom means the power by God to differentiate God-self from God), and God's act is also an affirmation of God's being (divine freedom means the power of God as Other than God-self to love or affirm God-self in the difference of this separation or order). Said otherwise, Rosenzweig describes an event wherein God's existence is founded in the affirming order of God's freedom. Being found in this order does not mean an emergence from a dialectical deduction out of an act of God's freedom. Rather, it means specifically the negation of God's originary freedom or the "not otherwise" into what Rosenzweig calls an "attribute"[40] of power. In this sense, divine freedom delimits the infinite negation of this originary negation and orders this drive or power into the character of a God who exists such that God's energy "is no longer caprice but essence. God the creator is essentially powerful."[41]

The transformation of the originary freedom or "not otherwise" is not a strict negation of this freedom into an antithesis of itself but an affirmation as well because this tendency or drive is affirmed into a feature of the existing God. Law does not produce conflict, and as we saw in "Atheistic Theology," action does not excise. If a dialectical logic presupposes that movement or change involves excision or reduction according to the drive and will of an essence that perdures over and against all else, lawful action or freedom effects change without reduction. Lawful action exposes elements as they exist within an order of other elements. Revelation is orientation. In this particular case, orginary freedom is no longer independent or disordered from divine nature. As such, it is delimited or restricted, and ordered in and by its exposure as an attribute of God as creator. To be ordered and exposed as divine power, originary freedom remains—now named, now identified, and now "revealed."

What Rosenzweig often calls the process that moves from introversion to extroversion is here recognized as an event of divine law or free delimitation and divine grace or affirmation. Of course, the same movement of delimitation and affirmation affects the originary nature, but we will not see the effects of divine freedom upon this nature until we investigate the reversal of God in "Revelation." Nonetheless, it will be the case that in both instances, Rosenzweig describes what it means to say that the God that remains is a God who experiences, at least to the extent that God experiences God-self as the one who makes the world. Existence means revelation. It means the having been acted upon by divine freedom. To be revealed is to be exposed in this affirmation and order.

Of course, for Rosenzweig, as for Schelling, such exposure of God to God-self gives rise to divine self-consciousness or wisdom. The very mechanisms of revelation, law, and grace render divine wisdom possible. As seen from the subjective side, the free God gains objective knowledge of God-self as ordered and affirmed or "revealed" as creator. "The creative power of the manifest God manifests itself in serene vitality, and the caprice of the concealed God reposes at the base of this power." God manifests, or reveals himself to himself, as Creator who exists out of an event of freedom. And although Rosenzweig does not directly link this self-manifestation of God for God to an explicit account of divine self-consciousness, the move to self-manifestation may be likened to Schelling's account of divine self-consciousness whereby divine wisdom means divine reflection upon the object of God's ordering and affirmation. Given the philosophical overlap between the act of divine self-manifestation in Schelling and Rosenzweig, we can identify this sort of divine knowledge as not only a form of wisdom but as a mode of judgment as well because this account of divine self-consciousness offers a philosophical articulation of the character of wisdom we earlier recognized in our analysis of the God of the Sabbatical year in Leviticus 25. As we saw in that discussion, to reflect upon an order or a law is to issue a judgment. In both the biblical and philosophical accounts, divine wisdom is, therefore, a reflection upon lawfulness or a judgment. Moreover, as our reading of Leviticus 25 also indicated, the link between divine wisdom and divine law generates a judgment that both precedes any demand for atonement and perdures throughout and subsequent to atonement. I will discuss this character of divine wisdom *qua* sabbatical judgment in greater detail in the discussion of the nature of the divine-human encounter in Chapter 6.

Viewed *objectively*, however, or from the vantage point of God as creator, knowledge means the awareness or narration of *having been acted upon* by divine freedom, or what is the knowledge of having been ordered and affirmed. This is the second sort of knowledge here made possible that when applied to knowledge of world and persons, will characterize the healthy understanding described by "The New Thinking," to which I will now turn.

WORLD OF PROVIDENCE

The preceding narrative of God's self-revelation as creator resembles Schelling's account in the *Weltalter*. With Rosenzweig's account of the role of divine freedom in the creation of the world, we move away from the *Weltalter*. For Schelling, God's creation of the world remained part and parcel of God's self-revelation, and all reality, world, and persons participated in the divine self-activity. Rosenzweig, however, begins *The Star of Redemption* with a three-part challenge to the philosophy of essentialism, the effects of which are clear in "The New Thinking." Neither God, world, nor man is narratable strictly within the life of the other. If God creates the world, therefore, God creates the world as other. Nonetheless, in the creation of the world as other, God operates with the same logic of freedom manifest in God's relation to God-self as other. It is, as we have seen, characteristic of God that God relates to another through the freedom of law and grace; and in the *Star*, we see the impact of this divine freedom upon the world as created.

According to the negative cosmology of the world offered in the early sections of the *Star*, the world that we do not know is what Rosenzweig here and in "The New Thinking" refers to as the metalogical world or the "plastic cosmos." Not the world of being nor the universal All that one finds in some versions of idealism, the metalogical world here deduced is a self-contained world characterized by a *logos* or law (the "yea") that orders the reality of the distinctive and plural (the "nay") into species, genus, or what Rosenzweig refers to as the "individual" (the ordered particular). Such is the world that irreducibly remains available only to our intuition after the ontological ground-clearing. What happens to this world in the event of divine freedom? As with God, the self-contained world is transformed into a world amidst a network of relations. Divine freedom extroverts the world, and each of the aspects of the world is negated and affirmed in this event.

First, the world's essence or *logos* becomes the universality of existence. If as essence, *logos* was universally applied within the plastic cosmos, now this essence is universally applied as existence. The world's essence is turned outward, facing what is not world, and in this case, God. But turned outward, self-contained universal essence becomes dependent universal existence. Existence is *logos* ordered in relation to and delimited by God. It is the effect of the "no" or differentiation of world from God as this distinction is affected by God's own act of ordering. The world, Rosenzweig says, is always in "constant need for renewal"[42] by God. As existence, it is and must be "seized by the power of God."[43] The world is not God, and therefore needs God to exist.

Second, the particularity of the plastic cosmos (the nay) is also extroverted and ordered as it now constitutes the very universal or essence of the world. Of course, as the universality of existence, the world is not only delimited in the freedom of God—that is, determined as "not" God—but it is also affirmed by God. The world needs the divine renewal day by day, but it does truly exist. As such, therefore, the world is a sign of God's power or providence. If only God's freedom guarantees that the sun will rise in the morning every morning, it is nonetheless the case that it is the sun which rises. "The creature consciousness of the world . . . of being created . . . materializes in the idea of divine providence."[44]

According to the *Star*, God's actions on the world and the signification of these actions or providence in the lawful character of the existence of the world function as a prognostication of a deeper revelation of God that transpires in the unique encounter between God and persons. The particular nature of this encounter between divine freedom *qua* the revelatory God and human beings *qua* loved constitutes the centerpiece of my analysis of the logic of law. For this reason, in addition to the fact that Rosenzweig's "The New Thinking" does not address this particular relationship but analyzes persons only within the larger, more general context of the foundedness of the world in the order and love of the free God, I will defer my discussion of Revelation and love for later. In what remains of my discussion of "The New Thinking," I would like to illuminate the general features of the world view presented in this essay and the *novum* that it offers for an understanding of the meaning of knowledge or wisdom.

THE STRUCTURE OF WISDOM

Having supplemented our reading of "The New Thinking" with the account of divine freedom that it presupposes, we may now recognize how the irreducible realities of God and world, exposed by the ontological cancellation of the essay, are ordered and found in the freedom of God. Their irreducibility on the one hand and availability to interaction on the other presuppose a logic of law, the origins of which can be identified as the act of divine freedom. The environment or world-view presented by "The New Thinking" is one in which each of the elements acts upon and responds to the others within the matrix of the lawfulness and affirmation of God who freely instituted their existence.

What then does knowledge of the world look like in this world-order? For my purposes, there are two important features characteristic of the knowledge of the New Thinking, or the logic of the law: The knowledge of this wisdom is not inherently polemical; and this knowledge is free and rational in so far as it permits at once the assertion of truth claims and presupposes the ability and importance of recognizing the possibility of a position outside of and different from one's own. The knowledge of the logic of the law presents the possibility of an emancipation of knowledge from power as control and introduces a new correlation between knowledge and power as pragmatic action and rightful or lawful response.

The Ills of Polemical Knowledge What do I mean when I say that the knowledge of the New Thinking is not inherently polemical? I have given many examples of polemical knowledge throughout the book, but the fuller presentation of the economy of revelation, existence, and order provided by "The New Thinking" essay permits a wider consideration of the relationship between knowledge and power as control on the one hand, and knowledge and power as free and lawful on the other. Consequently, this broader scope also invites consideration of the reach and ramifications of both

The New Thinking and the Order of Wisdom 165

approaches to knowledge in a way that I have not yet provided. In "The New Thinking," Rosenzweig writes

> [T]he new philosophy does nothing else but make the "method" of healthy human understanding into the method of scientific thinking. Wherein, then lies the difference between healthy human understanding and sick human understanding which . . . sinks its teeth into something that it will not let go before it "has" it in its entirety? [Healthy human understanding] can wait, can keep on living. . . .[45]

In the terms just described, polemical knowledge is "sick." We might risk reading Rosenzweig's terminology as a prognostication of Michel Foucault's analysis of how knowledge as the agency of the power for control propagates the diagnosis of disease along with Foucault's assessment of what knowledge emancipated from power might be. Knowledge is sick when it diagnoses sickness but withholds the possibility of recovery. In this section, first I will use the clear connection between Rosenzweig's account of the sick understanding and Foucault's analysis of knowledge as domination to clarify the character of knowledge as polemical; and second, consider what in both thinkers' estimation amounts to the possibility of knowledge unleashed from the drive of polemical logic.

Like "Atheistic Theology," the more extended account of being found in the order of God provided in the "The New Thinking" introduces a forceful move away from the intellectual by-products of the liaison between knowledge and power as control. If confident in the security of its own irreducibility, the healthy understanding "waits" and receives the activity of another, the sick understanding panics under the false impression of loss and reacts with the urgency for control. Epistemologically speaking, control registers in at least two obvious expressions: the essentialism of a metaphysics of presence on the one hand, and a single historical narrative of the progression of truth from a stable origin forward to a secure *telos* on the other hand. Both expressions demonize and render as diseased elements that do not match with and cannot be co-opted into the categories of an essentialist picture of what is, or an essentialist history of what has been and will be. If we have already understood how knowledge as control excepts what it cannot control as heresy, the assignation of heresy as disease exposes the extent of the danger and violence licensed by a dialectics of desire as it motivates the operations of knowledge and the classification of what is and should be. The sick understanding as described in "The New Thinking" has the potential to inflict damage far beyond the scholarly quibbles over reason or revelation, Hegel or Feuerbach. And although Rosenzweig does not spell out the extent of the possible damage inflicted by polemical knowledge, these ramifications do receive a first airing in Foucault's own commentary on Nietzsche and his and Nietzsche's joint recognition of the passion of control to insist upon an "exact essence of things" indicting "error" as illness or danger.

As the restless operation of control, Nietzsche says that knowledge expresses

> . . . instinct, passion, the inquistor's devotion, cruel subtlety, and malice. It discovers the violence of a position that sides against those who are happy in their ignorance, against the effective illusions by which humanity protects itself, a position that encourages the dangers of research and delights in disturbing discoveries . . . this historical analysis of this rancorous will to knowledge reveals that all knowledge rests upon injustice (that there is no right, not even in the act of knowing, to truth or a foundation for truth) and that the instinct for knowledge is malicious. . . .[46]

In short, Foucault illuminates, falsehood has no rights. It is dismissed *tout court*. If the knowledge of the New Thinking is not inherently polemical, it not only gives the lie to the self-certainty of the dominant logic of our intellectual histories and our classifications of ideologies, the "difference" between 1800 and 1900, Athens versus Jerusalem, the secular and the theological, and so on, but it also exposes the ugliness of its exceptionalism and the real dangers introduced by it toward that which it brands false and incurable.

Rosenzweig's "The New Thinking" introduces the seeds of this account, but Foucault's work expands upon its reach beyond the indictment of error or foolishness and into the incurability of wrong bodies, wrong emotions, wrong relations, wrong cultures, and wrong populations. When power presupposes insufficiency and operates to control or manage loss, it cannot contain its efforts to hold on to and possess what it fears it will lose. And if the greatest challenge to such power is whatever as unruly cannot be mastered, possessed, or regulated, power responds by indulging its self-established right to deem the uncontrollable, the unforgivable, and the expendable. Foucault's work is famous for its ability to unfold the dangerous by-products of this logic when applied to the material life of persons. Here, I will provide only a brief sketch of how the logic of exceptionalism permeates the range of human spheres of existence in my effort to amplify the gravity of a turn to a logic of law now exposed in "The New Thinking."

Of the many examples of the material effects of exceptionalism, we might point to three: namely, Foucault's analysis of the *Hôpital Général*, the asylum, and the nature of bio-power. In *Madness and Civilization*, Foucault says,

The New Thinking and the Order of Wisdom 167

[I]t is common knowledge that the seventeenth century created enormous houses of confinement; it is less commonly known that more than one out of every hundred inhabitants of the city of Paris found themselves confined there, within several months."[47]

From the start, Foucault tells us that "the institution set itself the task of 'preventing mendicancy and idleness as the source of all disorders.' "[48] Nonetheless, the reality and meaning of this institution is more insidious, according to Foucault. "Throughout Europe, confinement had the same meaning. . . . It constituted one of the answers the seventeenth century gave to an economic crisis that affected the entire Western world: reduction of wages, unemployment, scarcity of coin. . . ."[49] Testimonies to the failure of the powers-that-be to diminish and control the force of poverty, European houses of confinement forcibly gathered the excepted and unacceptable elements of society including "the poor, the unemployed, prisoners and the insane . . ." into what Foucault refers to as a "semi-judicial structure . . . [out of which] no appeal [would] be accepted."[50] Founded in 1656, the *Hôpital Général* exemplified an institution of control that not only materialized into the lives of real persons but pretended disingenuously to offer a recovery for the rejected. Indeed, Focuault makes clear that "from the very start, one thing is clear: The Hôpital Général is not a medical establishment."[51] It offered no means for recovery and admission was tantamount to indictment. More a police institution, its fundamental purpose was the separation of those who were deemed valuable to society from those deemed invaluable to society under the auspices of a regulatory-legal discernment of each category. The poor and excepted would be fed in confinement but only at the cost of their rights and freedom.

If the house of confinement enacted exceptionalism in the name of controlling the unruliness of poverty, the asylum institutionalized exceptionalism to control the unruliness of attitudes and emotions. Materially enacting the declaration of heresy by organizing a separation of "right thinking" from "wrong thinking," "healthy thinking" from "diseased thinking," the asylum used its "power" to coerce persons through the exposure of moral norms and judgments rather than through the physical force of gathering bodies into a police-like environment. According to Foucault's analysis, asylums maintained a number of highly effective techniques and mechanisms for identifying and sustaining the grave difference between the mentally accepted and the mentally rejected. After being committed, persons were accused of moral ineptitude and encouraged to feel guilt and anxiety. Such persons were further encouraged to confessional announcements of their depravity. Regularly "observed" by clinicians, patients were taught to identify themselves as insane. Clinical procedures offered no chance for reparative insight but only the deeper recognition of guilt and worthlessness. Like the Confinement House, asylums operated less as medical institutions and more as *faux* juridical institutions wherein

> [M]adness is ceaselessly called upon to judge itself. But beyond this, it is at every moment judged from without; judged not by moral or scientific conscience, but by a sort of invisible tribunal in a permanent session ... the decore of justice, in all its terror and implacability, will thus be part of the treatment and ... the asylum as a juridical instance recognized no other. It judged immediately, and without appeal.[52]

Of course, the asylum was nothing without its clinicians and the diagnosis of depravity correlated with the unshakeable "authority" of the professional. The asylum relied on a professional army of experts, doctors, and psychologists, uniquely capable of "seeing" the signs of madness, recognizing the ills of the insane, and judging the worth of those whose emotional life departed from the "norm." If, however, Foucault adds

> [T]he medical profession is required, it is as a juridical and moral guarantee, not in the name of science ... if the medical personage could isolate madness it was not because he knew it, but because he mastered it; and what for positivism would be an image of objectivity was only the other side of this domination.[53]

Therefore, any unique expert insight reflected less the development of a unique scientific training and more the expert's personal desire for and/or the unwillingness to let go of the power of determination easily expressed through the diagnosis and expulsion of any other, whose fundamental mental or emotional difference might compromise the situation of power so delicately but now institutionally sustained. An aura of authority accompanied the professional; and over time, Foucault discerns, this aura was transferred outside the asylum and on to the medical establishment. "In the patient's eyes, the doctor becomes a thaumaturge, the authority he has borrowed from order, morality, and the family, now seems to derive from himself."[54] When free to develop beyond the level of intellectual judgment, exceptionalism materialized and institutionalized promotes the legitimization of a tyrannical rule of law devoid of rights for and recognition of those it rules.

Finally, exceptionalism can reach beyond the indictment of individual economic value or belief and opinion. Exceptionalism can tyrannize whole populations characterized as other, diseased, and worthless. When it does, the domination of knowledge gives rise to the domination in war and the destruction of life altogether. According to Foucault, the power conditions that legitimize war as a materialization of exceptionalism have changed as a result of changes in the degree of control afforded by technology. If prior to the rise of technology, political power afforded sovereign leaders the freedom to take life away from those who in one way or another challenged their absolute control, the development of technology opened a new venue for the exercise of power: the power to control the productivity of life as proliferated through the new techniques that produce and secure it. The end-game of power remains the same—the means of asserting it and the impact on people has changed. If subject to the sovereign's power persons formerly lived in fear of the possession of their life (materially, spiritually, existentially), modernization transferred the location of coercion to the regulation and control over persons' contributions to the production of life/power. Foucault identifies how this shift appeared in the alteration of justificatory accounts of war from wars of defense (of the sovereign/state) to wars for the welfare of the "life" of the people. Within the context of what Foucault calls "bio-power," persons must "kill . . . in order to go on living."[55]

Still, the willingness to fight another whole people for the sake of protecting one's own so-called ways and means of life constitutes only one aspect of the coercion of political power. All aspects of life can be commodified and rendered valuable to those in power. All aspects of life can become testimonies to the security and veracity of the one or ones who authorize the truth. Consequently, all aspects of life must be regulated, observed, or watched; accounted for; and ultimately, co-opted as the rightful possession of the political power over and against the ownership and rights of living persons. "Such a power has to qualify, measure, appraise, and hierarchize, rather than display itself in its murderous splendor; it does not have to draw the line that separates the enemies of the sovereign from his obedient subjects; it effects distributions around the norm. . . ."[56] Normalization and quantification become valuable tools in the exercise of power; and in this way, bio-power influences all aspects of society—its sciences, its culture, its religion—ultimately imprisoning persons into a scientific and symbolic arena that persistently evacuates the individual, the personal, and the contingent.

Recovering Knowledge, Recovering Power The preceding review of Foucault's analyses reveals the material and not only intellectual impact of knowledge as control or knowledge driven by polemic. Exceptionalism seeps into entire institutional, political, and cultural matrices of life, and as will become clear, has determined the very context—and, consequently, the logic—of Jewish-Christian relations. It is the central contention of this book that Jewish and Christian relations can improve only if first, the dialectics of desire at work within them is exposed; and second; if and when Jewish-Christian conversation operates with a new logic. For his part, Foucault's work contributes to the first task but does little to contribute to the second.

For Foucault, the antidote to a hermeneutics of expertise in all its expressions (intellectual and institutional) is "genealogy." Genealogy unmasks truth wherever it seeks an uncompromising and insistent hold. Beyond this, genealogy documents the failure of truth to sustain a hold and marks its repeated lapse into "error." It illuminates movements and patterns of falsification born of the contingencies that disrupt the knower's drive to stability and certainty—to origins and ends. Humanity, Foucault remarks, "installs each of its violences in a system of rules and thus proceeds from domination to domination."[57] For its part, genealogy earmarks these trends and looks closely at events and their particularities so that

> [T]he purpose of history, guided by genealogy, is not to discover the roots of our identity, but to commit itself to its dissipation. It does not seek to define our unique threshold of emergence, the homeland to which metaphysicians promise a return; it seeks to make visible all of those discontinuities that cross us.[58]

Consequently, genealogy produces a carnival account of history and events, mocking presumptuous idealizations of occurrences and their monuments. Moreover, it systematically dissolves identities. It strips persons of the delusions that buttress their points of stable self-recognition. And, finally, genealogy exposes the underbelly of desire as it drives the pursuit of knowledge. It "dissolves the unity of the subject" and shows the extent to which "knowledge does not slowly detach itself from its empirical roots . . . to become pure speculation subject only to the demands of reason . . . [but] rather . . . creates a progressive enslavement to its instinctive violence."[59]

In contradistinction to an exceptionalism that promotes diagnosis at the expense of rather than for the welfare of the patient, Foucault calls genealogy a "curative science,"[60] which has more in common with medicine than philosophy. Perhaps this is because for Foucault, genealogy diagnoses in order to see what is, whereas exceptionalism diagnoses to see what it wants. Still, it is worth challenging Foucault's identification of genealogy with a curative science. Does genealogy render recovery possible, or is it simply an announcement of the disease without a real solution? If so, does not genealogy's commitment to heterogeneity and the dissolution of monumental thought perpetuate a culture of accuracy, albeit an accuracy of the contingent over and against an accuracy of essence? It appears to me that this is the case. The bravery and insight of Foucault's keen documentation of power constitutes an invaluable contribution, but any "antidote" that denies the vitality of this power and attempts to nullify it renders itself vulnerable to the very charges it launches against essentialism.[61] We might articulate the problem more clearly by saying that Foucault's genealogy eliminates truth. It occupies the strange territory of on the one hand, denying the validity of truth-claims altogether, and on the other hand, insisting upon its own certainty against truth. It illuminates all error except the error of the "truth" that "lauds error." Logically speaking, this epistemological mishap shows us that a vital response to the hermeneutics of expertise cannot fully annihilate desire. It cannot fully destroy the labor of truth-making without undermining itself in the process. But how can a response to exceptionalism sustain desire without polemic? How is it possible to diagnosis the tendency by desire to overreach itself into certainty and also offer an authentic repair? As we will see, the repair offered in the logic of the law is not a repair at all but an opportunity for desire and the will for truth to function *as* desire. Desire is not truth but a longing for it. A logic of the law lets desire remain within the limits of what it is.

To appreciate the transposition of desire into a logic of law requires a review not only of the implications of the New Thinking but a more focused account of the encounter between the free God and the free person. I will offer an account of the implications of the New Thinking here and reserve the detailed account of the divine-human encounter for the next chapter.

Like Foucault's genealogy, the knowledge that we articulate in the order of God is temporal. This knowledge moves, in that this knowledge reacts to rather than attempts to control the actions of others. Consequently, the knowledge of the logic of the law is not a knowledge of fixed concepts but a knowledge of snapshots. It marks a perpetual filming of encounters as they continually alter in the freedom of their movement. Consequently, when applied to a variety of intellectual disciplines, whether it is history, sociology, psychology, political science, or philosophy, the logic of the law sponsors an openness to change and a display of forces as they interact: for example, human beings responding to historical events (history) or natural events (science), or human beings engaging with each other collectively (sociology, economics, politics) or relating to one another emotionally (psychology). From the vantage point of the logic of the law, each of these disciplines receives a new lease on discovery, rooted as each is in a watching that does not delimit a correct characterization or definition of any given analysis. In this way, the logic of the law gifts these disciplines with a past, a present—and, most significantly, a future. They can change, they have changed, and they will change as persons and the world alter in time. If the hermeneutics of expertise insists upon the rights to an unbridled freedom over and against the character of a changing reality, the logic of the law, like Foucault's genealogy, unmasks the illegitimacy of this effort and emancipates knowledge from the limits it imposed.

On the other hand, when beginning this chapter, I noted that any unbridled assertion of truth is always accompanied by its apparent opposite: the reality of anxiety, the unavoidability of guilt, and the denunciation of persons' desires for the particular truths they hold. Given the contingent nature of reality, even sponsors of single-minded truths and their historical and institutional monuments will experience the alienation of portions of themselves and their experiences in the uncompromising accounts that they present. When all is said and done, a hermeneutics of expertise not only renders anxious and worthless those whom it diagnoses as wrong, but it also renders any given individual's particular experience and creative announcement of themselves as, at best, insignificant, and at worst, punishable. If the logic of the law can provide an alternative to the "sick understanding" without becoming mired in an epistemological hall of mirrors like we have seen in Foucault's genealogy, it is only because it is able to offer a basis for the rightful expression of individuals' claims in the very context of the changeability of temporal encounters. Truth must be possible, and truth must be licensed or lawful. Wherein does the logic of the law identify the basis for the dignity of or right to truth?

The key, philosophically, as we have discussed, can be found in the notion of the "something that remains" after the ontological cancellation. There is something irreducible, and we can now understand the philosophical benefits of our deduction from the identification of the three somethings that remain in "The New Thinking" to the activity of divine freedom out of which each arose and continues to arise. We now appreciate how the reality of God, world, and persons as we encounter them is a reality given in the freedom of God; and as such, it is a reality simultaneously gifted and ordered because as we have seen, it is the order and lawfulness of existence that permits the retention of existence. It is law that gifts. God's freedom performs affirmation through order, that which is can only be so far as it is given and so far as it is distinct. Consequently, we can see that the rightfulness of a something that exists derives from the lawfulness of its being what it is and not being what something else is.

The New Thinking and the Order of Wisdom 173

From here, we can understand how the logic of the law not only sponsors the changeability of knowledge/s but encourages the announcement of (temporary) truths as well. Truths alter with time, the argument is, but it is *truths* that alter. Communities make assertions. Disciplines advance bodies of knowledge. Persons identify with families and peoples and histories. The logic of law will not dismantle our curriculums or our disciplines or our efforts to locate ourselves in communities. Nor will it deny these rights to others. The logic of law recovers truth, and it recovers power within the context of a lawful pragmatism.

By a lawful pragmatism, I mean an account of knowledge and power that exposes the coordination between desire or power and the rights of others as exercised in the production of knowledge and in the functioning of social structures. Epistemologically speaking, if the logic of the law maps encounters, it does not map encounters from a bird's-eye view. It does not advance a body of knowledge other than that generated by persons with varying perspectives—and, most significantly, varying interests. We are interested in the world we live in, and consequently, we are interested in the world that we make.

> The knowing from which something comes out, just as with a cake, something must also have been put in. . . . Even in truth itself, the ultimate . . . an "and" must stick; otherwise than the truth of the philosophers, which may know only itself, it must be truth for someone. . . . And it thereby becomes a necessity that our truth becomes manifold and that "the" truth transforms itself into our truth. Thus truth ceases to be what "is" true and becomes that which has to be verified as true.[62]

The preceding quote from Rosenzweig sounds similar to the pragmatism of the American philosopher William James, who in his famous essay, "Pragmatism's Conception of Truth," wrote

> Pragmatism . . . asks its usual question. "Grant an idea or belief to be true," it says, "what concrete difference will its being true make in any one's actual life? How will the truth be realized? What experiences will be different from those which would obtain if the belief were false? What, in short is the truth's cash-value in experiential terms? . . . The possession of truth, so far from being here an end in itself, is only a preliminary means towards other vital satisfactions. . . ."[63]

One might say that the difference between Foucault and James has all to do with the difference in their appetite for our passions. James's the "Will to Believe" is a testament to our "right" to believe what we want under certain circumstances.[64] The desire to know is not something to be ashamed of or anxious over, as in Foucault. Of course, both James and Foucault are correct. Our desire plays an inextricable role in our knowledge, and at times, it behaves violently, and at times, contributes creatively. The logic of the law does not nullify desire but recognizes it as the motive and motor of our perspectives. But for the logic of law, this desire acts. It does not control, and it does not have to control. Desire controls when suffering scarcity. Desire controls when nothing remains. Even James cannot successfully argue against the possibility of a desire that overreaches; and consequently, cannot generate the basis for a pluralism of mutual recognition between persons and communities of varying interests.[65] The logic of the law, on the other hand, emerges from the being found in the order of God and out of the sufficiency of the divine affirmation—God's "yes" to what differs in its order. Divine freedom licenses our desire, and in turn, desire acts in its own freedom to promote and articulate itself. The irreducibility of God and the irreducibility of world and the irreducibility of other persons check this drive and sustain it as the drive of a particular perspective. Truth is recognized as the common sense and healthy account of the person or persons issuing the claim in that particular temporal, localized encounter.

Consequently, the logic of the law retains truth or recovers truth and not only the truth of the one who asserts a claim but the truth of another as well. It invites a full account of the recognition of another's position in a fashion that we saw alluded to but not entirely possible in the neo-Hegelianism of the late Gillian Rose. A vital knowledge, Rose understood, is a lawful knowledge—a knowledge that admits the self's need for recognition and the rights of the other for recognition. But the freedom to make claims and the possibility of the mutual recognition of others' claims requires a prior source of legitimacy what Rose herself refers to as "grace" when despite her virulent attack on theologies of "holy cities," she nonetheless recognizes the need for law as a site of transcendence and says, "Law is abundant and abounding: it is not the contrary of grace. . . ."[66] As discussed in Chapter 3, Rose references this link between grace and law to explain how and why persons can sustain their commitment to social life despite the inevitable anxiety that it produces. As we as earlier, however, even though Rose recognizes the philosophical requirement of grace, devoid of a robust theology of revelation, she cannot demonstrate the link between this grace and the law such that it can provide relief to the dialectical context between persons under the law. From Rose, therefore, we learn that we cannot arrive at the possibility of mutual recognition from one another alone. Left to ourselves, we are driven by desire.

However, unlike Rose's account of the law, the logic of the law reveals that we are not alone. We cannot reduce God and world to ourselves. Human intersubjectivity is not sufficient and cannot subsume the alternative realities of God and world. Human sociality meets with a freedom exterior to itself, a freedom of world, and ultimately, a freedom of God, which promotes the perpetual affirmation that roots my freedom and the freedom of others as well. Divine self-knowledge or wisdom performs or enacts the freedom of the law and the law of freedom, and it is this wisdom that renders an affirmative and creatively changing body of human knowledge possible.

Moreover, this epistemological reorganization of desire and social recognition affords a recovery of the reality of power as well. The epistemological reorganization of the logic of the law derives from the presupposition of powers. If within the logic of law, existence is free, as I have argued, then it is also the case that existence is power. It is the power to act as the "something that remains" within a network of free and ordered relations. When in this paradigm, power is adjudicated by the very conditions of its own existence—namely, the freedom of God—power need not be sacrificed; it need not be excepted by a thorough-going critique of knowledge as interest, as represented by Foucault's account of genealogy. In the context of the logic of the law, power is action. It is worth distinguishing between this concept of power as action and the notion of power as control premised upon the inability of desire to fulfill itself that we have seen exercised in our examples of exceptionalism.

Within the logic of the law, power means the ability to freely identify the excesses of desire unadjudicated—what epistemologically amounts to what I have called "ground-clearing," or what Foucault calls "genealogy." When applied to actions, such ground-clearing registers as political critique or resistance to tyrannical expressions of power. However, if the logic of the law goes farther than Foucault's genealogy epistemologically, it also goes farther in offering a new view of action or power as something other than political critique. Funded by a surplus of divine freedom, action within the logic of the law is not contingent upon the contest between itself and tyrannical power. Said otherwise, there are two different ways for persons to recognize and/or critique tyrannical forces of power. Foucault's account suggests an insidious dialectic between critique and tyranny. This dialectic is rooted in an acceptance of the fundamentally anarchic and thereby tyrannical character of desire or power. Consequently, the denunciation of power as anarchic deprives resistance or critique of its own power, leaving it weak and parasitic upon the forces of tyranny to which it reacts. Within the logic of the law, however, critique or resistance to an abuse of power is funded by an alternative source of power from the freedom of God. Within the logic of the law, it is more accurate to say that what we might first refer to as a critique of an abuse of power is better understood as a recognition of a failure of power by those who attempt to impose their will upon others. Control, as I have suggested, is not power. Control is a reaction to a lack of power—a lack of rights or freedom—and therefore manifests itself in theoretical and practical expressions of exceptionalism that inevitably except or alienate those who seek to protect themselves through it.

Within the logic of the law, consequently, the ability to critique or resist control derives not from a reaction to control but from a consciousness of the limits and rights of desire as found in the order of the free God. So grounded, critique transforms into or is enacted as the possibility of free action. Theory and practice are inseparable because both are rooted in the freedom of their lawful power. This account of power in the logic of the law shares much in common with the account of power in the work of Talal Asad, and in order to give an example of what this power looks like, we might turn to a brief discussion of two examples of Asad's analysis of the nexus between religion, power, and rights.

The first example I want to look at is found in Asad's critique of Clifford Geertz's analysis of religion. In the essay, "The Construction of Religion as an Anthropological Category," Asad offers an analysis of Geertz's "Religion as a Cultural System," in which Geertz offers his classic definition of religion. The point of Asad's article is to expose the nature and function of power in Geertz's own effort to define religion. Asad's analysis of Geertz's dance with power resembles the earlier account of the critique of power from the perspective of the logic of the law. In Asad's estimation, Geertz's definition of religion is an assertion of power as control—an assertion of power that exposes the lack of power. Asad presents two reasons for this view. First, Geertz asserts his definition of religion within the context of and as a reaction to his assessment of the power of secularism. No doubt, Geertz's definition is an expression of force, but it is not an expression of power because it is a response to the loss of power by religion within secular society. Second, Asad argues, Geertz is unaware of his own assertion of or attempt to assert power. Neither does he recognize his effort to define religion as control, nor does he recognize it as a rightful reaction to the usurpation of the role of religion by the secular. In Asad's estimation, therefore, Geertz's assertion of what constitutes religion is an exercise in the defeat of power and the substitute of it by control and fear.

By alternative, Asad suggests that the way to "have" power is to admit power or to be "found in power." Geertz fails to recognize the *sitz im leben* of symbols and their currency. He does not recognize that he is found in power, and that they are found in power, and that the key to power is the self-awareness of these locations and their forces. But what is this power in contrast to the aforementioned? It is the power of action. It is the power of forces that affect what is found within them—the power that "acts" upon a something found or affected by it. Power in this sense is freedom and not impotence. If control denies or avoids force, power presupposes the recognition of the reality and possibility of action and deed. To be found in power is to be affected by it and to recognize the opportunity to reciprocally act in response.

Asad exposes the difference between power and coercion again in a second example from the article, "French Secularism and the Islamic Veil Affair," which discusses the French government's law prohibiting veil wearing by Muslim women. In this article, Asad discusses how the French government attempts to define the meaning of the veil as an effort to control its society but fails to admit the assertion of "control" that it here performs. By contrast, Asad, the reader, and Muslim women demonstrate the meaning of power as recognition and power as action—in this instance, the power that recognizes the force of the French government. To recognize the French government's act as an act of power is the key to transforming the passivity of control into a free act of response. This is not only because knowledge or awareness is "power," if you will, but more so because the recognition of the forces of power in one's midst serves as a catalyst for the *re-actions*—of those affected by it. By exposing the forces within this particular location of power, Asad's article emancipates its readers, and the Muslim women in France themselves, to act back: to act in return. One good expression of power deserves another, and what emerges is an exchange of free actions instead of a clandestine exercise in control and impotence on both sides.

Asad's analysis calls for an exposure of power as freedom, just as I have presented in the logic of the law. Actions and interactions of this sort are not conflict driven because they presuppose the existence of the actions of others. When action is not stolen from under the authority and tyranny of another's illegitimate monopolization of power, it need not act "against" or in an effort to tear down the forces with which it engages. Conflict arises from a lack of power not from what Rosenzweig calls an "open field of actuality,"[67] which permits actors to behave freely as regulated by the rights of all to perform freely.

Judaism, Christianity, and the World   The preceding discussion brings us full circle back to Rosenzweig's and Rosenstock-Huessy's early conversations concerning the responsive nature of knowledge. We can now appreciate how both sides of a telling are always right in that both offer an exposition of the "what happened." Moreover, and equally as important, we can also appreciate how even though both sides of a telling can be right, neither account can *definitively* [although it can provisionally] falsify the other. The logic of law offers the legitimacy of a freedom of accounts without the tyranny of any one of them. The delimitation by the law is not a source of conflict (violence) for the one who narrates but the condition of the possibility of the freedom to narrate. If I am free to assert my claim as true, there is little benefit to the additional insistence upon the falsehood of the other.[68] Of course, within the order of God's freedom, there is no other mode of truth outside the truths of events—the proclamation of the operations of God's freedom as it is played out in our relations. Consequently, there is no other truth to lose. As we recall, it is on this point that Rosenzweig parted company with Rosenstock-Huessy. Although the two friends claimed agreement regarding the dialogical character of knowledge, only Rosenzweig sustained his commitment to this account and developed it in his New Thinking. By contrast, Rosenstock-Huessy identified Christ as the central meaning of history, and this, as we saw, constituted a point of no return for their personal dialog on the one hand and the prospects of a successful Jewish-Christian dialog on the other. I leave, therefore, this discussion of the New Thinking with a few introductory comments regarding the radical suggestions it presents for a new reading of Jewish-Christian relations from a logic of law before providing a more expansive discussion of this topic in Chapter 6.

The central premise of this volume rests upon the identification of what is commonly referred to as *supersessionism* (the notion that the gospel supersedes or replaces the Jewish covenant) and the logic operating within the dialectics of desire. Given the preceding discussion, we can now begin to appreciate the benefits of the approach to knowledge characteristic of the logic of the law for the particular question of the knowledge pursued in Jewish-Christian relations. Two features immediately present themselves with this analysis. To start, Christian-Jewish relations easily fall prey to supersessionism because supersessionism is an expression of the dialectics of desire. Where the latter is present, the former is inevitable. Consequently, a nonsupersessionist Jewish-Christian dialog must be nonsupersessionist all the way down. By this, I mean that a nonsupersessionist Jewish-Christian dialog will abide by standards that will inform Jews' relations to Christians and Christians' relations to Jews along with both of their relations to the non-Jewish and the non-Christian world. As will become clearer, this does not mean that the Jewish-Christian relationship does not possess unique characteristics. It does mean, however, that neither can assert a polemical position over and against non-Jews or non-Christians and still sustain an anti-supersessionist position. In "The New Thinking," Rosenzweig introduces a few brief remarks regarding a Judaism and Christianity within the logic of the law that will contribute to the more extended account that I will present of their nonsupersessionist apologetic relationship as I discuss it in Chapter 6.

In "The New Thinking," Rosenzweig introduces the logical structure of Judaism and Christianity as historically revealed traditions. His brief allusions to both revolve around three points: Neither Judaism nor Christianity need be fanatical; this does not mean that either tradition needs be subject to the standards of an external reality; and Judaism and Christianity do relate to one another polemically at times. Each does retain an ability to overreach in its claims.

As argued, the logic of law, rooted in the event of divine freedom, engenders an existential irreducibility that grounds and shapes a rationality of lawful truth-making and social recognition. When applied to Jewish and Christian relations, perhaps one of the most refreshing by-products of such an orientation consists in the alteration of the relationship between Judaism, Christianity, and what has in the same breath been referred to as paganism, too often demonized as the arch-enemy of both historically rooted, revelatory traditions. In "The New Thinking," Rosenzweig remarks, "the special position of Judaism and Christianity consists precisely in this: that even if they have become religion, they find in themselves the impulses to free themselves from their religiosity and to leave the specialness and its surroundings in order to find their way back to the open field of actuality."[69] The argument here is that Judaism and Christianity are special in their ability to free themselves from the necessity of identifying with such a label. As I discuss in greater detail, the logic of the law demands a reconsideration of the meaning of election as it operates within both traditions. At the heart of the logic of the law is a crucial and philosophically unprecedented correlation between the notion of election as a unique, yet not fanatical or polemical, relationship between the revelatory God and the community who receives this revelation. Although many within the Jewish thought canon have sought to demonstrate the rationality of election, none have located the rationality of election squarely within the character of divine revelation and its reception itself but have either demythologized the meaning of revelation altogether (for example, Maimonides, Cohen, Levinas) or have separated the rational aspect of election from the revelatory content and located it within the rational character of a created world, which provides a rational "ground" or condition for a subsequent revelation (Novak).

The logic of the law is a logic of revelation. As indicated by "The New Thinking," existence is revealed, and there is no created order not already taken up in and affected by the freedom and revelation of God. Wisdom is, therefore, God's free and lawful actions revealed to both the world and to persons; and all encounters, regardless of whether they are between persons and the world or between persons and God take place within the context of God's revelatory acts. "Should God have waited for mount Sinai, or even Golgotha?"[70] Rosenzweig asks in the "The New Thinking." "Clearly he did not . . . as little as paths lead from Sinai or from Golgotha, on which He can be reached with certainty, so little can He have denied himself the [possibility] of encountering even the person who sought Him on the trails around Olympus."[71] Revelation is not exclusively for Jews or for Christians, but neither is it an absolute outpouring of divine exposure into one location or another. Divine revelation is the action of divine freedom as it orders and affirms exterior existences. It can be correlated neither with natural law on the one hand nor theological positivism on the other.

If, however, Judaism and Christianity exist in the context of the order of divine revelation, this means that any version of a nonsupersessionist Judaism[72] or Christianity must go all the way down. By this, I mean that not only will the logic of the law reposition Judaism and Christianity with respect to each other, but it will also incorporate both of them into a nonpolemical orientation with respect to other possible truth claims. Recall, for example, Rosenstock-Huessy's assertion that "the stubbornness of the Jews is today no longer a Christian dogma. Christ today has people enough in his church to crucify him! . . . Today there are States and the Church where formerly there were peoples and the Synagogue."[73] In one fell swoop, Rosenstock-Huessy dismisses Judaism on account of its inability to verify Christianity in its [Judaism's] falsehood and introduces paganism as the new best heresy to assert oneself against. Consider on the other hand a variation of the same logic of exceptionalism toward non-Jewish and non-Christian traditions in Michael Wyschogrod's work as described by Kendall Soulen. "For Wyschogrod, theologically significant conversation between Jews and Christians is possible because both Judaism and Christianity acknowledge 'a movement of God toward humankind as witnessed in Scripture' a movement that engages humankind in God's election of Israel." As I will discuss further in the next chapter, Wyschogrod's attempt to bridge the divide between Judaism and Christianity through the assertion of a common truth nonetheless sustains a polemic between both traditions and the remainder of "non-elect" persons and communities. Both instances present the logic of supersessionism even when it is not (apparently) applied to the adversarial relationship between Judaism and Christianity.

Instead, the logic of the law initiates a new mapping of old categories that orders Judaism and Christianity within the wider world of God's freedom and thereby licenses us to ask for new historical accounts of the relationships between Judaism, Christianity, and the non-Jewish and non-Christian worlds they have participated in. At the very least, this ordering of Christianity and Judaism in the world promises new directions for the academic study of both traditions. On the one hand, the logic of the law resembles the move away from genealogies and toward the possibility of a robust and detail-specific analysis of religious data replete with comparisons between this data and the data from other religions and nonreligious cultures seen in the work of Jonathan Z. Smith.[74] On the other hand, the location of Judaism and Christianity in the logic of the law also resonates with the emancipation of religious studies from the commitment to a prior definition of religion found in the work of Talal Asad.[75] If Asad's methodological dismissal of definitions of religion was lodged in his review of Geertz's own attempt to define and ultimately safeguard the phenomenon of religion over and against what Geertz took to be an encroaching secularism, Asad's response illuminates the implicit dialectics of desire at play in Geertz's analysis whereby an essential and defined difference could be posited between the "religious" and the "secular." By exposing this dynamic in Geertz's method, Asad opens the possibility of an analysis of religion that like the logic of the law calls into question the perpetual contest between religion and secularity presupposed in Geertz's definitional approach to the study of religion.

At the very most, the location of Judaism and Christianity within the wider order of the revelation of God presents the possibility of a higher level of existential and dialogical engagement between both traditions and the non–Judeo-Christian world around them. Although the ultimate objective of this project is to demonstrate a new basis for a Jewish-Christian apologetic, the active range of divine freedom in the world means an alteration in the nature of Judaism and Christianity's participation in pluralist environments. With this claim, however, it becomes important to revisit a comparison between the rational character of the logic of the law and the rational character of natural law—and in particular, the minimalist account of natural law as both the ground and delimitation of revelatory traditions offered by David Novak that in his view renders Jewish and Christian participation in a multicultural environment possible and desirable. I want to reserve the lengthier analysis of Novak's views on Jewish-Christian relations for comparison with my own more developed account of Jewish-Christian apologetics in Chapter 6. Suffice it to say for now, however, that philosophically and theologically speaking, the fundamental difference between by the logic of the law and Novak's account of natural law and its possibilities for multicultural participation has to do with the character of law as natural or revelatory in both of our accounts.

As analyzed in Chapter 3, Novak's account of natural law links natural law (the reality of another to delimit the sovereignty of my own assertions) to what he refers to as "theological desire." Natural law, in Novak's language, intends revelation. Nonetheless, natural law is not revelation: It derives from human intersubjectivity and, consequently, delimits self-certainty without offering recognition of the self's truth-claims. As I suggested in Chapter 3, Novak's distinction between natural law and revelatory law permits the retention of a contest between law and desire; and therefore, if believers' truth-claims are asserted on the basis of their desires [even theological desires], these very claims become delimited by the minimal standards of a natural law, which is none other than the identification of persons making claims as finite and ineligible as presenters of absolute truth. The assertion that believers should not be able to make absolute truth-claims is in and of itself not a problem. What is a problem is the extent to which the agency of delimitation upon revelatory truth claims is outside of and/or other than these claims themselves. Said otherwise, religious believers, in this context, are rational only when they subject their truth-claims to the limits of a law that casts doubt upon their veracity. Desire in this account remains unreconciled, unadjudicated, and unjustified. Natural law cannot admit its legitimacy, just as Foucault's genealogy rendered desire dangerous always. In the case of Novak's analysis, the consequences of this model of law appear in the character of the conversation that he considers possible within a multicultural setting.

Although it is the case that Novak's account of religion in a multicultural space has challenged John Rawls's classic prioritization of the "right" over the "good," or just procedure over thick description teleological accounts of the good as viable points of discussion within a pluralist public square, Novak roots his challenge to Rawls in his account of the link between natural law and theological desire as it not only intends but is singularly manifest within the actual content of a revealed tradition. Said otherwise, natural law never exists in established, positive principles shared by a hypothetical nonteleologically invested rational community, according to Novak, but constitutes the negative limits implicit within any positive revelatory claim.

> Universal thinking by very particularly formed persons seems to be an imaginative attempt to constitute a world that would be the case if I were not part of the singular culture in which I now have been living concretely. But does this world actually correspond to anything we have really experienced? Any attempt to locate some universal moral phenomena is so vaguely general as to be normatively useless.[76]

Consequently, in Novak's account, natural law cannot be severed from revelation, and this undermines Rawls's effort to separate the two (at least in his early work). However, Novak's assertion of the "good" over the "right" is an overstatement because elsewhere, he clearly states that the "locus of concern" of natural law is "the question of truth, which, in its critical function, is primarily a negation of the arrogant pretensions of humans acting as if they themselves were infinite."[77] Natural law is not the *telos* of positive law but strictly the limit or minimal conditions necessary for positive law to function justly. Natural law never determines the positive content of particular traditions. Consequently, to the extent to which natural law offers a basis for either comparative ethics and/or multicultural conversation generally speaking, it does so only with respect to the overlap in minimal conditions shared by varying traditions and not with respect to positive claims or assertions about revelation or anything else for that matter.

The upshot of all of this is that from this perspective, revelatory claims cannot be admitted into rational conversation. They are lawful not by virtue of what they claim but only with respect to what they do not claim. Revelatory claims can be held, consequently, only in fear and trembling—in the anxiety or concern that one might attempt to overreach in one's presentation of them. The problem with Novak's account is a problem shared by all accounts of dialectical theology or dialectical thought wherein reason is identified with and outsourced by the character of human finitude. When law emerges from an intersubjective account, it is not free. Only law that arises from divine freedom installs the rights and legitimacy of truth-claims motored by desire.

Within the logic of the law, Jews and Christians are free to participate in a multicultural conversation whose contents include the free assertion of revelatory claims delimited and affirmed by their articulation in the context of the larger order of revelatory wisdom. Read from the perspective offered in "The New Thinking," therefore, we might note that although Rosenzweig indeed suggested that God did not have to wait for Sinai or Golgotha to reveal God-self, this does not mean that neither Jewish nor Christian testimony are valuable, legitimate, and consequently rational and well suited for presentation to others. Applied to his own work, Rosenzweig admits that *The Star of Redemption* is both a philosophical and a Jewish book. It is philosophical because God did not wait for Sinai. It is Jewish because just as

> ... for a Christian, the words of the New Testament would have come to his lips instead of my world ... to me these came. And ... this is, to be sure ... a Jewish book: not one that deals with "Jewish things," for then the books of the protestant Old Testament scholar would be Jewish books; but rather one for which, to say what it has to say ... the old Jewish words come ... like things in general, Jewish things have always passed away; yet Jewish words, even when old, share the eternal youth of the word, and if the world is opened up to them, they will renew the world.[78]

Of course, the fact that Judaism and Christianity may positively assert themselves in a nonsupersessionist expression both to the other and to others more broadly conceived does not mean that neither retains the tendency to overreach and wax dogmatic. As his analysis of what he referred to as "chosen people theology" in the early essay, "Atheistic Theology," demonstrated, Judaism and Christianity can attempt a theological reduction and assert themselves mythologically as theological sufficient. But "chosen-people theologies," or the Christian equivalent that he refers to as "life-of-Jesus theologies," guarantee a polemical and nonpersuasive approach to others. Attempts by both traditions to reduce the theological to a human experience or apprehension coterminously bolster their efforts to demonize the difference presented in other traditions or cultures. More importantly, by siphoning off what they might deem unacceptable, they isolate themselves from aspects of themselves, recoverable only after the exercise of demonization comes to an end, and each tradition permits itself to be adjudicated by the lawful order which alone justifies its claims. We might note, however, that the antidote to Jewish-Christian enmity is not a *faux* tolerance but a recognition of the reality of enmity as an indicator of an unadjudicated desire operative within the fashioning of truth-claims. Undoubtedly, as we will see, both Judaism and Christianity have the means to adjudicate their own deviations from lawful testimony. In point of fact, as I will show, their common appreciation for revelatory wisdom and lawful order even permits the one to incite this adjudication in the other, but I get ahead of myself with these points, and they will be developed more extensively in the next chapter.

PART THREE

Justification in the Law and Jewish-Christian Apologetics

SIX

The Law of Freedom, the Freedom of the Law

Persons Found in the Order of God

The preceding discussion and analysis has introduced the blueprint of the logic of the law as I see it emerge in Rosenzweig's post-Schelling account of the freedom of God. With the discussion of how the freedom of God acts as law and grace upon God as other and world as other, we reach the centerpiece of this analysis: the account of the encounter between divine freedom and human persons. This discussion constitutes the heart of my analysis because as an application of the logic of law to the encounter between God and persons, it offers a reinterpretation of the biblical account of the divine human relationship or what is later called *election*. One of the key arguments of this book is that one cannot casually invoke a doctrine of election without rigorous scrutiny regarding the structure presupposed, and in particular, the character of freedom and rights herein implied. Therefore, at stake in this philosophical reinterpretation of the biblical account of election is a repair of the profile of divine freedom and human freedom in the divine-human encounter. The argument here, already anticipated by the review of the logic of the law earlier, is that freedom and law are not diametrically opposed but reciprocal concepts so far as they emerge first from an act of divine freedom and subsequently infuse the performance of human freedom. We might say that theological freedom transpires through law and that law is, therefore, an expression of freedom. By correlation, persons are free in the law, and human freedom is lawful. In what follows, I will use Rosenzweig's *The Star of Redemption* as a jumping off point for exposing this philosophical reading of the biblical doctrine of election with two objectives in mind: the exposure of the difference between this account and other accounts of election wherein the said link between freedom and law is not sustained; and the establishment of the philosophico-theological groundwork for a Jewish-Christian apologetic or free learning predicated upon the principle of justification through the law.

THE REVELATORY GOD

The encounter between the free God and persons founded in the order of the free God begins with an account of the disclosure through the law and affirmation of God's freedom upon Godself as revealer. Rosenzweig discusses this conversion of God's exteriorization into revealer in the famous Part II of *The Star of Redemption*. There, Rosenzweig reminds us that just as it was "original freedom . . . the untrammeled passion of the mythical God, which burst forth from the concealed God into the light of the new days as divine creative power . . . so too the *moira* of God, that fateful divine essence, now seeks a path into the open. . . ."[1] Earlier juxtaposed against the working of divine freedom within the concealed God of the negative theological account, divine nature had been largely responsible for sustaining the concealment of God within God-self prior to the effects of the divine act of freedom, at least so far as Rosenzweig's negative deduction determined. Now, it is this impulse to divine inertia that undergoes alteration through God's free encounter with God's being. Divine freedom issues, as we recall, a "yes" and a "no" in its impact upon this feature of divine being, and in this case, divine inertia or fate is transposed into divine love "for love alone is at once such fateful domination over the heart in which it stirs and yet so newborn, initially so without a past, so wholly sprung from the moment which it fulfills and only from that moment."[2] As the "yes" and the "no" of divine freedom upon its own nature, divine love is that fateful impulse formerly committed to removing God from all that is other now motivating God to an "ever new self-denial, unconcerned with whatever may have preceded or be yet to come ... wholly offspring of the immediately present coup d'oeil, the live-in moment."[3] With this conversion from divine fate to divine love, God's freedom generates God's complete manifestation not only to the world as in creation, but now more specifically to human persons. Of course, such a revelation "does not posit anything" so far as all revelation, is act or event and never proposition. Despite the coming into manifestation achieved in creation, the creator God nonetheless "threatened to lose himself ... behind the infinity of creation." Consequently, the revelation of God in love means "the opening of something locked, none other than the self-negation of a mere mute being. ..."[4]

REVEALED PERSONS

If the coming to be of the revealer God transforms the creator God into a God who loves, what takes place in the interaction between the freedom of God as revealer and human persons? How do persons come into existence as the recipients of this freedom? Before answering this question, we must answer the epistemologically prior question: namely, who is the person that we do not know? As we have discussed, Rosenzweig applies Schelling's negative theological deduction to a negative cosmological deduction and here to a negative anthropological deduction. We do not know persons. As we recall, Rosenzweig, like Schelling, maintains that a negative deduction produces two different sorts of negatives: a positive-negative: namely, a deduction of a positive human nature that exceeds our apprehension; and a negative-negative: namely, a deduction of a person whose nature always negates anything at all. In the case of persons, the positive negative consists in an affirmation of the ephemerality of human existence: It is finite. On the other hand, the negative negative—the deduction of persons whose nature always negates anything at all—appears here as freedom: more specifically, a freedom of will in contrast to the divine freedom of deed. Together, the negative deduction provides an account of persons as finite beings with free will. Still, these two elements react one to another as was the case with God, and to the extent that human freedom strives to overwhelm its essence as finite, persons in Rosenzweig's account become identified as selves acting to secure their own peculiarity—as, Rosenzweig says, "in defiance"[5] of anything else. Rosenzweig's deduction leads to the profile of a tragic hero, driven to preserve his own particularity: a particularity that over and against the universal, arises strictly in the peculiarity of love (*eros*) and/or the supreme individuality of a person's death (*thanatos*). Always driven inward, the tragic self "knows nothing outside itself: it is inherently solitary. . . . How is it to manifest its solitude, this stubborn self-reliance, other than precisely by keeping silent . . . the heroic is speechless. . . ."[6]

The divine-human encounter begins with this profile of persons as secluded in finitude and driven away from relation and exteriority. Book II of the *Star* offers a narration of the event of God's interaction with humankind as testified to by the biblical writers. Here, Rosenzweig retells the narrative of divine revelation found in the Song of Songs. Rosenzweig describes an event of unprecedented love from an Other that because it is love, and therefore exterior, cannot be controlled by the recipient and can only be referred to by the beloved through her desire for more. The effect of divine freedom as "yes" and "no" or affirmation and lawful difference first registers as the conversion of the free defiance of the secluded self into the freedom of a humble self. What was once pride or freedom now registers as "awe"[7] or proclamation for the "grace of a Superior"[8] who offers this unprecedented love. Persons are affirmed [grace] in divine freedom as ones who can testify to the awe of God. On the other hand, the freedom of God affects a difference between God and persons—a difference that secures this affirmation, rendering it free from reduction [law]. With regard to persons loved by God, this amounts to the difference between the love of God as ceaseless and selfless, and the love of persons who love only as they are loved and only through their desire for more love.

The *novum* in Rosenzweig's account of divine revelation as love concerns the two-fold character of this love as expressed by God on the one hand and as received by persons on the other. Divine love is indiscriminate, complete, and wholly present. The beloved in turn experiences a feeling of "awe together with a feeling of dependence and of being securely sheltered or of taking refuge in the arm of eternity. . . ."[9] Yet, the reception of divine love is momentary and fleeting. Radical dependence means uncertainty concerning the return of this love. Confident in the love she has received, the beloved nonetheless experiences this confidence through her desire for more love. Experientially, the beloved can attest to having received love. Epistemologically and linguistically, she can only describe and witness to it through the language of desire. Recipients of revelation experience divine love as theological desire.

This desire, grounded in an event of divine exteriority, motivates and supports a temporalized process of pragmatic verification, and the beloved and ultimately her community engage in a perpetual process of discerning and announcing their desire for God. By definition, desire points to the object that it longs for in the context of its absence. Hinged between certainty and doubt, desire is often expressed through an interrogative: a Where is God? In contrast, however, to atheistic doubt or skepticism, this interrogative joins with the pragmatic reach that grounded in the eventfulness of the divine gift can proclaim that God is "here." Testimony of this sort publicizes divine love supporting a pragmatic performance of divine descent. Religious life in Rosenzweig's account consists in the pendulum swing between an individual or community's desirous cry for the presence of divine love and the verification that God is here, pragmatically sustained in the hope made reasonable by the [initial and possibly repeated] event of the divine gift.

With this two-sided account of the revelation of divine love, Rosenzweig coins his own version of religious materialism. Divine revelation speaks to and transforms the material and historical life of recipients. Divine love greets human desire. Theological desire navigates between human need and theological witness, and history is the playing field for the encounter as desires change with time. "Desires," Rosenzweig says, "are the messengers of confidence."[10] Longing and confidence meet in wishes or hope, and collective hope is defined by attentive listening. Persons are not asked to believe in a God whose projected reality falsifies their needs as long as the needs projected are accepted and verified by the community. In his essay, "Rennaissance of Jewish Learning," Rosenzweig describes the character of this community life and learning and says

> At a university the student is faced with the edifice of a science that is complete in general outline and only needs development in detail; it lies outside the student, and he must enter it and make himself at home in it. This movement, however would begin with its own bare beginnings, which would be simply a space to speak in and time in which to speak. . . . To begin with, don't offer them anything. Listen. And words will come to the listener, and they will join together and form desires. . . . Desires that join and men that join together: Jews—and an attempt is made to supply them with what they ask for . . . those who know how to listen to real wishes may also know perhaps how to point out the desired way. . . . For the teacher able to satisfy such spontaneous desires cannot be a teacher according to a plan; he must be much more and much less, a master and at the same time a pupil . . . he himself must be able to "desire". . . . The teachers will be discovered in the same discussion room . . . as the students.[11]

Theological discourse links the language of desire with the proclamation of God. This explains why and how Rosenzweig will say that "the thought of the choseness of the Jewish people is the prerequisite for thought as well as life ... the monstrous actuality of Jewish being has created for itself a self-protection...."[12] Jewish thinking arises from the materiality of the Jewish people and their will to self-preservation. Rosenzweig's chosen people resembles Spinoza's description of the biblical community, earlier discussed, whose polity and self-understanding reflect the sum total of its needs in history. The overlap between Rosenzweig and Spinoza arises from their shared anthropology of human desire. We have not yet seen how Rosenzweig's use of the category of revelation differentiates his account of the chosen people from Spinoza's biblical community. For that, we will need to go beyond an account of the divine love of revelation and deeper into an assessment of the character of divine freedom enacted through the event of revelation.

DIVINE FREEDOM AND DIVINE COMMAND ETHICS

The preceding review of divine revelation focused on the encounter between God's love and human desire. There is, however, good reason to further tease out the significance of the act of divine love distinct from its reception via human desire because this is where Rosenzweig parts company with Spinoza. As infinite substance, Spinoza's God generates reality but does not relate transactionally and temporally to any particular part of it. By contrast, Rosenzweig's God reveals and relates to persons through an act of love. However, divine love does more than affirm human desire. It also introduces persons to the reality of God's freedom. This encounter with divine freedom imposes an ethically and legally structured awareness of alterity into believers' theological testimony.

On the one hand, all temporal interactions between persons, God, and world exemplify acts of freedom. Experience, as shown, presupposes the separation or the freedom of the elements from each other. Additionally, divine freedom also takes on the character of the freedom of authority over human persons. Divine love asserts a claim on those who receive it. By challenging their prior understanding of reality, divine love commands their attention away from themselves. The content of the command consists in nothing more than the demand to acknowledge the love offered by testifying to God as revealer, creator, and redeemer. Still, the encounter with divine sovereignty transposes testimony into a commanded concern to love something other than oneself. That obedience to the command transpires in the context of the nature and reality of human desire only demonstrates the humanity of the divine command in Rosenzweig's account. Joined with divine command, theological desire funds the discernment of the community's concerns or needs in the name of obedience to the revelatory and commanding God. Revelation grounds a version of divine command ethics whereby God commands through love and humans obey because they are loved.[13]

Rosenzweig's divine command ethics also translates into a command to love the neighbor as a sign of the freedom of God's love. The encounter with divine alterity paves the way for covenantal participants to behave ethically toward other persons. This extension into an ethics of alterity distinguishes Rosenzweig's revelatory ethics from Cohen's deontological ethics of the self and Spinoza's ethics of self-preservation. Both Cohen and Spinoza put forth versions of the ethics of self-perfection. Cohen's self pursues compassion and love for the other as part of the infinite task of the self away from guilt toward moral perfection. Likewise, Spinoza identifies virtue with the tireless will to power of the self in its pursuit of the intellectual apprehension of God or nature. By contrast, Rosenzweig's ethics of love is motivated by the imperative (and desire) to testify to God.

How does this attention to the other transfer to a love for persons in the love of the neighbor? In Rosenzweig's account, love of the neighbor arises from the beloved's desire and the imperative to testify to God as one who not only loves this one soul but whose love extends to all souls and animates and redeems the world. Faith in God's redemption implies that the neighbor is loved by God just as I am loved by God. If, however, the neighbor is loved by God, I must try to treat her as one loved by God. This translates not only into the sustained effort to care for the neighbor who knows she is loved but also for the neighbor who cries out before the absence of God. In response, the believer performs her faith in God's redemption, declares that God is present, and treats the neighbor as one loved by God—that is, with the care required for meeting her particular needs.

At this juncture, we must stop our account and offer an assessment of its ramifications. Will this account open the door to a nonpolemically intended divine-human relationship, or does it repeat the structure of the logic of sacrifice described in Chapter 1? At first glance, a few red flags appear, which demand careful scrutiny. Two facts are most glaring: The account revolves around the operations of human desire and therefore demands that we look carefully to see whether the play of human desire does or does not resemble the play of human desire in either Foucault's or Novak's accounts; and the account profiles an encounter between divine command and human desire and requires an investigation into whether in this meeting, divine command overshadows human desire and human freedom: what is the flip side of the dialectics of desire.

Perhaps this argument against divine command ethics is best stated as follows: If we love others just because we love God, does not this mean that we love the other only because she is an extension of our desire to see God and not for herself? And if we love God as an extension of our own desires, doesn't this mean that we really love the neighbor only as an extension of our own love for ourselves and our desires? Isn't Rosenzweig's divine command ethics guilty of the same sort of solipsism I have identified in Spinoza's thought? In his excellent book, *Jewish Philosophy and the History of Messianism*, Martin Kavka raises this challenge to Rosenzweig's divine command ethics. There, he argues that Rosenzweig's "I love the neighbor because he is like me" ethical principle comes dangerously close to Hegel's ethics of self-recognition in the other. Because, Kavka says,

> [T]he I is already constituted before its encounter with the neighbor, and its love (for Rosenzweig) or forgiveness (for Hegel) of the other person is simply a recognition of itself in the other . . . I do not only call my neighbor "You" . . . I call him "soul" I call him "I." The neighbor is part of the song of myself. After revelation, the soul is never called into question. Rather, by foisting its love upon the world, it ensures that it will never be critiqued by anyone or anything in the world, by any worldly form.[14]

Kavka's critique focuses upon the prospect of the tyranny of human desire. As we have shown, however, this apparent tyranny of human desire always produces its seeming opposite, the guilt and anxiety that grips individuals in the operation of this very over-assertion. Is Kavka right? The answer is yes, at first—and then, no.

We might begin to respond to Kavka's challenge by pointing to a difference between the human desire for more of "me" and the theological desire for more of God. Yes, it is true that Rosenzweig's believer sees the other as an extension of her obedience to God and her love/desire for God. However, the believer's desire is not only subjective: It is theological as well. The recognition of "soul" in the other is only partly a repetition of my own desire. It is also a recognition of the alterity that transposed my desire from out of itself and toward a greater sovereignty. Divine command and love institute a conversion in the one loved. Consequently, there is always an excess—a transcendent alterity pointed to but never represented in the neighbor. This is not the case in the Hegelian model presented by Kavka. Hegelian self-consciousness presupposes the full realization of oneself in another self: that is, the ultimate and complete manifestation of Absolute

Spirit. Selfhood hereby projected and recognized achieves a totalization unavailable in the love of the neighbor as testimony. If part of the self-projection on to the other is a projection of her dialectical pointing toward the God beyond God, she cannot ever recognize herself fully: that is to say, fully appropriate the other into herself. The soul that she attempts to project always exceeds her own appropriation.

What about Kavka's follow-up point?—that Rosenzweig's believer's self is as soul, already established in its relationship to God, never to be altered or affected by its relationship with other persons and therefore free to pursue its new self's desires without limit. Said in the language of this book, even if the individual's desire is theological, doesn't the significance of its role render it impervious to delimitation or challenge? Aren't, in other words, religious believers beyond reproach and thereby incapable of honoring the rightful claims of nonbelievers? In what follows, I will argue against Kavka's charge that the believing self is never challenged in her testimony or that her theological proclamation is free of order or limit. How it is ordered and how such ordering permits it to remain open to and educate itself about the history and desires of other cultures requires a closer review of the impact of God's freedom as affirming law upon the divine-human relationship. In point of fact, the failure to articulate the lawfulness of divine freedom will give credence to Kavka's critique. It was the very weight of this critique of my first book, *Revelation and Theopolitics*, that first prompted me to write this volume. If *Revelation and Theopolitics* sought to present the benefits of dialectical theology for Jewish-Christian relations, this book announces the limits of such an approach insofar as dialectical theology neglects a robust account of how divine and human love are ordered in the freedom of divine law.

The Freedom of the Law and the Law of Freedom

Given the analysis of the logic of the law from our discussion of the New Thinking, we can already discern how the structure of revelatory freedom funds a reciprocal challenge to Kavka's concern over the tyranny of theological desire. Recourse to the structure of the logic of law reminds us that the existence of God, world, and persons is predicated upon an act of divine freedom through which God freely exteriorizes God-self toward that which is other. Unique to the character of divine freedom, however, is its ability to position God both in difference from and in affirmation of that other toward which it reaches. As I have shown in my discussion of both Schelling's *Weltalter* and Rosenzweig's appropriation of it, any other account of divine freedom would diminish the character of this sort of freedom as pure act beyond being. Applied to persons, therefore, God's freedom marks simultaneously the difference between God and persons and the affirmation of persons in this demarcation. More specifically, divine freedom differentiates itself from and simultaneously affirms human desire such that it is not rendered insufficient or valuable only by virtue of its tireless reach for union with God but rather identified—and, as I discuss more, judged as sufficient and affirmed as what it is: desire. To better understand how the divine-human revelatory encounter permits human desire to be simultaneously affirmed and delimited requires a closer review of the phenomenology of the revelatory exchange itself.

FREEDOM OF THE LAW

As noted, the revelatory encounter between God and persons is an event of divine command, and we identified the commanding character of revelation as a possible red flag of the logic of sacrifice. In reviewing this claim, we must reconsider the nature and/or meaning of the divine command. What did it mean to say that God commanded persons to "love God"? In Rosenzweig's version, the command to love God is a commentary on the difference between divine love and human love. Said otherwise, the command to love God means nothing more and nothing less than the impact of the imperative that derives from the alterity of the divine irreducibility. But of course, persons, in this account, become privy to divine alterity through the event of receiving unprecedented love. Consequently, the command emergent from the encounter with alterity is tantamount to the imperative, "Receive and recognize this love!" Structurally speaking, the argument is the Derridean one, which indicates that if a gift is truly a gift in that it is given prior to and regardless of the response of the one who receives, then inevitably, the gift is an expression of alterity.[15] Consequently, the event of receiving a gift is tantamount to the event of receiving a command from one who is other than oneself or a call to "Note the alterity of this gift!" or "Receive the gift!" The divine command is the link between gift and law enacted by divine freedom. It is a simple reflection of the alterity or difference between God and persons implicit within the event of God's exterior affirmation of persons as loved. We might say it this way: If the content of the divine command is "Love me," the meaning of this command is "God loves persons freely without reducing them to the divine essence." The command (*Gebot*) refers, therefore, not only to the imperative itself but to the logic or structure that this imperative implies. The command is interpreted through the law which it enacts and to which it refers.

The recognition of the divine command as participatory within the logic of law marks the great difference between a strictly dialectical theology of election and one emergent from the nexus of divine freedom and lawfulness. In this context, divine command no longer functions to dialectically negate that which fails to conform to its standard.[16] Rather, within the order of divine freedom, divine command mandates a recognition of a divine-human difference, which is the condition of the possibility of human freedom. If God were not other, we would not be free.

To appreciate the point better, we might say that the divine command is not for God but for us. According to the logic of a nonreductionist affirmation, God can only affirm us in positing a difference between himself and us. Therefore, God commands or stands as other to us so that we may be affirmed. Most significantly then, divine law is not God's means of acquiring power over and above human persons. It is the way that he reaches toward us. Divine law does not stand in contest with human desire but functions to secure its freedom and/or its rights.

In his account, Rosenzweig illustrates how God offers love without regard for any human response. God's love is not generated from want or desire but is a pure gift offered only for the sake of its recipients.

> Only the love of a lover is such a continually renewed self-sacrifice/ . . . The beloved accepts the gift . . . the lover, however, extorts his love from the very marrow of himself . . . every branch breaks out of the trunk and no longer knows anything of the tree, which it denies.[17]

Could God's love include an element of self-interest? Rosenzweig says no. Want or desire take time. But God's love is "completely fulfilled in the moment in which it exists."[18] It is "always and wholly of today . . . this love is the eternal victory over death."[19] Divine love as command simply reflects the lawfulness of being found in the order of God, a lawfulness that is not antagonistic toward or in violent competition with the humans who are ordered within it, but that affirms and determines the sustainability of their existence and vitality.

THE LAW OF FREEDOM

Given the logic of the law, covenantal life should not translate into a battle between human desire and divine command. In this context, persons ought to be able to adhere to or obey God's command freely, without the embattlement between one's interests for oneself and the imperative to testify to God. Testimony to God and the affirmation of human need should affirm one another. However, if divine freedom impacts upon human persons as affirmation and delimitation, this must also mean that human desire must not overreach itself. What does it mean for human desire to overreach? It means that as desire, it aspires beyond itself to its own fulfillment. Any desire that pretends that it can and/or does achieve its *telos* is a desire that overreaches itself as desire and fulfillment and not simply desire. However, desire is free only in its inability to achieve self-fulfillment, particularly when the fulfillment of desire emerges from a selfless-exteriority in which this desire may retain a rightful hope. This argument consists of two key claims: The law of grace limits and/or orders human love and/or the believer's testimony; and the law of grace is not only an ordering but also a judgment, in the sense of a "discernment" of human desire. While, I will suggest, nonrevelatory law claims to limit desire only to in fact be ruled by desire, revelatory law both limits and discerns desire so far as it arises from a transcendence not subject to the play of desire.

Claim 1: Revelatory law orders theological desire and testimony. Let us recall Kavka's critique of Rosenzweig's believer. The soul, Kavka says, "is never called into question. Rather, by foisting its love upon the world, it ensures that it will never be critiqued by anyone or anything in the world, by any worldly form."[20] Kavka's critique explains why the believer's testimony needs to be ordered. As the marriage between the reception of a momentary love by God and an historically evolving set of individual and community desires, theological testimony is always particular with respect to the content and historicity of its proclaimers. That means, however, that one person's testimony and/or one's tradition's testimony is not necessarily a relevant theological expression to another person or community. To anarchically and indiscriminately "foist" one's love on to the world without regard for the particularity and limit of one's theological proclamation is in effect to deny the very character of this proclamation as an expression of a particular individual or community's desire. It is to act as if my desire is not just that—*my desire*. But the structure of revelation already orders desire so that it cannot at once deny its own nature and still participate in the covenant relationship.

Recall Rosenzweig's exposition of the lawful difference between divine and human love. Only human love operates as desire and desire is only human. The condition of the possibility of a free human desire is also the limit against its pretense to become something other than my desire. To the extent that desire overreaches and pretends its own fulfillment and truth, it denies the condition of its freedom and undermines itself. As we have recognized in the work of Rosenstock-Huessy, Agamben, and even Foucault, the history of the dialectics of desire offers many examples of the self-undermining effect of unbridled desire. To excise the law from desire is to confuse and dissolve desire into its *telos*. I am not arguing that revelatory desire is incapable of self-nullification or overreaching. Rather, I am suggesting that desire can remain only if it is lawful. Without divine freedom and law, desire will always annihilate itself in its effort to overreach either in its pretense to be truth or in its denunciation of its worth upon its failure to do so. In the context of revelation, the divine-human relationship limits desire by identifying it as desire and nothing else.

JUSTIFICATION THROUGH THE LAW: ABIDING IN OUR NEED

Let me now turn to claim #2, that the law of divine grace not only limits desire (like nonrevelatory law) but as free in its relation to desire, judges or discerns but does not excise the character of human desire.

As we have seen and unlike the three examples of nonrevelatory law discussed in Chapter 3 (Spinoza, Rose, and Novak), revelatory law is free from the desire that it orders. Neither is it like Spinoza's law, the handmaiden of human desire; nor like Rose's broken middle, the embattled buffer to human conflict; nor, finally, like Novak's natural law, the gatekeeper of our finitude. Ever generated by God's grace, revelatory law is not vulnerable to strains or periods of antinomianism. It does not have to earn its freedom to order. In contrast to human persons who generate the law despite their interests, God does not offer the law despite himself but as a freely and lovingly offered gift.

But the free law of revelation also grants a freedom in the law for those who follow it. As the only law thus far considered that does not give into desire's pretense for self-fulfillment, revelatory law is, arguably, the only law that frees persons to authentically desire and hope for the recognition they long to have. Theological testimony that adheres to this law legitimizes believers' right to have their desires without burdening them with the inauthentic obligation to fulfill fully those desires themselves. To live within the order of revelation allows believers the freedom to hope in God's love on the one hand and releases them from the despair that consistently caps their efforts to make the world a home by themselves. The law of revelation frees persons to be who they are, believers who testify to the God they long for in history. It provides what Rosenzweig refers to as a "candid exposition . . .

of one's own self"[21]—or, we might say, issues a judgment of human desire insofar as it discerns or judges the character and legal status of this desire. As the judgment or the exposure of human self-awareness, revelatory law offers persons the tools with which they may live authentic and well-ordered lives. Let me show how this works in application to Rosenzweig's account of the community of believers.

Who is the community of believers? It is, as we may recall, the community of persons who collectively discern and announce each other's hopes or wishes in the context of their obedient testimony to the God of revelation. Communal Jewish life in Rosenzweig's account is part process of community identity formation (What are our collective desires?) and part active testimony and verification of God. What effect does the law of revelation have on this community life? Said simply, it historicizes the community's collective wishes, identifying members of that community as persons engaged in an ongoing hermeneutical effort to discern and announce their testimony as it changes in time. Revelatory law frees believers to advance new interpretations of the forms of their witness: that is, their texts, their prayers, their community laws, their literary and imaginative self-expressions. By contrast, it falsifies efforts to freeze the community's theological self-understanding. The law of revelation reminds communities that their exercise of verification is by definition, never ending. It offers a candid judgment of the character of religious life as the theological longing and hope that cannot provide the object of its own desire. As judgment, the law of revelation inserts a futurity into the community's religious expression—an intrusion of the messianic that, interestingly enough, tempers or calms religious life as it judges it as desire. Judaism has, Rosenzweig argues, generally thought historically. It has "heeded the call of the occasion. . . ."[22]

> One did not become a Jewish thinker in the undisturbed circle of Judaism. Here, thinking did not become a thinking about Judaism which was simply the most self-evident thing of all, more a being than an "ism," but rather it became a thinking within Judaism a learning, thus ultimately not fundamental but rather ornamental thinking.[23]

The New Thinking does not assert universal propositions. It adjudicates claims and therefore learns over time. It is and ought to be free thought that reflects the free law of revelation.

When viewed from the perspective of the limits of a dialectics of desire, the freedom and affirmation of the law installs a calm over those who stand in the order of divine freedom. In contrast to the extremes of illegitimate tyranny on the one hand and anxious self-diminishment and guilt on the other, persons found in the order of God are justified or accepted as right in and through the law. When divine freedom operates graciously through the form of divine law, it secures a basis for the rights of those it acts upon. In this context, persons can, in Rosenzweig's words, "abide"[24] or remain. The law affords an existential and moral sabbatical or rest without contest. And if in Chapter 4, we appreciated the post-atonement moment of the Sabbatical and Jubilee announcements, here we can also appreciate the post-atonement abiding within the logic of the law.

From the perspective of the logic of the law covenantal life is marked by moral striving. It is marked by the command to testify to God's tireless and selfless concern and by the imperative to discern the needs of the community whose testimony always reflects their individual and collectively verified needs. Still, unlike the dialectics of desire that stretch desire past its own limits and/or denounce it for its failures to achieve its own claims, the logic of the law encourages persons to work freely on their own behalf and on behalf of the revelatory God. In this law, persons are judged, but they are judged by a God who is free from the judgment he issues and who judges for us and not against us. In this context, judgment is normative but the standard of law through which it judges reflects the "what" and "who" humans are in their freedom. It exposes the extents and limits of human rights as persons interact with other persons, the world, and God within the order of the law. If in this account of election, the messianic judgment is now, this is because divine judgment installs a repose for those who dwell within it—a repose of living within the wisdom of the free God who enacts the gracious and lawful difference between his love and ours. The logic of law transposes the meaning of judgment, and within the time of God's discernment, persons and communities inherit an existential and moral justification of who they are within the historicity and finitude of their efforts.

A NONTELEOLOGICAL JUDAISM

Before moving to a discussion of the epistemological and apologetic significance of justification through the law, I would like to close this section with a consideration of the impact of this theology of the law and covenantal life upon an interpretation of Jewish legal life. In Chapter 7, I will offer a discussion of the impact of the logic of the law upon the life of Christian witness.

All throughout this chapter, I have sought to highlight the paradigm-altering character of divine freedom both in Rosenzweig's account and in my own view of the logic of the law. As mentioned in the introduction to the volume, this is a book about freedom, the shape of freedom, and the demands of freedom. Inspired by the character of God's sabbatical freedom and refueled by Schelling's and Rosenzweig's accounts, the volume celebrates what I refer to as the third moment in a triad of theological freedoms pointed to first in *Revelation and Theopolitics* and then in *Liturgy, Time and the Politics of Redemption* and now here. Viewed together, each volume attests to the power and reach of divine freedom and the impact of that reach upon human life. *Revelation and Theopolitics* outlined the character of God's freedom as radically other and commanding of a life of communal testimony. *Liturgy, Time and the Politics of Redemption* described the freedom of God to draw near us in our prayer. This book illuminates the freedom of God to issue judgments or order wisely. Earlier, we have glimpsed the character and reach of that freedom. For revelatory rooted communities, being found in the order of God means the license and demand to sustain a collective attunement to the needs of one's community.

In *Revelation and Theopolitics*, I described *halakhic* life in the framework of the testimony to divine command. In this discussion, I noted the extent to which *halakha* or particular Jewish laws operate as human responses to divine love. By this, I meant that the generation of specific laws and religious responses generally speaking (including, therefore, prayer, midrash, and others) constitute Jewish expressions of covenantal love. Given that human witness takes on the form of the proclamation of love for God in the expression of the human cry for more of this love, I demonstrated how *halakhic* life is synonymous with the proclamation of divine justice. As testimony, *halakha* witnesses to God's elective love. As theological desire, *halakha* witnesses to the community's need for God's elective love. Unlike the profile of Jewish life granted by either Spinoza or Cohen, a theology of divine command and love vitalizes a Jewish historical materialism whereby *halakha* functions as the lens of Jewish communal desire in its witness to God's covenantal love.

The extended account of the logic of law offered in this discussion does not alter this profile of Jewish materiality and *halakhic* change. However, the logic of the law illuminates what I have called the sabbatical character of this religious life. As is well known to scholars of Rosenzweig's work, there is a tension in Rosenzweig's writings regarding the relationship between Jewish life, historicity, eternity, and redemption. Although early scholarship on Rosenzweig's thought too quickly interpreted Rosenzweig's description of the Jews as the "eternal people" to mean that for Rosenzweig, Jewish life did not function historically, later Rosenzweig scholars have recognized the temporal character of all existence in Rosenzweig's account and understood therefore that Rosenzweig's designation of the Jews as the eternal people was not meant to dehistoricize them.[25] The account here brings both views together in a new coordination. If the *halakhic* life of testimony is clearly a temporal activity of discerning the community's needs through history, the logic of the law affirms that such an exercise of temporal discernment and proclamation is not driven by, and therefore distinguished from, a future teleological or redemptive fulfillment.

However, to argue that the logic of the law undoes the teleological expectation of the life of witness does not mean that the logic of the law undoes its redemptive significance. Rather, the logic of the law houses the *halakhic* life of testimony and discernment in the shelter of the divine affirmation. On the one hand, it indicates that from the human perspective, there will never be anything other than a testimony of theological desire in the context of God's affirming law. On the other hand, it offers the assurance that given God's affirming law and the freedom it affords human life, there is no other *telos* to desire. Historical existence is no longer pitted against redemptive fulfillment. Historical existence is redemptive fulfillment because the logic of the law offers a rest and/or an affirmation to the human, the divine, and the world in the freedom of their interactions. In terms of performance, Jewish life proceeds in time. In terms of meaning, Jewish life endlessly repeats the freedom of election in the order of God. History rests and rest is historical.

In *Revelation and Theopolitics*, I pointed to Rosenzweig's account of the repetition of the liturgical calendar as both a simulacrum of eternal time and as a gesture of perpetual repentance for the temptation of those who overreach in their testimony. There, I argued that

> Rosenzweig's description of the Jewish and Christian liturgical cycles shows how their repetitive ritual cycles effect a testimony of repentance insofar as both traditions establish festivals that mark and proclaim their faithful and desirous temporalizations of God's presence in our world . . . [and] both . . . contextualize these commemorations and temporalizations in the context of a yearly liturgical cycle whose repetition challenges the linearity and therefore the proclamations within the story they tell.[26]

This volume's attention to the logic of law offers a deeper explanation of the function of liturgical cycles. When viewed from the perspective of the logic of law, we can better appreciate the extent to which the annual repetition of the liturgical cycle expresses the rest or the repose afforded the life of testimony as it is found in the order of divine freedom. In this context, liturgical repetition expresses the rest of the divine order and is not an anticipation of another eternity. If liturgical repetition acts as an eschatological limit, it does so only by referring to the realized eschatology of the order of law that it reflects and within which all proclamation transpires. By the same token, we can also appreciate how my designation of liturgical repetition as a kind of testimony of repentance that delimits the ambitions of theological proclamation refers less to a punitive or excising limit upon the particular proclamations and more to the lawful limit of the nature of this testimony as human and only human. If liturgical repetition is repentant, it repents by repeating the order of the law, which renders testimony possible and not by casting doubt upon the exercise of religious life and devotion altogether.

By way of summary, a theology of the law restores the perpetual present of Jewish covenantal reality. As such, it emancipates Jewish life from any sort of progressive account of history without dematerializing or dehistoricizing any facet of its communal life. As was the case for the knowledge of the New Thinking, generally speaking, the impact of the logic of the law upon Jewish self-understanding is enormous. From this context, no expression of Jewish testimony can be deemed more meaningful than any other. No particular period of time in Jewish history constitutes a more or less significant episode in its salvation history. The logic of the law mandates a fluidity and creativity with regard to Jewish religious and cultural expression and does not require its service to a larger goal, whether that is union with the divine intellect or the restoration of the Temple or the reign of universal monotheism. Jewish life serves no ultimate or final end other than the exercise of its free and self-consciously performed testimony within the larger order of God's freedom.

Justification Through the Law: Truth Telling and Apologetics

TESTIMONY JUSTIFIED THROUGH THE LAW

If, as I have discussed, the logic of the law is a logic of freedom, then we cannot appreciate fully the scope and reach of a human freedom found in the order of God until we discern a community's freedom to admit exteriority into its testimony—a freedom to tell the truth without holding the truth. As already anticipated in my discussion of Rosenzweig's "The New Thinking," the logic of the law not only alters the meaning of knowledge and the self-understanding of historically-based revelatory traditions, but it also presents an entirely new logic for Jewish-Christian relations as well. Such a logic derives not only from the general structure of what it means to be found within the order of God. It derives even more specifically from the preceding redescription of the concept of divine election. More specifically, the transformation of Jewish-Christian relations predicated upon this redescription of the structure of election derives from the concept of "justification through the law" as described earlier. Although such a notion may at first glance appear disorienting to Christians, it has been the work of this volume to expose the role of law as the order of God as the point of logical reorientation for a nonpolemical account of revelatory religion. I will take up a more detailed discussion of the meaning of the logic of law within a Christian theological perspective in the next chapter.

Prior, however, to discerning the link between the lawful freedom of revelatory witness and the capacity to admit exteriority into this testimony, we must first examine the epistemological status of theological truth-claims within the nonteleologically driven covenantal encounter described earlier. At the heart of my argument is the claim that a theological truth-claim is justified, rationally, only if it operates within the law of divine freedom. The application of this standard of rationality will forge a significant distinction between what I refer to as truth-telling and truth-holding, a distinction that will be central to the formulation of a new Christian and Jewish apologetic exchange.

Justifying Belief Traditionally speaking, apologetics refers to the defense of one's beliefs to persons who do not share one's beliefs. Apologetic thinking has to do with defense. Of course, all claim making has to do with defense if by *defense*, we mean that the assertion of a claim as true requires some justification without which the claim would be either considered false, or at the very least, meaningless. Consequently, the conditions of the possibility of a successful apologetics are the same as the conditions of the possibility of truth assertions.

What then does it mean to be able to defend one's truth? What makes a truth-claim defensible? In my analysis of Rosenzweig's New Thinking and my presentation of the logic of the law, I laid out the basic standards and features of truth asserting as they function within the being found in the order of God. Truth-claims about the world, as we recall, were possible in the context of the recognition of the freedom of all to assert varying and changing claims premised upon changing interactions. Now, however, we are privy to a more detailed account of the divine-human relationship and the character of human desire within this relationship. Equipped with this information, we are in a better position to examine not only what it means to defend a truth generally speaking, but what it means for a historically based revelatory tradition to defend its truths about God.

In a well-known essay, "Apologetic Thinking," Rosenzweig discusses what it means for historically based revelatory communities to defend their theological claims. Although Rosenzweig does not explicitly tie his account of apologetic thinking in this essay to what he elsewhere refers to as the New Thinking, "Apologetic Thinking" is an application of the logic of the law on to theological assertions. Read from this perspective, apologetic thinking means adjudicated thinking—a thinking and assertion of religious claims defensible only when justified in, that is, both delimited and affirmed by the logic of the law. Let us take a closer look at this famous essay.

In "Apologetic Thinking," Rosenzweig refers to Jewish examples. Nonetheless, the points he makes pertain to both Judaism and Christianity as historically based revelatory communities. Jewish thinking (and, by extension, Christian thinking) begins with what Rosenzweig calls its "monstrous actuality."[27] By "monstrous actuality," Rosenzweig means that Judaism begins with real people, experiencing an actual historical event out of which emerges a set of impressions that shape or constitute the basis of Jewish existence or Jewish peoplehood. Speaking in the language of the earlier account, Jewish thinking (like all thinking) begins with the desire for self-preservation. Specifically, both Judaism and Christianity seek to preserve themselves by associating themselves with a certain identity. Jews, Rosenzweig suggests, conceive of themselves as a material people, and Christians conceive of themselves as a testimonial and spiritually defined community.

> The monstrous actuality of Jewish being has created for itself a self-protection. . . . But what here has a protective and actuality-preserving effect would have had to have a paralyzing effect on life in a community which in its essence is purely spiritual . . . for example, the Christian church. In the latter . . . the constant reformulating of Christological dogma, again and again, becomes the inner condition for the external continuation of the community.[28]

If, however, Jewish thinking begins with Jewish existence and Christian thinking begins with Christian proclamation, does—and if so, how—Jewish and Christian thinking develop further? There is no doubt that both traditions must develop beyond repeated attestations of their own identity because both traditions see themselves as responses to a divine event. Our analysis of "Atheistic Theology" has already demonstrated how the attempt to ignore or reduce the divine intrusion into a strictly human account inevitably undoes itself. The theological element within Jewish or Christian thinking moves both thought exercises past the limits of their own identitarian-driven assertions and therefore inserts an element of rationality or exteriority in the dynamic of their thought. The question before us concerns the nature of this rationality and its impact upon the self-identitarian narrative of each tradition.

What, we can speculate, would this rationality or encounter with exteriority look like if we followed the logic of dialectical theology? If apologetic thinking were rooted in dialectical theology alone, the insertion of the divine reality upon the Jewish and Christian identitarian accounts would challenge the justification of each equally. Both Judaism and Christianity offer examples of theologies that presuppose the dialectical alterity of God over and against human assertion.[29] Generally speaking, dialectical theology can apparently account for the reality of the divine intrusion into the strictly human and/or identitarian narrative. However, dialectical theology can account for only the intrusion of this exteriority at the expense of the justification of the human account. In this case, myth is certainly overcome but theology [the free human articulation of the reality of God] is also negated by the dramatic alterity of the theological reality that it cannot justifiably express. A dialectical account of the admission of the theological into Jewish thinking or Christian thinking simply inverts the logical failure of myth by reducing the human to the divine. By contrast, apologetic thinking must permit both: a recognition of theological reality along with the justification of a human narrative of this event. How can this be possible?

In "Apologetic Thinking," Rosenzweig distinguishes between good and bad apologetic thinking. About bad apologetic thinking, he says

> [I]t seems to me that the danger of all apologetics lies much more in the fact that one takes one's own, which after all, one knows oneself, in its full breadth and depth of actuality, while the foreign, of which one has only "taken notice," for the most part only as it occurs in a book, i.e., therefore precisely as an ideal.[30]

Said otherwise, absolute truth-claims predicated upon the desire of the knower alone constitute bad thinking. However, from the perspective of the logic of the law, the divine intrusion into the human narrative inevitably justifies the human account if and only when the person issuing the claim recognizes the limited and non-absolute reach of her claim, rooted as it is in her desire and therefore in her (and her community's) particular historical position. By logical extension, such a believer also recognizes that she cannot reduce all other possible truth-claims to the dustbin of falsehood. To recognize the historicity of my claim is tantamount to an admission of the possibility of another's own claim. Within the logic of the law, the condition of the possibility of truth is the recognition of the possibility (not the actuality) of someone else's truth.

Rosenzweig addresses this same point when he contrasts the bad apologist, who seeks to defend her claim as universalizable, with the good apologist, who can admit the "lie."

> Defending can be one of the noblest human occupations. Namely, if it goes to the very ground of things and souls and, renouncing the petty devices of a lie, ex-culpates with the truth, nothing but the truth . . . it would not at all be a defense in the usual sense, but rather a candid exposition, yet not of some cause, but rather of one's own [self].[31]

The good apologist can admit the possibility of the truth of another's claims along with the *possibility* of the falsehood of her own and the "lie" that is implicit in her effort to assert the universality of her own claim. With this admission, the good apologist frees herself from any guilt inevitably tied to the covert attempt to prop up one's truth as universalizable. To prop up one's truth as universalizable incurs guilt because it defies the very conditions of the freedom to assert a truth at all. By contrast, exposure of one's desire to lie frees or "exculpates" one from the possibility of guilt. In this way, apologetics presents a post-repentant and post-atonement reasoning. Apologetic thinking exposes the truth of human truth-telling: It offers what Rosenzweig says is a "candid exposition . . . of one's own self"[32] as justified by the order in which one is both delimited and affirmed as a proclaimer of theological truth. Consequently, to defend oneself means neither to demonstrate one's absolute rightness nor to atone for one's wrongness. Rather, it means to articulate the clear standards and/or terms for one's assertions—what in this case are the terms of the free law that simultaneously endow believers with the right to proclaim historically and with the recognition of the possibility of the truth of another's position. Apologetic thinking, therefore, presupposes a link between theological truth telling and the admission of exteriority into my original claim. It is to this issue that I now turn.

Admitting Exteriority What is the nature of the connection between theological truth telling and the admission of exteriority into an original claim as it is presented by both Rosenzweig's "Apologetic Thinking" and my extended analysis into the logic of the law? We might answer this question by further developing the line of thought presented earlier whereby we recognized the link between an apologetic defense and the ability to recognize who and what one is within the affirmation and limits of revelatory law. To defend oneself rationally does not mean to assert or nullify oneself over and against another. In fact, my defense of myself has no bearing on whether I am either more right or more wrong than another. From the perspective of the logic of law, defense translates into self-understanding within lawful difference rather than the exercise of conflict. Apologetic thinking is theological thinking within the judgment of divine wisdom. It performs the self-consciousness of one's existence within the lawful order of God's freedom.

The Law of Freedom, the Freedom of the Law 209

If, however, apologetic thinking defends through a "candid exposition of self," it is also the case that apologetic thinking defends through an exposition of the possibility of the truth of another's claims. Persons achieve the calm of self-recognition when they consider the possibility of another's claims. In fact, Rosenzweig argues, the refusal to admit this possibility leads to self-alienation. There are two postures of truth holding over and against truth telling. One, as we have discussed, is the insistence upon the universalizability of one's own claim. The second is the logically linked demonization of another's claim. Both, Rosenzweig asserts, result in the self-alienation of the proclaimer on the one hand and in the diminishment or full potential or her narration on the other hand. Why? To answer the question, we might recall Rosenzweig's earlier cited claim that

> It seems to me that the danger of all apologetics lies much more in the fact that one takes one's own, which after all, one knows oneself, in its full breadth and depth of actuality, while the foreign, of which one has only "taken notice," for the most part only as it occurs in a book, i.e., therefore precisely as an ideal.[33]

Such efforts are doomed to failure because the idealization or demonization of another commits the defender to a stable profile of her own beliefs ultimately idealizing and limiting her own range of beliefs and needs just as much as she delimits those of the one she demonizes. In the name of attempting to secure one's own truth, one limits one's truth, freezes it, and disables the proclaimer from freely expanding upon or adding to this truth as she is affected by changes in time. Of course, to isolate a truth from change is to render it less useful for those who hold it. In the process, persons become divorced from themselves and their historical reality. The condition of the possibility of my freedom through time is the possibility of a truth claim that differs from the one I currently attest. Freedom remains incommensurate with polemical thinking.

In "Apologetic Thinking," Rosenzweig turns to a discussion of the work of two early-twentieth-century Jewish thinkers, Max Brod and Leo Baeck, to evidence this refusal to engage with the possibility of another's claims within one's own tradition. Both identify Judaism with a particular definition and render this definition impervious to outside claims. Both thinkers, Rosenzweig shows, insist upon a single definition of Judaism—and, in particular, Judaism's relation to the law. But, Rosenzweig argues, the insistence upon a fixed account of the law in both thinkers results in a thorough-going loss of the meaning of the law within Judaism altogether. By this, Rosenzweig means that regardless of the dichotomy forged by either thinker—Judaism is "law," and Christianity is "spirit"; or, Judaism is "reason" and Christianity "faith"—

the tendency to dichotomize Judaism over against either Christianity or a variant account of Judaism (in this case, Brod's to Baeck's, or Baeck's to Brod's) results in an inauthentic understanding of Jewish law as both a marker of Jewish particularity and a testament to Jewish finitude, or limit. Brod, in particular, celebrates the law but renders law impervious to exterior factors or influences. The consequence is a narrow perspective on the law that denies law its worldly value, leaving it "completely at the nationalistically agitated surface of the problem. . . ."[34] Baeck has the opposite problem so far as his account errs on the side of announcing Judaism's common human essence at the expense of appreciating the particularity of the law. Despite its more universal appearance, Baeck's account is motivated by the same desire for familiarity and the same resistance to the challenge of the particular other as Brod's account. Humanism is always a guise for refusing to recognize authentic difference.

However, the upshot of the refusal to admit an engagement with another tradition or exteriority is ironically the very opposite of the intent. Exposure to an exteriority challenges the alienation of self that I endure for the sake of preserving my familiarity because the other that I disdain (or differentiate myself from) becomes the reminder of who I am—an individual or member of a community who testifies to a belief freely in the changing course of history. The recognition of the other and the admission of the antagonism between us that permits me to recognize the extent to which I too dearly hold on to my proclaimed truth both afford me greater self-understanding. Both inspire an account of myself or a self-defense that "ex-culpates"[35] the lie of my inauthentic assertion.

From this perspective, apologetic thinking exposes how standard efforts at defense are ultimately unsuccessful in disclosing and/or securing the innermost they seek to protect. Within the logic of the law, apologetic thinking negotiates between the fact of the particular and its perpetual indebtedness to the exterior. The usual negotiation between these often results in repression, control, antagonism, and/or anemic assertions of commonality. However, the logic of the law offers participants a self-conscious awareness of this negotiation with which they actively may guard against the hubris of false claims of certainty without nullifying the justification of a theological claim made within the affirmation and limits of the law.

OVERCOMING TOLERANCE AND EMBRACING ENMITY

Freedom within the law means freedom to admit the possibility of exteriority. What does such freedom look like when applied directly to Jewish-Christian relations? What is the character of a nonpolemically driven Jewish-Christian apologetics?

My discussion of a Jewish-Christian apologetics will proceed in three stages: an analysis of the question of tolerance and its relation to an apologetics within the law; an analysis of enmity and its role in Jewish-Christian relations; and a discussion of the content of an apologetics within the law, or what is better referred to as a new Jewish-Christian learning. Here, I will address the first and second points. I will discuss the third point in the next section.

Tolerance Judaism has had a long and complicated history with the notion of tolerance as it emerged within late medieval and early modern Western Europe. Ever since the work of Moses Mendelssohn, Jews have longed to reap the benefits of state-sponsored legal acceptance without having to forfeit the opportunity to critique the intellectual and cultural limits of enlightenment professed tolerance.[36] In a rather neglected essay, "Lessing's Nathan," Rosenzweig uses the pretense of a commentary on Lessing's play, "Nathan the Wise," to present an argument regarding the meaning of the modern concept of tolerance as applied to Jews.[37]

The history of the concept of tolerance has three important chapters, according to Rosenzweig's account: the medieval, the modern, and the one we currently occupy. No doubt, Rosenzweig admits, medieval attitudes and treatment of Jews were paradoxical. On the one hand, medieval attitudes toward Jews erred by identifying the people with their institution or religious house. "The human being is not Judaism, Christianity.... This is why the Middle Ages had to collapse and the 'purely human' enter."[38] And yet, later in the same essay, Rosenzweig notes, "In the Middle Ages the Jews were tolerated more, in modern times less than the others, that is a characteristic feature for the change of the concept of tolerance."[39] How to account for this?

In contrast to the Middle Ages, modernity premised tolerance on humanism. All persons are worthy of acceptance as human beings. But, Rosenzweig objects, "how empty is this presupposition of the one humanity, as long as human beings are not willing ... human beings know it, of course, and in spite of it hate one another."[40] Humanism is superficial. It thinly veils a resistance born of particularity and difference. We may, Rosenzweig suggests, recognize our common humanity. Even so, we retain an enmity for the other. A tolerance premised on common humanity leaves prejudices and misunderstandings intact amounting to an anemic manifestation of the universal. By contrast, the Middle Ages asserted no such commonality but identified Jews by their religion. No doubt, medieval Jews lacked political rights, but at least, Rosenzweig suggests, they were recognized as a separate and irreducible community and not rendered invisible by humanism's empty universals.

What then are we left with? "The new solution to the problem of tolerance [is], 'only because you are Edom may I be Yaakov.'"[41] What does this mean? On the one hand, the new solution cannot be a simple return to the Middle Ages. "We look backward but not in such a way that we would sacrifice our living life again to the life-destroying image of a holy institution."[42] Like Lessing and Mendelssohn before him,[43] Rosenzweig understands that tolerance must recognize Jewish particularity. Still, this must be a particularity of the living people and not the institution. Particularity and humanity must be linked. "The human being is more than his house but not the unhoused one not the 'pure,' that is, the naked human being . . . rather only the housed one."[44] But how is it possible to produce this connection between particularity and humanity?

Rosenzweig's comments are cryptic and undeveloped. Still, we can build some elements of an argument from the text. On the one hand, the "only because you are Edom may I be Yakov" indicates a rejection of the superficial and reductionist identification of sameness found in humanist accounts of tolerance. Edom and Yakov are not the same. Exposed here is the quest for familiarity and comfort at work in false claims of tolerance for the other. A superficial nod at an empty point of commonality guards traditions from coming to terms with their own self-constitutions.

> Look at Nathan. . . . Here is the naked human being, whose familiarity is celebrated. . . . It is a great symbol for this shallowness in the concluding scene where the archetypal difference of man and woman is denied in favor of the cool, fish-blooded brotherliness and sisterliness. The flatness of the family scene of the conclusion: uncle at best.[45]

Modern tolerance refuses to unpack its own presuppositions—its own drives. It remains unphilosophical or irrational in its insistence on security.

Instead, authentic tolerance begins by marking a difference between the two particulars—a difference that can generate varying models of relation, none of which are abstract or inconsequential. As different, the two particulars may be at odds, may overlap, may run parallel to or attract each other. There may be between them "an organic coherence, organic beside-, against-, and with-one another (only the particular case can teach which of these three)—of Jewish and Christian human beings, . . ."[46] but they cannot relate indifferently to each other under the false pretenses of a common essence. "No more the co-existence of two statues, no longer the indifferent confusion that one tried earlier to read out of Nathan the Wise."[47]

Enmity One final implication emerges from Rosenzweig's rather cryptic "if only because you are Edom may I be Yakov": namely, the suggestion that identity emerges here not only from difference but from the antagonism between two different identities. To say that the identity of Yakov presupposes the identity of Edom is to suggest that the particularity of the one is linked to its antagonism with the other. Neither can engage freely in their own self-making without first contending with the adversarial nature of their reaction to the other. If a preemptive identification of common humanity waxes inauthentic and ineffective as a basis for tolerance, the exposure of enmity toward the other constitutes a sign of the irreducibility of lawfulness within which any identity alone perdures. This position echoes a theme already announced in *The Star of Redemption*. "Before God, then, Jew and Christian both labor at the same task. He cannot dispense with either. He has set enmity between the two for all time, and withal has most intimately bound each to each."[48]

In both texts, Rosenzweig shows how enmity between identities impacts each tradition's labor of verification. There is, Rosenzweig argues in the *Star*, a link between Christian identity and Christian anti-Judaism. Why? Because the Christian hatred for the Jew is a guise for Christian self-hatred: a hatred that derives from the Christian's realization that her own truth arises from Judaism originally. Christian truth is not self-sustaining nor self-originating. It is indebted to a past and is not absolute. Nonetheless, Rosenzweig argues, Christianity's recognition of the nature and source of this anti-Judaism is what permits Christianity to endure. Without its indebtedness to Judaism, Christianity would rest secure in its proclamation and forego the labor of truth that it pursues "on the eternal way."[49] The recognition of its anti-Judaism not only historicizes Christianity but offers Christianity a future of free expression and continued change. The recognition of enmity stimulates the free determination of the tradition in time. The same is true with respect to Judaism's antagonism toward Christianity. Judaism and Christianity are implicated in each other's authentic labor of verification. To recognize this mutual indebtedness does not launch the two traditions into a dialog but stimulates both traditions to develop freely in time.

Logically speaking, the argument is rooted in the structure of the admission of exteriority into one's own tradition. If, according to the logic of law, my freedom requires your freedom, then the inverse must be the case as well: If you are not free, I am not free. Let me unpack this. At this juncture, I have established that the freedom of one person requires the freedom of the other. However, enmity means the demonization of another's claim as irredeemably false. Enmity involves the assertion of an unalterable claim.

As we have seen many times, however, the assertion of an unalterable claim undermines rather than supports the desire for self-preservation. Polemical thinking registers as an exceptionalism, which in one form or another compromises the "who" and the "what" that seeks self-certainty. Exceptionalism might secure some fraction of an individual or a group's desire for self-preservation but only by sacrificing whatever it deems inessential. Enmity is a sign of polemical thinking, and polemical thinking undoes its own aims. Consequently, enmity moves persons toward justification through the law because on pragmatic grounds alone, persons seeking to preserve their identity will understand the need to recognize another's identity as the very condition of the possibility of their own freedom.

But this realization also helps explain Rosenzweig's additional suggestion that human beings are "made" and not found.

> No more the coexistence of two statues, no longer the indifferent confusion that one tried earlier to read out of Nathan the Wise, no: organic coherence, organic beside-, against-, and with-one-another . . . of Jewish and Christian human beings. To build them up, to *make* human being, not to remember that we *are* human beings. . . . And that is why it is imperative to preserve the houses of spiritual life. . . .[50]

According to the logic of the law, identity is not static. An individual or community "is" what the individual or community will "become" freely. To be a Jew is in this respect to be a "Jew in the making." To be a Christian is to be a "Christian in the making," and we can say that the identity of each is partly determined by the encounter with exteriority. Of course, this is simply another way of saying that identity stands within the law—within the order of the irreducible existence of another.

The Fear of Syncretism Before leaving this analysis of an apologetics within the law, it is important to dispel two points of skepticism: the charge of syncretism on the one hand, and the charge of relativism in the midst of "evil" on the other.

The argument presented thus far indicates that a healthy apologetic relation between Judaism and Christianity consists of more than the reminder by another tradition of the limits or possible pretenses of one's own truth-claims. As well, I have argued that an apologetics within the law encourages the free inquiry into another's possible truths on the grounds of the fact that this possibility constitutes the possibility of my own proclamation. However, does such inquiry open the doors to the appropriation of another tradition's truths? Does the admission of my "lie," or what is my insistence upon the universality of my claim, mean an admission of another's truth?

In his essay, "Jewish-Christian Relations in a Secular Age," David Novak points out the apparent danger of this kind of syncretism as applied to the Catholic Church's effort to apologize to the Jewish people for its failure to react sufficiently to the Nazi-executed murder of the Jewish people. In this interesting piece, Novak argues that the Catholic Church should and can repent before God for its failings but cannot and should not be expected to issue an apology to the Jewish people. Why? Because the Catholic Church, Novak says, has the right to refuse the influence of any external standard in determining the content of its own testimony. He says, "Religious traditions are in a constant state of development and renewed self-understanding. But the criteria of development, the standard for change, are based upon what is within. . . ."[51] Would I agree? Yes and no.

The content of a community's testimony is determined by that community. A community never has to consult another in order for its testimony to be valid insofar as the logic of the law protects the rights of the desires of any community to its testimony. By extension, as we have discussed, the logic of the law does not erase but exercises well-ordered boundaries between communities. To admit the "lie" does not oblige one to admit another tradition into one's own.

However, the overlap between my view and Novak's ends here. In my account, apologetic thinking does not mean the admission of your truths into my testimony, but it does mean the openness to changes in history as a potential influence on my testimony. If admitting the lie means admitting that my testimony always changes with time, it can also mean admitting the possibility of a historical intrusion. Whether or not this historical contribution becomes woven into the community's testimony is determined by the process of verification of the community. That the community should be open to historical intrusions means, however, that Jewish and/or Christian "learning,"[52] and/or thinking is not always identitarian but should also be inquisitive and open to other modes of publication as they express themselves. It can, as Rosenzweig says, "lift [itself] beyond the living needs of [its] thinking. . . ."[53] Apologetics premised on the truth of historicity as judged by the free law of revelation sponsors a multicultural curriculum.

A Word on Evil If concern regarding syncretism of claims constitutes the skeptic's first challenge to an apologetics within the law, the question of the admission of the possibility of evil claims constitutes the second. It is one thing, the objector might argue, to understand the correlation between my freedom and the rights of another so long as that other is not evil or deemed evil within the discourse of my community. But what happens to the correlation when the condition of the possibility of my freedom is the freedom of persons or a community who is evil? Is my freedom contingent upon their freedom?

To respond, let me first state that the correlation between my freedom and another's freedom is not tantamount to my inability to express a judgment; in this case, a negative judgment upon the beliefs of another tradition or person. Recall, it is identity and the right to issue claims that is secured in the justification of the law. It is precisely a community's right to its judgments that the recognition of another provides. Still, there are two qualifications that need stating. First, the condition of the possibility of my judgment *that* another is evil is the freedom of the other to be evil or to present positions freely regardless of how these positions are judged by others. To realize this, however, is to realize something larger: namely, that the condition of the possibility of my moral judgment is nothing other than the freedom of God. My community has the right to issue a moral claim only insofar as it stands under the final or ultimate judgment of God. If another community, whose freedom constitutes the condition of the possibility of my own, expresses this freedom in what I deem to be an evil way, they do so under the freedom and judgment of God, and consequently, the final judgment regarding their rights/status is not mine to make. Any judgment that I make about them is provisional: It is temporary; it is subject to the conditions of justification within the law, and therefore, although my community may issue a moral judgment, it cannot issue a universally determinative moral judgment for such judgments are possible only within the freedom of God.

JEWISH-CHRISTIAN LEARNING

Jewish-Christian Relations after the Holocaust Apologetics within the logic of the law is nonpolemical and supports a new approach to Jewish-Christian relations. Throughout history, formal relations between Jews and Christians have been mired in a logic of exceptionalism whereby each tradition regarded the other from the vantage point of the contest for truth. Although it is the central claim of this book that both traditions have always retained the theoretical capacity to engage in a lawful learning of the other, history has facilitated the extent to which the relation between the two traditions has been vulnerable to the logic of sacrifice. We can see this evidenced in a range of examples from Justin Martyr's *Apology*[54] to Augustine's doctrine of the Jews[55] through to the status of Jews within medieval Christian society,[56] up to and including the philosophical engagement between Jews and Christians during the Enlightenment.[57]

It is widely noted that after the Holocaust, Jewish-Christian relations altered.[58] In particular, the Holocaust prompted Christian theologians to reassess Christianity's historical and theological relationship to Judaism. This turn is evident in a range of post-Holocaust Christian responses, including but not limited to the Catholic Church's *Nostra Aetate*, the work of Rosemary Radford Ruether, Gregory Baum, and John Pawlikowski.[59] In the wake of these reassessments, Jews and Christians developed a greater willingness to converse with each other. Of course, a simple increase in the frequency and willingness of Jews and Christians to speak with one another does not signal an authentic change in Jewish-Christian relations.

In fact, a good deal of the work performed in Jewish-Christian relations over the past 50 years has, despite its best intentions, remained structured by an exceptionalist logic. During this time, we can identify two different approaches to Jewish-Christian relations. The first approach is represented by the work of Kendall Soulen and Michael Wyschogrod, and the second approach is represented in the work of Joseph Soloveitchik and David Novak.

In their work, Soulen and Wyschogrod make significant strides in furthering a Jewish recognition of Christianity and a Christian recognition of Judaism. Both ground the possibility of Jewish-Christian relations in the identification of a family resemblance between the two traditions. In his work, Soulen invites Christians to recognize God's unique and meaningful relationship to Israel. This, Soulen argues, enhances Christian self-understanding and enables Christians to overcome their instrumentalist account of God's one-time dealings with this ill-disciplined people. For example, in *The God of Israel and Christian Theology*, Soulen says,

> The necessary correction is a frank reorientation of the hermeneutical center of the Scriptures from the incarnation to the reign of God, where God's reign is understood as the eschatological outcome of human history at the end of time. On this view, God's covenant with Israel in the midst of the nations does not come to end with Jesus Christ's resurrection, nor indeed with any event prior to the eschatological consummation of God's reign. Rather, God's history with Israel and the nations remains the constant and universal medium of God's ongoing work as the Consummator of the human family in the midst of creation.[60]

Like Soulen, Wyschogrod's account of Jewish-Christian relations is also premised upon the identity between the God of Israel and the God of

Christ. "The disagreement between Judaism and Christianity with respect to the incarnation . . . while not reconcilable, can be brought into the context within which it is a difference of faith regarding the free and sovereign act of the God of Israel."[61] This claim licenses Wyschogrod to open theological conversation with Christians on a whole range of topics, including incarnation, blessing, eucharist, Temple, and others. The identification of the God of Israel and the God of Christianity frees both theologians to explore the theological content of the other's tradition for the sake of gaining a better understanding of the God whom they worship.

Why is this not enough? Both Wyschogrod and Soulen remain bound to a truth-driven approach to Jewish-Christian relations. When describing Wyschogrod's approach to Jewish-Christian relations, Soulen showcases this shared feature of their work, and says,

> For Wyschogrod, theologically significant conversation between Jews and Christians is possible because both Judaism and Christianity acknowledge "a movement of God toward humankind as witnessed in Scripture" a movement that engages humankind in God's election of Israel. To be sure the two communities understand this movement in ways that unmistakably diverge, at least at certain points. Yet, the gulf that results is not so wide that understanding is impossible. Indeed as Wyschogrod holds, because the two traditions share certain common premises it is possible "for each side to summon the other to a better understanding of its own tradition." For Wyschogrod, Jewish-Christian relations concern something more important than "dialogue." They concern a common search for truth in light of the Word of God.[62]

Even though Wyschogrod and Soulen have identified a shared truth between Jews and Christians, this does not free them from exceptionalist logic but only relocates the exception as whatever set of beliefs fall outside of the rubric of God's electing and/or redemptive labor with Israel. The cornerstone of this approach is the value and significance of God's election of Israel. Participation in this election renders each tradition meaningful and valid. God loves the people Israel, and Christians are engrafted upon this primary love and participate in the blessings that God promised Abraham and his descendants. Where, however, does this leave either tradition's ability to recognize positions outside of this biblical paradigm? Outside positions assume value only insofar as they have a role in this narrative. But, this excludes the self-understanding of any non-Jewish or non-Christian position. The fact that Jews and Christians agree upon a truth claim does not help adjudicate either of the two traditions' relations to those outside the Judeo-Christian world view, and furthermore, it veils the range of residual points of contest between Judaism and Christianity that therefore also remain unadjudicated.

The second approach represented by the work of Soloveitchik and Novak argues contra Wyschogrod and Soulen that Jewish-Christian relations are most successfully rooted in each tradition's respect for the creator God and not on the grounds of a common understanding of the event of divine revelation and election. In the famous article, "Confrontation," Soloveitchik argues that there is a difference between a person's participation in general society and a person's religious community. All persons share a created status as members in the wider society but participation in one's faith-community is not translatable to others. It is impossible, he says,

> ... to speak of Jewish identity without realizing that this term can only be understood under the aspect of singularity and otherness. There is no identity without uniqueness. As there cannot be an equation between two individuals unless they are converted into abstractions, it is likewise absurd to speak of the commensurability of two faith communities which are individual entities.[63]

Consequently, Soloveitchik argues, the particular content of one's faith-community cannot constitute the basis for an encounter between persons of different traditions. To relate to one another, persons must approach each other within the sphere of shared commitments and shared truths—and, according to Soloveitchik, the arena of shared experience is the general society.

> [W]e, created in the image of God, are charged with responsibility for the great confrontation of man and the cosmos. We stand with civilized society shoulder to shoulder over against an order which defies us all. Second, as a charismatic faith community, we have to meet the challenge of confronting the general non-Jewish faith community. We are called upon to tell this community not only the story it already knows—that we are human beings, committed to the general welfare and progress of mankind, that we are interested in combating disease, in alleviating human suffering, in protecting man's rights, in helping the needy, *et cetera*—but also what is still unknown to it, namely, our otherness as a metaphysical covenantal community.[64]

David Novak's work further develops the structure of Soloveitchik's analysis through an analysis of the role of natural law within Jewish-Christian relations. Like Solovetichik, Novak insists that "the ultimate claims of Judaism and Christianity are mutually exclusive" but that "this need be the basis of hostile disputations only when it is assumed that Judaism and Christianity have no commonalities at all."[65] Also like Soloveitchik, Novak locates the point of commonality between the two traditions within the condition of human creatureliness. All persons are created in the image of God, Novak frequently argues. As such, persons function "naturally" and achieve awareness of their creatureliness within social relations that expose another person as a check upon the free reign of my desire or what is tantamount to my finitude. This limit upon our freedom, Novak refers to as natural law, and natural law therefore constitutes the minimal condition of justice emergent from the reality of social existence. Unlike other natural law theorists, Novak does not identify this minimal condition of justice with positive universal legislation but understands that different traditions express this limit within culturally specific terms. Within rabbinic Judaism, Novak identifies natural law with laws regarding the Noahide, but the identification between natural law and Noahide law is unique to Judaism and would not itself constitute a basis for Jewish-Christian dialog. What does constitute the basis for Jewish-Christian dialog is the commonality of the minimal condition of justice as expressed in varying forms by Jews and Christians and all persons whose cultures or traditions retain an awareness of a transcendent standard of justice. In this way, the common condition of natural law can, according to Novak, fund a tradition-based comparative ethics.

Still, like Soloveitchik, Novak's approach suffers certain significant limits. By premising Jewish-Christian relations upon a common truth regarding human creation, both thinkers inevitably foreclose the possibility of a Jewish-Christian conversation that reaches into the deepest truths of each tradition. Both thinkers bear the limits of an exceptionalist model that dismisses or renders invisible that which is not exposed within the confines of the chosen truth. Of course, neither Novak nor Soloveitchik begrudged this fact. Neither bemoaned the limits of a Christian understanding or recognition of Judaism because in their estimation, the price of such exposure was the loss of the exclusivity or uniqueness of Jewish truth claims. However, Soloveitchik and Novak were limited by a false-choice. One need not sacrifice self-preservation for the sake of the recognition of the other for it is only through the ability to recognize another that one retains the very conditions of one's existence.

Jewish-Christian Learning If, in Chapter 5, I outlined the nature of Jewish and Christian relations to non-Jewish and non-Christian culture within a logic of the law, the preceding detailed account of an apologetic thinking within law permits us to examine the specifics of a post-polemical Jewish-Christian engagement. The key to rerouting Jewish-Christian relations has to do with reorienting the terms of the conversation away from analyses of truth and toward the mandate to develop a curriculum of mutual education.

Of course, the mandate to educate presupposes the value of what is to be learned. A Jewish-Christian curriculum of mutual education presupposes the rights of both traditions to present and perpetuate their respective world views, and this is what the logic of the law renders possible. Beyond this, learning also presupposes the free desire to engage with and/or inquire into these alternative positions. Operating within the context of the logic of the law, Jewish and Christian learning performs the free inquiry into the full breadth of the claims made by the other tradition. As we have seen, the lawful rights of another do not, within the logic of the law, stand in conflict with my own interests. The law is free for me. It does not demand that I compromise my desire to meet its demands. Rather, my desire is secured in the recognition of the value of another's claims, and as a result, Jews and Christians have a mutual interest in learning about the full range of the other's religious expression. In this context, Jewish-Christian learning is not something that I do despite my desire to testify but as an extension of my testimony to the free and lawful God.

What does a curriculum in Jewish-Christian education look like? What forms of study might the full exposure of another's tradition take when Jewish-Christian relations are no longer predicated upon the discernment and protection of truth-claims? In what follows, I will offer four examples of this sort of Jewish-Christian education.

The Challenge of History and Parallel Problem Solving One of the greatest benefits of a nonpolemically driven apologetics arises from the freedom it presents for Jews and Christians to benefit productively from the work and experiences of the other tradition as this tradition responds to historical challenges. In other words, an apologetics within the law justifies and encourages each tradition to study and learn from one another's history. There are many examples of this sort of engagement. We might consider, for example, a Christian study of the Jewish mode of responding to the destruction of the Temple through the range of textual and legal reactions. A free and open Christian study of this Jewish response could produce a number of significant benefits for Christians: Christian analysis of the Jewish textual response could educate Christians to a range of hermeneutical possibilities for contending with ruptures between historical experience and primary sacred texts; Christian analysis of the Jewish theological response to the destruction of the Temple could enhance Christian theological understanding of mourning, survival, and renewal; Christian analysis of the Jewish responses to the loss of the Temple could deepen a Christian understanding of rabbinic Judaism, that form of Judaism that Christianity has most neglected and with which it has stood in the greatest contest for the history of Jewish-Christian relations.

One of the greatest examples of Jews learning from a Christian historical response can be found in the impact of Martin Luther King's 1960's civil rights movement upon Jewish participation, generally speaking, and upon the involvement of Abraham Joshua Heschel, in particular. In her essay, "Praying with their Feet: Remembering Abraham Joshua Heschel and Martin Luther King," Heschel's daughter, Susannah Heschel, speaks of King's impact upon her father, and says,

> The relationship between the two men began in January 1963, and was a genuine friendship of affection as well as a relationship of two colleagues working together in political causes. . . . King encouraged Heschel's involvement in the Civil Rights movement. . . . When the conservative rabbis of America gathered in 1968 to celebrate Heschel's sixtieth birthday, the keynote speaker they invited was King. When King was assassinated, Heschel was the rabbi Mrs. King invited to speak at his funeral.[66]

Both King and Heschel reaped enormous benefits from their relationship, and their relationship deepened Jewish-Christian relations. Unoccupied by the need to persuade the other, each supported the other's work, and each acquired a deeper understanding of the similarities between their two traditions. Heschel reflects upon this, and says,

> Theologically as well as politically, King and Heschel recognized their own strong kinship. For each there was an emphatic stress on the dependence of the political on the spiritual, God on human society, the moral life on economic well-being. Indeed, there are numerous passages in their writings that might have been composed by either one. . . . Both Heschel and King . . . spoke of God in similar terms, as deeply involved in the affairs of human history.[67]

The capacity to engage in this sort of study of the other's historical responses reinvigorates the value of the study of religious history for each tradition. Such an approach avoids disingenuous claims to objective neutrality because both parties present themselves as committed believers. Within the logic of the law, the particularity of each tradition is justified by virtue of the irreducibility of the other. The presentation of particular differences does not obstruct free inquiry but encourages it.

Theology Jewish and Christian learning can and should include theology. By theological learning, I mean that Jews and Christians are free to inquire into the full range of the fundamentals of each other's tradition. Ever since the 1990s, a rich friendship has developed between Wyschogrod and

Soulen, and although I do not agree with their approach to Jewish-Christian relations, *practically speaking*, their theological exchanges offer a fine example of the benefits of this sort of learning when taken out of the context of their truth-driven approach to Jewish-Christian relations. In these exchanges, Soulen and Wyschogrod demonstrate how Jewish-Christian theological exchange opens one's perspective of the other tradition and enhances one's self-understanding in the process. In his essay, "Incarnation and God's Indwelling in Israel," Wyschogrod studies and discusses the incarnation of Christ and links the incarnation with God's care and desire to be near the body Israel. In one fell swoop, Wyschogrod educates Jews about the incarnation of Christ and helps Jews recall the nearness of God within their own biblical tradition. By the same token, Soulen's book, *The God of Israel and Christian Theology*, teaches Christians about God's election of Abraham as an election into divine care and blessing. In this way, Soulen not only asks Christians to consider how Jews experience God's election *qua* "blessing," but he also permits Christians to reconsider the purpose of Christ's election as part and parcel of God's wider interest in the blessing and care of all his children. By teaching Christians a Jewish concept, Soulen expands Christian self-understanding on its own terms. While, therefore, Soulen and Wyschogrod premise their engagement upon a shared appreciation for the truth of the God of Israel, the sort of examination each presents of the other's central theological categories could easily operate within the logic of the law and could, therefore, in this context, be emblematic of a more expanded free curriculum of learning between the two traditions.

Scriptural Study When the pursuit of truth is no longer an issue, Jewish-Christian learning frees both traditions to study each other's sacred texts together. Let me give you a brief example from texts that I have discussed earlier in the volume. In Luke 4, Jesus says, "The Spirit of the Lord is upon me, because he has anointed me to preach good news to the poor. He has sent me to proclaim release to the captives and recovering of sight to the blind, to set at liberty those who are oppressed, to proclaim the acceptable year of the Lord."[68] In this sermon, Jesus quotes from the book of Isaiah (61:1, 2) and invokes the concept of the Jubilee year. Of course, the notion of the Jubilee year derives from Leviticus where the Jubilee year offers a year of rest for the land and a redistribution of wealth for its inhabitants.

> And you shall hallow the fiftieth year, and proclaim liberty throughout the land to all its inhabitants; it shall be a jubilee for you, when each of you shall return to his property and each of you shall return to his family. . . . [I]n it you shall neither sow, nor reap what grows of itself. . . . You shall not wrong one another, but you shall fear your God; for I am the Lord your God.[69]

Luke's Jesus does not mention Leviticus or the link between the Jubilee and the land. A Jewish-Christian text study would enable Christians to recognize the significance of the land for any Jewish account of the Jubilee and would begin a process whereby Christians might begin to repair their often-confused assumptions about the Jewish concern for the land. By the same token, Jews have much to gain by rereading Leviticus 25 alongside Luke 4. Jews read Leviticus through the lens of rabbinic texts, and according to the rabbis, the Jubilee year is no longer performed because Jews no longer live in the land with the Temple. Consequently, Jews often forget the meaning of the Jubilee and the important statement that it makes about God's concern for the poor. Jews who read about Jesus' emphasis upon God's interest in healing the poor can be reminded of this facet of their love for God.

Are Jews engaged in Jewish-Christian text study allowing the New Testament to trump rabbinic texts? Are Christians bypassing the authority of the later dogmatic and exegetical traditions? No. As an expression of the Jewish community's historical testimony, rabbinic texts always retain an authority for the Jewish community that non-Jewish texts cannot have. That the New Testament can enhance Jewish self-understanding does not mean that Jews will turn toward it to understand their community's historical desires and specific relationship to God. On the other hand, it is the case that the very appreciation of divine freedom that renders Jewish-Christian learning possible can temper rabbinic claims to exclusive Jewish self-understanding. If God is free, the divine prerogative does not rest strictly upon the rabbis to the exclusion of other Jewish expressions of God's encounter with the people Israel. Certainly, the same holds true for Christians eager to retain the authority of later Christian dogmatic and exegetical writings. In point of fact, Jewish-Christian text study can have an emancipatory effect upon Jews and Christians themselves, whereby Jews and Christians of all expressions are justified in the diversity and irreducibility of their accounts with no brand or approach retaining a monopoly on truth. Scriptural learning can help repair long-standing internal debates over the significance of one denomination or exegetical tradition against another. The logic of the law dismantles denominationalism's self-certainty. A scriptural engagement between Jews and Christians that earmarks the irreducible worth of the other traditions' interpretation can also earmark the worth of another denomination or exegetical strategy within one's own tradition.[70]

Liturgical Learning Finally, Jewish-Christian learning frees members of each tradition to learn from one another's liturgical lives. It may once again be the case that such learning opens forgotten aspects of Jewish and Christian prayer. Religious scholars, myself included, have remarked upon the nearness to God experienced in the Eucharist and the similarities between this encounter and the participation of the community of rabbis in studying Jewish texts.[71] Moreover, Jews who have read, for example, the Book of Common Prayer gain a much deeper understanding of the meaning of the presence of God through Christ in a Christian's daily life and may also walk away with a greater appreciation of the beauty and depth of daily Jewish prayer. For many years now, Christians have studied about the Seder and its founding narrative in the book of Exodus and have deepened their understanding of the character of political emancipation afforded by God's acts in history with the Jewish people. Such examinations have funded Christian re-readings of the meaning of the Eucharist and have inspired a Christian return to theo-politics in a post-secular age.[72]

Although Jewish and Christian liturgical teaching is not new, the development of a curriculum in each tradition's liturgical life within the logic of the law guarantees that liturgical exchange does not promote a hidden agenda of persuasion and is not driven by an interest in the reform or renewal of the meaning of each tradition's liturgical life.[73] To the extent that a free inquiry into each tradition's liturgical life does promote reform or reflection within one's own community, such a benefit accrues only because of the freedom with which the learning transpires and is not the premise for the learning because such a premise easily devolves into polemical thinking.

Each of the preceding four areas of a Jewish-Christian curriculum of learning presents countless possibilities for a vital engagement between Jews and Christians as rooted within the logic of the law. This type of curriculum has many practical benefits and can generate and/or support joint efforts to respond to a whole host of current challenges, including but not limited to ethical problem solving, economic loss, and political and religious conflict resolution. Within the logic of the law, each of these engagements acts as a practical witness to the freedom of God as love and law—a freedom of the God who is "with us" in the difference and affirmation of our humanity as it labors to testify to this God in history.

SEVEN

Christianity and the Law: The Law as the Form of the Gospel

At this stage of our discussion, the central argument of the volume has been presented. Despite the preponderance of theologians and philosophers whose thought has been patterned after a logic of sacrifice and exceptionalism, the theology of the biblical text coupled with the philosophical analyses of Schelling and Rosenzweig expose a logic of law—a logic emergent from the biblical conception of election that funds a nonpolemical account of power and apologetic relations between Jews and Christians, and between Jews, Christians, and the wider society.

This exegetically and philosophically presented blueprint of the law now in place, we must inquire into the viability of a logic of the law for Christian theology. If, as I have argued, a logic of the law reveals the nonpolemical character of election, what place does such a logic have within Christian theology, and can a Christian theological recuperation of the law offer a similar basis for a Christian apologetics? The central purpose of this chapter is to defend this claim by way of an analysis of the meaning of law within Karl Barth's *Church Dogmatics*. More specifically, I will argue that Barth's

Christianity and the Law: The Law as the Form of the Gospel 227

claim that the "Law is the form of the Gospel" funds a Christologically based articulation of the logic of the law.

To say that Barth's theology honors and requires law does not mean that it presupposes and/or requires the performance of Jewish law. What then does it mean? Throughout the past 30 years, a number of Jewish scholars have tackled Barth's theology because, in large measure, of the covenantal focus of his Christology. It might appear useful to consult these Jewish interpretations of Barth's work by, for example, Michael Wyschogrod or David Novak, in order to excavate a Barthian theology of the law. However, our analysis must look elsewhere because neither Wyschogrod nor Novak provide a detailed account of Barth's concept of the law as the form of the gospel. Wyschogrod focuses his attention on Barth's scripturalism,[1] while Novak attempts to discern a natural law theology in Barth's work,[2] but neither recognizes the central link between revelatory gospel and law as first articulated by Barth in II.2 of the *Dogmatics* and then discussed at length throughout the remaining volumes of this work. Instead, I want to approach my analysis of the role of law in Barth's theology by way of an interpretation offered by a different and much more critical Jewish scholar—Jacob Taubes—whose *The Political Theology of Paul* I discussed briefly in Chapter 1.

Jacob Taubes and the Critique of Theology

In an infrequently discussed article, "Theodicy and Theology: A Philosophical Analysis of Karl Barth's Dialectical Theology," Taubes presents a critical analysis of Barth's *Church Dogmatics* as a glaring example of the inextricable link between theology and theodicy. If, Taubes suggests, Barth's earlier second edition of the *Epistle to the Romans* attempted to disengage theology from an exercise in divine and human self-justification and tyranny, theology (in general) and Barth's incarnational Christology (in particular) thwart this critical move by collapsing any substantive difference between the divine and the human in the context of a redemptive scheme that essentializes and props up both as fully self-justified. Taubes's reading of Barth's later work rests on a fundamental misreading of Barth's theology of divine freedom and divine law and offers a unique opportunity to appreciate not only the mechanics of Barth's account of divine freedom but the manner by which they give rise to the contextualization of divine and human freedom within the free and affirming limits of the law.

HERESY AND ITS PROPONENTS

Taubes's analysis of Barth's work reflects Taubes's commitment to what he coins a "messianic logic" most easily identifiable in the writings of St. Paul on the one hand and the messianic ideology surrounding Sabbatei Zevi (1626) on the other hand. Before piecing together Taubes's messianic logic with his reading of Barth, it is worthwhile to recall my earlier discussion of Taubes's *The Political Theology of Paul* in Chapter 1 of this book. There, I turned to Taubes's *The Political Theology of Paul* to illuminate the exceptionalism in the work of Rosenstock-Huessy and Giorgio Agamben. I used Taubes's keen recognition of the exercise of "outbidding," whereby governed by the desire to present and secure the absolute legitimacy of a particular set of beliefs, an individual or community delegitimizes or sacrifices the claims of others. Taubes's insightful account of the role of desire in claim making helped identify the logic of sacrifice in Rosenstock's Christological essentialism and in Agamben's account of *pistis* or messianic "faith" in the "as not." Consequently, Taubes's account of the Pauline desire for legitimacy in the face of the normative ideological and legal systems of his day offered a critical lens through which to recognize Rosenstock-Huessy's and Agamben's lack of historical and epistemological self-consciousness regarding the character of their so-called emancipatory programs.

In Chapter 1, I suggested that much of the significance of Taubes's work for contemporary Jewish-Christian relations has to do with his identification of the role of desire within certain appropriations of the model of biblical election. As is clear by now, this book argues that Jewish-Christian dialog cannot proceed in earnest by simply identifying the shared covenantal origins and structure of each tradition unless a rigorous analysis of the logic of law—or the nexus between freedom and law operative within the biblical concept of election is exposed. Taubes's analysis of Pauline messianism contributed to casting a critical eye over knee-jerk accounts of election and exposed the drive for legitimacy and consequent impulse for outbidding that has characterized the inner motivation of Jewish-Christian dialogue for most of its history. The key to understanding Taubes's critical analysis of the logic of sacrifice within certain presentations of biblical election has to do with his identification of Paul as a Jewish heretic when heresy is understood as an intra-traditional mechanism for responding to historical catastrophe. If, in other words, the logic of sacrifice requires the expulsion of the heretic in order to sustain the legitimacy of the truths it presents, Taubes's analysis of Paul refuses this expulsion and insists upon the reintegration of the heretic and his ideas back into the dominant world view.

According to Taubes, scholarship has long over-dramatized the polemical divide between Pauline theology and Judaism. In Taubes's estimation, Martin Buber's characterization of the difference between Pauline *pistis* and Jewish *emunah* offers a prime example. In Buber's account, Paul is held responsible for the inauguration of a not only a new object of religious belief but a new model of religious life premised upon the conversion of an individual in faith over and against the life of *emunah*, or the natural saturation in a community that "engulfs and determines him."[3] In Buber's view, *pistis*—or the belief "in" something—is Greek in contrast to *emunah*, or community dwelling which is biblical. Paul becomes the ring leader of the Athens-Jerusalem divide now translated into Christological terms.

Taubes's criticism of this classic Pauline-Jewish divide is now well supported by biblical scholarship. Among the scholars who have noted the internal Jewish context of Paul's writings are Krister Stendhal, E. P. Sanders, John Gager, and others. The sheer fact, according to Taubes, that "the word 'Christian' . . . doesn't yet exist for Paul"[4] is only the tip of iceberg with regard to the dismantling of this stereotype. Beyond this, a careful reading of Paul's writings underscores the extent to which Paul understood his theology as internal to the Judaism of his day.

"My thesis," Taubes says, "is that Paul understands himself as outbidding Moses."[5] On the one hand, outbidding suggests a positive comparison between two types. Paul sees himself as like Moses. On the other hand, outbidding also suggests the out-doing of the prior example as an insufficient expression of this type. Paul sees himself as a better Moses than Moses. Paul, Taubes argues, "stands before the very same problem [as] . . . Moses."[6] While the Moses of Exodus stood before God seeking the legitimacy of the people Israel, Paul stood before God begging for the justification of the people Israel again. In each instance, Taubes reflects, "the people have sinned"[7] first with regard to the incident of the golden calf and second with regard to the rejection of Jesus as Messiah. Regardless of the particular sin, both leaders find themselves in the position of needing to respond to what in Taubes's view constitutes an historical catastrophe—a tear in the seam of the redeemed nexus between God and his people, and both leaders use a transvaluation of ideas: that is to say, present a dramatic and polemical challenge to the dominant notions of the *status quo* to effect the action required as a response to this historical reality. In the first instance, Moses recognizes the injustice of his people, and in his effort to relegitimize them, demands a transvaluation of the primacy of divine justice into the primacy of divine mercy. Moses stands up to God and challenges his power and his "justice": "*Elohim hayyim* is a polemical formula,"[8] Taubes notes (having learned this, he claims, from Carl Schmitt). At once, therefore, Moses positions himself as both polemical heretic and leader of the nation. From the vantage point of the system of divine justice, the people ought to be sacrificed for the sake of their sin. The system privileges the just and excludes the unjust. Moses rejects this exceptionalism and interprets their sin as evidence of the fundamental divide between history and the fulfillment of divine justice in the world. Moses *qua* heretic walks away not only as leader of the nation but as the only authentic reader of history as well.

Paul, Taubes thinks, functions similarly. Like Moses, he is concerned to legitimize the people of God in their sin, here linked with the crucifixion of Jesus as the Messiah. The Messiah has been crucified. Messianic redemption has failed to take place in the realm of history, and the people are responsible for this tear in the redemptive structure. In the wake of this catastrophe, the people must atone and be forgiven. They must have some way to contend with the dramatic rupture within their historical experience. Where can they find this legitimization and repair their sense of justified participation in their world? Can they have recourse to the dominant world view of their day: that is, view themselves as the people Israel as understood by the mainstream community? No, from the perspective of the *status quo*, persons proclaiming the catastrophe of the crucified messiah are fanatical heretics, outside the fold of the normative approach to the divine-human relationship. The normative tradition, Taubes suggests, cannot sustain itself against the falsifying power of this historical event and so declares those for whom it has the power to undermine the promise of divine redemption as heretics excluded from the norm. Like Moses, Paul resists this exclusion and foists himself *qua* heretic back into the tradition. However, for reasons stated earlier, such an imposition cannot come in the form of a repetition of Paul's place within normative Judaism but can only assume the form of a transvaluation of the values of that normative position, here a transvaluation of the status-producing role of *nomos* within the Jewish-Hellenic cultural and political alliance of the day. Paul is like the biblical Moses on the one hand, but the anti-type of the Moses presented by the tradition that developed from him on the other hand. Both boldly reject the exceptionalism implicit in their own traditions, an exceptionalism funded by the tradition's insistent denial regarding history's perpetual falsification of the prophetic possibility.

We can now see, perhaps more clearly than before, how Taubes's analysis of Paul offers a strong critique of the exceptionalism linked to the ossification and essentialism of Judaism and/or Christianity as religious traditions or ideologies. Within this context, the heretic is hailed as the voice of exteriority demonized by the *status quo*, the agent of what Taubes refers to as a

Christianity and the Law: The Law as the Form of the Gospel 231

negative political theology, or the advancement of a historically self-conscious documentation of the tendency by all traditions and/or ideologies to negate the falsifying reality of events.

Taubes's analysis of Paul mollifies the long-standing polemic between Pauline Christianity and first-century Judaism on the one hand, and perhaps more significantly, challenges the tradition of Jewish-Christian enmity that has developed in its wake. Still, we must ask, if Taubes's messianic logic presents a more sober and realistic account of the character of the Pauline-Jewish polemic, has it done enough to depolemicize Jewish-Christian relations overall, or does it reinstall the logic of sacrifice and exceptionalism it seeks to repeal? In what follows, I will argue that despite Taubes's contribution, his celebration of the heretic as the singular voice of exteriority "in the fold" ultimately justifies a regular transvaluation of values against the "norm," or what is the perpetuation of a dangerous pattern of enmity and polemic as the mainstay of a tradition's capacity for self-critique. Said otherwise, if Taubes hails the heretic as the only voice of critique, he is hereby committed to a kind of scorched-earth account of the exercise of admitting exteriority into our traditions. Traditions do not admit exteriority and contend with it via a process of internal change but are inevitably and only overtaken by the undermining voice of the so-called heretic whose criticism dismantles the validity of the world view as a whole. If Rosenstock-Huessy and Agamben exclude the inessential from the essential, Taubes imposes the inessential back onto the essential still operating, however, within the same dialectic between believer and heretic, excluder and excluded, typical of the logic of sacrifice. Neither can Paul *qua* heretic ever be authentically folded back into the tradition, nor can the tradition ever authentically reinterpret itself through the lens of the heretic's exterior cry for acceptance. The dialectic of exception remains regardless of whether it is the believer or the heretic who is the more prized. Taubes's celebration of the heretic does little to alter the reality of polemical thinking despite the relocation of it to an intratraditional rather than intertraditional phenomenon.

In fact, Taubes's account of the inevitable exclusion of the Pauline community from the normative Jewish society of the day not only documents but justifies Paul's polemical, but in this case, antinomian posture over and against Judaism. The logic here is as follows: The normative community from which one seeks legitimization is itself *qua* essentialist, illegitimate, or impervious to critique. Granted the *status quo*'s refusal to admit exteriority or critique, polemical renunciation of the dominant world view constitutes the only possible reaction. Normative world views that refuse the interruption of history and the input of those who experience it wax tyrannical and leave no option for critique save rebellion in the form of ideological warfare. With this position, Taubes identifies the point of difference between his account of "negative political theology" and that presented by Carl Schmitt. As Aleida Assmann suggests,

> Schmitt's position . . . claims that there are no "immanent" categories to which a political order could appeal for its legitimacy. On this point Schmitt and Taubes (as well as the Paul Taubes has in mind) appear to agree. But while Taubes (and Paul) derive from this the conclusion that there are no legitimate political orders whatsoever (but only legal orders)—this point of view regards itself as "negative political theology"—Schmitt retains the postulate of the representative political order, which draws its legitimacy from the divine sovereignty which it has made manifest.[9]

Paul in Taubes's account is no politician. Neither is he a prophet nor a philosopher. Instead,

> [H]e clambers out of the consensus between Greek-Jewish-Hellenistic mission-theology . . . Paul is a fanatic! Paul is a zealot, a Jewish zealot. . . . He is totally illiberal . . . this is someone who answers the same thing in a completely different way, that is, with a protest, with a transvaluation of values. . . . This is incredible and compared to this all the little revolutionaries are nothing. . . .[10]

Paul's Gospel amounts in Taubes words to nothing less than a political "declaration of war,"[11] and by war, Taubes does not mean a provisionally destructive tool used to ultimately restore a stable order but rather a chaotic response to catastrophe that presupposes the insidiousness of all orderly attempts to fend off the forces of history in the name of the retention of power. Critique can never operate as successful apologetics but always destroys what it challenges.

This perspective presents enormous problems for Jewish-Christian relations, and we can see this in Taubes's own thought in the essay, "The Issue between Judaism and Christianity: Facing Up to the Unresolvable Difference," written in 1953. Here, Taubes lays out what he presents as the irreconcilable point of enmity between Judaism and Christianity, an enmity that goes all the back to the originary exercise of Pauline outbidding. Although Taubes's position may undermine the long-standing assessment of the difference between *emunah* and *pistis* best represented in Buber's account, it is nonetheless the case that from the perspective of a Pauline account of Christianity, the two traditions remain fundamentally at odds over the issue of the law. It is the law more than monotheism, Taubes asserts, that constitutes the central and defining element of Judaism through time. And consequently, he argues, that if

[C]hallenges not to Judaism's monotheism but to the validity and interpretation of the Law, shake the Jewish religion and community to their foundations ... [Then a]ny messianic claim represents such a challenge because it claims to have ushered in an age in which the Law is superseded.[12]

If, on the one hand, such a perspective raises the possibility of internal Jewish polemics along the lines of Sabbateinism, it is also the case that it sustains a polemic between Judaism and Christianity so far as the latter develops out of what is originally an internal and then external messianic/heretical movement. Undoubtedly, Taubes argues, *halakha* is more than legalism. Nonetheless, as diverse a category as it is and regardless of how compatible *halakha* is with varying expressions of Judaism—for example, rational, mystical, and otherwise—it nonetheless sets the perimeters of what counts as normative and exterior to normative Judaism."*Halakha* is not an empty vessel into which any sort of contents can be poured. It has its limit in the divine law and Messianism in any form must necessarily transgress that limit."[13] By extension, then

Judaism must reject Christianity's interpretation of itself [that is, of Judaism] ... Christian history, as I have said, constitutes no "mystery" for the Jewish religion. Christianity represents a crisis that is "typical" in Jewish history and expresses a typical Jewish "heresy": antinomian Messianism-the belief that with the coming of the Messiah, not observance of the Law, but faith in him is required for salvation.[14]

What then can we say about Jewish-Christian relations from a Taubesian perspective? Clearly, for Taubes, there is no path to a healthy apologetic for either tradition. Inevitably, Judaism and Christian remain in opposition toward each other. Still, Taubes suggests, such enmity is better than the alternative, a *faux* tolerance premised upon some liberal identification of commonality whether this is identified as monotheism, love, or ethics. Much worse than a perpetual tug of war between the two traditions is an inauthentic appeal to a form of liberal redemption that denies the vitality of the heretical push and pull between the two. That Christianity emerges from the liberating honesty of Paul's reaction to normative Judaism is, consequently, only one side of the story, after all. Jews, for their part, Taubes suggests, have good reason (namely, that reason cannot authentically mollify the differences between them) to reassert their characteristic commitment to law and to justice. By virtue of its brutal honesty and its persistent refusal to accept the imposition of another world view's exceptionalism, enmity constitutes the only trustworthy indicator of the insistence upon historical realism over and against hegemonic fantasy.

[T]he controversy between the Jewish and Christian religions points to the perennial conflict between the principle of law and the principle of love. The "yoke of the Law" is challenged by the enthusiasm of love. But the "justice of the Law" may, in the end, be the only challenge to the arbitrariness of love.[15]

As I have noted several times before, Taubes's keen recognition of the tension and enmity between Judaism and Christianity, even as this tension is whitewashed in liberal efforts at reconciliation, constitutes a significant contribution of his work toward moving Jewish-Christian relations forward. The enmity between the two is a reality. The fork in the road between Taubes's position and the position presented in this book concerns the possibility of a relationship between the two traditions after the reality of the enmity is acknowledged, and ultimately, the determination of that possibility is theological in nature.

At the end of the day, Taubes's indebtedness to the dialectic of sacrifice derives from his inability to see religious traditions and/or their theologies as anything other than self-validating and impervious to critique. Taubes's analysis of the need for legitimization and the inevitable failure to fully secure it is a reflection of the logic of his particular brand of the positive and coercive character of political theology. Theology is always political, and politics is always theological. Taubes's skepticism regarding the hidden agendas at work in all expressions of order exposes a tyranny or capriciousness identified at once with the divine and the human. Political or orderly structures which, *qua* essentialist, refuse possible falsification by the challenges of history often tout their power as divinely installed, divine chosen, divinely sanctioned. Divine capriciousness frequently translates into the privileging of the few over the many. Expressed as either favoritism toward the elect or anger toward the rejected, divine fancy secures and legitimizes what are *de facto*, illegitimately sustained systems of power. By extension, therefore, and ironically enough, divine caprice expresses itself in human deification. Consequently, the less-than-holy alliance between divine caprice and human tyranny props up each element against the forces of falsification. Mapping the movements of the divine and the human, theology inevitably endorses the terms of this unholy alliance and can do little but articulate the mutual verification of each element's illicit claim for self-justifiability and caprice. In this way, as Aleida Assmann attests, "legitimacy is denied to all sovereigns of this world, be they imperatorial or theocratic."[16] And contrary to the grandiose claims of hegemonic systems, there is, Taubes insists, a fundamental "futility of creation. All of this is . . . to be found in Romans 8: the groaning of the creature . . . [and] that's what Benjamin is talking about. That is, the idea of creation as decay . . . without hope."[17]

We see Taubes's assessment of the limits of theology most explicitly in his 1953 article, "Theodicy and Theology: A Philosophical Analysis of Karl Barth's Dialectical Theology."[18] The primary objective of the article is to critique the incarnational theology of Barth's *Church Dogmatics* as apologetics in the worse sense of the word: that is, the unexamined defense of the portrait of divine redemptive activity. Still, a second and almost equally significant goal of the essay is to challenge what appear to be the new possibilities implicit in dialectical theology for announcing the catastrophic difference between the divine and the human—or what would be tantamount to a theologically authentic account of the impossibility of redemption.

THE VIRTUES AND VICES OF DIALECTICAL THEOLOGY

In *The Political Theology of Paul*, Taubes describes Karl Barth's second edition of the Romans commentary as "one variant in the collapse of German cultural Protestantism. About this edition, Karl Barth says, No stone has stayed in its place. . . ."[19] And earlier in his essay on Barth and theodicy, Taubes says similarly, "it seemed that Karl Barth's *Romans* was not theology but 'religious literature' and therefore not theodicy. . . . An attempt at theology without theodicy!"[20] Dialectical theology like that described by Barth in his second edition to the *Epistle to the Romans* offers an important test case for theology, generally speaking. With its emphasis upon the dramatic and radical difference between the divine and the human, it performs theology as the announcement of crisis rather than theology as the assertion of redemption. As a theology of crisis, dialectical theology in Taubes's view poses the possibility of a theological announcement of the impossibility of redemption—a theology after prophecy, a theology of sin and tireless critique. In this way, dialectical theology comes daringly close to a theological undoing of theology as usual. Still, Taubes remains skeptical. Perhaps when all is said and done, dialectical theology cannot reach this far—perhaps just at the brink of its announcement of the crisis, it pulls back and rejoins the ranks of apologetic thinking, reiterating, after all, the ultimate union and reciprocal justification of God and world in the scheme of the redemptive hope. Will, Taubes asks, "the theological negation of the mundane conventional order be able (as a permanent element of critique) to prevent an ambiguous use of the dialectical *sic et non*?"[21]

The answer, according to Taubes, is "no." As close as Barth's dialectical theology comes to exposing the structure of an anti-theology theological analysis, a closer analysis of Barth's *Romans II* exposes an implicit presupposition of redemption and/or what is according to Taubes the identity between the divine and the human that constitutes this redemptive structure. The key to this discovery, Taubes argues, is to identify what in Barth's *Romans II* operates as the self-consciousness of the condition of crisis. Persons, Barth indicates, are aware that "I am as the new man not only he who I am not, but I am also he, who I am not."[22] Said otherwise, I gain the awareness of that which I am not *qua* the old Adam only through the dialectical consciousness of the new Adam. Redemption and/or the liberation from death constitute the condition of the possibility of my ability to undergo the crucifixion of the flesh. "Only because man is already spirit, can he experience himself crucified in the flesh."[23] That persons have this "experience" and reflect upon this experience suggests an epistemological bird's-eye view or point of consciousness outside the destruction and dissolution of the death that consequently denies the primacy and/or originality of this experience but exposes its indebtedness to a decidedly opposite spiritual condition. Consequently, Taubes concludes that "behind the dualism between the Creator and the creature lurks the original identity between the divine and the human."[24] Dialectical theology cannot sustain the account of dramatic difference between the human and the divine. Its articulation of the difference between the two reflects a transitional condition the originary and final condition of which is a reconciliation of the separated elements.

"The spectre of Hegel haunts Barth,"[25] Taubes concludes from his analysis of *Romans II*, and the force of this critique only strengthens with his reading of Barth's later work. In this discussion, Taubes does admit that there is an apparent difference between Barth's account of divine freedom and Hegel's position on divine necessity. Technically, the Barthian commitment to divine freedom ought to sustain the possibility of a check against the ultimate identity between the divine and the human. Barth's recourse to an actualism of divine freedom could, in other words, offer a candid announcement of the dramatic difference between the divine and the human, a candid account of the character of divine caprice, and at the least, the possibility of the failure of the realization of redemption within the scope of human history.

In fact, Taubes argues this recourse to the Barthian conception of divine freedom amounts to little given Barth's insistence upon the inextricable link between divine freedom and divine grace. According to Taubes, Barth's God always enacts his freedom in the name of his love, and in the *Church Dogmatics*, it is the incarnation of the divine in the body of Christ that acts as the medium through which this divine love is expressed and manifest. In this reading, the incarnation over-determines the character of the divine event or freedom that activates it. "In Barth's late period, the symbol of incarnation does eclipse the catastrophic quality of history. . . ."[26] A God who loves and loves without limit is no different from a God of Reason that *qua* Spirit realizes itself affirmatively in all that is other. Taubes's reading of Barth parallels my reading of Agamben such that the character of divine love privileges or favors indiscriminately, on the one hand, and leaves open the possibility of the exception and exclusion of what does not participate in the nearness of divine favor on the other hand. Either way, love has no limit, and the conditions are set for a tyranny of the loved and a tireless and ultimately futile campaign for legitimacy by the unloved. Barth's theology of divine freedom promotes election unchecked. If *Romans II* presented even a hint of antithesis between the divine and the human, Barth's later work guarantees that "in the act of love God makes himself the object of his own wrath,"[27] denying the distance and challenge to all things human with the favoritism of a love that restores the illegitimate power of the divine-human union guaranteed by the incarnation of Christ.

Once again, and now with reference to the theology of Karl Barth, Taubes implicates theologies of election within the dangers of essentializing thought. Recourse to covenantal thought alone, we learn from this analysis, cannot repair the exceptionalism commonly linked to philosophical essentialism. If, for Taubes, essentialism of both kinds requires an appreciation of the role of the heretic within the patterned repetition of normative traditions, the central argument of this book locates access to exteriority within the logic of the law. More specifically, this book questions Taubes's insistence upon the capriciousness of the divine and identifies a logical nexus between divine freedom and divine law that affirms and delimits persons in their desire. As Chapters 4, 5, and 6 have demonstrated, it is the logical connection between the enactment of divine freedom and the law through which exteriority and/or critique is rendered possible along with the perpetuation of a tradition as it moves through and responds to historical change. Within this context, critique is neither heretical nor polemical but an expression of the limits that define the character of religious life as it freely responds to and documents its ongoing interactions with God and world. If thus far I have identified the structure of this logic by recourse to the biblical text on the one hand and the theo-philosophical analysis of divine freedom in Schelling and Rosenzweig on the other hand, in this chapter, I will illustrate the logic of law within Barth's *Church Dogmatics*. Such an illustration will not only demonstrate the limits of Taubes's messianic logic—and in particular, Taubes's failure to identify the biblically rooted structure of divine freedom—but it will moreover call into question Taubes's reading of Barth's work and present an interpretation of Barth's theology by means of which we may recognize a Christian theology of the law.

Barth's Theology of the Law: The Law as the Form of the Gospel

As compelling as Taubes's account of the demand for the heretic is, his messianic logic refuses to stretch and entertain a more philosophically complex and biblically authentic account of the exercise of divine freedom. The consequences of such a failure in hermeneutical and theo-philosophical imagination spiral into an overall indictment of what it means for persons to have rights and for institutions to be justified in their adjudication of these rights. Together with Taubes's scathing critique of liberalism goes any recourse to a theological basis for rights—and institutional justification, in particular. Given Taubes's specific indictment of Barth's work as contributing to this crisis, it is important to identify how *contra* Taubes, Barth's account of divine freedom and law installs a theological basis for divine and human accountability.

My discussion of Barth's account of divine freedom as the basis of what I will refer to as the theology of law in his *Church Dogmatics* will proceed in two stages, which mirror my analysis of the logic of law in Chapter 6. First, I will present the nexus between freedom and law in Barth's account of the nature of the divine command in order to expose what Barth means when he says that the law is the form of the gospel. Second, I will examine the corresponding condition of human life within the context of its relationship with the divine, or what I will refer to as the justification within the law of the Church community in its existential and epistemological or theological expressions.

DIVINE FREEDOM, DIVINE LAW

According to Taubes, theology manipulates. It is always disingenuous in its irrepressible effort to assert illegitimate power both divine and human. In turn, this promotes the insatiable human need for legitimization characteristic of exceptionalist logics. The earlier review of Taubes's *Political Theology of Paul* and his essay on Barth suggests a two-pronged analysis of divine

Christianity and the Law: The Law as the Form of the Gospel 239

freedom as either the tyranny of divine justice that sets in motion the polemical relationship between the "righteous" worthy of reward and the "unrighteous" deserving of punishment or the freedom of divine love as favoritism, which in its wake, dichotomizes between the "elect" and the "rejected," the "loved," and the "forgotten."

Barth's theological account differs from Taubes's with regard to both expressions of divine freedom. As was true for Rosenzweig, Barth's account of divine freedom centers upon and is uniquely manifest in the character of the divine command as a command to love God. Barth's analysis of the command of God appears in volume II.2 of the *Church Dogmatics*, and it is here that we see in Barth the same account of the nexus between freedom and law that we saw in Leviticus 25, together with the philosophical analyses presented by Schelling and Rosenzweig.

Briefly stated, my argument identifies the nexus between freedom and law in Barth's account of the divine command such that freedom is never unadjudicated, and law is never coercive. So linked, the relationship between freedom and law expressed in the divine command presents a theological basis of human rights grounded in the affirmation of the human in the order of the difference between itself and the divine. Generally speaking, Barth's discussion of the divine command reveals a more complex understanding of divine freedom as both the sovereignty to command along with the freedom to care for that which is other than itself, and by logical extension, unveils the implicit lawfulness characteristic of both modes of expression. On the one hand, as we will see, God's freedom *qua* command is delimited because it is "for us." On the other hand, as divine and thereby radically other, the freedom of God's love takes place within the order of the "difference" between the divine and the human. As discussed in Chapter 6, command constitutes the only form that the "gift" of love can take.

What, Barth asks, is the unique feature of the divine command? What distinguishes it from other commands? It is, he says, "the form by which the command of God is distinguished from all other commands [which] . . . consists in the fact that it is permission—the granting of a very definite freedom."[28] By this, Barth means that unlike other commands, the divine command not only requires obedience but affirms or offers grace to those whom it commands such that they may freely and with ease align themselves with it. Said in the terms earlier described, the divine command commands us to receive divine love. To obey the command is to permit oneself to be loved. But to be commanded to receive love is to be commanded to perform that which we most need and most desire. It is to be commanded to do that which we freely seek or to be given permission to "live before Him . . . in peace and joy. . . . We have not to do that which contradicts but that which corresponds to His grace *as it is directed to us* (*emphasis*, mine)."[29] The divine command, Barth suggests, is "for us," and it is precisely this focus that constitutes the basis of it as a claim upon us.

On what grounds, Barth asks, are persons compelled by the divine command? What is its basis as a claim? Do persons perform the divine command only from fear, or is it rooted in a different justification? *Contra* Taubes's interpretation, Barth's presentation of the reality of divine sovereignty demonstrates how such sovereignty asserts a rightful claim upon its recipients by virtue of its gracious affirmation of the difference between the divine and the human. That the divine command is justified or makes a valid claim upon its recipients by virtue of this extension toward them does not suggest a limitation upon divine power. Rather, it is the central argument of this book that the justification of the divine command as a claim derives precisely from the very character of God's freedom. As we saw in our discussion of Regina Schwartz's *The Curse of Cain*, only a God delimited by his own need for power would insist upon a claim for the sake of buttressing that power. But the biblical God of Leviticus 25, the God of Schelling, and the God of Rosenweig is a God who is free in his assertion of power to draw near to those with whom he seeks to relate within an ordered context. By commanding persons to receive divine love, God affirms human difference; he does not negate it. Undoubtedly, a command by virtue of its origin from the transcendent and dramatically other God, the divine command does not coerce. Rather "it sets us free . . . with it the Sabbath always dawns. . . . The command of God wills only that we, for our part, accept that God in Jesus Christ is so kind that He accepts us just as we are. . . ."[30] Although in the second half of my discussion of Barth's theology of the law, I will look carefully at the existential and theological impact of the freedom of the law for members of the Church community, any description of the command of God and its validity presupposes the freedom and affirmation that it provides for the hearers and the doers of the command. Compelled and claimed by the divine command and its mandate to receive the love of God, persons dwell in a Sabbath beyond judgment, beyond sacrifice, and in the freedom to rest in the order that defines them. The law is the form of the *gospel*. "As Paul and also James formulated it, the Law itself is the 'law of liberty' and its telos, its intention, its general sum and substance, can be understood only when it is understood as the law of liberty."[31]

However, if God's freedom *qua* divine command is always expressed and rendered valid as an expression of divine love, it is also the case that the freedom of God to love that which is other than Godself is always ordered.

For Barth, divine grace is always lawful. It always occurs in the context of the difference between the divine and the human. It is and can only ever be expressed as the divine command that articulates this difference. The *law* is the form of the gospel.

> It is as we may believe in God that His claim confronts us in the loftiness and dignity of the obligation and which derives automatically from the gift that He has made us, a gift as incomprehensible as it is unfathomable. . . . The Law is completely enclosed in the Gospel. It is not a second thing alongside and beyond the Gospel. It is not a foreign element which precedes or only follows it. It is the claim which is addressed to us by the Gospel itself and as such, the Gospel which we cannot really hear except as we obey it.[32]

Barth's discussion of the basis of the divine claim dispels charges of theological favoritism launched against him by Taubes.

> The fact that God is gracious to us does not mean that He becomes soft, but that He remains absolutely hard, that there is no escaping His sovereignty and therefore His purpose for man. To know His grace is to know this sovereignty. And obviously to accept His grace can only be to acknowledge this sovereignty and therefore the duty of obedience to Him, or briefly, to become obedient to Him.[33]

It is the case that divine love affirms those whom it reaches. It is not the case that it offers them the right to self-justification. Divine love is not an access route to human tyranny but the opposite: an expression of the unique authority of the free God, who in this freedom commands the affirmation of that which he is not. Revelation is always ordered.

A mirror image of the analysis of freedom and law already presented in this volume, Barth's presentation of the law as the form of the gospel depolemicizes the divine-human relationship. More specifically, the lawfulness of divine freedom operative in Barth's account of divine command bypasses the exceptionalism that inevitably results from Taubes's more limited assessment. According to Taubes, the capriciousness of divine justice dramatically differentiates between the righteous and the unrighteous. For Barth, by contrast, divine command gifts all into righteousness. As the form of God's love, God's command renders all persons equally privy to the freedom and capacity for obedience. God's command is not a tool through which God trumpets his own justice but renders it available for enactment by us all. By the same token, if for Taubes, divine love translates into a dichotomization of the loved over against the unloved, the elect in contrast to the rejected, Barth's account of the lawfulness of the gospel militates against an unbridled favoritism that privileges the chosen over the forgotten. Presupposing the commanding and authoritative transcendence of the sovereign God, divine election equalizes persons as they stand before this authority and does not privilege some over others. God's love delimits human power. It demarcates the difference between it and the divine such that the collapse into reciprocal sources of tyranny like that announced in Taubes's scheme cannot possibly emerge.

The depolemicizing nature of the nexus between freedom and law within the divine command is illustrated by Barth in his reading of the narrative of the rich man in Mark 10:17–31. The narrative appears to pivot upon a dichotomization between the rich man who insists upon his righteous performance of the biblical commandments and the disciples, who he says

> . . . have indeed left all and followed Him. They have therefore done what the rich man was incapable of doing. . . . They are therefore, on the way to eternal life, as they are assured in v. 30. Twice it is stated emphatically that Jesus "looked on" them. He is looking at His own. It is the look of the One who knows that they are His own, and also how and why they are.[34]

The rich man is disobedient, the disciples obedient. The rich man is left, and the disciples comforted in the nearness of God. But Barth says the narrative of the rich man illustrates the law as the form of the gospel. If so, this must complicate the above dichotomy so far as God's love militates against the absolute judgment of a divine justice in the name of God's interests alone and because God's sovereignty works against the exclusivity of the divine favor of those who follow near Him. And this is exactly what Barth unearths from the text. Granted, the rich man "disobeys" Jesus in his insistence upon his righteousness, but this behavior does not exclude him from God's righteousness as it is extended to him now and always in the future. "Jesus looked upon him and loved him," Barth notes. We cannot

> . . . agree with Calvin [who claims that] . . . Jesus loved him as God loved Aristides and Fabricius on account of their civil virtues . . . [Rather] . . . He loves him; i.e. He reckons him as His; He does not will to be without him . . . the Law is obviously the form of the Gospel; the judgment declared by the Law is the shape taken by the grace of God.[35]

Divine judgment under the freedom of the law operates as discernment and not exclusion. The demand that he follow "to which he is not equal . . . does not cease to be the form of the good tidings addressed to him that his Judge is his Friend and Helper. . . ."[36]

Christianity and the Law: The Law as the Form of the Gospel 243

On the other side, the nexus between freedom and law in the divine command registers a corrective upon election understood as a choice in favor of some rather than others. The disciples who trumpet themselves as loved by Jesus misunderstand the law of the gospel that places them, like the rich man, within the order of the difference between the divine and the human.

> The interchange between Jesus and Peter in Mk. 10:28–31, which brings the whole story to a conclusion ends in v. 31 with the significant saying; "Many that are first shall be last, and the last first". . . . We do not hear of the saved and the lost, or of those who are within and those who are without, or of participants and not-participants, but of a serious, and yet for all its seriousness not an absolute, difference within the same sphere. The disciples with their obedience, which they do not owe to themselves, but to the divine ability bestowed on them, are now first and the rich man, in virtue of his human inability, is one of the last. . . . Yet both participate in both presuppositions. The relationship between the former and the latter is reversible in virtue of the presuppositions that are true for both. The rich man, who is now the last, could become a first on the strength of the divine ability, which is not withdrawn even from him but available even for his use. And the disciples, who are now the first, could become the last in virtue of their own human inability which resists the divine ability.[37]

From the divine perspective, there is no real difference between the righteous and the disobedient or between the saved and the rejected. To be precise, if the divine acceptance of persons in the law alters the classic distinction between the elected and the rejected,[38] this is not only because the law is the form of the gospel, if you will, but more originally because God has assumed the sacrifice of himself through Jesus as the required offering. Seen from this vantage point, Barth's account of the law of the gospel presupposes an originary sacrifice within the divine self, and in this fashion, differs from Schelling and Rosenzweig's accounts. There is, one could argue, a Christological essentialism at the very source of Barth's theology of the law. That this is the case and that this identification of the originary sacrifice with Jesus as Christ constitutes the core of Barth's thought will, as I will show, impact somewhat upon the extent to which his theology can advance a free curriculum of learning with persons who are not part of the Christian community. At the same time, however, it is also the assumption of rejection by God through Christ, which sets the stage for the full election and/or affirmation of all persons within the divine order. As Joseph Mangina puts it,

> Barth's specific version of double predestination is this: in Christ, God chooses death for himself and life for us. God loves in order that we might win. "The

elect" and the "the rejected" are not two groups of people. Rather, Barth refers all such language primarily to Jesus himself. He is the elect, the beloved chosen by God from all eternity. But for what was he chosen? He was chosen to die. As the elect, he is precisely the rejected one— . . . Jesus Christ takes the place of sinners not . . . God himself assumes the burdens of rejection for our sake.[39]

If a Jewish logic of the law bypasses a logic of sacrifice altogether, a Christian logic of the law takes hold post-sacrificially such that despite the originary sacrifice by God of God, Christians may nonetheless experience the same peace and repose in this post-sacrificial condition and therefore assume a similarly nonpolemical relation to nonbelievers as persons for whom an originary sacrifice was not and is not theologically required.

JUSTIFICATION IN THE LAW: EXISTENTIAL FREEDOM

At the heart of the analysis of this book is the correlation between the freedom of God in the law and the freedom of human persons within that same law. It is the identification of this correlative freedom that permits and inspires the dramatic alteration in apologetic relations available to Judaism and Christianity in view of their accounts of revelatory order. Despite the centuries of Christian antipathy to Jewish law, Barth's analysis of Christian life is undeniably structured by the law. We receive the gospel in the law, and we experience the law through the gospel. The objective of this discussion is to examine the character of freedom in the law described by Barth in his description first of the existential and then later of the theological dimensions of Christian life.

As I have made clear throughout the volume, the structure of a logic of law provides a non-exceptionalist approach to intersubjective social relations between believers and nonbelievers. Symptoms of exceptionalism include guilt, anxiety, and the desire for control each of which support and sustain polemical thinking. My excursus on Leviticus 25 rooted the logic of the law in a discussion of the Sabbatical year, and I have returned to this motif repeatedly to illustrate the sort of repose rendered possible in a non-sacrificially structured divine-human encounter.

The goal here is to demonstrate how Barth's conception of the law as the form of the gospel permits the same sort of repose—a repose made possible through the logic of the law as it operates within the reconciling exercise of divine freedom. The *Church Dogmatics* is filled with innumerable references to the character of freedom and peace afforded life in Christ. However, there is a repeated and often-neglected connection in these references between the character of Christian freedom and peace and the notion of the law as the form of the gospel. To see the impact of the latter upon the former, we can turn first to Barth's brief discussion of the nature and prioritization of what are traditionally referred to as the justification and sanctification of persons in Christ. Like all human experiences, justification and sanctification refer to a divine act, and in this case, two divine activities: namely, the humiliation of God through the assumption of our rejection, and the blessing and or exercise of divine grace reflected in the exaltation of persons—in short, divine judgment and divine liberation. But what Barth asks is the relationship between these two moments, these two prerequisites of our reconciliation?

It is often asserted that a fundamental difference between Barth's *Commentary upon the Romans*, 2nd edition and his later *Church Dogmatics* has to do with a reversal in Barth's emphasis upon the theological-anthropological significance of atonement in the first and an emphasis on the possibility of sanctification in the latter.[40] When all is said and done, I think it is fair to accept Taubes's final account of the relationship, which suggests that ultimately, both texts recognize atonement as an element in the higher and more complete realization of sanctification. Where Taubes's reading of Barth goes astray has to do with the meaning of this movement from atonement to sanctification in Barth's work. As we recall, Taubes cites this movement in *Romans II* and the later work to document the tyrannical tendencies of Barth's overall theology of redemption. But, Barth's account of the relationship between the atonement and sanctification of persons through God's election of Jesus Christ operates within the lawfulness of the gospel, and as such, works against the divinization of the human, which Taubes associates with redemptive schemes.

Contrary, Barth says, to trends in older Protestant dogmatics that stress the correlation between and an *ordo salutis*—an order of salvation and a moral and psychological account of human spiritual development from justification toward sanctification—a Word of God theology does not separate the actions or order of the God who coterminously justifies us in his humiliation and "in his exaltation sanctifies us."[41] Divine judgment is never separate from and/or fails to participate within the sanctification of persons. It is contrary to the notion of divine freedom to suggest otherwise for a God whose judgment of persons failed to develop fully into their sanctification would be limited in his freedom to judge freely or execute justice "for us." This does not mean that there is no difference between judgment and sanctification. Clearly "it is one thing that God turns in free grace to sinful man, and quite another that in the same free grace He converts man to Himself."[42] Nonetheless, Barth insists upon the inextricability of the two moments, and even more importantly, upon the primacy of sanctification as the goal of the two activities together. "What is the forgiveness of sins . . . if it is not directly accompanied by an actual liberation from the committal of sin? . . . As God turns to sinful man, the conversion of the latter to God cannot be lacking."[43] Recall, if you will, that God assumes our rejection. Any judgment that perdures is no longer a judgment of wrath but a judgment of discernment—a judgment within the form of the law that earmarks the eternal order of divine sovereignty and human obedience. "[I]n relation to the relationship between justification and sanctification are we not forced to say that teleologically sanctification is superior to justification? . . . It is obvious that we cannot help putting and answering the question in this form."[44]

To speak of the teleological significance of sanctification is to speak of the "Sabbath that always dawns for persons in Christ."[45] The logical nexus between freedom and law as it appears in this ratio of justification and sanctification creates the same sort of rest and self-consciousness afforded persons in Rosenzweig's account of revelation as orientation. Here we find an echo of the themes of release from anxiety and guilt and acceptance of human material and spiritual need.

Sanctified by God, we "abide like branches in a vine . . . standing in Jesus Christ. . . ."[46] Morally, we are liberated to perform the command of God. Existentially, we are not plagued by either our inability to obey or by the burden of fulfilling our needs.

> Be not anxious! Be not afraid! In these two imperatives any separation between Gospel and Law is absolutely impossible. The desire to be for ourselves is not salvation but perdition, and it is from this that the command frees us. It is therefore, full of the Gospel, full of grace, full of God's friendship for man. . . . This is the tree which is really pleasant to the eyes and to be desired.[47]

Justified and sanctified, we can live freely as we are without the expulsion of our material or spiritual needs.

JUSTIFICATION WITHIN THE LAW: THE TRUTH AND FALSEHOOD OF CHRISTIAN WITNESS

In Deuteronomy 29:28, it says, "The secret things belong unto HaShem our G-d; but the things that are revealed belong unto us and to our children for ever, that we may do all the words of this law." Frequently, this verse is used to support the view that Judaism neither sponsors a theological tradition nor funds the pursuit of divine wisdom. Needless to say, the Jewish

Christianity and the Law: The Law as the Form of the Gospel 247

tradition has not always taken this for granted. Included in the Jewish biblical canon are texts labeled "wisdom literature," including Job, Ecclesiastes, and Proverbs. Moreover, a lengthy list of Jewish philosophers from Saadia Gaon to Hermann Cohen has developed philosophical accounts of Jewish wisdom. But how does the pursuit of wisdom relate to "the things that are revealed . . . [and] all the words of this law"? Of course, it has been the primary focus of this book as a whole to assert a direct relationship between law and wisdom and by extension apologetics. In this section of my discussion of Barth's *Dogmatics*, I will turn to Barth's discussion of the nature of Christian truth found in his account of Jesus as Logos, or Jesus as the true witness, to establish the correlation between law and wisdom in Barth's presentation of the character and structure of Christian witness. As I will show, Barth's account of the structure of Christian witness mirrors Rosenzweig's account of the nature of knowledge within the event of revelation such that for both thinkers, persons are justified in their claims within the law of divine revelation. In the first part of this discussion, I will excavate Barth's analysis of the link between wisdom and law through an examination of his exegesis of the Book of Job. In this discussion, I will compare Barth's interpretation of the Book of Job with my own, where I show how the nexus between law and wisdom in the two traditions constitutes a point of reconciliation between Jewish and Christian conceptions of law and leads the way to the establishment of a nonpolemical Jewish-Christian apologetics. Following my discussion of Barth's interpretation of Job, I will conclude my analysis of the logic of the law in Barth's *Dogmatics* with a discussion of his account of the truth of Christian witness within the structure of the law.

Reconciling Wisdom and Law: An Excursus on the Book of Job Commentaries upon the Book of Job within the Jewish philosophical tradition leave readers with a troubling antinomy between law and wisdom.[48] There is little doubt that Maimonides, for one, did not seek to place the pursuit of knowledge and the life of the law against each other. Nonetheless, as discussed in Chapter 2, without an extended account of the nature of divine freedom, Maimonides' effort to correlate *halakha* and knowledge of God does not fully succeed. Frequently, Maimonides appears to view *halakhic* behavior as a means to a higher *telos* (philosophical wisdom), and his interpretation of the Book of Job offers a good example of this problem.

Maimonides discusses Job in Chapters 22–23 of v. 3 of *The Guide of the Perplexed*. Immediately in Chapter 22, Maimonides sets up the dichotomization that will govern his reading of the text in his description of Satan as one who "roamed all over the earth . . . [such that] there is no relationship whatever between him and the upper world."[49] As well, Satan is not only restricted to roam over the Earth, but in Maimonides' reading, he is also forbidden to gain dominion over the soul, "he has been given dominion over all terrestrial things, but . . . he is kept away by a barrier from the soul. . . . This is the meaning of 'only spare his soul.'"[50] Describing Satan in these terms sets the stage for the Jobian drama of the liberation of the soul from a life of terrestrial concerns.[51] Maimonides equates the life of the soul with the life of "truth" and the ways of the world with "error," and he reinforces this dichotomization in his description of Job. "The most marvelous . . . thing about this story is . . . that knowledge is not attributed in it to Job. He is not said to be a wise . . . man. Only moral virtue and righteousness in action are ascribed to him. . . ."[52]

In the article, "Maimonides, Spinoza and the book of Job," Edwin Curley suggests that such a view corresponds to what Maimonides says in 3.17. "I believe that providence is consequent upon the intellect and attached to it. . . ."[53] God is more interested in the wise than the moral. Moreover, to the extent that God offers deserts for the wise, such deserts are not material but the rewards of overcoming the need for material things. "True happiness, which is the knowledge of the deity, is guaranteed to all who know Him and a human being cannot be troubled in it by any of all the misfortunes in question. . . ."[54] If we take this (what Curley calls the "intellectualist position") as Maimonides' central reading of the book of Job, we may conclude that Maimonides reads Job as a wisdom tale that teaches us that true knowledge is speculative and not moral and also that its rewards are immaterial—beyond this world and its concerns. Wisdom is, therefore, disassociated from righteousness, the law, and materiality. Therefore, as Curley puts it, "Job's problem . . . is that he is 'one of those ignoramuses who observe the commandments' (3.51) . . . but whose belief in God is based . . . not on philosophical argument."[55]

This is not the only possible reading of Maimonides commentary on Job,[56] however, because in Chapter 23, Maimonides suggests that the point of the book is to show that "divine governance of, divine providence for, and divine purpose with regard to, natural matters differ from our human governance of, providence for and purpose with regard to the things we govern, we provide for and we purpose."[57] Here, we find an example of Maimonides' rejection of analogical thought applied to the question of divine providence. In this reading, Job's error has to do with his earlier misunderstanding of the application between human expectations of reward and merit and divine reward and merit. This, as Curley says, is an error in "equivocal predication"[58] such that the point of, for example, God's final address to Job is to illustrate the fundamental difference between the nature of divine governance and providence and human conceptions of these same concepts. If this is the correct reading, what is the impact of this upon Maimonides' construal of the relationship between wisdom and law?

On the one hand, Curley argues that Maimonides' position does not correspond to the teaching of the law because by that teaching, he means the notion that God sees to it that performing the law breeds materially positive consequences. But we might still ask whether with this position, Maimonides maintains the significance of the law even if he rejects the notion of law within a logic of reward/punishment. We might, for example, consider, as Curley does, the possibility that Maimonides combines the two positions. This might mean that persons perform the law and rightfully expect merit but cannot expect to understand what merit is from a divine point of view, given the analogical breakdown between human and divine understanding. This is an interesting compromise because it does not, like the intellectualist reading of Maimonides, suggest that Maimonides prioritizes some form of positive philosophical speculation or wisdom over righteousness or the law. Nonetheless, this approach to Maimonides' reading still separates performance of the law from wisdom even when wisdom is here identified as the pursuit of negative theology. They remain two separate and irreconcilable activities. One's pursuit of the law has no impact upon one's understanding, particularly because by performing the law, one expects some form of merit that the challenge to equivocal predication guarantees is in error.

Of course, as Curley points out, the incommensurability between persons' need to expect and imagine reward and the challenge to equivocal predication included in the compromise suggests that the compromise is not a real compromise between the two positions because for persons' expectations regarding merit to be anything other than absurd, there must be some expectation of overlap between the two conceptions of merit. Consequently, Curley dismisses this compromise possibility, in particular because it does not comport with the general tendency in Maimonides' *Guide* to favor of a strict account of negative theology.[59]

At this point, we are left with two possible accounts of Maimonides' interpretation of the Book of Job: either the "intellectualist position" or the "negative theological position." According to Curley, the latter is quite close to what Maimonides labels the "Asha'rite position," which as he describes it, not only denies any connection at all between well-being and merit as human beings and a divine conception of merit but insists upon the absolute justice of the divine will at all times. If the negative theological view challenges the rationality of any link between law and material well-being, the Asha'rite view goes even farther, suggesting the highly conceivable and perfectly acceptable coordination of human suffering and divine justice. Curley is divided as to which of these two count as Maimonides' central reading of Job, and he suggests that the intellectualist view counts as his exoteric position and the Asha'rite view his esoteric one. For my purposes, neither account permits a reconciliation between law and wisdom. If the intellectualist position prioritizes wisdom over law, the negative theological position instrumentalizes law as a tool to be used for the work of negative theology. Yes, Maimonides admits the importance of the law, but he also asserts that "the goal of the commandments . . . is to quell the impulses of matter . . . and allow the mind to concentrate on the true end of the human species which involves solely the mental representation of the intelligible."[60] The law is neither, an end in itself, nor is it synonymous with the ultimate end that is wisdom, and finally, at its most useful, it remains dissociated from the value of material life but designed instead to "quell the impulses of matter." As we will see, I disagree with Maimonides' two possible accounts of the meaning of wisdom and with his account of the law as second to the pursuit of wisdom on the one hand and a vehicle for quelling rather than meeting material need on the other.

Lucky for us, neither of these possible accounts of Maimonides' reading of Job makes good sense of the text. Maimonides' disengagement of law/righteousness from wisdom is challenged by God's endorsement of Job's righteousness.[61] Additionally, God rewards Job materially in correlation with his new found wisdom such that material success is also linked to righteousness.[62] This is not to suggest that there is a causal relationship between Job's righteousness and his material well-being. On this, I agree with Maimonides. However, there are other ways of understanding the link between Job's righteousness in the law, his wisdom, and his material well-being than that of the reward and punishment scheme, which Maimonides rejects. I hope to show an alternative to this in what follows.

In the work of Emanuel Levinas, Maimonides' emphasis on philosophical speculation meets its contemporary adversary—illustrated nicely by their dramatically different accounts of the figure of Job. In the essay, "Transcendence and Evil," Levinas argues that the Book of Job is not a theodicy nor a book of Wisdom. It does not teach us a truth about God or ontology but rather something about the transcendence of evil: namely, that "it hits me within my horror at evil and thus reveals—or already is—my association with the Good."[63] Not only does Levinas disassociate wisdom from morality, but he also distinguishes ethics from the "law" and sees a difference between himself and Phillip Nemo on this point. "Nemo identifies the ethical . . . with the Law, while the evil which awakens us to the You of God would be precisely a challenge to the Law. . . ."[64] Evil as portrayed in the Book of Job leads us back—as the whirlwind speeches remind Job, to the awareness of a primordial responsibility that we have to another—a responsibility whose origin we cannot remember but to which we are all the more obligated on account of its transcendence over our memory or cognition.

My concern to weave a third possibility between these extremes arises from my confidence that the Jewish tradition offers an invaluable recasting of the notion of wisdom as the innermost meaning of the law, a notion neglected by Jewish philosophy largely because of its reticence to permit Jewish thought a full encounter with a biblically grounded and theologically dramatic account of divine revelation. The notion that a tradition of Jewish wisdom or reasoning arises not instead of or as prepared for by *halakha* but directly from an awareness of the order implicit within Jewish law recaptures a religiously vital account of reasoning that overcomes the long-standing antinomy presented by the philosophical tradition. Even more significantly, as I have shown, a wisdom emergent from a knowledge of the meaning of the law funds a new and refreshing basis for Jewish apologetic thinking. That the link between wisdom and law present within Jewish texts and thought is also, as I will show, implicit within a certain Christian conception of the relationship between the gospel and law not only helps repair the centuries old polemic between Jews and Christians regarding the law but also identifies the unique role of "law" in a Christian apologetics.

So, let us return to the Book of Job. What is it that Job does not know? The central argument here is that Job does not know how to defend himself. More generally, Job does not understand law well enough to make and present successfully a legal claim on his own behalf. There are two elements included in this overall failure. One, Job does not know how to communicate his own defense; and two, although incapable of communicating his own defense, Job insists upon his own defense and positions himself as judge over questions of his innocence. Let me explore each of these in turn and discuss the ramifications of this failure.

In many respects, the Book of Job is about peace or rest. Rest comes, however, only when needs are met: social, physical, political, economic, and so on. Job is restless. "Truly the thing that I fear comes upon me, and what I dread befalls me. I am not at ease, nor am I quiet; I have no rest; but trouble comes."[65] The theme of how words are used also appears throughout the text. And Job says, "Oh that my words were written down . . . engraved on a rock forever. . . ."[66] Job has difficulty speaking, and his words fail him constantly. If only, he says, they could be written down, perhaps they might present his claims effectively. But alas, they are not, and he cannot effectively present his position. Over and over again, defense morphs into mockery. Unable to speak transparently, Job's discourse to his friends and to God waxes caustic, and yet the ineffectiveness of his attacks produces the need for more. "Teach me and I will be silent;" he says to his friends, "make me understand how I have gone wrong. How forceful are honest words! But your reproof, what does it reprove . . . do you think that you can reprove words . . . ? You would even cast lots over the orphan and bargain over your friend. . . ."[67] "How forceful are honest words?" he asks, but where are there any? The friends' words are not honest, he claims, but neither are his own. Teach him, he tells his friends, and he will listen to their insights, but he ignores them and insists upon his innocence. More apropos of his actual position, he yells out to them, "As for you, you whitewash with lies. . . . If you would only keep silent, what would be your wisdom!"[68] "Your maxims are proverbs of ashes, your defenses are defenses of clay. . . ."[69] But Job's sarcasm is ineffective, and communication breaks down. "I am, a laughingstock to my friends, I who called upon God and he answered me, a just and blameless man, I am a laughingstock."[70] Job cannot issue a claim in his own defense and cannot be heard.

The same pattern of failed communication, mockery, and additional miscommunication continues in Job's discourse with God. His speech is filled with empty promises. "Let me have some silence and I will speak. . . ."[71] "I would speak to the Almighty. . . ."[72] "Only grant two things to me, then I will not hide myself from your face. . . . Then call, and I will answer. . . ."[73] But once again, his efforts are to no avail, and Job resorts to mockery.

> What are human beings, that you make so much of them, that you set your mind on them . . . will you not look away from me for a while. . . . Why do you not pardon my transgression and take away my iniquity? For now I shall lie in the earth; you will seek me but I shall not be.[74]

The joke will be on God for although "he mocks at the calamity of the innocent,"[75] it is Job who mocks in return. By Chapter 29, Job's failures to defend himself result in the final soliloquy—his final plea addressed neither to God nor the friends—a defense without a hearing.

Job's inability to defend himself stands in awkward tension with his proclamations to the contrary. Clearly incapable of positing a claim on his own behalf, he positions himself nonetheless as legal judge—authoritative over matters of righteousness and wickedness, innocence and guilt. Job's insistence that he is "a laughingstock to my friends, I who called upon God and

Christianity and the Law: The Law as the Form of the Gospel 253

he answered me, a just and blameless man, I am a laughingstock" exposes this tension in his own position. Self-certainty overrides social acknowledgment. "I will defend my ways to his face . . . I have indeed prepared my case. . . ."[76] He can and he will, he insists, justify himself before God. "There an upright person could reason with him, and I should be acquitted forever by my judge."[77] God will decree it. Still, if he is so certain, why the need for a judge? Job renders *himself* justified, so why does he need a trial at all? Of course, the trial he imagines is a farce, the verdict already clear. Yet, what would defense mean without a trial? What would it mean to defend oneself if there were no one to issue a defense to? Clearly, Job does not understand the meaning of justification. And by justification, I mean that neither does Job understand what it is to be justified—that is, to be made right or have one's defense recognized by another—nor, however, is Job "justified" in a second sense. He cannot and does not understand how to hold and present a justifiable claim. Truth and legality are deeply interwoven. One can only hold a claim successfully when one can defend oneself of that claim before another.

In his famous book, *Who is Man?*, Abraham Joshua Heschel speaks of this link between epistemological and legal justification. Persons, Heschel tells us, are not self justifying. Something has worth only when there is more than one to judge, and our lives have value only when we are in relation to someone else. But value constitutes order. Different things have different values, and the relation or logic of the values generates a map or an order of value. Consequently, Heschel holds persons are justified when they participate in an order not of their own making or projection. "Man is not sufficient to himself . . . life is not meaningful to him, unless it is of value to someone else."[78] We cannot tell the truth about ourselves. We must ask the question about our human nature precisely because we cannot logically take "account" of ourselves and our claims alone. We can only take account of ourselves when we are ordered in a mapping that extends beyond ourselves. This is what Job does not know.

Linked to Job's confusion about justification is a misconception regarding the nature of freedom: his own and God's. On the one hand, Job's judicial self-certainty presupposes a dynamic that pits his freedom against God's freedom. In his own mind, Job's freedom is rational, and God's freedom capricious—even violent. ("Thine hands have made me . . . yet you destroy me."[79]) And yet, a closer look shows the logic of Job's construal. Job choreographs a misconception of the antagonistic nature of divine freedom. If he is right, then God is inevitably wrong. But by declaring himself just, Job honors no freedom other than his own. Self-endowed with judicial authority, Job denudes God of freedom. Of course, such declarations amount to naught, as we've seen, and his final soliloquy ends, "Oh that I had one to hear me! . . . Oh, that I had the indictment written by my adversary . . . I would bind it on me like a crown . . . I would give him an account of all my steps; like a prince I would approach him. . . ."[80] But Job does not understand the law, and his self-pronouncements dissolve into unrealized hypotheticals; and in the very midst of his own desperate appeal, he admits, "I do not know myself."[81] Chapter 32 starts, "these three men cease to answer Job because he was righteous in his own eyes . . . Job justified himself rather than God."[82]

In the very interesting article, "Does Job love God for naught?," Susannah Ticciati also discusses Job's confusion about the law. Ticciati specifically points out the shiftability in Job's discourse about righteousness and wickedness. Pointing specifically to verses 9:20 and 9:21, Ticciati shows how each verse suggests a different model of righteousness premised upon the inclusion of the word "if." Whereas in 20a, we see, "If I am innocent, my own mouth would condemn me, though I am blameless, he would prove me perverse," there is no "if" in v. 21—just a declaration "אֲנִי־תָם." 20a juxtaposes righteousness with perversity, whereas v. 21 presents a claim only to *tam* or purity. Ticciaiti gleans from this a shiftability in Job's own expression of righteousness: the first representing a righteousness in juxtaposition to disobedience—that is, a righteousness within the system of law; the second suggesting the "remainder" that prevails after the binary dissolution between righteousness and perversity—an integrity or purity beyond the law. Ticciati argues that the fact that "that the distinction between the two terms [righteousness and wickedness] cannot be maintained unambiguously,"[83] and therefore, "cancel one another out"[84] is confirmed by v. 22, "he destroys both the perfect and the wicked." Here, however, it is *tam*, which "is grouped with '*rsh*' as its contrary within the legal system." In this way, Ticciati argues, "the distinction between *tam* and *tsdqu*, that which is beyond the law and that which is defined within it, is seen to be a distinction within *tam* itself."[85] There is no way to speak of *tam* without speaking of the legal system from which it is the remainder. Nonetheless, the remainder transcends the system, and more importantly, exposes what Ticciati refers to as the arbitrary violence required to sustain it. Fluency in meaning evidences lack of stable origin. Devoid of a stable origin, the legal system is preserved through force alone—the freedom of divine caprice—and in her reading, it is precisely this freedom of divine caprice and coercion "against which" Job wrestles. Conflict is a requisite reaction to divine coercion. Job exposes the violence implicit within and at the base of the law "an arbitrariness which is in fact to be equated with God—that forms the deeper dimension or "more of the Covenant and severs it from its equation with the system of the law."[86]

However, for Ticciati, Job's discovery of the arbitrary freedom of the God who supports the law introduces Job's deeper wisdom concerning the freedom and caprice of divine election. In this view, the whirlwind speeches present Job with "the gratuity of God's creation . . . God's election of creaturely reality."[87] Job's exposure to both expressions of radical freedom funds an awareness of the "radical precedence of God's electing will"[88] or wisdom. Job's "integrity"—or the deeper meaning of his *tam*—reflects, therefore, his willingness to wrestle with the system and subsequently uncover this notion of radical freedom. Moreover, according to Ticciati's logic, Job can discover the character of God's radical freedom only by asserting his own. The discovery of God's freedom arises only from the contest of each party's flexing their own sovereign muscle. Discovery of divine freedom, in Ticciati's estimation, is correlative to what she refers to as Job's "simultaneous self-discovery and self-making."[89] The instability of Job's self—the process of self-making—reveals the instability of the divine self. One expression of "ungrounded freedom" reveals another.

I have spent some time outlining Ticciati's reading because the differences in our accounts highlight my argument regarding the nexus of law and wisdom. Ticciati and I both recognize the instability in Job's account of the law. Nonetheless, Ticciati and I read the instability of his account of the law very differently. Like me, Ticciati appreciates the link between wisdom and an awareness of divine sovereignty. As well, Ticciati boldly suggests that wisdom is linked to an understanding of the meaning of covenant. Job learns, in her account, that covenant presupposes God's radical freedom in active exchange with our own. We differ concerning the role of law in wisdom and covenant and its relation to divine freedom. Ticiatti's argument dissolves into a painful antinomianism whereby the law is a sign of divine coercion and ultimately "transcended" by the piety of Job's unwillingness to accept it. Job's freedom is the freedom against the law, but in her account, God's freedom is also a freedom against the law—a freedom devoid of order that spontaneously supports or undoes order as it will.

There are, however, a number of problems with Ticciati's account. Logically speaking, the largest flaw is her claim that Job's free, philosophical doubt correlates with a knowledge of indeed, uncovers a wisdom about God's own freedom. In fact, as we will see, I also hold that Job's refusal to accept the party line presented by the "friends"—or what is his expression of philosophical doubt—is a good thing, and part and parcel of the kind of wisdom presented in the text. However, in Ticciati's account, Job's philosophical doubt breeds enmity between himself and the friends and God. Ticciati maintains that philosophical doubt inevitably breeds conflict—the conflict that uncovers freedom. It appears to me, however, that a philosophical doubt that breeds conflict is not authentic doubt, and Job is guilty of insufficient doubt. He replaces the self-certainty of the friends' world view with the self-certainty of his own innocence. Such doubt, fully and thoroughly applied to his own claims, would have helped Job overcome the restlessness characteristic of perpetual conflict.

Logically speaking, Ticiatti's correlation between Job's freedom and God's freedom breaks down. Job does not acknowledge divine freedom at all. That Job stands in conflict with God suggests that in Job's estimation, he is correct, and God is incorrect. Only Job is self justified. Only Job is free. There is no acknowledgment of the radical or absolute character of divine freedom here at all. More than anything, Ticiatti's Job seems to pay attention to what she claims is the undoing of the law—an undoing that offers Job just the opening he needs to assert his own authority, or what she refers to as his own making and self-discovery. In a word, wisdom devolves into Job's knowledge of himself.

The key to Ticciati's error consists in her failure to acknowledge two different logics at play in the narrative. Ticciati attempts to bridge Job's account of divine enmity with Job's awareness of divine election. This mires her in an additional confusion whereby the God who elects the created world is also a God of violence who coerces order and sustains conflict with his creation. The covenantal God becomes antinomian and coercive. However, such a perspective is the natural conclusion of a person who already rejects the law. One who rejects the law will clearly posit the law as the ungrounded enemy. But this odd coalition of concepts unravels when we simply admit that Job's own logic is faulty and that the point of the narrative is to juxtapose and not correlate it with the revelation in the whirlwind speeches. The instability in Job's account of the law reflects Job's lack of understanding of the innermost meaning of the law—an innermost meaning that neither dissolves the law nor transcends the law but reveals its place in the divine order and the freedom and peace afforded by a consciousness of this order. Knowledge of the meaning of the law in this sense constitutes wisdom and wisdom affords an overcoming of restlessness not only for Job personally but for his ability to relate and "defend" or present himself to God and others.

Christianity and the Law: The Law as the Form of the Gospel

What does Job learn in the whirlwind speeches? Most succinctly, Job learns that performing the law can and needs to be linked to wisdom. That Job is positively favored because of his performance of the law is clear by God's own statements to this effect. The wisdom he gains does not stand in contrast to but rather constitutes an exposure of the deeper or innermost meaning of his performance of the law. In Chapter 38, God wastes no time telling Job that his account of law and defense is flawed, "Who is this that darkens counsel by words without knowledge? . . . I will question you and you shall declare to me."[90] Job has inverted the order of the law, the order of justification. God questions, and then you declare: not the reverse. Job does not understand that he is justified only through the law—that he stands within an order and a set of relations that he has not created.

Chapter 38 offers a detailed account of the order presupposed by the law. "Where were you," God asks, "when I created this order?"[91] Less an announcement of power, God's illustrations are meant as teachable moments the purpose of which is to show Job that he is not the source of order and value and that his worth or justification is not his own. God alone occupies this position, and Job is ordered by and accounted for in God's creation and not the reverse. Of course, the exposure of this wisdom repairs Job's prior misunderstanding. It explains his inability to defend himself to his friends and God. It explains his inability to issue an account of himself that is convincing and stable. Here, Job learns that the stability of his worth, the possibility of his defense, and the prospect of peaceful relations with others all derive from his place within this order; and with this revelation of the nature of wisdom, he turns a corner and announces to God, "I am of small account."[92]

The wisdom Job accrues not only teaches him that the law justifies. It also teaches him that the justification through the law is not burdensome and does not demand that he sacrifice either who he is or what he needs. Wisdom is not at odds with human need and desire. Rather, the wisdom of law affords a peace that stands in significant contrast to the restlessness and enmity characteristic of Job's prior life. If earlier chapters detailed the conflict with God and friends, the Book of Job closes with Job's quiet listening. He is comforted. He regains family, health, and all that he needs for a long and comfortable life. The wisdom of the law offers peace. It offers the rest that is available to one who understands his positive place within the order of things. To say that Job is not the source of his own justification is not to say that he has no worth but rather that his worth is assured in this larger context. God redeems Job's possessions but only as they are ordered by the freedom of the God who creates and reveals.

If the Book of Job is a book about wisdom, it is a book about the nexus between wisdom and law and the repose of self-consciousness that it offers those to whom it is revealed. But such a peace, I have argued earlier, creates unique conditions for an authentic apologetic reasoning—an authentic ability to present oneself freely to others without persuasion, without control, without the need for self-justification. At the end of the book, we are told that Job prays for his friends. What at first may seem a condescending gesture assumes an entirely different meaning within the context of the knowledge of justification and law of which Job is now aware. Presented at this point in the narrative, Job's ability to pray is not illustrative of a self-satisfied knowledge of what counts as true for others. Rather, Job's prayer functions as an expression of his ability to "hear" the needs of his friends and then pray to God that these needs be met. This prayer presupposes his ability to listen to the needs of his friends, to be open to their claims as expressions of their desires, and such an ability links directly to the wisdom he has accrued. The candid exposition afforded him concerning his own desires, their credibility on the one hand, and his inability to fulfill them himself on the other, offers Job a strikingly positive position for listening to the claims and/or longings of others. Sociality and in particular, the ability to render oneself authentically privy to the claims sponsored by another requires a freedom to disengage from the weight of one's own desires. Wisdom affords an exposition of desire in the context of an order of divine fulfillment. Job no longer holds his own claims. He is justified through the law and need not retain his justification over against the claims of another. Wisdom invites recipients to enjoy the desires of another as a testament to the lawfulness in which persons are ordered. In the case of Job, it gives rise to prayer—what in this instant constitutes the liturgical recognition of the wisdom of the law.

By way of summary, then, the argument here demonstrates how the Book of Job sponsors a marriage between wisdom and law unrecognized by the large swath of the Jewish philosophical tradition. The dichotomization of wisdom and law in the Jewish philosophical tradition is unfortunate not only because it pits the Jewish tradition against itself but also because it ignores the positive apologetics possible from the reparation of the two categories.

Barth's Commentary on Job Given Barth's account of the law as the form of the gospel, it should come as little surprise that his reading of the Book of Job greatly resembles my own and illustrates the nexus between law and wisdom that when applied to apologetic thinking, presents a model for nonpolemical Jewish-Christian engagement.

Barth's commentary on the Book of Job is included within his larger discussion of the link between Christ's role as Reconciler and Christ's function as Revealer of the Logos and the Bearer of Wisdom IV.3.1 of the *Dogmatics*, entitled "The Falsehood and Condemnation of Man." Barth's reading of the Book of Job illustrates the connection between his analysis of the law as the form of the gospel and the Christian appropriation of truth and/or the epistemological status of Christian witness. That Barth's discussion of Christian knowledge in general and Job's knowledge (or ignorance) in particular is directly linked to Barth's own account of law is evidenced in Barth's initial (and perhaps unexpected) announcement at the start of his discussion concerning the tradition of Christian antipathy toward the law and his unbridled effort to reinstitute the meaning of the law in the Christian message.

> [T]he conception[s] of the Gospel and the Law . . . belong to the basic substance of my dogmatics. . . . There are still far too many things which I cannot understand in the counter-thesis advanced with varying degrees of sharpness and consistency by authors that the Gospel and the Law differ and are even antithetical in significance and function. . . . I do not understand with what biblical or inherent right, on the basis of what conception of God . . . they can speak . . . not of one true and clear Word of God but of two Words. . . . I do not understand how there can be ascribed to Paul a conception of the Law of God by which he admittedly does not agree with the self-understanding of the Old Testament.[93]

What according to Barth makes the law so significant in the context of the discernment of Christian witness or knowledge? How does the law as the form of the gospel impact upon testimony? By way of introduction, let me say that if in Barth's view, the gospel constitutes the *content* of divine love and the possibility of persons' love and witness in response—that is, their obedience—the law *orders* this testimony and gives rise to an awareness of the context or deeper meaning of this obedience and election or what is the awareness of one's place within the divine order. Once revealed, the ordered context of this testimony exposes the structure of justification or truth telling: namely, that within the divine law, persons are not justified in and of themselves but only within the order of this law in a way that mirrors both the philosophical account of the logic of law and the biblical account of the nexus between wisdom and law presented in the earlier interpretation of the Book of Job. Witness to the gospel counts as wisdom only when exercised with the lawfulness of divine justification.

According to Barth, the effort to explain Christian knowledge presupposes Jesus Christ as both Logos and as elected man or witness. That human knowledge is justified only in the law has all to do with the nexus between law and freedom as it operates within these two aspects of the Christological presentation of truth. This holds true for Job as well, whom Barth refers to as a witness in-the-making. Consequently, we must begin our examination of Barth's interpretation with an account of the meaning of Jesus Christ as Logos and Witness.

The logical structure of Barth's analysis of Christian witness is established in his discussion of Jesus as the Prophet or ultimate bearer of the Word of God or Logos in IV 3.1. Much of Barth's discussion fleshes out the import of the connection between Jesus as the agent of reconciliation and Jesus as the one who, in this capacity, reveals wisdom and compares this role with the prior role of the prophets on the one hand and the history of Israel as a bearer of the Word of God on the other hand. For my purposes here, the central aspect of this discussion consists in Barth's assertion of the primacy and uniqueness of Jesus as the Word of God. Jesus' Word, Barth says, "is the light of life . . . He is the one and only light of life. . . . Everything which we have to say concerning the prophetic office of Jesus Christ rests on this emphasis. . . ."[94] Immediately, Barth acknowledges the sort of concern such a claim engenders. Apparently, he concedes, such a claim is "a hard and offensive saying which provokes doubt and invites contradiction. . . ."[95] Isn't it, he asks, "an unfriendly and quarrelsome . . . principle . . . a proclamation of unconcealed intolerance and therefore an intolerable disruption of the co-existence of men of different outlooks[?]"[96]

Barth's unapologetic announcement of the exclusivity of Jesus Christ as the only light places us directly in the middle of our attempt to discern the place of the law within his theology. Looking back, we can recall Rosenzweig's "is God supposed to have waited for Sinai or even for Golgotha?"[97] Divine freedom, in Rosenzweig's thought, is not exclusively linked to one particular religious or historical expression. Consequently, the logic of the law as it operates within the New Thinking requires a recognition of the *possibility* of the truth of the claims of others as these claims assume a variety of particular linguistic expressions. According to Barth, by contrast, divine freedom expresses itself uniquely in the person and flesh of Jesus.[98] What impact does this determination have upon the logic of the law as a mechanism for a nonpolemical assertion of theological knowledge? Clearly, Barth's theology presents an expectation and hope for the universal witness to Christ. God's act through Jesus as Christ is for all humanity, and a Christian in Barth's account is one who enters into fellowship with God in Christ and who lives his/her life in the service and ministry of this particular fellowship.

Christianity and the Law: The Law as the Form of the Gospel 261

Any account of Barth's theology must recognize this theological determinism. However, to speak of a theological determinism with regard to God's eternal election in and of Jesus Christ is not to speak of a determinism within human articulations or proclamations of this Word. To do so is to ignore Barth's account of the law as the form of the gospel as I have described it earlier and as it appears in his particular account of the role of Jesus Christ in his prophetic office: that is, as the content and agent of divine truth or wisdom.

Barth states the point this way. The claim that Jesus Christ is the one and only light of life and Word of God "is a Christological statement. . . . It looks away from the non-Christian and Christian alike to the One who sovereignly confronts and precedes both as the Prophet."[99] Said in the terms of the logic of the law, the claim that Jesus Christ is the one and only prophet is a claim that manifests the law of difference between the divine Word and any other human word. Although in Barth's estimation, the assertion of this claim reflects an unadulterated sovereignty associated with God and by God in Jesus Christ as Electing God, it does not however provide any such basis of certainty or self-justification for persons who attempt to repeat it and/or appropriate it as a claim. As an expression of the law of the gospel, the exclusivity of the claim installs a judgment that is a discernment of the difference between the Word of God as uniquely spoken or revealed in God and/or Christ and human proclamation. "Thus," Barth says,

> [T]he criticism expressed in the exclusiveness of the statement affects, limits and relativses the prophecy of Christians and the Church no less than the many other prophecies, lights and words relativised and replaced by it. . . . What it says concerning the impotence of all other prophecy which attempts to rival its own is valid only in analogy to, and in consequence of, the fact that first and supremely it is true of the Christian sphere.[100]

Herein, I will detail the precise conditions for a Christian proclamation of the Word of God within the limits of the law. The purpose of this discussion is to highlight how the exclusive sovereignty of Jesus Christ as Logos establishes the lawful standard of the gospel as the unique Word of God in contrast to any human testimony.

If, however, Jesus Christ is the reconciler who reveals the Logos and the law of the truth of the gospel, he is also as the man rejected and elected by God, the only "true witness" to this same Word. At once, Jesus is Logos and witness to the *logos*. He is, therefore, the justifying law of all proclamation and the one completely justified in this law. To speak of Jesus *qua* elected man as the one justified in the law is to speak not only of this man's recognition of the Word of God in its sovereignty. It is as well to speak of this man as the recipient of the divine love—this man affirmed in the law through whose affirmation or reception of divine grace all persons are elected into fellowship and love of God. That, therefore, Jesus constitutes the "true" witness' derives from this unique position as ordered within and affirmed by the law of the gospel. About Jesus' life, Barth says that

> [I]t is a life offered up to God. . . . To this there corresponds externally and visibly, in the attitude and acting of His life, the fact that it is lived in the sphere of God's order and according to the direction of His command. . . . He does not belong to Himself. He does not direct or control His own possibilities. . . . It is in doing this that He proves Himself to the true Witness.[101]

Still, this is only one aspect of Jesus' proclamation as the true witness. Yes, he stands within the law. Yes, he acknowledges the sovereignty of the divine Word, but he also stands affirmed within the law of the gospel, and with this affirmation, may speak justifiably, may testify to the Word of God. "Jesus Christ does speak; for as He speaks God speaks."[102] If it is the case that as rejected, Christ is the one who suffers the silence of the passion and whose word as human is rejected by the judgment of the crucifixion, he is also the one elected and liberated in God now capable of testimony in the law.

According to Barth, we may best understand each of these two aspects of Christian truth—the divine *logos* and the human witness—if we view them through the category of freedom. Freedom, he says, "is the form and character of the intercourse between true God and true man enacted in this man. This is what makes Him the Witness of the truth, the true Witness."[103] As *logos*, God freely presents his Word as truth; and as elected man, Jesus freely testifies to the exclusivity of this Logos. But freedom, Barth reminds us, is never capricious—neither the divine expression of the superiority of his Word nor the freedom of the human announcement of its reception of this truth. Both aspects of the expression of the Word of God are adjudicated by the law. If the divine Word reigns superior over all human repetition and expression, it is nonetheless a Word "for us" a Word, whose validity and authority derives from the liberation it offers to those who are other than God in his sovereignty. The same can be said for the freedom of Jesus' testimony. Affirmed by God's love, Jesus' witness achieves validity only when justified within the law of the uniqueness of the divine Word. Both the divine assertion of the truth and the human apprehension and testimony to it are possible only within the order of the law. The law determines the conditions of the possibility of the gospel as truth.

Christianity and the Law: The Law as the Form of the Gospel 263

With this Christological account of the law as the form of truth, Barth navigates away from a logic of sacrifice. Neither does God offer his truth so that we will be indebted to him, nor do we attest to it to avoid punishment. The nexus between law and freedom in the presentation of the truth of the gospel renders the difference between the divine and the human within the affirmation of both participants.

> It would be the most dreadful and frivolous misunderstanding—the lie which opposes the true Witness—if we were to understand and explain this connexion of the two determinations in terms of a *Do* and *Des*, a Credit and Debit, a balance and debt. It consists rather in the fact that on both sides freedom is the form and character of the intercourse between true God and true man. . . .[104]

As the bearer and witness to wisdom, Christ installs a logic of law through which Christian wisdom is free in the law and not the by-product of an ontological collapse of the divine into the human or the human into the divine.

It is in the context of this discussion of the nature of "true witness" that Barth introduces his reading of Job. For Barth, Job is a witness in the making, and his process exposes the nature of wisdom and its crucial link to the law. If we begin again by asking, "What does Job not know for Barth?," we will see that Barth's interpretation deeply resembles my own. According to his account, Job is an authentically obedient man—an obedient man whose obedience is like Christ's pure in form at the start and pure in form at the close but mired in a suffering obedience in between. Job knows how to be obedient but does not understand the lawfulness implicit within this obedience. This lack of knowledge or wisdom appears explicitly in Job's insistence on defending himself, his insistent disordering of the lawfulness of the law he himself performs. He rightly, in Barth's terms, "maintains his righteousness before God. But he blatantly sets himself in the wrong by arrogantly advancing the righteousness as a claim that God should be righteous before him, to his human eyes and according to his human thoughts and standards."[105] Unlike Kierkegaard, we cannot, Barth argues, admit that Job is excused and justified in his contest against God. "This is going too far . . . Job is guilty in this regard. . . ."[106] Job inverts the law of divine justification and perverts his own defense.

On the other hand, Barth asserts that there is more to Job than this inversion of the law and ignorance. Job, he notes, is unstable in his manipulation of the law. Even he doubts it: He admits its futility. He understands, in Barth's account, that he has to do with God, and try as he may to justify his own assertions, he stands before a God for whom such self-defense is null and void. Job is a witness in the making; his doubt regarding his own self-justification presses him to uncover the truth—a truth concerning divine lawfulness that he does not yet know but knows that he must search out. Job, then, is both right and wrong. "If he were not on the way, he could not stumble and fall."[107] Barth's reading contrasts starkly with Maimonides'. Whereas Maimonides severs the link between Job's righteousness and his subsequent wisdom, Barth offers the more covenantally coherent account of the nexus between righteousness and wisdom whereby neither righteousness nor obedience is reduced to knowledge, nor knowledge emptied into ethical responsibility. Wisdom for Barth, as for me, deepens the meaning of election when by election we understand the loving dispensation of the law to persons who are justified and made free within it.

Consequently, Barth's interpretation of the whirlwind speeches more resembles my interpretation than it does Maimonides'. As I do, Barth interprets the early verses of the whirlwind speech as a reversal of Job's account of the law. Job, God indicates, is wrong in his defense. He is wrong in his accusation against God. He is immediately "put in his place by God, and yet, because it is God who does this, he is put in a good place. The equilibrium of his right and wrong is broken."[108] Revealed in the speeches, according to Barth, is the lawful context and meaning of the covenantal relationship. "Thus the perennial nature of the relationship of the election and the covenant between God and himself, himself and God, is revealed and made public by the One who is Lord and Judge in this relationship."[109] The truth of election is the lawfulness of the divine justification and the Book of Job teaches how the divine wisdom of the God who orders acts as a commentary upon the nature of the God of election and the character of the life of covenant. It is Job's predicament that he cannot link wisdom with revelation and/or the command to righteousness. He cannot reconcile the freedom of God's power to order the world with the love of the God who elects and loves his treasured possession.

> It is not in relation to the Subject Yahweh that the problem of Job arises. It is in relation to Him that he knows and clings to the fact that in what befalls him he has to do with God. It is on the basis of this knowledge that he disputes with God. The disputing or problem, however, arises from Yahweh's being as Elohim and Shaddai, from the majestic and almighty operation of Yahweh in relation to him.... [And yet,] the answer which Yahweh gives to Job necessarily consists in the fact that Yahweh makes Himself known as Elohim-Shaddai, as the One who even in the enigmatic character of the rule of His majesty and omnipotence is still the God of the particular election of Israel and therefore of Job, and therefore the Lord with whom he cannot dispute and whom he cannot try to set

right, but in face of whom he can only keep silence. [With this] however, Yahweh restores and re-establishes the unity . . . and thus gives Job the freedom to abandon as inappropriate and indeed impossible for the elect of Yahweh the accusation against this predication and work which is unwittingly directed against Yahweh Himself.[110]

The whirlwind speeches repair this rift between love and freedom—between a covenant of obedience and the truth or wisdom about God. In both Barth's interpretation and my own, the antinomy between praxis and knowledge and between this world and the next is healed through the logic of the law. Obedience implies truth, and the love of God in election characterizes the freedom of God in his order.

What then about God's description of the animals and the nature that constitutes the remaining content of the whirlwind speeches? As I did, Barth interprets God's description as an announcement of the divine order.

> The cosmos which Yahweh calls upon to testify is, of course, an echo of the voice of His own Word concerning His autonomy of power which is operative in these forms and in which He evades the power of man, His immanent autonomy (lawfulness) of purpose which man cannot catch or follow in his own explanations, respect for which is the presupposition of all the realization of man's freedom in his own sphere.[111]

Here, too, God's account teaches Job his place within the order—an order that as Barth also notes is revealed by God without coercion, without fear, without contest. God offers law freely, for us, so that we may be made free within it. He does not, Barth argues, present

> His blind superiority to man [*contra* Ticciati] but His questioning whether man can really think that the cosmos is his cosmos and belongs and listens to him. Can he really think that it is ordered according to his ideas, wishes purposes and plans. . . ? Not of itself, but as God causes it to speak as His creation, the cosmos puts to man a question which he can only answer in the negative.[112]

A witness in the making, Job's reception of the divine revelation of law renders him wiser and more deeply committed to the righteousness he formerly performed.

Given the parallels in these two interpretations, it is worth exploring whether Barth's theology yields a similar apologetics rooted in the law. We can begin to flesh out an answer to this question in a review of Barth's closing remarks concerning the nature of falsehood in his commentary on the Book of Job.

If truth in Barth's account refers to the form and content of the gospel, falsehood constitutes a neglect of the form regardless of the content of the claim presented. The ability to pronounce the gospel does not, according to Barth, exhaust wisdom. Falsehood constitutes a departure from the lawfulness of a claim. The one who utters a "false" claim does not, Barth says,

> ... question the truth ... the liar ... confesses the truth of God, the truth of man, Christian truth. The only thing is that it has become untruth since in his mouth it can only be the truth which is taken in hand and inspired and directed by him.[113]

Falsehood is, as Rosenzweig would say, a refusal "to admit the lie" concerning one's certainty in holding truth. It is a refusal to permit one's truth to withstand the adjudication of the law inextricably linked with the gospel in Christ's own witness, a refusal born of the desire to know that one has mastery over one's claims. Still, exposure to the truth of Christ's witness dislodges our claims to self-certainty. Man "seeks to define the order himself and issues an ideal picture of the being, order and mystery of the world as seen and understood by man—but who but man has given this picture its factuality and normativeness?"[114]

Barth turns to his interpretation of Job's friends to illustrate this character of falsehood. Unlike Job who trembles in his self-certainty, the friends are zealous defenders of God. Divine apologists, they plunge deeper and deeper into falsehood with every "right" claim they make. Secure in their self-justification, they hubristically speak for God, and not surprisingly, their defense falls on deaf ears. They communicate to no one. Neither do they impress God, nor do they convince Job. They speak of God but on their own behalf. Their communication fails, and they are left isolated from God and others, redeemed only by a sacrificial intervention by Job at the end of the narrative. Only by witnessing the order implicit within Job's sacrificial offering (that is, "all this comes from God") can the friends achieve the awareness of their lie and glimpse the nature of the truth in which they are justified.

Barth also links falsehood to ahistoricality. Recognition of the law is concomitant with recognition of the temporality or historicality of one's claims. The friends by contrast, Barth points out, "preach timeless truths"[115] impervious to change and challenge. But the truth of the law requires a historical self-consciousness of one's claims—an awareness of the changeability of how one expresses one's desires (theological, in this case). As law, wisdom prohibits the free assertion of eternal truths. Inevitably, the friends' insistence upon the timeless character of their truths only contributes further to their self-alienation and failed communication. Dogmatism is not conversation's best friend. The friends' refusal to historically contextualize their own claims results in their inability to listen to anyone else. There is, Barth says, no limit or law on their assertions, and therefore, there is no room for anyone else to make a contribution. Truth is closed, and seen from this perspective, all other persons function only as instruments. Either they bolster the certainty of the claimant with their agreement, or they get in the way and must be dismissed or contested in disagreement. As instrumental, persons are always just a moment away from incurring the enmity of the liar. There is no basis for true fellowship or authentic listening. Still, in the end, it is the liar who cannot rest. Despite her failure, she ceaselessly pursues the justification of a truth that alienates others who do not share her quest. Such, Barth tells us, is the problem of Christian speaking when afflicted by falsehood. But falsehood, he tells us, does not have the last word. The Word of Christ is more powerful than the words of those who speak the gospel as liars, and Christians, he says, can hope and pray that like Job they will have their lie unmasked and assume a life of justification under the law.

This is as far as Barth goes in his discussion of commentary on the Book of Job. Left here, we may anticipate a Barthian account of the nexus between wisdom and law within Christian witness, but Barth leaves this discussion of what he calls the structure of Christian witness for the second half of volume IV.3. In the final section of this chapter, I will present this account and show how it underwrites an apologetic reasoning not unlike the one I have developed in prior chapters.

THE STRUCTURE OF CHRISTIAN WITNESS

According to Barth, the fundamental purpose of Christian life is to witness to God in service or ministry. By now, we understand that there are lawful perimeters that govern the validity of Christian witness. But what exactly does such testimony within the law look like, and how does the presentation of this testimony impact upon the relationship between Christians and non-Christians? Said otherwise, what, according to Barth, does it mean to be a Christian? What sort of a claim does a Christian make, and how does the issuance of such a claim distinguish her from others?[116]

To be a Christian, Barth suggests, is to live within a certain vocation or in response to the presupposition of "the event in which the grace of God which justifies man before Him and sanctifies him for Him finds its counterpart in the gratitude of man."[117] Of course, Barth insists, this vocation arises from a prior history within God

> ... in which Jesus Christ did His work and spoke His Word ... but primarily in Himself, in His pre-temporal, supra-temporal and post-temporal eternity. ... Primarily in God Himself man stands already in the light of life ... no man is rejected, but all are elected in Him to their justification, their sanctification and also their vocation.[118]

What does this choice for man's vocation say about the nature of being a Christian and the character of Christian claim-making?

Barth's initial musings about the meaning and status of being a Christian point back toward the logic of the law. Yes, a Christian is one who has been called by God eternal, and yes, a Christian is hereby justified and sanctified. However, this very same Christian relies upon the eternal repetition of this divine election: that she has been elected by God in the past means that she will need to be elected continuously in the divine act throughout the future. Her election and her determination as a Christian are not matters of her own assertion that she can then hold over and against the assertions of others. The opposite is the case, according to Barth:

> [I]s it not inevitable, then that our self-understanding as Christians should constrain us on this side, together with our knowledge of the existence of Jesus Christ in its universal significance, to an openness towards others. ... For all the seriousness with which we must distinguish between Christians and non-Christians, we can never think in terms of a rigid separation. All that is possible is a genuinely unlimited openness of the called in relation to the uncalled. ... To live on this basis, in this openness and readiness, in this "tolerance" towards the non-Christian, is not then a particular virtue. He would not be called himself if he did not self-evidently and naturally (as a Christian) live on this basis.[119]

Rooted in the primacy of the lawfully regulated act of divine election, Christian vocation depolemicizes Christian non-Christian relations. But if this is the case, what can a Christian say? If she cannot identify herself as one who holds a particular truth, what constitutes the difference between herself and the non-Christian in Barth's account?

There is undoubtedly, according to Barth, a real difference between Christians and non-Christians, but the difference between the two has little to do with any particular action or claim issued on the part of the believer. To be a Christian, Barth suggests, is to have been set "in attachment to [God through] ... the liberating power of his Word. ..."[120] The term *Christian* refers specifically to

> ... one who belongs in a special way to Jesus Christ. ... The special way in which Christians belong to Him, however, is that their existence. ... is determined ... by their faith in Him, by their liberating and yet also binding and active knowledge that all men and therefore they themselves belong to Him. In the active knowledge of this faith of theirs they anticipate the form of existence which one day is to be that of all men. ....[121]

From this perspective, a Christian is a person who has *access* to a particular truth or knowledge regarding universal human fellowship in Christ but who does not generate this knowledge herself.

"Ye have not chosen me"—whether by accepting a tradition or exercising your own judgment "but I have chosen you. ..." (John 15:16). Christian knowledge happens to and for a Christian.

> We have seen how this comes about, namely, by his illumination to active knowledge which as such is his awakening. Since this is an act of God, of Jesus Christ, of the Holy Spirit; since it is the active Word of God effectively spoken to him, it is established that his distinction from others is definitely not grounded in himself, nor put in his own hands, let alone made over to him as a possession. ... His distinctiveness stands or falls with the fact that it is freely given him and that he receives it as a grace with pure gratitude *which advances no claim* [emphasis, mine]. ... In the event of vocation he is led to this insight. And in it he is made over and freely delivers himself *de facto* to the One to whom He belongs *de iure*. ... He finds himself placed, and thus places himself, in the hands of the One to whom as owner there belongs the sole and total responsibility and care for his existence. ....[122]

Said in other terms, the knowledge or wisdom attested to by a Christian abides, Barth argues, by a particular structure. If Christian witness and proclamation is a product of the having been attached to and brought into fellowship with Christ, there is in Barth's own language a "law of freedom" or a "controlling principle"[123] that structures this coming to truth. With Barth's announcement of the structure, or what I refer to as the logic of Christian knowledge, we come full circle in our response to Taubes's account of Barth's work. Such a structure, Barth asserts, explains how Christian proclamation navigates between the two extremes of Christian quietude and other-worldly eschatological expectation and a this-worldly Christian moralism or self-certainty. If one asks after the meaning or value of Christian proclamation, the tendency by thinkers is to point either toward its eschatological significance or to a "a self-glorifying Christian moralism which tries to be [the primary] principle itself. ..."[124] That, according to Barth, neither of these approaches constitutes the overriding structure within which Christian knowledge abides illustrates how different Barth's account of witness is from the dichtomization between crisis theology and self-worldly justification described by Taubes in his analysis of Barth's early and later work.

The structure of Christian witness is the law as the form of the gospel, and it is this principle that mediates between the two extremes of a Christian knowledge. According to Barth, it is the principle that

> [T]hey are the beloved of God who may love Him in return. They have the freedom as His children to converse with Him as their Father . . . in and through all this they are what they are, have what they have and do what they may do. . . . As those who in distinction from others are and have and may do these things and rejoice in the fact, Christians are in the world and yet they confront the world standing at the side of the God who acts and reveals Himself in Jesus Christ.[125]

Neither strictly eschatological nor strictly this worldly, the apprehension or awakening of Christians to the truth of the gospel is possible in our time through the active and gracious revelation of God. The structure of Christian witness and the condition of its free and lawful possibility is the nexus between the freedom and the lawfulness of God in fellowship with those who have been made attached to him.

If, therefore, a Christian is one who by attachment by God apprehends the divine revelation, then a Christian is one who testifies to this truth in the lawfulness or order of this revelation. Certainly, she is one whose apprehension of truth translates into the praise or witness to the divine revelation or *logos*.[126] More importantly for this discussion, however, she is one whose apprehension as witness or testimony is always justified or defensible only by virtue of the prior act of God and never in and of itself. They are, Barth says,

> . . . made by Him His witnesses . . . not for the vain increase of their knowledge of men, the world and history by this or that which they now come to know of God . . . but witnesses who can and must declare what they have seen and heard like witnesses in a law-suit. Their calling embraces not only the fact that God gives them knowledge and that he calls them to this knowledge but also the fact that He summons and equips them to declare what He has given them to know. . . . He gives them the freedom, but also claims and commissions them to confess that they are hearers of His Word. . . . This is their *raison d'etre*. . . .[127]

Without the gospel, there would be no Christian wisdom. Without the law, such wisdom would not be justified. Christian witness is as much a liturgy of love as it is a liturgy of the law, and because it is both, it presents unique opportunities for and categorically undermines the possibility of anything but a free, nonpolemical engagement with the non-Christian.

A CHRISTIAN APOLOGETICS WITHIN THE LAW

I must confess the gospel, Barth says. I must because I am commanded, and I must because I am free. However, my confession of the gospel transpires within the law, and this means that when I confess the gospel, I do so nonpolemically. There are two reasons for the nonpolemical character of Christian confession. The first is because within the law, I may tell or proclaim the truth, but I do not hold or possess it. Consequently, I am not the judge or the one who discerns truth. My articulation of the gospel is always justified only within the order of the difference between God's own Revelation and Speaking of the Word and my reception of this Word through God's lawful love. If by apologetics, we mean the "defense" of the truth to the nonbeliever, then I cannot behave apologetically. However, it has been the task of this book as a whole to present a different conception of apologetics whereby I may freely present my claim without polemically defending it against another's, and we can now recognize this same structure of apologetics in Barth's theology. As in Rosenzweig's thought, the condition of the possibility of the validity of my own proclamation also guarantees the condition of the possibility of another's assertion, and therefore, I cannot proclaim the absolute falsehood of another's claim without compromising the possibility of my own. In other words, the possibility of the other's assertion can, as it does in Rosenzweig's thought, act as a check against my tendency to what Barth calls "domesticate" the living truth of the Gospel. Along these lines, Barth admits that

> [W]e have also claimed that there are no good grounds not to accept the fact that such good words may also be spoken *extra muros ecclesiae* either through those who have not yet received any effective witness to Jesus Christ and cannot therefore be reckoned with the believers who for their part attest Him, or through more or less admitted Christians who are not, however, engaged in direct confession or direct activity as members of the Christian community....[128]

The limit upon our possession of the truth requires that we remain open to the *possibility* of the "true words" by these others.

> The community which lives by the one Word of the one Prophet Jesus Christ, and is commissioned and empowered to proclaim this Word of His in the world, not only may but must accept the fact that there are such words and that it must hear them too, notwithstanding its life by this one Word and its commission to

preach it. . . . Does it not necessarily lead to ossification if the community rejects in advance the existence and word of these alien witnesses to the truth . . . it must really hear them, *although without prejudice to its own mission.* . . . [emphasis, mine][129]

Focusing in particular on Barth's phrase, "without prejudice to its own mission," it is important to remember that the mandate to remain open to these possible truths is not predicated upon the goal of appropriating these possible truths but rather constitutes a praxis of the law—an exercise in executing the very structure of the Christian proclamation of the gospel. We must hear these possibilities on their own terms and as possible within their own right and "without prejudice" to the community's own mission. This is not to say that Christian communities cannot opt to consider these attestations as relevant proclamations within their own community life, or as what Barth calls "parables of the kingdom."[130] It is to say that such an appropriation does not drive the recognition of their possibility but constitutes only a potential by-product of what is a lawfully required aspect of Christian proclamation. On the same grounds as the condition of the possibility of their own proclamation of truth, Christians not only may benefit from hearing these assertions but must hear and remain open to the possibility of these claims lest they fundamentally deny the sovereignty and authority of God.

The second reason why Christians can, in Barth's view, engage in nonpolemical encounters with others is because they have the freedom to do so.[131] As was the case with Rosenzweig's account of human life, so it is with Barth's that the nexus between law and freedom emancipates persons from exercising the fulfillment of their needs and/or desires. As detailed throughout the volume, the assertion of truth-claims and the persuasion of others constitute a mode of social recognition or the fulfillment of one's desire to be acknowledged. The structure of Christian life within the law offers a different approach to the human quest for recognition so far as divine election permits persons the freedom to be who and what they, affirmed within the order of God. Divine election releases persons from the burden of establishing strategies of self-recognition and from the need to persuade others to appropriate their own particular claims. There is, in Barth's theology, a direct correlation between the sense of peace and repose characteristic of Christian life and the Christian ability to engage freely with others without persuasion and control. Within the law of freedom, "the Christian is not liberated as such from vigorous activity and action, but from all the wishful thinking, self-justification and demanding which do not further this but rather poison and impede it."[132] Christian empowerment no longer rests with Christian imperialism but with the freedom to stand affirmed within the law of the gospel. So placed,

> [the Christian] has absolutely nothing to postulate. . . . He is delivered from the torturing necessity of always having to postulate the limited success and results of his action, the acknowledgment, encouragement and estimation of his person and efforts by those around. . . . He may never free himself from the sway of the rule that he may indeed ask for what he is to receive, but may not demand it, and therefore does not need to do so. . . .[133]

Like Job, the Christian who lives within the law of the gospel has gained self-awareness—the self-consciousness of her historicity and the historicity of her assertions—an understanding of herself as a recipient of and not a generator of truth. As such, she stands prepared to see and hear others in this same position. She not only does not view others as instrumental to her existential security, but she is uniquely prepared to listen without agenda to their needs and desires as they are expressed in their respective claims. While Barth does not state this explicitly, one can, I believe, deduce a link between Barth's analysis of the love of the neighbor and the character of witness within the law. We are, Barth tells us, commanded to love the neighbor. More specifically, to love the neighbor is to recognize the neighbor, in her humanity, as a sign or testimony to Christ. In the event that the neighbor is one who has not encountered Christ, the Christian has, Barth says, an obligation to testify to God or Christ before her so that she may know of God's grace in this way. In this way, to love the neighbor is to pray for her as one who is cared for in the grace of God. However, the ability to pray on behalf of another presupposes a recognition of the particularities of that other—an awareness of her need. In this context, the free listening to the other that, structured in the law, I am freely capable of doing is of enormous help. It is, in this analysis, the very structure of my Christian life that prepares me to listen freely so that then and only then can I issue a prayer that is not hegemonic—or as Barth says, "patronizing"[134]—but free and without agenda. Listening to the other constitutes a liturgy of the law that as inextricable from the life of Christian witness uniquely frees Christians to engage with the needs of others.

In closing, what do we walk away with from this examination of Barth's theology of the law? First, we walk away with a realization of how both Jewish and Christian theology can contribute to repairing a long-standing antinomy between law and wisdom in both traditions. More specifically, we walk away with the perhaps somewhat surprising realization that Barth's theology of the Word is uniquely suited to contribute to this repair—more so than a long list of Jewish philosophers for whom covenantal theology is an inadmissible basis for Jewish life and thought. Second, however—and perhaps most importantly—the identification of a Barthian theology of the law charts a new course for repairing a deeper schism: namely, the polemic between Judaism and Christianity on the significance and meaning of the law. The point of my work is not to suggest that Barth is a defendant of *halakha* as performed by Jews. It is, however, to offer a strong argument for why Christian theologians can no longer engage in a tireless and negative campaign against the law when understood as the ordering principle of the Gospel. When viewed from this perspective, a Christian recognition of the law does not move Jewish-Christian relations forward by attempting to identify elements of biblical law within Christian life. Rather, the argument here is that a Christian theology of the law that demonstrates the order of witness renders Christianity more capable of listening to the claims of all non-Christians, Jews included. That the feature that permits Christianity this free openness to exteriority is a feature that it has inherited from the world view of the Hebrew Scriptures, or that a Christianity that comes to terms with the elements of Judaism within it is better prepared to engage with the world is a reflection upon the implicit rationality of biblical reasoning as it manifests itself in both traditions.

NOTES

1. SACRIFICING ELECTION: DIVINE FREEDOM AND ITS ABUSES

1. In his Introduction to the letters, Harold Stahmer presents this view and says, "Conversation, dialogue, speech set against speech was the method and medium wherein, at one stage in their lives, a Jew and a Christian discovered their respective identities and a common framework for answering their age's particular brand of spiritual agnosticism and academic and professional nihilism." Harold Stahmer, "Introduction" in *Judaism Despite Christianity: The 'Letters on Christianity and Judaism' between Eugen Rosenstock-Huessy and Franz Rosenzweig* (New York: Schocken Books, 1971), 4.

2. For historical reflections upon the letters between Rosenzweig and Rosenstock-Huessy, see Dorothy M. Emmit, "The Letters of Franz Rosenzweig and Eugen Rosenstock-Huessy," *The Journal of Religion* 25 (1945): 261–75. Also see Harold M. Stahmer, "'Speech-Letters' and 'Speech-Thinking': Franz Rosenzweig and Eugen Rosenstock-Huessy," *Modern Judaism* 14 (1984): 57–81.

3. Rosenstock-Huessy's focus upon the significance of Jesus as the Logos for reorienting thought away from the dominance of conceptual reason toward a recognition of the role of dialogue and speech described in his correspondence with Rosenzweig develops into one of the major themes of his later work. According to Harold Stahmer, "Rosenstock-Huessy has devoted most of his life in this century to 'gnawing upon the bone of speech.' (*Die Sprache des Menschengeschlechts*, vol. I, 739–810).... Problems of speech and language have been uppermost in his mind during this entire period and culminate in his *Die Sprache des Menschengeschlects* (2 vols. 1933–34). The same preoccupation permeates *Out of Revolution* (1938) and provides the heart of the plan for his two volume *Soziologie* (1956). The recent (1966) Harper Torchbook edition of *The Christian Future* or the *Modern Mind Outrun* is undoubtedly the most readily accessible brief introduction to this aspect of Rosenstock-Huessy's writings and is an ideal complement to many of the themes developed in *Judaism Despite Christianity*." (Stahmer, "Introduction," 19).

4. Both Rosenzweig and Rosenstock were familiar with Schelling's work and were interested in Schelling's notion of the "ages of the world" described in his *Philosophy of Revelation*. In particular, both Rosenzweig and Rosenstock-Huessy took interest in Schelling's focus upon the significance of Jesus' dialogical openness symbolized in what Schelling identified as the logos-centered (over and against the institutional) character of the final Johannine age. According to Harold Stahmer, "For Rosenstock-Huessy and Rosenzweig, the Johannine age would be an age ruled by the Word, and the traditional barriers between the sacred and profane would be eliminated." (Stahmer, "Introduction," 21). Moreover, both thinkers appreciated Schelling's recognition of the dialogical meaning of Jesus as the Logos as a crucial move away from the dominance of the conceptual found in the German idealism of Fichte and Hegel.

5. For example, Eugen Rosenstock-Huessy, *Speech and Reality* (Berlin: Argo Books, 1969) and *The Christian Future or the Modern Mind Outrun* (Berlin: Argo Books, 1981).

6. *Judaism Despite Christianity*, ed. Eugen Rosenstock-Huessy (New York: Schocken Books, 1971), 119.

7. Ibid., 122.

8. Ibid.

9. Ibid., 121.

10. That Rosenzweig had already shed his commitment to German idealism by the time of the letters is well documented. For a helpful account of Rosenzweig's early Hegelianism, see Otto Pöggeler, "Between Enlightenment and Romanticism: Rosenzweig and Hegel" in *The Philosophy of Franz Rosenzweig*, ed. Paul Mendes-Flohr (Hanover: Brandeis University Press, 1988). According to Paul Mendes-Flohr, in response to an invitation to assume a university lecturer position arranged by Friedrich Meinecke, Rosenzweig declined and explained that "the man who wrote *The Star of Redemption* . . . is of a very different caliber from the author of *Hegel un der Staat*." (Rosenzweig to Meinecke, 30 August 1920, in N. N. Glatzer, ed., *Franz Rosenzweig: His Life and Thought*, 2d. rev. ed., New York: Schocken Books, 1961, 62) in Paul Mendes-Flohr, "Franz Rosenzweig and the Crisis of Historicism" in *The Philosophy of Franz Rosenzweig*, ed. Mendes-Flohr, 157. For purposes here, it is worth noting that a 1913 conversation with Eugen Rosenstock-Huessy that temporarily convinced Rosenzweig to move away from the relativism of his Hegelianism to embrace the orientation of the real and the ideal afforded by revelation constitutes one important historical marker of this shift in Rosenzweig's thought. According to Stahmer, "Rosenzweig's decisive rejection of Idealism, following his crucial encounter with Rosenstock in 1913, and his increasing preoccupation with the significance of revelation, was intensified in the course of his study of Schelling's writings. . . ." (Stahmer, "Introduction," 7).

11. Rosenstock-Huessy, *Judaism Despite Christianity*, 125.

12. Jacob Taubes, *The Political Theology of Paul*, trans. Dana Hollander (Stanford: Stanford University Press, 2004), 39. I will discuss Taubes's notion of outbidding in greater detail in a later section of this chapter.

13. Rosenstock-Huessy, *Judaism Despite Christianity*, 125.

14. Ibid., 141.

15. Ibid., 142.

16. Ibid., 144.

17. Rosenzweig's description of the Johannine era is quite different and stresses the openness of Christianity to the non-Christian world rather than a Christianization of the world. And he says, "The Johaninne completion has no form of its own. . . . The integration of the Russians into the Christian orbit was one of the great events of ecclesiastical history. The other was the liberation of the Jews and their admission into the Christian world. . . . Here hope . . . flows directly from the eternal people of hope . . . toward the Christian peoples. . . . And this time, instead of having to convert the heathen, the Christian must directly convert himself, the heathen within himself. Accordingly in this incipient fulfillment of the ages it is rather the Jew, accepted into the Christian world, who must convert the heathen within the Christian. . . . This Johannine Church is amorphous and necessarily unestablished. . . . Goethe is the first of its fathers . . . and indeed was—a pagan man. . . ." (Rosenzweig, *Star*, 285). In Chapters 5 and 6, I will discuss how it is the logic of the law that operates within Rosenzweig's vision of the Johannine era. For here, it is important only to recognize the extent of the Christian encounter with exteriority presented in this vision and mark the significant difference between this account and the one presented by Rosenstock-Huessy in the letters above.

18. Rosenstock-Huessy, *The Christian Future*, 68.

19. Agamben, *The Time That Remains*, 23

20. At this juncture, it is worth noting that for some readers there are "two Agambens." Antonio Negri originated this reading, which suggests that on the one hand there is the post-Foucaultian political critic of *Homer Sacer*; and on the other hand, the utopian Agamben of *The Coming Community* and *The Time That Remains*. A discernment of the veracity of Negri's reading of Agamben is beyond the scope of this chapter. However, Negri's observation seems to apply to scholarship on Agamben's work. Most work on Agamben's thought has focused upon his political analyses without consideration of his account of the messianic. For challenging reviews of Agamben's analysis of sovereignty, see William Connolly, "The Complexities of Sovereignty" in *Giorgio Agamben, Sovereignty and Life*, ed. Matthew Calarco and Steven DeCaroli (Stanford: Stanford University Press, 2007). A valuable exception to this strain in scholarship is William Rasch's "From Sovereign Ban to Banning Sovereignty," also in *Giorgio Agamben, Sovereignty and Life*. In his essay, Rasch discusses the nature of Agamben's messianic vision in relation to his analysis of the limits of the political and in relation to his analysis, therefore, of Schmitt in particular.

21. Giorgio Agamben, *The Time That Remains: A Commentary on the Letter to the Romans*, trans. Patricia Dailey (Stanford: Stanford University Press, 2005), 44. The actual term *aphōrismenos* appears in Romans 1:1.

22. Agamben, *The Time That Remains*, 45.

23. Ibid., 46.

24. Ibid.

25. Ibid., 50.

26. Ibid., 31.

27. Ibid., 27.

28. Agamben's account of the classless community has received significant criticism from a range of thinkers for its impracticality and impossibility. According to William Connolly, Agamben's vision smoothes the complexities and differences attending political logics enmeshed in cultural situations (Connolly, *Sovereignty and Life*, 30–31). William Rausch asks, "Why has this new community, freed from every ban, never been realized? It is, to be sure, an unfair question. Utopias should never be scrutinized. But it is a necessary question . . ." (Rausch, *Sovereignty and Life*, 105). I agree with Rausch's charge but as will become clearer, it seems to me that the problem with Agamben's messianism has less to do with the fact that it is nowhere to be found and more to do with the fact that it neglects a full recognition of the force of desire that motors it. Unrecognized, this desire produces a utopianism that excludes that which is not taken up into it.

29. Ibid., 57.

30. Ibid., 51.

31. Ibid., 69.

32. Ibid., 68.

33. Ibid.

34. Ibid., 77.

35. Ibid., 106.

36. Ibid., 115–16.

37. Ibid., 118–19.

38. Ibid., 121.

39. See John. G. Gager, *Reinventing Paul* (Oxford: Oxford University Press, 2000), and more recently, N. T. Wright, *Paul: In Fresh Perspective* (New York: Fortress Press, 2009).

40. Agamben, *The Time That Remains*, 120.

41. Ibid., 131.

42. Ibid., 133.

43. Jacob Taubes, *The Political Theology of Paul*, trans. Dana Hollander (Stanford: Stanford University Press, 2004), 39.

44. Ibid., 39.

45. Ibid., Appendix A, 98.

46. See, for example, Habermas's comments on the transcendental skills maintained by the social scientist in his *The Theory of Communicative Action*.

There he says, "If the social scientist has to participate virtually in the interactions whose meaning he wants to understand, and if, further, this participation means that he has implicitly to take a position on the validity claims of those immediately involved in communicative action. . . . [Then] he is moving within the same structures of possible understanding in which those immediately involved carry out their communicative actions. However, the most general structures of communication that speaking and acting subjects have learned to master not only open up access to specific contents. . . . These same structures also simultaneously provide the critical means to penetrate a given context, to burst it open from within and to transcend it, the means, if need be, to push beyond a de facto established consensus, to revise errors, correct misunderstandings, and the like. . . . It is this potential for critique built into communicative action that the social scientist . . . can systematically exploit. . . ." (Jurgen Habermas, *The Theory of Communicative Action: Reason and the Rationalization of Society*, vol. 1, trans., Thomas McCarthy [Boston: Beacon Press, 1984, 120–21]).

47. Schmitt makes this point in *Political Theology* when distinguishing his view from Locke, he says, "The peculiarity of the legal form must be recognized in its pure juristic nature. . . . The law gives authority, said Locke, and he consciously used the *law* antithetically to *commissio*, which means the personal command of the monarch. But he did not recognize that the law does not designate to whom it gives authority. . . . The legal prescription, as the norm of decision, only designates how decisions should be made, not who should decide. . . . But the pivotal authority is not derived from the norm of decision." Carl Schmitt, *Political Theology: Four Chapters on the Concept of Sovereignty*, trans. George Schwab (Chicago: The University of Chicago Press, 1985), 42–43.

48. Taubes, *Political Theology*, 87.

49. Rosenstock-Huessy, *Judaism Despite Christianity*, 133.

50. Ibid., 134.

51. While others have noted Schelling's influence upon Rosenzweig's thought—and in particular, Part I of *The Star of Redemption*—my emphasis upon his account of divine revelation as the primary aspect of his influence upon Rosenzweig is unique. For another account of Schelling's influence upon Part I of *The Star of Redemption*, see Robert Gibbs, *Correlations in Rosenzweig and Levinas* (Princeton: Princeton University Press, 199), 40–46. Gibbs does focus upon the influence of Schelling's account of freedom as the condition of the possibility of existence and knowledge of the "real," but he does not examine the theological dynamic in Schelling's *Weltalter* as a theology of creation that links divine existence, wisdom, grace, and law. Michael Morgan and Paul Franks offer helpful historical context for Schelling's influence upon Rosenzweig in Franz Rosenzweig, *Franz Rosenzweig: Philosophical and Theological Writings*, trans., Paul W. Franks and Michael (Indianapolis: Hackett Publishing Company, 2000), 25–47.

52. Ibid., 121.

53. Schelling wrote *The Ages of the World* over several decades and composed many versions of it during that time although he never completed it. The version here referred to is the one dated from 1815. For more information about the other versions and their translations, see Jason M. Wirth, "Translator's Introduction" to F. W. J. Schelling, *The Ages of the World* (New Albany: SUNY Press, 2000).

54. The purpose of this discussion is to extract a particular logic operative in Schelling's account of divine freedom. It is not to engage in comparisons between the *Weltalter* and Schelling's other work. Nor am I attempting to place Schelling in the philosophical context of nineteenth century German Idealism. For instructive accounts of both aspects of Schelling's thought, see Dale E. Snow, *Schelling and the End of Idealism* (New Albany: SUNY Press, 1996); Alan White, *Schelling An Introduction to the System of Freedom* (New Haven: Yale University Press, 1983); and *Schelling Now: Contemporary Readings*, ed. Jason M. Wirth (Bloomington: Indiana University Press, 2005).

55. Alan White comes closest to recognizing the link between the free divine act and divine existence; the subsequent identification between God's act and existence *and* divine self-knowledge or self-revelation (wisdom); and finally the crucial nexus between divine revelation, divine self-consciousness (wisdom), and divine ordering or lawfulness. In his *Schelling: An Introduction to the System of Freedom*, White says the following when discussing Schelling's 1809 essay, "Philosophical Investigations concerning the Essence of Human Freedom and Related Subjects," "In Schelling's technical sense, God 'exists' only following his primal act of self-reflection; prior to that act, God is not nothing (if he were, he could not act), but since he is fully undeveloped, he does not yet 'stand' (exsistere). . . . Understanding enters only with the self-reflection in which God distinguishes himself from the yearning by objectifying it. Through this reflection, God comes to 'see his mirror image,' 'the word' is spoken, and love and understanding come into existence. Understanding works to separate all that is implicit in the divine ground, while love works to hold together the elements that are thereby distinguished." (White, *Schelling*, 118–19).

56. F. W. J. Schelling, *The Ages of the World*, trans. Jason M. Wirth (New Albany: SUNY Press, 2000), 81.

57. Schelling, *Ages of the World*, 81.

58. Ibid., 39.

59. Ibid.

60. In *Schelling: An Introduction to the System of Freedom*, Alan White points out that among the post-Aristotelian thinkers most bound by this inability to correlate an absolute, perfect God with the reality of a contingent world, it was Spinoza who most occupied Schelling's attention. According to White, Schelling criticized Spinoza all throughout his career for presenting "the finite as following from the infinite with complete logical necessity. Spinoza presents the finite as related to the finite in the same way that the properties of individual

triangles are related to the essence of triangularity; just as the mathematician can derive the properties of all triangles by exhaustively thinking the idea of the triangle-without observing any real triangles—so too, according to Schelling's Spinoza, could any intellect capable of exhaustively thinking the absolute derive from it the fundamental characteristics of finite existence, even without taking notice of any real, finite beings (11:276; cf. Gpp, 75)." (White, *Schelling*, 160).

61. Ibid., 20.
62. Ibid., 25.
63. Ibid., 37.
64. Ibid., 45.
65. Rosenstock-Huessy, *Judaism Despite Christianity*, 148.
66. Ibid., 122.
67. Rosenzweig attributes the notion of "revelation as orientation" to Rosenstock-Huessy in his 1917 letter to Rudolph Ehrenberg, otherwise known as the "'Urzelle' to *The Star of Redemption*." "The previous year in correspondence with Rosenstock I asked him straight out what he understood by revelation. He answered: revelation is orientation. After revelation there is an actual, no longer relativized Up and Down in nature—'heaven' and 'earth' and an actually fixed Earlier and Later in time." Franz Rosenzweig, *Philosophical and Theological Writings of Franz Rosenzweig*, eds. Paul Franks and Michael Morgan (Indianapolis: Hackett Publishing Company, 2000), 49–50. As I suggest, however, Rosenzweig and Rosenstock-Huessy understood the link between revelation and orientation differently and the logic of the law exposed by this volume in part emerges out of the difference in these interpretations.
68. Rosenstock-Huessy, *Judaism Despite Christianity*, 134–35.
69. Franz Rosenzweig, "Apologetic Thinking" in *Philosophical and Theological Writings of Franz Rosenzweig*, 107.

2. MONOTHEISM AND EXCEPTIONALISM

1. Schwartz's work would not be possible without the influence of Sigmund Freud's *Moses and Monotheism*, which forced Jews (and then Christians as well) to come to terms with the specific and often violent emotional drives motoring the character of Jewish monotheism and Christological sonship. In *Moses and Monotheism*, Freud maintains that "if we admit for the moment that the rule of Pharaoh's Empire was the external reason for the appearance of the monotheistic idea, we see that this idea—uprooted from its soil and transplanted to another people—after a long latency period takes hold of this people, is treasured by them as their most precious possession, and for its part keeps this people alive by bestowing on them the pride of being the chosen people. It is the religion of the primeval father, and the hope of reward, distinction and finally world sovereignty is bound up with it. . . ." (Sigmund Freud, *Moses and Monotheism*, trans. Katherine Jones [New York: Vintage, 1955], 108). Freud's emphasis

upon the emotional benefits of an exclusivist monotheism offers the groundwork for Schwartz's biblical interpretation. Nonetheless, *Moses and Monotheism* does not pretend that the value of monotheism is reducible to its less than virtuous origins, and Freud maintains that "The people, happy in their conviction of possessing truth, overcome by the consciousness of being the chosen, came to value highly all intellectual and ethical achievements. . . ." (Freud, *Moses and Monotheism*, 109); and about Christianity; Freud suggested that "in certain respects the new religion was a cultural regression as compared with the older Jewish religion. . . . The Christian religion did not keep to the lofty heights of spirituality to which the Jewish religion had soared. The former was no longer strictly monotheistic. . . ." (Freud, *Moses and Monotheism*, 112). Implausible as it is, Freud's account of biblical monotheism, at the very least, recognizes a complexity in its form and function which as we will see is neglected in Schwartz's account.

2. Regina Schwartz, *The Curse of Cain: The Violent Legacy of Monotheism* (Chicago: The University of Chicago Press, 1998), 5.

3. Ibid., 103.

4. Ibid., 16.

5. Ibid., 21.

6. Genesis, 17: 7–8, Rabbi Nosson Scherman ed., *The Chumash*, ArtScroll Series (Brooklyn: Mesorah Publications, 1995).

7. Schwartz, *The Curse of Cain*, 35, 37.

8. See Genesis 17:8, cited earlier.

9. Schwartz, *The Curse of Cain*, 42.

10. Ibid., 55.

11. See Leviticus 25:20–23. "And if ye shall say: 'What shall we eat the seventh year? Behold, we may not sow, nor gather in our increase'; then I will command My blessing upon you in the sixth year, and it shall bring forth produce for the three years. And ye shall sow the eighth year, and eat of the produce, the old store; until the ninth year, until her produce come in, ye shall eat the old store. And the land shall not be sold in perpetuity; for the land is Mine; for ye are strangers and settlers with Me." Leviticus, 25:20–23, ArtScroll.

12. Schwartz, *The Curse of Cain*, 60.

13. Ibid., 86.

14. Ibid., 89.

15. Ibid., 86–87.

16. Ibid., 142.

17. In Moshe Halbertal and Avishai Margalit, *Idolatry*, trans. Naomi Goldblum (Cambridge, Mass.: Harvard University Press, 1992), 12.

18. Ibid., 18.

19. Ibid., 18.

20. Ibid., 20.

21. For example, they say, "[t]he Bible itself does not resolve the question of whether God has an image . . . [sometimes] biblical literature does ascribe an

image to God, for example when the priestly sources speaks of God as dwelling within the sanctuary. . . . These trends within the Bible are developed further in the *Shi'ur Komah* literature, a form of mystical literature from the second and third centuries that discusses the size of the parts of God's body . . . [and] the midrash on the Song of Songs tells us about traditions of God being seen. . . . The claim that God has no image was turned into one of the foundations of Judasim by Maimonides, [but] does not reflect either the Bible or the rabbinic tradition" (Halbertal and Margalit, *Idolatry*, 46–47).

22. Ibid., 110.
23. Ibid., 238.
24. Ibid., 170–71.
25. Ibid., 172–73.
26. Martin Jaffee, "One God, One Revelation, One People: On the Symbolic Structure of Elective Monotheism." *Journal of the American Academy of Religion* 69 (2001): 774.
27. Jaffee, "One God, One Revelation," 774.
28. Of course, one might argue that a brand of philosophical skepticism would not arm its adherents to the sort of intolerance rooted in self-certain philosophical assertions, but this retort loses its meaning because any philosophical skepticism that guards against intolerance would also be a philosophical skepticism incapable of asserting its own positive truth-claims. Revelatory commitments, however, as it is the task of this volume to show, permit persons to recognize truth without pretending to hold or possess truth. I will offer a more detailed philosophical account of this position in Chapters 5 and 6.
29. For scholarship that argues in favor of Maimonides' support for creation *ex nihilo*, see A.L. Ivry "Maimonides on Possibility" in *Mystics, Philosophers and Politicians*, ed., J. Reinharz and D. Swetschinki (Durham: Duke University Press, 1982), 67–84; and, of course, the work of Kenneth Seeskin, which will be discussed here: in particular, Kenneth Seeskin, *Maimonides on the Origin of the World* (Cambridge: Cambridge University Press, 2005). For scholarship in favor of Maimonides' support for either the Aristotelian doctrine of eternity or the Platonic creation *de novo* account, see Shlomo Pines, "Translator's Introduction" in Moses Maimonides, *The Guide of the Perplexed*, trans. Shlomo Pines (Chicago: The University of Chicago Press, 1963) (Aristotelian); Julius Guttman, *Philosophies of Judaism* (Philadelphia, 1964), 165–70 (Aristotelian); and Norbert Samuelson, "Maimonides' Doctrine of Creation," *The Harvard Theological Review* 84.3 (1991): 249–71 (Platonic). Although the large majority of Maimonidean scholars are divided into these two groups, Sara Klein Braslavy argues that Maimonides remained skeptical about both positions and never decided definitively between them. See Sara Klein Braslavy, "The Creation of the World and Maimonides' Interpretation of Genesis i–v" in *Maimonides and Philosophy*, ed., Shlomo Pines and Yirmiahu Yovel (Dordrecht: Martinus Nijhoff Publishers, 1986).

30. Leo Strauss is most famous for the esoteric reading of *The Guide of the Perplexed*, according to which, the most exoteric claims of the text serve political purposes, and only the esoterically concealed claims reflect Maimonides' true philosophical positions. See Leo Strauss, "How to Begin to Study the *Guide*" in Moses Maimonides, *The Guide of the Perplexed*, trans. Shlomo Pines.

31. Kenneth Seeskin, *Maimonides: A Guide for Today's Perplexed* (Springfield New Jersey: Behrman House, Inc.), 44.

32. Seeskin identifies this difference in his essay, "Metaphysics and Its Transcendence" in *The Cambridge Companion to Maimonides*, ed. Kenneth Seeskin (Cambridge: Cambridge University Press, 2005), 98.

33. Moses Maimonides, *The Guide of the Perplexed*, 2.25, 328.

34. Seeskin, *Maimonides on the Origin of the World*, 31.

35. Ibid.

36. Ibid., 31.

37. Ibid., 32.

38. Ibid., 26.

39. Ibid., 4.

40. So although Seeskin admits that a Maimonidean embrace of creation *ex nihilo* is not itself necessarily or absolutely true, Seeskin does maintain that Maimonides' qualified embrace of it nonetheless assumes the falsehood of either the Platonic or the Aristotelian position. Still, as we will see, Seeskin does not want to suggest that Maimonides' rejection of either of these two model registers as a rejection of the notion of divine Being or wisdom because according to Seeskin, wisdom and free will are not contradictory aspects of God's unity.

41. Maimonides, Seeskin tells us, offers his own take on Plato's account. He assumes a more active and robust description of Plato's Demiurge. Seeskin says, "Like his view of Aristotle, Maimonides' view of Plato is more thematic than historical. In general, he associates Platonism with three claims: (1) creation *ex nihilo* is impossible, (2) the world had a beginning and was created from preexistent matter, and (3) the heavens are subject to generation and destruction" (Seeskin, *Maimonides on the Origins of the World*, 38).

42. Maimonides, *Guide*, 2.13, 283.

43. Ibid., 58.

44. Ibid.

45. Maimonides, *Guide*, 1.52, 115.

46. According to Seeskin, "[u]nbeknownst to Maimonides, most of these arguments derive from Proclus or the *Theology of Aristotle*" (Seeskin, *Maimonides on the Origin of the World*, 78). See Proclus, *On the Eternity of the World*, ed. Helen S. Lang and A.D. Marco (Berkeley: University of California Press, 2001) for an English translation.

47. Ibid., 83.

48. Maimonides, *Guide*, 2.14, 288.

49. Ibid., 2.19, 302.

Notes to pages 63–66   285

50. According to Shlomo Pines, it is difficult to gauge the extent of the influence of the Mutakallimūn on Maimonides' thinking because on the one hand, "he does not hesitate clearly to express the respect he feels for philosophy and the intellectual contempt with which the theological efforts of the Mutakallimūn inspire him. . . ." (Pines, "Translator's Introduction, cxxiv), yet at the same time, he expresses sympathy with their account of the temporal creation of the world. For a detailed analysis of the influence of the Mutakallimūn on Maimonides, see Pines, "Translator's introduction" in Moses Maimonides, *The Guide of the Perplexed*, cxxiv–cxxxi.

51. Seeskin, *Maimonides on the Origin of the World*, 84.
52. Ibid., 86, and in Maimonides, *Guide* 3.25, 504.
53. Maimonides, *Guide* 2.19.
54. Seeskin, *Maimonides on the Origin of the World*, 88, and *Guide*, 1.69.
55. Ibid.
56. Although Maimonides does not directly reference a Plotinian account of the origin of the world as one of the three possible accounts, Plotinus' theory of emanation influenced Maimonides and is indirectly addressed in the *Guide* as an account of the origin of the world. For Seeskin's discussion, see Seeskin, *Maimonides on the Origin of the World*, 116–17.

57. Pines, "Translator's Introduction," in *The Guide of the Perplexed*, cxxvii.
58. Maimonides, *Guide*, 2.22, 319.
59. Pines, "Translator's Introduction," cxxviii.
60. Ibid.
61. Ibid. See Maimonides, *Guide*, 2.18, 3.25.
62. Ibid.
63. Ibid., cxxix.
64. Maimonides, *Guide*, 3.23, 492–93.
65. Ibid., 1.68, 163–64.

66. In the final sections of the *Guide*, Maimonides discusses union with God through intellectual apprehension. Although scholars have long debated what, according to Maimonides, constitutes the highest end of human life (see in particular the debate between Alexander Altmann, "Maimonides on the intellect and Scope of Metaphysics," in *Von der mittelatlerlichen zur modernen Aufklärung* (Tubingen: J. C. B. Mohr, 1987) 60–129; and Shlomo Pines, 'The Limitations of Human Knowledge Acoording to al-Farabil, ibn Bajja, and Maimonides," in *Studies in Medieval Jewish History and Literature*, ed., Isadore Twersky (Cambridge, Mass: Harvard University press, 1979, 82–109), the final chapters of the *Guide* point to an intellectual apprehension of and union with God, whereby human passions are set aside as expendable. In 3.51, Maimonides says, "We have already made it clear to you that that intellect which overflowed from Him, may He be exalted, toward us is the bond between us and Him. You have the choice: if you wish to strengthen and to fortify this bond. . . . And it is made weaker and feebler if you busy your thought with what is other than He.

Know that even if you were the man who knew the most the true reality of the divine science, you would cut that bond existing between you and God if you would empty your thought of God and busy yourself totally in eating the necessary or occupying yourselves with the necessary. You would not be with Him, then, nor He with you. . . ." Providence, therefore, benefits the intellectually active: "providence watches over everyone endowed with intellect proportionately to the measure of his intellect. Thus providence always watches over an individual endowed with perfect apprehension. . . ." (Maimonides, *Guide*, 3.51, 621, 624). Martin Kavka also argues that Maimonides' emphasis upon the intellectual life comes at the expense of the validity of the human life of the passions and the body and says, "Maimonides' account in the final chapters of the *Guide* of the intellectual love of God marks no departure from the Stoic account of joy described here. For intellectual love is rooted in the actualization of the human intellect, that which is essential to the human, properly 'ones' own. . . . the inward idealist move of Maimonidean teleology is a move that regards the created realm only as the necessary framing environment in which God's revelation takes place. It refuses to see the external world as intrinsically good. It does not know how to make the argument that if God is essentially goodness, then that which God creates (whether or not it is endowed with reason) must also have an essence that is essentially good. . . ." Martin Kavka, *Jewish Messianism and the History of Philosophy* (Cambridge: Cambridge University Press, 2004), 85.

67. Haim Kreisel, "Maimonides on the Eternity of the World," unpublished Association of Jewish Studies presentation (www.ajs.net.org).

68. Maimonides, *Guide*, 2.22, 319.

69. Ibid.

70. Kreisel, "*Maimonides on the Eternity of the World.*"

71. Ibid.

72. Ibid.

73. Maimonides, *Guide*, 1.53, 122.

74. Ibid.

75. F. W. J. Schelling, *The Ages of the World*, trans. Jason M. Wirth (New Albany: SUNY Press, 2000), 81.

76. Ibid., 39.

77. Ibid.

78. Ibid., 38.

79. Ibid.

80. See footnote 68.

81. The two different accounts here offered of how will and wisdom relate to one another have ramifications for Maimonides' and Schelling's account of divine self-knowledge. For both, divine self-consciousness means the identity between act and apprehension. In the *Guide* 1.68, Maimonides says, "God is an intellect in *actu*," and in the *Weltalter*, Schelling says, "hence that rapport

into which eternal freedom enters with nature is nothing but the eternal-coming-to-itself of the highest.... It comes to what is its own and knows it as its own proper nature ... but everything that should come to itself must seek itself. There must therefore be something in the Godhead that seeks and something that is sought.... Hence only thus can one think a consciousness that is eternally alive...." (Schelling, *Weltalter*, 45). However, the difference between the two is clear. If, for Maimonides, God knows all that is other through knowing Godself (Maimonides, *Guide*, 3.68) "through knowing the true reality of His own immutable essence, He also knows the totality of what necessarily derives from His acts" (Maimonides, *Guide* 3.68, 485), for Schelling, God knows Godself, through knowing what is Other within Godself. For Schelling, God only knows Godself as alive and manifest. The conditions of our knowing God are the conditions of God's knowing Godself. "Most people begin from wanting to explain a revelation of the Godhead. But that which should give itself must already have itself; what wants to articulate itself must first come to itself; what is manifest to others must already be manifest to itself" (Schelling, *Weltalter*, 45).

3. MODERN JUDAISM, LAW, AND EXCEPTIONALISM

1. David Novak's work does offer a detailed exposition regarding the meaning and philosophical import of revelatory law. However, we find his most detailed account of the relation between law and desire in his description and phenomenology of natural law which qua natural, is not revealed. For Novak, natural law intends revelation but it is not a result of divine revelation. For Novak's account of the meaning of revelatory law see David Novak, *The Election of Israel: The Idea of the Chosen People* (Cambridge: Cambridge University Press, 1995).

2. For a detailed examination of the impact of Spinoza's work on the German Enlightenment and the Jewish *Haskalah*, see Steven B. Smith, *Spinoza, Liberalism and the Question of Jewish Identity* (New Haven: Yale University Press, 1998). Smith's work acknowledges important differences between Spinoza's emphasis upon the power of the sovereign, his apparent favoritism of the elite over the masses along with his insistence upon the role of a public religion required to motivate the masses to obedience toward the state. Nonetheless, Smith does not pay sufficient attention to Spinoza's indebtedness to the theocratic and covenantal model of biblical Israel. Along the same lines, many Jewish scholars over-emphasize the apparent importance attached to autonomy in Spinoza and Cohen. For example, David Novak says, "The most radical preclusion of election comes from the philosophy of the archetypal modern Jewish renegade, Baruch Spinoza [whose] rationalist theology does not in fact constitute the event of revelation apart from the event of the human discovery of eternal truth.... And, as we shall see, two centuries after Spinoza, Hermann Cohen

attempted much the same thing although operating from a quite different philosophical base. Spinoza's radical project cleared the way for Jewish secularism and the atheism it fundamentally assumes" (Novak, *The Election of Israel*, 15). It is my contention, however, that this overemphasis on the humanism in Spinoza and Cohen's thought misses important differences in their positions on law.

3. Willi Goetschel's work on Spinoza and the role of the affections in the *Ethics* and the political writings constitutes an exception to this tendency. In his work, Goetschel pays particular attention to the role of the affections in Spinoza's thought as one of the central aspects of connection forged by later German thinkers, including Mendelssohn and Lessing. This identification of the importance of the affections helps Goetschel earmark the difference between Spinoza's understanding of human autonomy (or power) and a Cohenian notion of autonomy divorced as it is from the affections. In his *Spinoza's Modernity*, he says, "Spinoza's *Ethics* can . . . be understood as a philosophy of self-empowerment in the precise meaning of the term. His metaphysics rests upon a strong conception of individuality. . . . Although Spinoza redefines the concept of autonomy and freedom in a way that has led to the dismissal of his philosophy as reductive and determinist, his reformulation of human freedom and autonomy in terms of self-determination and self-preservation . . . breaks new ground for a dynamic conception of individuality that takes the psychosomatic constitution of human nature as the basis for the individual's open-ended potential for self-realization" (Goetschel, *Spinoza's Modernity: Mendelssohn, Lessing and Heine* [Madison: University of Wisconsin Press, 2004], 51).

4. This is in part because of the influence of Leo Strauss's interpretation of Spinoza's emphasis upon biblical Judaism and its themes of revelation, theism, and divine law as examples of Spinoza's esotericism or tendency to hide more traditionally radical elements of his thought (for example, naturalism, atheism, and amoralism) behind the guise of these traditional categories. See Leo Strauss, *Persecution and the Art of Writing* (Chicago: The University of Chicago Press, 1952).

5. Nancy Levene suggests a more nuanced account of Spinoza's account of revelation. Arguing against a Spinozistic dichotomy between reason and revelation, Levene suggests that on the one hand, "It is Spinoza's abiding claim that no standpoint is free of revelation . . . not because religion is true . . . not is it because one must believe in God. . . . Spinoza thinks that the narrow notion of revelation as the divine gift to a particular community of law or sacrality has the same significance as a human given law. But there is a wider notion of revelation in Spinoza's thought. . . . This is the notion that even the most universal, the most eternal, the most natural things—peace rationality, freedom, morality (God, or Nature)—originate from nothing . . . they come into existence—their creation, creativity, making, origination is the ground of, the essence, of existence itself. . . . Both religion (God) and reason (Nature) are revealed, created, made. . . ." (Levene, *Spinoza's Revelation: Religion, Democracy and Reason* [Cambridge: Cambridge University Press, 2004], 3).

Notes to pages 78–86   289

6. Baruch Spinoza, *Ethics* in *The Essential Spinoza: Ethics and Related Writings*, ed. Michael Morgan, trans. Samuel Shirley (Indianapolis: Hackett Publishing Company, 2006), 4.
7. Ibid., 7.
8. Ibid., 8.
9. Ibid., 16.
10. Ibid., 19.
11. Ibid., 26.
12. Benedict de Spinoza, *Theologico-Political Treatise*, trans. R. H. M. Elwes, (New York: Dover Publications, Inc., 1951), 201.
13. Spinoza, *Ethics*, 34.
14. Ibid., 35.
15. Ibid., 36.
16. Ibid., 32.
17. Ibid., 66.
18. Ibid.
19. "The greater the love wherewith one thinks the object of his love is affected toward him, the greater will be his vanity . . . he will endeavor as far as he can, to imagine the object loved as bound to him as intimately as possible, and this conatus, or appetite, is fostered if he imagines someone else desires the same thing for himself" (Spinoza, *Ethics*, 79).
20. Ibid., 88–89.
21. Ibid., 111.
22. Ibid., 106–07.
23. Spinoza, *Theologico-Political Treatise*, 204.
24. Ibid., 203.
25. Ibid., 209.
26. Ibid., 214.
27. Ibid.
28. Ibid., 76.
29. Ibid., 208.
30. Ibid., 209.
31. Ibid., 245.
32. For a provocative account of the meaning of Spinoza's excommunication, see Richard H. Popkin, "Spinoza's Excommunication" in Heidi M. Ravven and Lenn E. Goodman, ed. *Jewish Themes in Spinoza's Philosophy* (Albany: SUNY Press, 2002), 263–81.
33. For arguments emphasizing the connection between Spinoza's account of the divine affinity for the material world and the Jewish emphasis upon God's favor for His creatures, see both Lenn Goodman, "What Does Spinoza's Ethics Contribute to Jewish Philosophy," and Lee C. Rice, "Love of God in Spinoza" in Heidi M. Ravven and Lenn E. Goodman, eds., *Jewish Themes in Spinoza's Philosophy*, 17–93 and 93–107.

34. Ibid., 219.
35. Ibid.
36. Deuteronomy 10:12–13, Rabbi Nosson Scherman ed., *The Chumash*, ArtScroll Series (Brooklyn: Mesorah Publications, 1995).
37. Jon D. Levenson, *Sinai and Zion: An Entry into the Jewish Bible* (New York: HarperOne, 1987), 77.
38. Deuteronomy 30:11–14 (ArtScroll).
39. Ibid., 220.
40. For an interesting account of what this might look like, see Nancy K. Levene, "Judaism's Body Politic" in *Women and Gender in Jewish Philosophy*, ed., Hava Tirosh-Samuelson (Indianapolis: Indianapolis University Press, 2004), 234–62.
41. Nancy Levene makes this point and says that for Spinoza, "there is no sociality that is natural—we must paradoxically see that each has an origin: that nature and politics come into existence together, and thus are always disrupting and complicating each other. . . ." (Levene, *Spinoza's Revelation*, 8).
42. Spinoza, *Ethics*, 106.
43. Ibid., 142.
44. Ibid., 113.
45. Until recently, there has been little scholarship on Rose's work. In the past few years, two works have appeared that offer more comprehensive analyses of her thought: Vince Lloyd *Law and Transcendence: On the Unfinished Project of Gillian Rose* (New York: Palgrave Macmillan Publishing Company, 2009), and Andrew Shanks, *Against Innocence: An Introduction to Gillian Rose* (London: SCM, 2008).
46. Gillian Rose, *Mourning Becomes the Law: Philosophy and Representation* (Cambridge: Cambridge University Press, 1996), 74.
47. Ibid., 75.
48. Ibid.
49. Ibid.
50. For an extended analysis of Rose's reference to grace and its relation to her discussion of law, see my essay, "Theological Desire: Feminism, Philosophy, and Exegetical Jewish Thought" in *Women and Gender in Jewish Philosophy*, ed., Hava Tirosh-Samuelson. (Bloomington: Indiana University Press, 2004), 314–40.
51. Ibid., 36.
52. Gillian Rose, *The Broken Middle: Out of Our Ancient Society* (Oxford: Blackwell, 1992), 87.
53. David Novak, *The Election of Israel*, 128.
54. David Novak, "Philosophy and the Possibility of Revelation" in *Tradition in the Public Square: A Novak Reader*, eds., Randi Rashkover and Martin Kavka (Grand Rapids: Wm. B. Eerdmans, 2008), 15.
55. "Natural law . . . can be seen as what Kant called a 'border concept' (*Grenzbegriff*). On the surface, it functions like the idea of natural rights . . . but

unlike the idea of human rights, it does not claim to be self-constituting. By its real assertion of nature, it indicates that it is rooted in an order that transcends any immanent society. Here is where it parts company with liberalism and reconnects itself to the religions of revelation from whence it emerged. . . ." (Novak, *Natural Law in Judaism*, 25–26).

4. THE BIBLICAL THEOLOGY OF ABIDING

1. In his *The Death and Resurrection of the Beloved Son*, Jon Levenson presents a similar, if even more provocative account of the *akedah*. There, Levenson suggests that we see the *akedah* as a test through which Abraham will acknowledge the reality of the theological order within which he lives. In this way, the *akedah* does not operate as an exercise in exchange but rather Abraham's obedient repetition or announcement that his beloved son came from God and therefore belongs to God. Levenson, *The Death and Resurrection of the Beloved Son: The Transformation of Child Sacrifice* (New Haven: Yale University Press, 1995), 126.

2. Gerhard Von Rad, *From Genesis to Chronicles: Explorations in Old Testament Theology* (Minneapolis: Augsburg Fortress Press, 2005), 177.

3. Ibid.

4. Ibid., 180.

5. Ibid.

6. Ibid., 183.

7. Ibid.

8. Genesis Rabbah, I,10, *The Midrash*, trans. Rabbi Dr. H. Freedman (New York: The Soncino Press, 1983), v.1.

9. Moses Maimonides, *The Guide of the Perplexed*, vol. I, Shlomo Pines, trans. (Chicago: The University of Chicago Press, 1963), 125.

10. David Novak, *Covenantal Rights: A Study in Jewish Political Theory* (Princeton: Princeton University Press, 2000), 41.

11. "Man is not lost in his object only when the object becomes for him a human object or objective man. This is possible only when the object becomes for him a social object, he himself for himself a social being, just as society becomes a being for him in this object. . . . Thus man is affirmed in the objective world not only in the act of thinking, but with all his senses . . . human sense . . . comes to be by virtue of its object, by virtue of humanized nature." (Marx, "Economic and Philosophic Manuscripts of 1844," 88–89).

12. In "What is to be Done," Lenin referred to the "dictatorship of the proletariat" and said, "toilers need a 'state' i.e. the proletariat organized as the ruling class. . . . The exploited classes need political rule in order to completely abolish all exploitation. . . . The doctrine of the class struggle as applied by Marx to the question of the state and socialist revolution, leads inevitably to the recognition of the political rule of the proletariat, of its dictatorship . . . i.e.

of power shared with none . . ." (Lenin, *The Essential Works of Lenin*, 1987, 286–88).

13. Gerhard Von Rad, *Genesis: A Commentary* (Philadelphia: Westminster Press, 1972), 61.

14. Ibid.

15. Ibid.

16. Ibid.

17. Ibid.

18. Deuteronomy 7:7–8, Rabbi Nosson Scherman ed., *The Chumash*, ArtScroll Series (Brooklyn: Mesorah Publications, 1995).

19. Deuteronomy 4:37–38 (ArtScroll).

20. Martin Luther, *On Christian Liberty* (Minneapolis: Augsburg Fortress Press, 2003), 12.

21. Ibid., 10.

22. Ibid., 13.

23. According to Rubenstein, choseness is premised upon merit. Consequently, as chosen one either lives up to one's expected obedience, or one fails in this expectation and is rejected. Divine favoritism is the flip side of divine punishment, and neither Christians nor Jews can escape this logic. In a classic essay, "The Dean and the Chosen People," Rubenstein explains, "The Dean dramatized the consequences of accepting the normative Judeo-Christian theology of covenant and election in the light of the Holocaust. . . . If I truly believed in God as the omnipotent author of the historical drama and in Israel as his Chosen People, I had no choice but to accept Dean Gruber's conclusion that Hitler unwittingly acted as God's agent in committing six million Jews to slaughter." (Rubenstein, *After Auschwitz*, 3). Here, I want to emphasize the consequences of a Christian account of election devoid of a theology of law for Christian anti-Judaism. Certainly, however, Rubenstein's logic could be applied to Christians themselves, as discussed in Chapter 1.

24. Claus Westermann, *Genesis: A Continental Commentary* 12–36 (Minneapolis: Augsburg Fortress Press, 1995), 29.

25. Ibid., 12–36, 255.

26. See M. Weinfeld, "The Covenant of Grant in the Old Testament and in the Ancient Near East." *Journal of the American Oriental Society* 90 (1970): 184–203.

27. Gary N. Knoppers, "Ancient Near Eastern Royal Grants and the Davidic Covenant: A Parallel?"*Journal of the American Oriental Society* 116 (1996): 670–97.

28. See Louis Newman, "Covenant and Contract: A Framework for Jewish Ethics." *Journal of Law and Religion* 9 (1991): 89–112.

29. B. Sanhedrin 44a re: Josh 7:11.

30. Genesis 17:10 (ArtScroll).

31. Regina M. Schwartz, *The Curse of Cain: The Violent Legacy of Monotheism* (Chicago: The University of Chicago Press, 1997), 24.

32. Genesis 17:10–11 (ArtScroll).

33. Perhaps the most noteworthy is Joseph Blenkinsopp, *Wisdom and Law in the Old Testament: the Ordering of Life in Israel and Early Judaism* (Oxford: Oxford University Press, 1995). Identifying the link between wisdom and Torah law, Blenkinsopp comments that "Ezra himself is described as both priest and scribe and his principal concern is the study of the law (Ezra 7L10, etc.). Later still, the scribe Ben Sira is first and foremost a legal scholar (Ecclus. 32: 14–15; 39:1) and teaches his discipline in a school (51:23). Other teachers and sages were active during this long period, including Qoheleth and those whose sayings were brought together by the editor of Proverbs (I:6; 22:17; 24:33; 30:1; 31:1). Increasingly . . . the interpretation of and instruction in the law took centre stage and became the vital link with Judaism of the post-biblical period" (Blenkinsopp, *Wisdom and Law*, 12).

34. In his *The Tree of Life: an Exploration of Biblical Wisdom*, Roland E. Murphy expresses this common view and says, "The most striking characteristic of this literature is the absence of what one normally considers as typically Israelite and Jewish" (Murphy, *The Tree of Life*, 1).

35. Babylonian Talmud, *Baba Metsia* 86b; Complete Soncino Translation, (http://wilkerson.110mb.com/Tanhuma), Vayera, 2; *Pirqei Rabbi Eliezer*, 29.

36. In *The Gift of Death*, Derrida describes the paradox of the reception of a gift. "On the basis of the Gospel of Matthew we can ask what 'to give back' . . . means. . . . God decides to give back, to give back life, . . . once he is assured that a gift outside of any economy, the gift of death—and of the death of that which is priceless—has been accomplished without any hope of exchange, reward, circulation or communication. . . . Through the law of the father economy reappropriates the *an*economy of the gift as a gift of life or, what amounts to the same thing, a gift of death"—that is to say, a gift that we cannot fully demonstrate our reception for without reincorporating it into an economy of exchange (Derrida, *The Gift of Death*, 97).

37. Genesis 18:1 (ArtScroll).

38. Genesis Rabbah 18:7, Midrash.

39. Elliot Wolfson, "From My Flesh I would Behold God: Imaginal Representation and Inscripting Divine Justice, Preliminary Observations." *Journal of Scriptural Reasoning* 2 (2002). etext.lib.virginia.edu/journals/ssr/issues/volume2/number3/ssr02-03-e01.html.

40. See Genesis Rabbah 48:4–5, Midrash.

41. Genesis commentary (ArtScroll), 78.

42. Clearly, demonstrations of this sort could be both: that is, reflections of divine freedom and contingent responses to human action. Nonetheless, to the extent to which divine action does indicate a reward or punishment of Israel's actions, it does so contextualized still and always within this theological reality that at the end of the day, nullifies the absolute meaning of a reward and punishment scheme.

43. See Chapter 6 for an extended philosophical account of this analysis of the rights of others.

44. For a similar account of the covenantal basis of human rights, see David Novak's *Covenantal Rights: A Jewish Political Theory*. Although Novak's account does not expand upon the internal theological assumption of human rights, his analysis of the correlation between duties to God and the rights of persons who have those duties amounts to a similar perspective to the one presented in this account. In particular, see *Covenantal Rights* for Novak's structural account of duties and rights, 36–55.

45. For a careful analysis of Abraham's prerevelatory knowledge of God, see David Novak's *The Election of Israel: The Idea of the Chosen People* (Cambridge: Cambridge University Press, 1995), 115–38.

46. Novak, *The Election of Israel*, 121. Of course, this is not to imply that God's election of Abraham and his descendants is not marked by features unique to this relationship. It is to argue that the divine capacity for love is not exhausted by this relationship as is borne out by an analysis of the theology of divine creation.

47. Shevuous 25b, Shabbos 127a (Soncino).

48. Genesis 18: 20–23 (ArtScroll).

49. The Book of Job 38:4–10. *The New Oxford Annotated Bible with the Apocrypha*, Revised Standard Version, eds., Herbert G. May and Bruce M. Metzger (New York: Oxford University Press, 1977).

50. Genesis 18:3 (ArtScroll).

51. Genesis 18:27 (ArtScroll).

52. Genesis 18:18 (ArtScroll).

53. Deuteronomy 10:12–15 (ArtScroll). Also see Joshua 24:1–26.

54. Jon D. Levenson, *Sinai and Zion: An Entry into the Jewish Bible* (San Francisco: Harper & Row, 1985), 45.

55. BT Shabbat 88a. (Soncino). See also Mekhilta Derabbi Yishmael, Bahodesh, "I the Lord am your God (Exod. 20:2). Why were the Ten Commandments not proclaimed at the beginning of the Torah/A parable: what is this like? Like a human king who entered a province and said to the people: Shall I reign over you? They replied: Have You conferred upon us any benefit that you should reign over us? What did he do? He built the city wall for them, he brought in the water supply for them, and he fought their battles. [Then] he said to them: Shall I regin over you? They replied: Yes, yes." (Mekhilta Derrabi Yishmael Bahodesh 5, 6).

56. Levenson, *Sinai and Zion*, 42.

57. Ibid., 45.

58. Ibid., 27.

59. Ibid., 43.

60. Ibid., 38.

61. Jon D. Levenson, "The Theologies of Commandment in Biblical Israel." *Harvard Theological Review* 73 (1980): 32.

62. Levenson, *Sinai and Zion*, 45.
63. Hosea, 2:18, Ibid. 78.
64. Ibid.
65. Ibid.
66. Levenson, "The Theologies of Commandment in Biblical Israel," 28.
67. Psalm 119, cited by Levenson, "The Theologies of Commandment in Biblical Israel," 28.
68. Ibid., 29.
69. For an interesting account of the character and motive for *halakhic* change, see David Weiss Halivni, *Revelation Restored: Divine Writ and Critical Responses* (Boulder: Westview, 1998).
70. Exodus 23:10 (ArtScroll).
71. Leviticus 25:2–5 (ArtScroll).
72. Maimonides, *Guide*, Part 3, 553.
73. Metsudah: *Chumash/Rashi: A New Linear Translation*, trans. Rabbi Avrohom Davis; Nachum Y. Kornfeld, Abraham B. Walzer, eds. (NJ: KTAV Publishing House, 1997).
74. BT Tractate *Sanhedrin* 39a.
75. Leviticus 25:6–7 (ArtScroll).
76. Rashi, Leviticus 25:6 (Metsudah Chumash/Rashi).
77. Deuteronomy 15:1–3 (ArtScroll).
78. For this argument, see David L. Baker, "The Jubilee and the Millennium Holy Years in the Bible and Their Relevance Today." *Themelios* 24/1 (1998): 44–69.
79. See footnote 90 for a list of scholarly texts that analyze the theology of the poor in the Gospel of Luke.
80. Rashi, Leviticus 25:6 (Metsudah Chumash/Rashi).
81. Deuteronomy 31:8–13 (ArtScroll).
82. Deuteronomy 4:6 (ArtScroll).
83. Ibid., 26.
84. Levenson, "Theologies of Commandment in Biblical Israel," 28.
85. Patrick Miller, "Deuteronomy and Psalms: Evoking Biblical Conversation." *Journal of Biblical Literature*, 118/1 (1999): 14l.
86. Leviticus 25:8–13 (ArtScroll).
87. Leviticus 23:27–32 (ArtScroll).
88. For an excellent account of atonement within the biblical text, see Baruch Levine, *JPS Torah Commentary: Leviticus*, Jewish Publication Society, 2004.
89. *The Chumash*, The ArtScroll Series/Stone edition (Brooklyn: Mesorah Publications, Ltd., 1996), 155.
90. Leviticus 25:8–10 (ArtScroll).
91. Avot, 5:11, *The Pirkei Avos Treasury: Ethics of the Fathers: The Sages' Guide to Living With an Anthologized Commentary and Anecdotes* (Brooklyn: Mesorah Publications, Ltd., 1995).

92. Deuteronomy 29:15–69 (ArtScroll).
93. Novak, *Covenantal Rights*, 75–76.
94. Ibid., 102.
95. Isaiah 61:1–2 (RSV).
96. Bradley C. Gregory, "The Postexilic Exile in Third Isaiah: Isaiah 61:1–3 in Light of Second Temple Hermeneutics." *Journal of Biblical Literature*, 126 (2007): 475.
97. Ibid., 483.
98. Ibid.
99. Ibid., 487.
100. Ibid., 488.
101. Ibid.
102. Ezra 9:9 (RSV).
103. Ibid., 495.
104. Ibid.
105. Ibid.
106. Rosemary Ruether, *Faith and Fratricide: The Theological Roots of Anti-Semitism* (Eugene: Wipf and Stock, 1997), 41.
107. Ibid., 47.
108. Ibid., 55–56.
109. Ibid., 78.
110. Gregory, "The Postexilic Exile in Isaiah," 496.
111. Paul Hanson, *The Dawn of the Apocalyptic: The Historical and Sociological Roots of Jewish Apocalyptic Eschatology* (Minneapolis: Fortress Press, 1979), 60.
112. Ibid., 62.
113. Ibid., 64.
114. Ibid., 68.
115. Ibid., 73.
116. For a review of contemporary New Testament scholarship on Luke 4, see Joel B. Green, *Theology of the Gospel of Luke*; J. A. Sanders, "From Isaiah 61 to Luke 4," in *Christianity, Judaism and other Greco-Roman Cults: Studies for Morton Smith at Sixty* (SJLA12/1), ed. J. Neusnes (Leiden: Bril, 1975), 75–106; L. C. Crockett, "Luke 4:25–7 and Jewish-Gentle Relations in Luke-Acts," *Journal of Biblical Literature* 88 (1969): 177–83; Jeffrey S. Siker, "First to the Gentiles: A Literary Analysis of Luke 4:16–30," *Journal of Biblical Literature* 111/1 (1992): 73–90. For discussions regarding the Gospel of Luke's perspective on the Jews in general, see *Luke-Acts and the Jews: Eight Critical Perspectives*, ed., Joseph B. Tyson (Minneapolis: Augsburg Fortress Press, 1988). Also important is David L. Tiede, "Glory to the People Israel" in eds. Joseph B. Tyson, Richard P. Thompson, and Thomas E. Phillips, *Literary Studies in Luke-Acts* (Macon: Mercer University Press, 1998), and L. Brawley, "Luke-Acts and the Jews: Conflict, Apology and Conciliation" in the same volume. Also helpful is Kenneth Duncan Litwak, *Echoes of Scripture in Luke-Acts* (London: T & T Clark, 2005). For

discussions concerning the Lukan perspective on the poor and whether or not the Lukan Gospel espouses a prioritization of the poor, see D. P. Seccombe, *Possessions and the Poor in Luke–Acts* (SNTU, 6; Linz: A. Fuchs, 1982); R. B. Sloan, *The Favorable Year of the Lord: A Study of the Jubilary Theology in the Gospel of Luke* (Austin: Scholar Press, 1977); and W. Stegemann and L. Schottroff, *Jesus and the Hope of the Poor*, trans. M. J. O'Connell (New York: Orbis Books, 1986).

5. THE NEW THINKING AND THE ORDER OF WISDOM

1. Rosenzweig says that he saw *The Star of Redemption* as "the second book he [Schelling] tried to give" (Rosenzweig, *Der Mensch und sein Werk*, 148).

2. It is widely recognized that although Schelling's later work is credited for greatly influencing twentieth-century existentialist thought, it remained focused more upon the limits of idealism and less upon offering a vivid account of the human existentialist situation. Remarking upon this aspect of Schelling's work, Dale E. Snow suggests that at the end of the day, *The Ages of the World* was a failure philosophically "[b]ecause it amounts, in many ways, to a guided tour of the limits of philosophy." (Snow, *Schelling and the End of Idealism* [Albany: SUNY Press, 1996, 184]). Consequently, Snow suggests, the work of examining the implications of Schelling's account of divine freedom and non-Being would fall into the hands of later philosophers like Heidegger and theologians like Paul Tillich.

3. For a general introduction to "Atheistic Theology," see Paul Mendes-Flohr's "In 1914 Franz Rosenzweig writes the essay 'Atheistic Theology,' which criticizes the theology of his day," in eds. Sander L. Gilman and Jack Zipes, *Yale Companion to Jewish Writing and Thought in German Culture* (New Haven: Yale University Press, 1997), 322–26.

4. Franz Rosenzweig, "Atheistic Theology," in eds. and trans., Paul W. Franks and Michael L. Morgan. *Philosophical and Theological Writings* (Indianapolis: Hackett Publishing Company, Inc., 2000), 16.

5. Ibid., 17.

6. In their introduction to Rosenzweig's "Atheistic Theology," Paul Franks and Michael Morgan clearly articulate the link between Feuerbach and Buber in Rosenzweig's mind when they say that "Rosenzweig reads Buber in the tradition of Feuerbach. . . . Here is theology turned into anthropology. . . . According to Rosenzweig, Buber's racial, biological, and psychological account of the Jewish people claims that God is part of the mythology that derives from that people" (Franks and Morgan, *Philosophical and Theological Writings*, 6).

7. Ibid., 17.
8. Ibid.
9. Ibid., 18.
10. Ibid., 17.
11. Ibid., 19.

12. Michael Morgan and Paul Franks, "From 1914 to 1917" in *Rosenzweig: Philosophical and Theological Writings*, 31.
13. Ibid.
14. Ibid.
15. A number of scholars make note of the fact that even Rosenzweig's 1913 decision against converting to Christianity represents this reorientation in intellectual historical perspective because Rosenzweig's earlier decision to convert to Christianity was in part predicated upon his Hegelian-informed narrative of the historical triumph of Christianity in the west. Otto Pöggeler explains that "Hegel found his way to an affirmation of the state, but he regarded the world of the European states as a realization of the new liberty of Christian faith; because Rosenzweig understood his own time as founded by Hegel and Hegel's contemporaries, it was only a matter of logical consequence that he contemplated conversion to Christianity. . . ." (Pöggeler, "Rosenzweig and Hegel," 114).
16. For a clear and persuasive articulation of the difference between secularism and secularization theory, see José Cassanova, *Public Religions in the Modern World* (Chicago: The University of Chicago Press, 1994).
17. Rosenzweig is not the first to refer to the Johannine age and/or the Johannine church. As Alexander Altmann indicates, "The notion of Johannine Christianity formed one of the leading ideas of the German idealist movement . . . Peter is the apostle of the Father, Paul of the Son, and John of the Holy Spirit. John represents the church of a free, undogmatic Christianity" (Altmann, "Franz Rosenzweig on History," 125). Altmann's essay also elucidates the link between Rosenzweig's appreciation for the notion of the Johannine church and his move away from a Hegelian-dominated account of intellectual history. Already Altmann says, "in his letter to Hans Ehrenberg (dated 11 December 1913) Rosenzweig outlines the view that was to become characteristic of his entire historical thinking: The pagan Aristotle was no longer a power. Descartes, Spinoza and Leibniz cannot be considered pagans outside the Church but heretics within it. In Kant, Fichte, Schelling, Hegel, the heretics return to the fold of the Church. They regard themselves as Christian philosophers" (Altmann, "Rosenzweig on History," 126). In other words, philosophy no longer dominates and sublates religion and religion is no longer quarantined from philosophy. Interiority and exteriority are cancelled and each moment achieves position. Rosenzweig's later account of the Johannine age reflects this reorientation of intellectual history as applied to the narrative of secularization theory commonly identified with the work of Max Weber. For a discussion of Weber's secularization theory, see Max Weber, "Social Psychology of the World's Religions" in *Max Weber, Essays in Sociology* (New York: Routledge, 2009). I will discuss Rosenzweig's description of the Johannine age and its church more in Chapter 6.
18. As noted in Chapter 1, Rosenzweig attributes the notion of "revelation as orientation" to Rosenstock-Huessy as discussed in his letters to Rosenzweig

dated October 28 and October 30, 1916 published in *Judaism Despite Christianity*, and Rosenzweig informs Rudolph Ehrenberg of this indebtedness in his famous 1917 letter also known as the "Urzelle (Germ Cell) of *The Star of Redemption*."

19. Ibid., 19–21.

20. Franz Rosenzweig,"Urzelle to *The Star of Redemption*" in *Philosophical and Theological Writings*, 65.

21. Rosenzweig, "Atheistic Theology," 23.

22. Thus far, I have highlighted the connection between Rosenzweig's account of existence and Schelling's philosophical project. This is not to say that Rosenzweig's account of existence derived solely from his reading of Schelling's work. In May 1929, Rosenzweig wrote an essay called "Exchanged Fronts" (*Vertausche Fronten*), in which he described a famous confrontation between Ernst Cassirer and Martin Heidegger that had just taken place in the Swiss mountain resort of Davos. The debate, Rosenzweig argued, indicated a greater affinity between Heidegger's philosophical position and Rosenzweig's own New Thinking than Cassiser's. Rosenzweig's comments on the Davos debate have stirred a great deal of speculation regarding his indebtedness to Heidegger's account of human existence and finitude. Although it is well documented that Heidegger's student, Karl Lowith, denied any significant influence of Heidegger on Rosenzweig's thought, Peter Gordon's *Rosenzweig and Heidegger: Between Judaism and German Philosophy*, has reopened the case. In his book, Gordon argues against reading Rosenzweig as either a faithful believer or proponent of theology and stresses instead his interest in a "new thinking . . . new precisely because it aimed to wrest itself free of the traditional, theological category of eternity, even while it struggled to find theological purpose within the confines of human temporal life" (Gordon, *Rosenzweig and Heidegger*, 21). For Gordon, Rosenzweig's interest in the temporality of human life brings him closer to the work of Heidegger and the intellectual spirit of post–WWI Germany. Gordon's appreciation of Rosenzweig's interest in temporal existence is now more widely recognized than during the early days of Rosenzweig scholarship. Dana Hollander's *Exemplarity and Choseness* underscores this point when she, too, links her reading of *The Star of Redemption* to Rosenzweig's essay, "The New Thinking." See Dana Hollander, *Exemplarity and Choseness* (Stanford: Stanford University Press, 2008), 160–61. However, my account differs from Gordon's so far as he posits a strict divide between theological thought and existential reflection upon the temporality of human living and knowing. Gordon's emphasis upon existentialism dismantles Rosenzweig's carefully constructed marriage between philosophy and theology, referred to as the New Thinking. What makes the New Thinking new is not simply that it moves away from traditional theology but rather that it does so by proposing a new way to speak of theology and its relationship to human existence and knowledge.

23. Franz Rosenzweig, "The New Thinking," in *Philosophical and Theological Writings*, 115.

24. Ibid., 118.
25. Ibid., 119.
26. Ibid., 121.
27. Ibid., 123.
28. Ibid.
29. Ibid., 124.
30. Ibid.
31. Ibid., 125.

32. As Alexander Altmann has expressed it, "In idealist philosophy history culminates in the complete self-realization of God, the absolute Spirit. In Schelling's words, 'The last period is one of complete realization, i.e., the complete humanization (*Menschwerdung*) of God. . . . Then God will be indeed all in all, and pantheism will be true.' (F.W. J. Schelling, '*Stuttgarten Privatvorlesungen*' (1810) in *Sämmtliche Werke*, vol. 7, pt. 1 (1860), 484)," Altmann, "Rosenzweig on History" in *The Philosophy of Franz Rosenzweig*, 137. Like me, Altmann contrasts Schelling's residual idealism with Rosenzweig's theology for which "providence, therefore cannot mean the self-realization of God. It means the love of God expressed in revelation." Ibid., 137.

33. The influence of Schelling's *Weltalter* in Rosenzweig's Part I is not the only major philosophical influence in Rosenzweig's account. As has been well documented, Rosenzweig also uses the logical language of Hermann Cohen's mathematical infinitesimal to detail the logic of the two sorts of negations (the positive negation and the "negative" negation). According to Robert Gibbs, Rosenzweig makes use of Cohen's infinitesimal logic to justify speaking of these intuited elements as hypothetical possibilities and not merely abstract, imagined concepts. Here, Cohen's mathematics helped because Cohen contra Kant, insisted upon using infinitesimal calculus to demonstrate how "something" hypothetical can derive from "nothing"—or in other words, how knowledge emerges from pure reason and has no necessary recourse to empiricism. Rosenzweig is not orthodox about his appropriation of Cohen's logic, but as Gibbs tells us, "When he refers to the two forms of proceeding as the 'yes' and the 'no,' he draws on both Schelling and Cohen; however when he links these words with the neighbor and the escapee, respectively, he opts for Cohen and the infinitesimal" (Gibbs, *Correlations*, 51). At the end of the day, however, Rosenzweig's recourse to Cohen's infinitesimal logic is of less concern for this project than Rosenzweig's use of Schelling's account of divine freedom because it is this account which we see in Rosenzweig's description of the move from the intuited elements into "existence" or what Schelling referred to as the move from negative to positive philosophy. In this move, Rosenzweig departs dramatically from Cohen whose account of lived philosophy remains committed to the realization of the Idea of God in contrast to Rosenzweig's New Thinking. A full account of the relationship between Rosenzweig and Cohen exceeds the bounds of the project, but there is ample and excellent scholarship now available on this topic.

See: Dana Hollander, *Exemplarity and Choseness: Rosenzweig and Derrida on the Nation of Philosophy* (Stanford: Stanford University Press, 2008) and Martin Kavka, *Jewish Messiansim and Philosophy* (Cambridge: Cambridge University Press, 2002).

34. Franz Rosenzweig, *The Star of Redemption*, trans. William W. Hallo (New York: Holt, Rinehart and Winston, 1971), 29.
35. Ibid., 31.
36. Ibid.
37. Ibid.
38. Ibid., 40.
39. Ibid., 113.
40. Ibid., 113.
41. Ibid.
42. Ibid., 121.
43. Ibid.
44. Ibid., 120.
45. Rosenzweig, "The New Thinking," 123.
46. Michel Foucault, "Nietzsche, Genealogy, History" in the *Foucault Reader*, ed., Paul Rabinow (New York: Pantheon Books, 1984), 95.
47. Foucault, "Madness and Civilization," *Foucault Reader*, 124.
48. Ibid., 129.
49. Ibid., 131.
50. Ibid., 125.
51. Ibid.
52. Foucault, "The Birth of Asylum," *Foucault Reader*, 154–55.
53. Ibid., 160.
54. Ibid., 163.
55. Foucault, "The Right of Death and Power over Life," *Foucault Reader*, 260.
56. Ibid., 266.
57. Foucault, "Nietzsche, Genealogy, History," *Foucault Reader*, 85.
58. Ibid., 95.
59. Ibid., 96.
60. Ibid., 90.
61. In her excellent essay, "What is Critique? An Essay on Foucault's Virtue," Judith Butler poses a challenge to my critique of the limits of Foucault's account of genealogy. Butler argues that Foucault's account of critique does not result in a nihilism regarding truth on the one hand, and a salvaging of the "truth" of the errancy of all absolute claims on the other hand. The key to Butler's position is her identification of a praxis of virtue constitutive of Foucault's account of critique such that critique means not only the ability to recognize the investment of the self in absolutizing ideological systems, but also the freedom of the self to ask "how not to be governed like that"—or what amounts

to a practical "objecting to an imposition of power" (Butler, "What is Critique?," 8). Although Butler's retrieval of Foucault has identified a more robust view of the power of the self in its role as the agent of critique, she nonetheless presents a view of the self divided against itself and alienated from its own power. In her account, the desire of the self to resist the being governed "like that" stands against the desire of the self to precisely "be governed like that." Butler retrieves Foucault only by reconnecting his view of freedom to an Enlightenment account that links freedom with resistance alone, leaving emancipated persons at odds with institutions and world-views and traditions. Alternatively, I am arguing in favor of a notion of freedom within a world view—a freedom of desire for norms along with a freedom to alter or change norms through time.

62. Rosenzweig, "The New Thinking," 135.

63. William James, "Pragmatism's Conception of Truth" in *Pragmatism and Four Essays from the Meaning of Truth*, ed. Ralph Barton Perry. (New York: The New American Library, Inc., 1974), 133–34.

64. In the "Will to Believe," James says, "The thesis I defend is, briefly stated, this: Our passional nature not only lawfully may, but must decide an option between propositions, whenever it is a genuine option that cannot by its nature be decided on intellectual grounds; . . ." (James, "The Will to Believe," 11).

65. This is why one of the most significant critiques of James's defense of religion is its naïve optimism. James's inability to recognize the negative effects of desire means that his pragmatism cannot contend with the problem of enmity between persons or communities. According to James, the assertion of our passions in favor of the religious hypothesis constitutes a rightful exercise of our passions precisely because a pragmatic embrace of the religious hypothesis generates real experiential cash-value. However, religious beliefs may simultaneously be useful for those who verify them but problematic for others who do not. James's blindness toward the capacity of desire to overreach itself means that he cannot provide an approach to adjudicating instances of this sort of conflict. For James's arguments regarding the utility of this embrace of our religious desires see William James, "Is life Worth Living" in *The Will to Believe*. Also see William James's *The Varieties of Religious Experience* (New York: New American Library, 1958) and finally, "The Will to Believe" in *The Will to Believe and Other Essays in Popular Philosophy* (New York: Dover Publications, 1956).

66. Gillian Rose, *Mourning Becomes the Law* (Cambridge: Cambridge University Press, 1997), 87.

67. Rosenzweig, "The New Thinking," 130.

68. In Chapter 6, I will discuss the problem of evil as it arises in this context.

69. Rosenzweig, "The New Thinking," 130.

70. Ibid., 130.

71. Ibid.

72. We usually identifiy supersessionism with Christianity, but Judaism can be supersessionist as well. David Novak makes this point in his article, "From Supersessionism to Parallelism in Jewish-Christian Dialogue." There he says, "When practiced by learned Jews . . . Jewish counter-supersessionism can be as plausible as Christian supersessionism. Working out of a committed and knowledgeable background from within the Jewish tradition, these Jewish theologians do not constitute Judaism to be the antithesis of Christian. Rather, they constitute Christianity to be the antithesis of Judaism" (Novak, *Talking With Christians*, 9).

73. Eugen Rosenstock-Huessy, ed., *Judaism Despite Christianity* (New York: Schocken Books, 1971), 141.

74. See Jonathan Z. Smith, *Drudgery Divine: On the Comparison of Early Christianities and the Religions of Late Antiquity* (Chicago: The University of Chicago Press, 1994). In his discussion of scholarly modes of studying Christianity in antiquity, Smith distinguishes between comparative and genealogical analyses of religion and says, "In the case of the study of religion, as in any disciplined inquiry, comparison in its strongest form brings differences together within the space of the scholar's own intellectual reasons. It is the scholar who makes their co-habitation—their sameness—possible not 'natural' affinities or processes of history. Taken in this sense, 'genealogy' disguises and obscures the scholar's interests and activities allowing the illusion of passive observation." Smith, *Drudgery Divine*, 51. By suggesting that genealogy pretends to assert natural differences or similarities between traditions, Smith points to what above I describe as an assumption of ontological uniqueness or position, which gives a tradition the license to articulate its own uniqueness and dominance over and against other traditions either historically or comparatively. It is worth noting, however, that Smith identifies "comparative" work with the scholar alone. Consequently, Smith and I disagree with regard to whether believers can act as "scholars" *qua* believers or whether they must shed their believing commitments in order to engage in nongenealogically informed studies of religion.

75. See Talal Asad, "The Construction of Religion as an Anthropological Category," in Michael Lambek, *A Reader in the Anthropology of Religion* (Oxford: Blackwell Publishing, 2002).

76. David Novak, "Natural Law, Universalism and Multiculturalism" in *Tradition and the Public Square: A Novak Reader*, ed. Randi Rashkover and Martin Kavka (Grand Rapids: Wm. B. Eerdmans, 2008), 157.

77. Ibid., 155–56.

78. Ibid., 131.

6. THE LAW OF FREEDOM, THE FREEDOM OF THE LAW

1. Franz Rosenzweig, *The Star of Redemption*, trans. William W. Hallo (New York: Holt, Rinehart and Wintson, 1971), 159.

2. Ibid., 160.
3. Ibid.
4. Ibid., 161.
5. Ibid., 167.
6. Ibid., 77.
7. Ibid., 168.
8. Ibid.
9. Ibid.
10. Franz Rosenzweig, "Rennaissance of Jewish Learning" in *On Jewish Learning*, ed. N. N. Glatzer (New York: Schocken Books, 1965), 69.
11. Ibid., 68–69.
12. Franz Rosenzweig, "Apologetic Thinking," in Franz Rosenzweig: *Philosophical and Theological Writings*, eds. and trans., Paul Franks and Michael Morgan (Indianapolis: Hackett Publishing Company, 2000), 96.
13. For a detailed exposition of the relationship between divine love and divine command in Rosenzweig's thought, see Martin Kavka and Randi Rashkover, "A Jewish Modified Divine Command Theory." *Journal of Religious Ethics* 32:2 (Summer 2004): 387–414.
14. Martin Kavka, *Messianism and Jewish Philosophy* (Cambridge: Cambridge University Press, 2004), 152–53.
15. In *The Gift of Death*, Derrida says, "The crypto-or mysto-genealogy of responsibility is woven with the double and inextricably intertwined thread of the gift and of death; in short of the gift of death. The gift made to me by God as he holds me in his gaze and in his hand while remaining inaccessible to me, the terribly dissymmetrical gift of the *mysterium tremendum* only allows me to respond and only rouses me to the responsibility it gives me. . . ." (Derrida, *The Gift of Death*, 33).
16. This constitutes the difference therefore between the notion of command within the logic of the law and the notion of command associated with the gift referred to above in Derrida's *The Gift of Death*. According to Derrida, the asymmetrical character of the gift imposes a mandate of sacrifice upon the recipient. The recipient is commanded to receive or recognize the gift, but she is incapable of receiving it fully without co-opting it into the orbit of her desire thereby compromising her recognition of its alterity. As shown here, however, the logic of the law links divine command with the affirmation of persons' desire such that the one does not cancel the other. As discussed in what follows, the divine command is "for us." It is the means whereby God affirms persons in their difference from God. In this respect, the divine command constitutes a theological sign of God's care for persons and not their self-sacrifice.
17. Rosenzweig, *Star*, 162.
18. Ibid., 164.
19. Ibid.
20. Kavka, *Jewish Messianism*, 153.

21. Rosenzweig, "Apologetic Thinking," 107.
22. Ibid., 98.
23. Ibid.
24. Recall Rosenzweig's interpretation of the sacrifice of Isaac in his November 8, 1916 letter to Rosenstock-Huessy, where he says, "The two sacrifices, that on Moriah and that on Golgatha have this in common, then . . . that nothing was got out of them (since what was sacrificed is identical with what was given back), but the sacrifice itself becomes in effect the abiding object of faith, and thereby that which abides" (Rosenzweig, *Judaism Despite Christianity*, 134).
25. See Peter Eli Gordon, *Rosenzweig and Heidegger: Between Judaism and German Philosophy* (Berkeley: University of California Press, 2005) and Dana Hollander, *Exemplarity and Choseness: Rosenzweig and Derrida on the Nation of Philosophy* (Stanford: Stanford University Press, 2008).
26. Randi Rashkover, *Revelation and Theopolitics: Barth, Rosenzweig and the Politics of Praise* (London: T & T Clark, 2005), 103.
27. Rosenzweig, "Apologetic Thinking," 96.
28. Ibid.
29. We might, on the one hand, point to certain interpretations of Maimonides' negative theology, which maintain an insurmountable distance between the recognition of the reality of God and the human formulation of this reality. On the other hand, we could point to Karl Barth's strict theology of the negation of human theological discourse in his famous *Epistle to the Romans* for a Christian example. In Chapter 2, I offered a careful analysis of Maimonides' theology and the ramifications of the assertion of this radical divide between the divine and the human. In Chapter 7, I will present a discussion of Barth's theology and Barth's own dramatic move away from a purely dialectical perspective in favor of a God whose freedom affirms the reality of that which it transcends.
30. Ibid., 99.
31. Ibid., 107.
32. Ibid.
33. Ibid., 99.
34. Rosenzweig, "Apologetic Thinking," 104.
35. Ibid., 107.
36. Mendelssohn was critical of any kind of enlightenment tolerance that dissolved the unique significance of religion in general and Judaism in particular for the state. Near the end of *Jerusalem*, Mendelssohn warns, "There are some who want to persuade you that if only all of us had one and the same faith we would no longer hate one another for reasons of faith, of the difference in opinion, that [in such a case] religious hatred and the spirit of persecution would be torn up by the roots and extirpated. . . . Beware friends of men, of listening to such sentiments without the most careful scrutiny. They could be snares

which fanaticism grown impotent wants to put in the way of liberty of conscience brothers, if you care for true piety, let us not feign agreement where diversity is evidently the plan and purpose of Providence. . . . Let everyone be permitted to speak as he thinks, to invoke God after his own manner. . . ." (Mendelssohn, *Jerusalem*, 137–39).

37. Willi Goetschel does discuss Rosenzweig's essay in relation to Lessing's thought in an essay, "Lessing and the Jews." Here, Goetschel identifies the link between Rosenzweig's emphasis upon Jewish and Christian particularity and the indebtedness and hostility Christianity has toward Judaism and Lessing's attitudes toward tolerance and the role of religion in society. Goetschel challenges the common portrait of Lessing as an advocate of enlightenment humanism, and in his longer study of Lessing in *Spinoza's Modernity: Mendelssohn, Lessing and Heine*, argues that for Lessing, a Christianity that reflects on the manner by which it has asserted its identity "need no longer be disguised and therefore illicit. Instead, acknowledgment of the Jews will enable Christians to grasp the gift of tradition without having to cover it up as a theft. In short, Christians need the Jews not as scapegoats, but instead to come to a better, more enlightened and ultimately more profound understanding of their religion" (Goetschel, *Spinoza's Modernity*, 193).

38. Franz Rosenzweig, "Nathan's Lessing," in *Cultural Writings of Franz Rosenzweig*, ed. and trans., Barbara E. Galli (Syracuse: Syracuse University Press, 2000), 106–07.

39. Ibid., 110.

40. Ibid., 106.

41. Ibid., 107.

42. Ibid.

43. For a detailed account of Mendelssohn and Lessing's relation to the Enlightenment ideals of tolerance, see Willi Goetschel, *Spinoza's Modernity: Mendelssohn, Lessing, and Heine* (Madison: University of Wisconsin Press, 2004).

44. Rosenzweig, "Nathan's Lessing," 107.

45. Ibid., 108.

46. Ibid., 107.

47. Ibid.

48. Rosenzweig, *Star*, 415. It is worth noting that my reading of Rosenzweig's account of the enmity between Jews and Christians differs from the common wisdom on this subject, and in particular, from the position described by Leora Batnitzky in *Idolatry and Representation: The Philosophy of Franz Rosenzweig Reconsidered*. Whereas in my view, Rosenzweig's account of the enmity between Jews and Christians is not his last word on Jewish-Christian relations but one element in the development of the relationship of order and rational respect afforded by the New Thinking, Batnitzky emphasizes the structure of enmity as the fundamental character of the relation between the two in Rosenzweig's account. She says, "For Rosenzweig, the relationship between individual

human beings and the relationships between an individual and God have a possibility open to them that the relationship between Judaism and Christianity does not have. This is precisely the possibility of love. The Jewish-Christian relationship . . . is forever marked by the enmity that God has set between them. . . ." (Batnitzky, *Idolatry and Representation*, 160). I agree with Batnitzky that the New Thinking does not promote love between Jews and Christians. As well, I agree with Batnitzky that Rosenzweig's account of the relationship between Jews and Chrsitians as described in *The Star of Redemption* emphasizes the enmity between them. However, I do not think that either of these factors suggests that Rosenzweig's New Thinking does not ground a rational relationship between the two traditions within the logic of the law, particularly, if one reads *The Star of Redemption* alongside Rosenzweig's summary account of it in his essay, "The New Thinking."

49. Rosenzweig, *Star*, 415.

50. Rosenzweig, "Lessing's Nathan," 107–08.

51. David Novak, "Jewish-Christian Relations in a Secular Age" in *Talking With Christians: Musings of a Jewish Theologian* (Grand Rapids: Wm. B. Eerdmans Press, 2006), 175.

52. Rosenzweig, "Apologetic Thinking," 99.

53. Ibid., 103.

54. Justin Martyr's *Apology* offers a good example of the early Church's instrumentalist account of the Jews as the negative prognostication of the truth of Christ. In the *Apology*, he says, "For why should we believe a crucified man that he is First-begotten of the Unbegotten God, and that he will pass judgment on the whole human race, unless we found testimonies proclaimed about him before he came, and was made man, and see that things have thus happened? For we have seen the desolation of the land of the Jews, and the men of every nation who have been persuaded by the teaching that comes from his apostles and have turned away from the old customs in which they lived, wandering astray—that is ourselves since we know that the Gentile Christians are more numerous and truer than those from among the Jews and Samaritans" (Martyr, *Apology* in *Readings in Christian Doctrine*, 22).

55. Although Augustine argued against the persecution of the Jews, he supported this position by way of his account of the Jews as the witnesses to the faith preached by the prophets and to the divine judgment—a witness that *de facto* also attested to the validity of Christianity. For detailed investigations of Augustine's doctrine of Jewish witness as it develops throughout his work, see Jeremy Cohen, *The Living Letters of the Law: Ideas of the Jew in Medieval Christianity* (Berkeley: University of California Press, 1999), and more recently, Paula Fredriksen, *Augustine and the Jews: A Christian Defense of Jews and Judaism* (New York: Doubleday, 2008).

56. Robert Chazan characterizes life for Jews in medieval Christendom and says, "The missionizing campaign mounted by the Church was external and

obvious. Jews could readily recognize this externally imposed threat and were forced to mobilize their resources to combat it." (Chazan, *The Jews of Medieval Western Christendom 1000–1500*, 245). According to Chazan, some Jews launched anti-Christian polemical responses: for example, Jacob ben Reuben, who wrote *Milhamot ha-Shem*. Christian disputations or challenges to the Jews regarding the Messianic status of Jesus emerged in this period as well, the two most famous being the Barcelona Disputation of 1263 and the later Tortosa Disputation of 1391. As Chazan details, the Tortosa Disputation in particular placed enormous pressure on Jews to convert and effectively produced a large number of Jewish conversions at that time. (Chazan, *The Jews of Medieval Western Christendom*, 252).

57. Even the Enlightenment-educated Jewish philosopher Moses Mendelssohn was challenged by the Swiss pastor J. C. Lavater either to disprove the truth of Christianity or to convert and Mendelssohn's famous book *Jerusalem: Or On Religious Power and Judaism* is in large measure an apologetic defense of Judaism not only over and against the Kantian exclusion of Judaism as a religion within the limits of reason alone but over and against Christian calls for his conversion as well. See Randi Rashkover, "Overcoming Tolerance: Mendelssohn on Jewish-Christian Relations." *Jewish Studies Quarterly* 16 (2009): 118–45.

58. In *A Dictionary of Jewish-Christian Relations*, Edward Kessler and Neil Wenborn remark on this point and say, "Since the beginning of the 20th century the relationship between Judaism and Christianity has changed dramatically.... However, it was the impact of the Holocaust, the creation of the State of Israel, the development of the ecumenical movement and the work of the Second Vatican Council (1962–65) which in combination made the changes more widespread" (Kessler and Wenborn, *A Dictionary of Jewish-Christian Relations*, xiii).

59. See Gregory Baum, *Christian Theology After the Holocaust* (London: Council of Christians and Jews, 1977); Rosemary Radford Ruether, *Faith and Fratricide: The Theological Roots of Anti-Semitism* (Eugen: Wipf and Stock, 1996); and Eugen B. Korn and John T. Pawlikowski eds., *Two Faiths, One Covenant?: Jewish and Christian Identity in the Presence of the Other* (The Bernardin Center Series) *(New York: Rowan and Littlefield, 2004)*.

60. Kendall Soulen, *The God of Israel and Christian Theology* (Minneapolis: Fortress Press, 1996), 138.

61. Michael Wyschogrod, "Why Was and Is the Theology of Karl Barth of Interest to a Jewish Theologian?" in *Footnotes to a Theology: The Karl Barth Colloquium of 1972*, ed., Martin Rumscheidt (SR Supplements; Waterloo, Ont.: Canadian Corp. for Studies in Religion, 1974), 100.

62. Kendall Soulen, "An Introduction to Michael Wyschogrod" in Michael Wyschogrod, *Abraham's Promise: Judaism and Jewish-Christian Relations* (Grand Rapids: Wm. B. Eerdmans, 2004), 14.

63. Joseph B. Soloveitchik, "Confrontation" in *Tradition: A Journal of Orthodox Thought* 6 (1964): 2.
64. Ibid.
65. Novak, *Talking With Christians*, 30–31.
66. Susannah Heschel, "Praying with Their Feet: Remembering Abraham Joshua Heschel and Martin Luther King," *PeaceWork: Global Thought and Local Action for Non-violent Social Change*, 37 (2006–2007) (http://www.peacework magazine.org/praying-their-feet-remembering-abraham-joshua-heschel-and-martin-luther-king).
67. Ibid.
68. The Gospel of Luke 4:18–19, *The New Oxford Annotated Bible with the Apocrypha*, Revised Standard Version, eds., Herbert G. May and Bruce M. Metzger (New York: Oxford University Press, 1977).
69. Leviticus 25:10–1, Rabbi Nosson Scherman, *The Chumash*, ArtScroll Series (Brooklyn: Mesorah Publications, 1995).
70. Peter Ochs's work in particular offers an account of both how and why Jews and Christians (and Muslims) may engage in the study of each other's sacred texts. According to Ochs, Scriptural Reasoning is most pressingly rooted in the willingness of members of these traditions to recognize that a "binary claim [with] the pragmatic force of a mark of societal disruption" is one way that a community signals to another that, in fact, "something is amiss." (Ochs, "A Philosophical Warrant for Scriptural Reasoning," *Modern Theology* 2006, 4). This can mean a number of different things. First, it may mean that a point of long-standing enmity between two traditions causes problems for both traditions and therefore members of each tradition recognize the value of analyzing the logics at play in the problematic claim. Second, it may mean that a societal disruption in one tradition enables another tradition to recognize how a failure in its own logic upholds and supports the binary claim in the other tradition. Scriptural Reasoning is also supported by (but not rooted in) participants' recognition that their own scriptures do issue a similar hypothesis—namely that "we are to care for those who suffer." (Ochs, "A Philosophical Warrant for Scriptural Reasoning," 4). If, in other words, there is a scriptural (hypothetical) overlap at work between Jews, Christians, and Muslims engaged in Scriptural Reasoning, it is not founded on the claim that they are Abrahamic traditions but rather on the commitment that they mutually entertain the hypothesis that we are to care for those who suffer. Certainly, Jews, Christians, or Muslims who have no desire to engage in collaborative problem solving may choose not to engage in Scriptural Reasoning. However, the fruits of participation to date far exceed the requirements for engagement. Scriptural Reasoning encourages religious traditions to practice and develop a body of wisdom that is distinguishable from "knowledge" construed as the accrual of true propositions. This wisdom is deeply embedded in a language and lived practice arising from a pragmatically asserted theology of creation and of the God who draws near and

who promises to "be with us" as we hope for ways to redeem suffering. Ochs's account of the pragmatic thrust of Scriptural Reasoning presents a non–truth-driven approach to Jewish-Christian relations that bears much in common with the logic of the law here presented. So understood, Scriptural Reasoning operates as one expression of how the logic of the law can manifest itself in varying forms of Jewish-Christian encounter. For two other useful accounts of the pragmatic orientation of Scriptural Reasoning, see Nicholas Adams, *Habermas and Theology* (Cambridge: Cambridge University Press, 2006) and David F. Ford, *Christian Wisdom: Desiring God and Learning in Love* (Cambridge: Cambridge University Press, 2007).

71. Randi Rashkover, "The Semiotics of Embodiment: Radical Orthodoxy and Jewish-Christian Relations" in *Journal of Cultural and Religious Theory* 3 (2002) (http://www.jcrt.org/).

72. For a rich example of a rereading of the meaning of the Eucharist in light of the Jewish narrative of the Exodus, see Scott Bader-Saye, *The Church and Israel After Christendom* (New York: Wipf and Stock, 2005).

73. For an example of what a detailed reciprocal Jewish-Christian exposure to the world-altering potential of each other's liturgical practices, see Randi Rashkover and C. C. Pecknold, eds., *Liturgy, Time and the Politics of Redemption* (Grand Rapids: Wm. B. Eerdmans, 2006).

7. CHRISTIANITY AND THE LAW: THE LAW AS THE FORM OF THE GOSPEL

1. Michael Wyschogrod, "Why Was and Is the Theology of Karl Barth of Interest to a Jew?" *Footnotes to a Theology, the Karl Barth Colloquium of 1972*, Corporation for the Publication of Academic Studies in Canada, 1974.

2. David Novak, "The Rabbis, Paul and Karl Barth" in *Talking With Christians: The Musings of a Jewish Theologian* (Grand Rapids: Wm. B. Eerdmans, 2006).

3. Jacob Taubes, *The Political Theology of Paul*, trans. Dana Hollander (Stanford: Stanford University Press, 2003), 6.

4. Ibid., 39.

5. Ibid.

6. Ibid., 47.

7. Ibid., 37.

8. Ibid., 31.

9. Aleida Assmann, "Afterword" in Taubes, *The Political Theology of Paul*, 139.

10. Ibid., 24.

11. Ibid., 13.

12. Jacob Taubes, "The Issue Between Judaism and Christianity: Facing Up to the Unresolvable Difference," *Commentary Magazine* (1953): 7.

13. Ibid., 7–8.

14. Ibid.

15. Ibid., 10.
16. Assmann, "Afterword" in *The Political Theology of Paul*, 12.1.
17. Taubes, *The Political Theology of Paul*, 72.
18. Jacob Taubes, "Theodicy and Theology: A Philosophical Analysis of Karl Barth's Dialectical Theology," *Journal of Religion*, Volume XXXIV (1954).
19. Ibid., 64.
20. Taubes, "Theodicy and Theology," 243.
21. Ibid., 233.
22. Ibid., 237.
23. Ibid.
24. Ibid., 238.
25. Ibid., 233.
26. Ibid., 240.
27. Ibid., 242.
28. Karl Barth, *Church Dogmatics*, II.2, trans. G. W. Bromiley, J. C. Campbell; ed., G. W. Bromiley, T. F. Torrance (Edinburgh: T & T Clark, 1957), 585.
29. Ibid.
30. Ibid., 587–88.
31. Ibid., 593.
32. Ibid., 557.
33. Ibid., 560.
34. Ibid., 624.
35. Ibid., 617.
36. Ibid., 618.
37. Ibid., 629.
38. For an interesting and new account of Barth's analysis of the elected and rejected, see Mark R. Lindsay, *Faith and Theology: Barth, Israel and Jesus*, (Barth Studies, Aldershot, Ashgate, 2007). With particular regard to Barth's analysis of the election of the Jews, Lindsay asserts—and I would agree—that although it may undoubtedly be said that "Barth's language at this point is undeniably ill-conceived . . . the theological argument behind the terminology is in fact far more sympathetic to Israel than Barth's language suggests"(Lindsay, *Faith and Theology*, 95).
39. Joseph Mangina, Karl Barth: *Theologian of Christian Witness* (Louisville: Westminster John Knox Press, 2004), 71.
40. Perhaps the most noted proponent of the belief that Barth's work underwent a radical change from dialectical theology of crisis to a positive theology of sanctification rooted in the *analogia fidei* is Hans Urs von Balthasar. For this view, see Hans Urs von Balthasar, *The Theology of Karl Barth*, trans. John Drury (New York: Holt, Rinehart and Winston, 1971).
41. Karl Barth, *Church Dogmatics*, IV.2, ed. Geoffrey Bromiley, Thomas Forsyth Torrance; trans. G. T. Thompson and Harold Knight (London: T & T Clark, 2004), 503.

42. Ibid.
43. Ibid., 505.
44. Ibid., 508.
45. Barth, *Dogmatics*, II.2, 587.
46. Ibid, 600.
47. Ibid.
48. According to Robert Eisen, "Jewish interest in Job seems to have been particularly acute in the Middle Ages" although philosophical attention to the Book of Job occupied the attention of only a small group of medieval Jewish philosophers "most of [whom] were influenced by Maimonides. . . . These commentators were thus the first interpreters in Judaism to provide readings of Job that were both comprehensive and philosophical" (Eisen, *The Book of Job in Medieval Jewish Philosophy*, 4). Of course, contemporary Jewish thinkers have also demonstrated philosophical interest in the *Book of Job*, including Emmanuel Levinas and Joseph Soloveitchik.
49. Moses Maimonides, *The Guide of the Perplexed*, volume III, trans., Shlomo Pines (Chicago: The University of Chicago Press, 1963), 487.
50. Ibid., 488.
51. There is a wide range of interpretations concerning the meaning of Satan in Maimonides' account, but according to Robert Eisen, "medieval commentators on Maimonides are practically unanimous in the view that Satan is a representation of the principle of privation, which is the absence of a natural form in an object that might normally possess it and is therefore responsible for the process of decay and corruption in the physical world" (Eisen, *The Book of Job in Medieval Jewish Philosophy*, 51).
52. Maimonides, *Guide*, 3.487.
53. Ibid., 3.474.
54. Ibid., 3.492–93.
55. Edwin Curley, "Maimonides, Spinoza and the Book of Job," in *Jewish Themes in Spinoza's Philosophy*, eds., Heidi Ravven and Lenn Evan Goodman (Albany: SUNY Press, 2002), 157.
56. Although according to Robert Eisen, there is a very strong tendency among modern interpreters of Maimonides that "Job learns a psychological immunity from suffering and that this is equated with providence"—that is, what is tantamount to an intellectualist account of Job's transformation. Eisen, *Job in Medieval Philosophy*, 58.
57. Maimonides, *Guide*, 3.497.
58. Curley, "Maimonides, Spinoza and the Book of Job," 166.
59. Maimonides, *Guide*, 1.56, 1.131.
60. Maimonides, *Guide*, 3.433–32.
61. And the LORD said unto Satan: "Hast thou considered My servant Job, that there is none like him in the earth, a whole-hearted and an upright man, one that feareth God, and shunneth evil?" Job 1:8 (RSV).

62. "Now therefore, take unto you seven bullocks and seven rams, and go to My servant Job, and offer up for yourselves a burnt-offering; and My servant Job shall pray for you; for him will I accept, that I do not unto you aught unseemly; for ye have not spoken of Me the thing that is right, as my servant Job hath. . . . So the LORD blessed the latter end of Job more than his beginning; and he had fourteen thousand sheep, and six thousand camels, and a thousand yoke of oxen, and a thousand she-asses. He had also seven sons and three daughters. And he called the name of the first, Jemimah; and the name of the second, Keziah; and the name of the third, Keren-happuch. And in all the land were no women found so fair as the daughters of Job; and their father gave them inheritance among their brethren. And after this Job lived a hundred and forty years, and saw his sons, and his sons' sons, even four generations. So Job died, being old and full of days. Job, 42:8–12 (RSV).

63. Emmanuel Levinas, "Transcendence and Evil" in Phillippe Nemo, *Job and the Excess of Evil*, trans. Michael Kigel (Pittsburgh: Duquesne University Press, 1978), 178.

64. Ibid., 178.

65. The Book of Job, 3:25–26, *The New Oxford Annotated Bible with the Apocrypha*, Revised Standard Version, eds., Herbert G. May and Bruce M. Metzger (New York: Oxford University Press, 1977).

66. Ibid., 19:23.

67. Ibid., 6:24.

68. Ibid., 13:5.

69. Ibid., 13:12.

70. Ibid., 12:14.

71. Ibid., 13:13.

72. Ibid.

73. Ibid., 13:20.

74. Ibid., 7:17–21.

75. Ibid., 30:18.

76. Ibid., 13:15–18.

77. Ibid., 23:7.

78. Abraham Joshua Heschel, *Who Is Man?* (Stanford: Stanford University Press, 1965), 57.

79. Job, 10:8 (RSV).

80. Ibid., 31:35–37.

81. Ibid., 9:15–22.

82. Ibid., 32:1.

83. Susannah Ticciati, "Does Job Fear God for Naught?," *Modern Theology*, 21 (2005): 360.

84. Ibid., 359.

85. Ibid., 360.

86. Ibid., 361.

87. Ibid., 364.
88. Ibid.
89. Ibid.
90. Job, 38:1–3 (RSV).
91. Ibid., 38:4.
92. Ibid., 40:4.
93. Karl Barth, *Church Dogmatics: The Doctrine of Reconciliation*, IV.3.1, ed. G. W. Bromiley, T. F. Torrance (London: T & T Clark, 2004), 370.
94. Ibid., IV.3.1, 86.
95. Ibid., 87.
96. Ibid., 89.
97. Franz Rosenzweig, "The New Thinking," trans., Alan Udoff, Barbara Galli (Syracuse: Syracuse University Press, 1998), 91.
98. In an article, "The Freedom of God in the Theology of Barth," George S. Hendry challenges the logical consistency of Barth's analysis of divine freedom with regard to its Christological determinism. "Was," he asks, "God free to choose to be other than the God of grace in Jesus Christ? . . . God's election of himself in Jesus Christ is the primordial act of the being of God, and as such it excludes alternative choices. . . . If this is the primordial act of the being of God which he has done of himself and with himself, there is no warrant for speaking of it as a choice." George Hendry, "The Freedom of God in the Theology of Barth," *Scottish Journal of Theology*, 31 (1978): 229–44. Undoubtedly, Barth asserts a Christological determinism which compromises his account of divine freedom. The point of my analysis is to demonstrate that this limitation does not override the relationship between freedom and law within Christology whereby the conditions of a free Christian witness and apologetics are still met.
99. Barth, *Dogmatics*, IV.3.1, 91.
100. Ibid.
101. Ibid., 381.
102. Ibid., 410.
103. Ibid., 382.
104. Ibid., 382.
105. Ibid., 406.
106. Ibid., 407.
107. Ibid.
108. Ibid., 427.
109. Ibid.
110. Ibid.
111. Ibid., 431.
112. Ibid., 432.
113. Ibid., 436–37.
114. Ibid., 449.
115. Ibid., 457.

Notes to pages 267–73   315

116. For a helpful analysis of the concrete character of the Christian ethical witness emergent from the freedom of God, see Rev. W. A. Whitehouse, "The Command of God the Creator: An Account of Karl Barth's Volume on Ethics," *Scottish Journal of Theology* 5 (1952): 337–54.

117. Barth, *Dogmatics*, IV.3.2, 482.
118. Ibid., 484.
119. Ibid., 494.
120. Ibid., 529.
121. Ibid., 526.
122. Ibid., 536–37.
123. Ibid., 556.
124. Ibid., 558–59.
125. Ibid., 562.

126. Elsewhere, I discuss the nature of this witness in detail. See Randi Rashkover, *Revelation and Theopolitics: Barth, Rosenzweig and the Politics of Praise* (London: T & T Clark, 2005).

127. Barth, *Dogmatics*, IV.3.2, 576.
128. Barth, *Dogmatics*, IV.3.1, 110.
129. Ibid., 115.
130. Ibid., 117.

131. To date, John Webster's *Karl Barth's Ethics of Reconciliation* (Cambridge: Cambridge University Press, 1995) remains the most theologically astute analysis of the correlation between the role of divine freedom and human moral agency in Barthian scholarship. Considering my emphasis upon apologetics on the one hand and my emphasis upon law on the other, my focus remains epistemic, whereas Webster's book attends to the dimension of moral freedom characteristic of the Christian witness.

132. Barth, *Dogmatics*, IV.3.1, 667.
133. Ibid., 668–69.
134. Ibid., 822.

REFERENCES

Adams, Nicholas. *Habermas and Theology*. Cambridge: Cambridge University Press, 2006.

Agamben, Giorgio. *The Coming Community*. Minneapolis: University of Minnesota Press, 1993.

———. *The Time That Remains. A Commentary on the Letter to the Romans*. Trans., Patricia Dailey. Stanford: Stanford University Press, 2005.

Altmann, Alexander. "Franz Rosenzweig on History" in *Philosophy of Franz Rosenzweig*. Ed., Paul Mendes-Flohr. Waltham, Mass.: Brandeis University Press, 1988.

———. "Maimonides on the Intellect and Scope of Metaphysics" in *Von der mittelatlerlichen zur modernen Aufklärung*. Tubingen: J. C. B. Mohr, 1987.

Asad, Talal. "The Construction of Religion as an Anthropological Category" in *A Reader in the Anthropology of Religion*. Ed., Michael Lambek. Oxford: Blackwell Publishing, 2002.

Assmann, Aleida. "Afterword" in *The Political Theology of Paul*, Jacob Taubes. Trans., Dana Hollander. Stanford: Stanford University Press, 2003.

Babylonian Talmud: Complete Soncino Translation. (http://wilkerson.110mb.com/Tanhuma).

Bader-Saye, Scott. *The Church and Israel After Christendom*. New York: Wipf and Stock, 2005.

Baker, David L. "The Jubilee and the Millennium Holy Years in the Bible and Their Relevance Today." *Themelios* 24/1 (1998): 44–69.

Barth, Karl. *Church Dogmatics*, v. II.2. Trans., G. W. Bromiley and J. C. Campbell. Eds., G. W. Bromiley and T. F. Torrance. Edinburgh: T & T Clark, 1957.

———. *Church Dogmatics*, v. IV.2. Trans., G. T. Thompson and Harold Knight. Eds., G. W. Bromiley and T. F. Torrance. London: T & T Clark, 2004.

———. *Church Dogmatics: The Doctrine of Reconciliation*, v. IV.3.1. Trans., G. W. Bromiley and T. F. Torrance. Ed., G. W. Bromiley. London: T & T Clark, 2004.

———. *Church Dogmatics* IV. 3.2. Trans., G. W. Bromiley. Eds., G. W. Bromiley and T. F. Torrance. London: T & T Clark, 2004.

Bibliography

Batnitzky, Leora. *Idolatry and Representation: The Philosophy of Franz Rosenzweig Reconsidered.* Princeton: Princeton University Press, 2000.

Baum, Gregory. *Christian Theology after the Holocaust.* London: Council of Christians and Jews, 1977.

Blenkinsopp, Joseph. *Wisdom and Law in the Old Testament: The Ordering of Life in Israel and Early Judaism.* Oxford: Oxford University Press, 1995.

Braslavy, Sara Klein. "The Creation of the World and Maimonides' Interpretation of Genesis i–v" in *Maimonides and Philosophy.* Eds., Shlomo Pines and Yirmiahu Yovel. Dordrecht: Martinus Nijhoff Publishers, 1986.

Butler, Judith. "What is Critique? An Essay on Foucault's Virtue." (http://tedrutland.org/wp-content/uploads/2008/02/butler-2002.pdf).

Cassanova, José. *Public Religions in the Modern World.* Chicago: The University of Chicago Press, 1994.

Chazan, Robert. *The Jews of Medieval Western Christendom 1000–1500.* Cambridge: Cambridge University Press, 2007.

Cohen, Hermann. *Religion of Reason Out of the Sources of Judaism.* Trans., Simon Kaplan. New York: Frederick Ungar, 1972.

Cohen, Jeremy. *Living Letters of the Law: Ideas of the Jew in Medieval Christianity.* Berkeley: University of California Press, 1999.

Connolly, William. "The Complexities of Sovereignty" in *Giorgio Agamben, Sovereignty and Life.* Eds., Matthew Calarco and Steven DeCaroli. Stanford: Stanford University Press, 2007.

Crockett, L. C. "Luke 4:25–7 and Jewish-Gentile Relations in Luke-Acts." *Journal of Biblical Literature* 88 (1969): 177–83.

Curley, Edwin. "Maimonides, Spinoza and the Book of Job" in *Jewish Themes in Spinoza's Philosophy.* Eds., Heidi Ravven and Lenn Evan Goodman. Albany: SUNY Press, 2002.

Derrida, Jacques. *The Gift of Death.* Chicago: The University of Chicago Press, 1996.

Eisen, Robert. *The Book of Job in Medieval Jewish Philosophy.* Oxford: Oxford University Press, 2004.

Emmit, Dorothy M. "The Letters of Franz Rosenzweig and Eugen Rosenstock-Huessy." *The Journal of Religion* 25 (1945): 261–75.

Ford, David. *Christian Wisdom: Desiring God and Learning in Love.* Cambridge: Cambridge University Press, 2007.

Foucault, Michel. "The Birth of Asylum" in the *Foucault Reader.* Ed., Paul Rabinow. New York: Pantheon Books, 1984.

———. "Madness and Civilization" in the *Foucault Reader.* Ed., Paul Rabinow. New York: Pantheon Books, 1984.

———. "Nietzsche, Genealogy, History" in the *Foucault Reader.* Ed., Paul Rabinow. New York: Pantheon Books, 1984.

———. "The Right of Death and Power over Life" in the *Foucault Reader.* Ed., Paul Rabinow. New York: Pantheon Books, 1984.

Fredriksen, Paula. *Augustine and the Jews: A Christian Defense of Jews and Judaism*. New York: Doubleday, 2008.
Freud, Sigmund. *Moses and Monotheism*. Trans., Katherine Jones. New York: Vintage, 1955.
Gager, John. G. *Reinventing Paul*. Oxford: Oxford University Press, 2000.
Genesis Rabbah, v. I, 10. *The Midrash*. Trans., Rabbi Dr. H. Freedman. New York: The Soncino Press, 1983.
Gibbs, Robert. *Correlations in Rosenzweig and Levinas*. Princeton: Princeton University Press, 1994.
Glatzer, N.N., ed. *Franz Rosenzweig: His Life and Thought*, 2nd. rev. ed. New York: Schocken Books, 1961.
Goetschel, Willi. *Spinoza's Modernity: Mendelssohn, Lessing and Heine*. Madison: University of Wisconsin Press, 2004.
Goodman, Lenn. "What Does Spinoza's Ethics Contribute to Jewish Philosophy?" in *Jewish Themes in Spinoza's Philosophy*. Eds., Heidi Ravven and Lenn E. Goodman. Albany: SUNY Press, 2002.
Gordon, Peter. *Rosenzweig and Heidegger: Between Judaism and German Philosophy*. Los Angeles: University of California Press, 2005.
Green, Joel B. *Theology of the Gospel of Luke*. Cambridge: Cambridge University Press, 2004.
Gregory, Bradley C. "The Postexilic Exile in Third Isaiah: Isaiah 61:1–3 in Light of Second Temple Hermeneutics." *Journal of Biblical Literature* 126 (2007): 475.
Guttman, Julius. *Philosophies of Judaism: The History of Jewish Philosophy from Biblical Times to the Philosophy of Franz Rosenzweig*. Trans., David Silverberg. Philadelphia: Double Day Anchor, 1964.
Habermas, Jurgen. *The Theory of Communicative Action: Reason and the Rationalization of Society*. vol. 1. Trans., Thomas McCarthy. Boston: Beacon Press, 1984.
Habertal, Moshe and Avishai Margalit. *Idolatry*. Trans., Naomi Goldblum. Cambridge, Mass.: Harvard University Press, 1992.
Halivni, David Weiss. *Revelation Restored: Divine Writ and Critical Responses*. Boulder: Westview, 1998.
Hanson, Paul. *The Dawn of the Apocalyptic: The Historical and Sociological Roots of Jewish Apocalyptic Eschatology*. Minneapolis: Fortress Press, 1979.
Hendry, George. "The Freedom of God in the Theology of Barth." *Scottish Journal of Theology* 31 (1978): 229–44.
Heschel, Abraham Joshua. *Who Is Man?* Stanford: Stanford University Press, 1965.
Heschel, Susannah. "Praying with Their Feet: Remembering Abraham Joshua Heschel and Martin Luther King." *PeaceWork: Global Thought and Local Action for Non-violent Social Change* 37 (2006–2007). (http://www.peaceworkmagazine.org/praying-their-feet-remembering-abraham-joshua-heschel-and-martin-luther-king).
Hollander, Dana. *Exemplarity and Choseness*. Stanford: Stanford University Press, 2008.
Ivry, A.L. "Maimonides on Possibility" in *Mystics, Philosophers and Politicians*. Eds, J. Reinharz and D. Swetschinki. Durham: Duke University Press, 1982.

Jaffee, Martin. "One God, One Revelation, One People: On the Symbolic Structure of Elective Monotheism." *Journal of the American Academy of Religion* 69/4 (2001): 753–76.

James, William. "Is Life Worth Living?" in *The Will to Believe and Other Essays in Popular Philosophy*. New York: Dover Publications, 1956.

———. "Pragmatism's Conception of Truth" in *Pragmatism and Four Essays from the Meaning of Truth*. Ed., Ralph Barton Perry. New York: The New American Library, Inc., 1974.

———. *The Varieties of Religious Experience*. New York: New American Library, 1958.

———. "The Will to Believe" in *The Will to Believe and Other Essays in Popular Philosophy*. New York: Dover Publications, 1956.

Kavka, Martin. *Jewish Messianism and the History of Philosophy*. Cambridge: Cambridge University Press, 2004.

Kavka, Martin and Randi Rashkover. "A Jewish Modified Divine Command Theory." *Journal of Religious Ethics* 32/2 (Summer 2004): 387–414.

Kessler, Edward and Neil Wenborn, eds. *A Dictionary of Jewish-Christian Relations*. Cambridge: Cambridge University Press, 2008.

Knoppers, Gary N. "Ancient Near Eastern Royal Grants and the Davidic Covenant: A Parallel?" *Journal of the American Oriental Society* 116/4 (1996): 670–97.

Korn, Eugen B. and John T. Pawlikowski, eds. *Two Faiths, One Covenant?: Jewish and Christian Identity in the Presence of the Other*. The Bernardin Center Series. New York: Rowan and Littlefield: 2004.

Kreisel, Haim. "Maimonides on the Eternity of the World." Association of Jewish Studies presentation. (http://ajs.net.org).

Lauterbach, Jacob Z., ed. *Mekhilta De-rabbi Yishmael: A Critical Edition*. 2nd ed. Philadelphia: Jewish Publication Society, 2004.

Lenin, Vladimir. *The Essential Works of Lenin: "What is to be Done and Other Writings."* New York: Dover Publications, 1966.

Levene, Nancy K. "Judaism's Body Politic" in *Women and Gender in Jewish Philosophy*. Ed., Hava Tirosh-Samuelson. Indianapolis: University of Indianapolis Press, 2004.

———. *Spinoza's Revelation: Religion, Democracy and Reason*. Cambridge: Cambridge University Press, 2004.

Levenson, Jon D. *The Death and Resurrection of the Beloved Son: The Transformation of Child Sacrifice*. New Haven: Yale University Press, 1993.

———. *Sinai and Zion: An Entry into the Jewish Bible*. New York: HarperOne, 1987.

———. "The Theologies of Commandment in Biblical Israel." *Harvard Theological Review* 73/1/2 (1980): 17–33.

Levinas, Emmanuel. "Transcendence and Evil" in *Job and the Excess of Evil*, Phillippe Nemo. Trans., Michael Kigel. Pittsburgh: Duquesne University Press, 1978.

Levine, Baruch. *JPS Torah Commentary: Leviticus*. Jewish Publication Society, 2004.

Lieber, Moshe and Nosson Sherman, eds. and trans. *The Pirkei Avos Treasury: Ethics of the Fathers : The Sages' Guide to Living with an Anthologized Commentary and Anecdotes*. Brooklyn: Mesorah Publications, Limited, 1995.

Lindsay, Mark R. *Faith and Theology: Barth, Israel and Jesus*. Barth Studies. Aldershot: Ashgate, 2007.

Litwak, Kenneth Duncan. *Echoes of Scripture in Luke-Acts*. London: T & T Clark, 2005.

Lloyd, Vince. *Law and Transcendence: On the Unfinished Project of Gillian Rose*. New York: Palgrave Macmillan Publishing Company, 2009.

Luther, Martin. *On Christian Liberty*. Ed., Harold Grimm. Trans., W.A. Lambert. Minneapolis: Augsburg Fortress Press, 2003.

Maimonides, Moses. *The Guide of the Perplexed*. vols. I, II, and IIII. Trans., Shlomo Pines. Chicago: The University of Chicago Press, 1963.

Mangina, Joseph. *Karl Barth: Theologian of Christian Witness*. Louisville: Westminster John Knox Press, 2004.

Martyr, Justin. "The First Apology of Justin, the Martyr." *Readings in Christian Thought*. Ed., Hugh T. Kerr. Nashville: Abingdon Press, 1966.

Marx, Karl. "Economic and Philosophic Manuscripts of 1844" in *The Marx-Engels Reader*. 2nd ed. Ed., Robert C. Tucker. New York: W. W. Norton & Company, 1978.

May, Herbert G. and Bruce M. Metzger, eds. *The New Oxford Annotated Bible with the Apocrypha*. Revised Standard Version. New York: Oxford University Press, 1977.

Mendelssohn, Moses. *Jerusalem: Or on Religious Power and Judaism*. Trans., Alan Arkush. Waltham, Mass.: Brandeis University Press, 1983.

Mendes-Flohr, Paul. "In 1914 Franz Rosenzweig writes the essay 'Atheistic Theology,' which criticizes the theology of his day" in *Yale Companion to Jewish Writing and Thought in German Culture*. Eds., Sander L. Gilman and Jack Zipes. New Haven: Yale University Press, 1997.

Miller, Patrick. "Deuteronomy and Psalms: Evoking Biblical Conversation." *Journal of Biblical Literature* 118/1 (1999): 3–18.

Morgan, Michael and Paul Franks. "From 1914 to 1917" in *Rosenzweig: Philosophical and Theological Writings*. Eds., Michael Morgan and Paul Franks. Indianapolis: Hackett Publishing Company, 2000.

Murphy, Roland, E. *The Tree of Life: An Exploration of Biblical Wisdom*. 3rd ed. Grand Rapids: Wm. B. Eerdmans Company, 2002.

Newman, Louis. "Covenant and Contract: A Framework for Jewish Ethics." *Journal of Law and Religion* 9 (1991): 89–112.

Novak, David. *Covenantal Rights: A Study in Jewish Political Theory*. Princeton: Princeton University Press, 2000.

———. *The Election of Israel: The Idea of the Chosen People*. Cambridge: Cambridge University Press, 1995.

———. "Jewish-Christian Relations in a Secular Age" in *Talking With Christians: Musings of a Jewish Theologian*. Grand Rapids: Wm. B. Eerdmans Press, 2006.

———. "Natural Law, Universalism and Multiculturalism" in *Tradition and the Public Square: A Novak Reader*. Eds., Randi Rashkover and Martin Kavka. Grand Rapids: Wm. B. Eerdmans Press, 2008.

———. "Philosophy and the Possibility of Revelation" in *Tradition in the Public Square: A Novak Reader*. Eds., Randi Rashkover and Martin Kavka. Grand Rapids: Wm. B. Eerdmans Press, 2008.

———. "The Rabbis, Paul and Karl Barth" in *Talking With Christians: Musings of a Jewish Theologian*. Grand Rapids: Wm. B. Eerdmans Press, 2006.

———. "From Supersessionism to Parallelism in Jewish-Christian Dialogue" in *Talking With Christians: Musings of a Jewish Theologian*. Grand Rapids: Wm. B. Eerdmans Press, 2006.

Ochs, Peter. "A Philosophical Warrant for Scriptural Reasoning." *Modern Theology* 22/3 (2006): 465–82.

Pines, Shlomo. "The Limitations of Human Knowledge According to al-Farabil, ibn Bajja, and Maimonides" in *Studies in Medieval Jewish History and Literature*. Ed., Isadore Twersky. Cambridge: Harvard University Press, 1979.

Pines, Shlomo, trans. "Translator's Introduction" in Moses Maimonides, *The Guide of the Perplexed*. Chicago: The University of Chicago Press, 1963.

Pöggeler, Otto. "Between Enlightenment and Romanticism: Rosenzweig and Hegel" in *The Philosophy of Franz Rosenzweig*. Ed., Paul Mendes-Flohr. Waltham, Mass.: Brandeis University Press, 1988.

Rasch, William. "From Sovereign Ban to Banning Sovereignty" in *Giorgio Agamben, Sovereignty and Life*. Eds., Matthew Calarco and Steven DeCaroli. Stanford: Stanford University Press, 2007.

Rashi. Leviticus 25:2. *Metsudah Chumash/Rashi, Vols. 1–5: Genesis, Exodus, Leviticus, Deuteronomy*. 2nd ed. Eds., Nachum Y. Kornfeld and Abraham B. Walzer. Trans., Rabbi Avrohom Davis. Jersey City, N. J.: Metsudah/KTAV Publishing House, Inc., 1997.

Rashkover, Randi. "Overcoming Tolerance: Mendelssohn on Jewish-Christian Relations" *Jewish Studies Quarterly* 16 (2009): 118–45.

———. *Revelation and Theopolitics: Barth, Rosenzweig and the Politics of Praise*. London: T & T Clark, 2005.

———. "The Semiotics of Embodiment: Radical Orthodoxy and Jewish-Christian Relations." *Journal of Culture and Religious Theory* 3/3 (2002). (http://www.jcrt.org/archives/03.3/rashkover.shtml).

———. "Theological Desire: Feminism, Philosophy, and Exegetical Jewish Thought" in *Women and Gender in Jewish Philosophy*. Ed., Hava Tirosh-Samuelson. Bloomington: Indiana University Press, 2004.

Rashkover, Randi and C. C. Pecknold. eds. *Liturgy, Time and the Politics of Redemption*. Grand Rapids: Wm. B. Eerdmans Press, 2006.

Ravven, Heidi M. and Lenn E. Goodman, eds. *Jewish Themes in Spinoza's Philosophy*. Albany: SUNY Press, 2002.

Rice, Lee C. "Love of God in Spinoza" in *Jewish Themes in Spinoza's Philosophy*. Eds., Heidi M. Ravven and Lenn E. Goodman. Albany: SUNY Press, 2002.

Rose, Gillian. *The Broken Middle: Out of Our Ancient Society.* Oxford: Blackwell, 1992.

———. *Mourning Becomes the Law: Philosophy and Representation.* Cambridge: Cambridge University Press, 1996.

Rosenstock-Huessy, Eugen. *The Christian Future of the Modern Mind Outrun.* Berlin: Argo Books, 1981.

———. *Die Sprache des Menschengeschlechts.* Berlin: Verlag Lambert Schneider, 1963 and 1964.

———. *Out of Revolution: Autobiography of Western Man.* Oxford: Berg Publishers, 1938.

———. *Speech and Reality.* Norwich: Argo Books, 1970.

Rosenstock-Huessy, Eugen, ed. *Judaism Despite Christianity.* New York: Schocken Books, 1971.

Rosenzweig, Franz. "Apologetic Thinking" in *Philosophical and Theological Writings.* Eds., trans., Paul W. Franks and Michael L. Morgan. Indianapolis: Hackett Publishing Company, 2000.

———. "Atheistic Theology" in *Philosophical and Theological Writings.* Eds., trans., Paul W. Franks and Michael L. Morgan. Indianapolis: Hackett Publishing Company, 2000.

———. *Der Mensch und sein Werk: Gesammelte Schriften.* Dordrecht: Martinus Nijhoff Publishers, 1984.

———. "Nathan's Lessing" in *Cultural Writings of Franz Rosenzweig.* Ed., trans., Barbara E. Galli. Syracuse: Syracuse University Press, 2000.

———. "The New Thinking" in *Philosophical and Theological Writings.* Eds., trans., Paul W. Franks and Michael L. Morgan. Indianapolis: Hackett Publishing Company, 2000.

———. "The New Thinking." Trans., Alan Udoff and Barbara Galli. Syracuse: Syracuse University Press, 1998.

———. "Rennaissance of Jewish Learning" in *On Jewish Learning.* Ed., N. N. Glatzer. New York: Schocken Books, 1965.

———. *The Star of Redemption.* Trans., William W. Hallo. New York: Holt, Rinehart and Winston, 1971.

———. "Urzelle to *The Star of Redemption*" in Franz Rosenzweig, *Philosophical and Theological Writings.* Eds., trans., Paul W. Franks and Michael L. Morgan. Indianapolis: Hackett Publishing Company, 2000.

Rubenstein, Richard. "The Dean and the Chosen People" in *After Auschwitz: History, Theology and Contemporary Judaism.* 2nd ed. Baltimore: The Johns Hopkins University Press, 1992.

Ruether, Rosemary. *Faith and Fratricide: The Theological Roots of Anti-Semitism.* Eugene, Oregon: Wipf and Stock, 1997.

Samuelson, Norbert. "Maimonides' Doctrine of Creation." *The Harvard Theological Review* 84/3 (1991): 249–71.

Sanders, J. A. "From Isaiah 61 to Luke 4" in *Christianity, Judaism and other Greco-Roman Cults: Studies for Morton Smith at Sixty.* SJLA12/1. Ed., J. Neusnes. Leiden: Brill, 1975.

Santner, Eric. *On the Psychotheology of Everday Life: Reflections on Freud and Rosenzweig.* Chicago: The University of Chicago Press, 2001.

Schelling, F. W. J. *The Ages of the World.* Albany: SUNY Press, 2000.

———. *Ausgewählte Schriften.* 6 vols. Ed., M. Frank. Frankfurt: Suhrkamp 1985.

Scherman, Nosson, ed. and trans. *The Chumash,* ArtScroll Series. Brooklyn: Mesorah Publications, 1995.

Schmitt, Carl. *Political Theology: Four Chapters on the Concept of Sovereignty.* Trans., George Schwab. Chicago: The University of Chicago Press, 1985.

Schwartz, Regina Schwartz. *The Curse of Cain: The Violent Legacy of Monotheism.* Chicago: The University of Chicago Press, 1998.

Seccombe, D. P. *Possessions and the Poor in Luke-Acts.* Studien zum Neuen Testament und seiner Umwelt. Linz, 1982.

Seeskin, Kenneth. *Maimonides: A Guide for Today's Perplexed.* Springfield, N. J.: Behrman House, Inc., 1991.

———. *Maimonides on the Origin of the World.* Cambridge: Cambridge University Press, 2005.

Seeskin, Kenneth, ed. "Metaphysics and Its Transcendence" in *The Cambridge Companion to Maimonides.* Cambridge: Cambridge University Press, 2005.

Shanks, Andrew. *Against Innocence: An Introduction to Gillian Rose.* London: SCM, 2008.

Siker, Jeffrey S. "First to the Gentiles: A Literary Analysis of Luke 4:16–30." *Journal of Biblical Literature* 111/1 (1992): 73–90.

Sloan, Rober B. *The Favorable Year of the Lord: A Study of the Jubilary Theology in the Gospel of Luke.* Austin: Scholar Press, 1977.

Smith, Jonathan Z. *Drudgery Divine: On the Comparison of Early Christianities and the Religions of Late Antiquity.* Chicago: The University of Chicago Press, 1994.

Smith, Steven B. *Spinoza, Liberalism and the Question of Jewish Identity.* New Haven: Yale University Press, 1998.

Snow, Dale E. *Schelling and the End of Idealism.* Albany: SUNY Press, 1996.

Soloveitchik, Joseph B. "Confrontation." *Tradition: A Journal of Orthodox Thought* 6/2 (1964): 5ff. (http://www.bc.edu/research/cjl/meta-elements/texts/cjrelations/resources/articles/soloveitchik).

Soulen, Kendall. *The God of Israel and Christian Theology.* Minneapolis: Fortress Press, 1996.

———. "An Introduction to Michael Wyschogrod" in Michael Wyschogrod, *Abraham's Promise: Judaism and Jewish-Christian Relations.* Grand Rapids: Wm. B. Eerdmans Press, 2004.

Spinoza, Benedict de. *Ethics* in *The Essential Spinoza: Ethics and Related Writings.* Ed. Michael Morgan. Trans., Samuel Shirley. Indianapolis: Hackett Publishing Company, 2006.

———. *A Theologico-Political Treatise.* Trans., R. H. M. Elwes. New York: Dover Publications, Inc. 1951.

Stahmer, Harold. "Introduction" in *Judaism Despite Christianity: The 'Letters on Christianity and Judaism' between Eugen Rosenstock-Huessy and Franz Rosenzweig*. Ed., Eugen Rosenstock-Huessy. New York: Schocken Book, 1971.
———. "'Speech-Letters' and 'Speech-Thinking': Franz Rosenzweig and Eugen Rosenstock-Huessy." *Modern Judaism* 14 (1984): 57–81.
Stegemann, W. and L. Schottroff. *Jesus and the Hope of the Poor*. Trans., M. J. O'Connell. New York: Orbis Books, 1986.
Strauss, Leo. "How to Begin to Study the *Guide*" in Moses Maimonides, *The Guide of the Perplexed*. Trans., Shlomo Pines. Chicago: The University of Chicago Press, 1974.
———. *Persecution and the Art of Writing*. Chicago: The University of Chicago Press, 1952.
Taubes, Jacob. "The Issue Between Judaism and Christianity: Facing Up to the Unresolvable Difference." *Commentary Magazine* (1953): 525–33.
———. *The Political Theology of Paul*. Trans., Dana Hollander. Stanford: Stanford University Press, 2004.
———. "Theodicy and Theology: A Philosophical Analysis of Karl Barth's Dialectical Theology." *Journal of Religion* 34/4 (1954): 231–43.
Ticciati, Susannah. "Does Job Fear God for Naught?" *Modern Theology* 21 (2005): 353–66.
Tiede, David L. "Glory to the People Israel" in *Luke-Acts and the Jews: Conflict, Apology and Conciliation*. Ed., Robert L. Brawley. Atlanta: Society of Biblical Literature, 1988.
Tyson, Joseph, B., ed. *Luke-Acts and the Jewish People: Eight Critical Perspectives*. Minneapolis: Augsburg Fortress Press, 1988.
Von Balthasar, Hans Urs. *The Theology of Karl Barth*. Trans., John Drury. New York: Holt, Rinehart and Winston, 1971.
Von Rad, Gerhard. *From Genesis to Chronicles: Explorations in Old Testament Theology*. Minneapolis: Augsburg Fortress Press, 2005.
———. *Genesis: A Commentary*. Philadelphia: Westminster Press, 1972.
Weber, Max. "Social Psychology of the World's Religions" in Max Weber, *Essays in Sociology*. New York: Routledge, 2009.
Webster, John. *Karl Barth's Ethics of Reconciliation*. Cambridge: Cambridge University Press, 1995.
Weinfeld, M. "The Covenant of Grant in the Old Testament and in the Ancient Near East." *Journal of the American Oriental Society* 90 (1970): 184–203.
Westermann, Claus. *Genesis: A Continental Commentary*, 12–36. Minneapolis: Augsburg Fortress Press, 1995.
White, Alan. *Schelling: An Introduction to the System of Freedom*. New Haven: Yale University Press, 1983.
Whitehouse, W. A. "The Command of God the Creator: An Account of Karl Barth's Volume on Ethics." *Scottish Journal of Theology* 5 (1952): 337–54.
Wirth, Jason, M., ed. *Schelling Now: Contemporary Readings*. Bloomington: Indiana University Press, 2005.

Wolfson, Elliot. "From My Flesh I Would Behold God: Imaginal Representation and Inscripting Divine Justice, Preliminary Observations." *Journal of Scriptural Reasoning* 2 (2002). (http://etext.lib.virginia.edu/journals/ssr/issues/volume2/number3/ssr02-03-e01.html).

Wright, N. T. *Paul: In Fresh Perspective*. New York: Fortress Press, 2009.

Wyschogrod, Michael. "Why Was and Is the Theology of Karl Barth of Interest to a Jewish Theologian?" in *Footnotes to a Theology: The Karl Barth Colloquium of 1972*. Ed., Martin Rumscheidt. SR Supplements. Waterloo, Ont.: Canadian Corp. for Studies in Religion, 1974.

Žižek, Slavoj, Eric Santner, and Kenneth Reinhard. *The Neighbor: Three Inquiries in Political Theology*. Chicago: The University of Chicago Press, 2006.

INDEX

abiding, 101–42; Barth on, 246; circumcision and, 117–19; creation and, 103–8; law and, 199–201; Sabbatical year and, 128; Schelling on, 39–42
Abrahamic covenant, 108–19
abundance, logic of, 127
action, Rosenzweig on, 155–84
active emotions, Spinoza on, 82
actus purus, Schelling on, 32–37, 73
Agamben, Giorgio, 15–30, 277*n*20
Al-Gahazli, 64
All, Schelling on, 36
allies, Spinoza on, 85
Altmann, Alexander, 298*n*17, 300*n*32
analogical thought, Maimonides on, 248
anti-idolatry: metaphysically rooted claims, 51–56; nonmetaphysically rooted claims, 50–51
apocalyptic sectarianism, Ruether on, 140–41
apologetics: Barth on, 268–69; Christian, 136, 226–74; Jewish, possibility of, 90–94; nonpolemical, 210–16; Rosenzweig on, 205–8; self-consciousness and, 42; truth telling and, 204–25. *See also* Jewish-Christian relations
Aristotle, 53, 57–59, 61–64
Asad, Talal, 176–77, 181
Assman, Aleida, 232, 234
asylum, Foucault on, 167–68
atheism, law of, 145–55
Athens-Jerusalem divide: and Maimonides, 52, 57, 60–64; Rosenzweig on, 151

atonement, Barth on, 245
attribute, Spinoza on, 79
Augustine, Saint, 216, 307*n*55

Baeck, Leo, 209–10
Barth, Karl, 226–74; Taubes on, 227–38
Batnitzky, Leora, 306*n*48
Baum, Gregory, 217
belief, justification of, 205–8
Bible: on abiding, 101–42; Barth on, 226–74; Jewish-Christian learning and, 223–24; on persons, 190; Spinoza on, 77–89; on theology of history, 135
Biblical citations: 1 Corinthians 7:29–32, 15; 2 Corinthians 3:14, 23; Deuteronomy, 25, 87, 108, 119–20, 128, 246; Exodus 19:17, 120; Ezekiel 16:60, 51; Ezra, 48–49, 138–39, 293*n*33; Galatians 1:15, 16; Genesis, 106–7, 110–14; Hosea, 50, 123; Isaiah, 103, 135–42, 223–24; Jeremiah 32:17, 104; Job, 66, 118–19, 247–67; John 15:16, 269; Leviticus 25, 125–26, 131–33, 282*n*11; Luke, 127, 142, 223–24; Mark 10:17–31, 242–43; Psalms, 104, 124, 129; Romans 8, 234–35
bio-power, Foucault on, 169
Blenkinsopp, Joseph, 293*n*33
blessedness, Spinoza on, 93
Brod, Max, 209–10
Buber, Martin, 146–47, 229, 297*n*6
Butler, Judith, 301*n*61

carnal Israel, Spinoza on, 77, 83–86
Cassirer, Ernst, 299n22
causal knowledge, Spinoza on, 80
Chazan, Robert, 307n56
Christ: Barth on, 243, 246–48, 259–63; Rosenstock-Huessy on, 11, 275n3
Christian, term, 268–69
Christian apologetics, 136, 226–74; law and, 271–74. *See also* Jewish-Christian relations
circumcision, 111–14; and abiding, 117–19; semiotics of, 115–19
Cohen, Hermann, 146, 287n2, 300n33
collective action, Spinoza on, 83–84, 92
command, divine, 192–95; Barth on, 239–43; and freedom and law, 195–204; Rosenzweig on, 154
communication: and apologetics, 272–73; Job on, 251–52, 258; Rosenstock-Huessy on, 10–11, 275n3
community: of believers, 200, 215; of learning, 191
conatus, Spinoza on, 81, 84, 91–92
confinement, house of, Foucault on, 166–67
Connolly, William, 278n28
contingency: Maimonides on, 60–64, 69; Spinoza on, 79
control: Foucault on, 166–69; versus power, 176
covenant: Abrahamic, 108–19; Agamben on, 22; life under, 201; Schwartz on, 46; Sinaitic, 119–25; Spinoza on, 86–89
creation: and abiding, 103–8; *de novo*, 58; *ex nihilo*, 57–58, 64–65; Maimonides on, 56–68; Rosenzweig on, 162–64; Schelling on, 34–35
Curley, Edwin, 248–50

delayed effect, Seeskin on, 62
democracy, Spinoza on, 84, 88
Derrida, Jacques, 21, 115, 293n36, 304n15
desire: and knowledge, 173–74; Novak on, 96–98; Rose on, 94–96; Rosenzweig on, 190–92; Spinoza on, 77–91. *See also* dialectic of desire

dialectical theology, Taubes on, 235–38
dialectic of desire, 27, 76–98, 143–44; Foucault on, 170; and freedom and law, 200–1
dialog: of doubt, 117–19; of gift/prayer, 115–17
diasporic Judaism, Spinoza on, 89
divine command, 192–95; Barth on, 239–43; and freedom and law, 195–204; Rosenzweig on, 154
divine difference, Schelling on, 71–72
divine freedom, 9–42; Barth on, 238–74; and desire, 174; dialectic of desire and, 143–44; and human persons, 187–225; Job on, 253–56; Maimonides on, 57, 63, 66; Rosenzweig on, 31–39, 155–84; Schelling on, 31–39, 72–73; and sin, 131–35; Taubes on, 227–38; Von Rad on, 104–5
divine image, 282n21; Novak on, 105–6
divine judgment, 131–35; Barth on, 242, 245
divine life, aspects of, 32
divine mercy, Maimonides on, 105
divine unity, Maimonides on, 68–75
doubt: dialog of, 117–19; Job on, 255–56

economics, 127, 133
Eisen, Robert, 312n48, 312n51, 312n56
election: Agamben on, 25–26; Barth on, 243; Job on, 255–56; logic of law and, 179–80; *versus* persuasion, 272; precautions on, 187; Rosenstock-Huessy on, 12; Rosenzweig on, 146–49; Taubes on, 237; Von Rad on, 103. *See also* exceptionalism
elective monotheism, 54
emotions, Spinoza on, 81–82
emunah, 22, 229
enemies, Spinoza on, 85
enmity, 212–14; Job on, 256; Taubes on, 232–34
error, idolatry as, 51–53
essence: Maimonides on, 59, 61–64; Rosenzweig on, 156–57, 163; Spinoza on, 79

essentialism, Rosenzweig on, 156, 162
estate, Agamben on, 17
evil, 215–16, 250–51
exceptionalism, 2; Agamben on, 16–30; Barth on, 241, 260; Foucault on, 166–70; logic of, 2, 7–98; Maimonides on, 56–68; modern Judaism on, 76–98; monotheism and, 43–75; Schwartz on, 45–49; Taubes on, 26–30; world view of, 14–16; Wyschogrod on, 218. *See also* election
exile, Gregory on, 137–38
existence: Maimonides on, 59, 61–64; Rosenzweig on, 152–55; Schelling on, 33; Spinoza on, 79
existential freedom, Barth on, 244–46
extension, Spinoza on, 80
exteriority: admitting, 208–10; and freedom, 213–14; Rosenzweig on, 206–7; Taubes on, 230–31

faith: Agamben on, 22–23; Buber on, 229; *versus* works, 108–9
falsehood, Barth on, 266–67
fear, Rosenstock-Huessy on, 10–11
Feuerbach, Ludwig, 147–50, 152, 165, 297*n*6
Fischer, George, 130
Foucault, Michel, 165–71
Franks, Paul, 150, 152, 297*n*6
freedom: and apologetics, 272–73; Barth on, 262, 265, 272–73; and exteriority, 213–14; Jubilee year and, 133; and law, 187–225; *versus* polemical thinking, 209–10; Rosenzweig on, 155–84; Sabbatical year and, 125–42; Taubes on, 236–37; theology of, Bible on, 101–42. *See also* divine freedom
Freud, Sigmund, 281*n*1

Gager, Paul, 23, 229
Geertz, Clifford, 176–77, 181
genealogy: Foucault on, 170–71; Smith on, 303*n*74
Gibbs, Robert, 300*n*33

gift, 304*n*16; dialog of, 115–17; and law, 196; Rosenzweig on, 197
God: Being of, Schelling on, 34; beyond Being, Maimonides on, 68–75; revelatory, 188–89; Spinoza on, 78–83; unknown, 70, 160. *See also under* divine
Goethe, J. W. von, 277*n*17
Goetschel, Willi, 282*n*3, 306*n*37
Gordon, Peter, 299*n*22
Gospel, Barth on, 226–74
grace: Agamben on, 16, 21–26; law of, 198–201; normativity of, 119–25; Rose on, 96, 174
Greek influence: and Maimonides, 52, 57, 60–64; Rosenzweig on, 151
Gregory, Bradley C., 135–38, 141–42

Habermas, Jürgen, 28, 278*n*46
HaChaim, Or, 116
halakha, 113, 121; as sign of covenant, 113–14; Taubes on, 233; and wisdom, 129. *See also* law
halakhic life, 122–24, 202–3
Halbertal, Moshe, 49–56
Hanson, Paul, 135, 141–42
healthy human understanding, Rosenzweig on, 157
Hegel, G. W. F., 147, 150, 194, 236, 298*n*15
Heidegger, Martin, 299*n*22
Hendry, George S., 314*n*98
heresy, Taubes on, 228–35
Heschel, Abraham Joshua, 222, 253–54
Heschel, Susannah, 222
history: Agamben on, 19–20; biblical theology of, 135; Foucault on, 170; intellectual, Rosenzweig on, 149–52; and Jewish-Christian relations, 221–22; Rosenzweig on, 154; and witness, 215
Holocaust, 109; and Jewish-Christian relations, 216–20
humanism, 210–11
human persons, 106; Barth on, 242–43; failings of, divine judgment and, 131–35; Heschel on, 253–54; order

330   Index

and, 187–95; revelation and, 189–92; Spinoza on, 80–83, 91

idealism, 300n32; Rosenzweig on, 158
identity, enmity and, 213
idolatry: as error, 51–53; metaphysically rooted claims, 51–56; nonmetaphysically rooted claims, 50–51
image, divine, 282n21; Novak on, 105–6
intellectual history, Rosenzweig on, 149–52
intellectual life, Maimonides on, 285n66
intolerance, monotheism and, 49–56
intuition: Rosenzweig on, 160; Spinoza on, 80–81
Islam, 63
Israel: and problem of sin, 131–35; restoration of, 135–42. *See also* Judaism

Jaffee, Martin, 43, 54–56
James, William, 173–74, 302n65
Jesus. *See* Christ
Jewish apologetics, possibility of, 90–94
Jewish-Christian relations, 9; Agamben and, 17; Barth and, 274; enmity and, 212–14; fear of syncretism and, 214–15; after Holocaust, 216–20; learning, 216–25; Luther and, 109–10; New Thinking and, 178–84; punishment theology and, 109; Rosenstock-Huessy and, 11–12; Taubes on, 231–34; tolerance and, 211–12. *See also* apologetics
Jewish law, Taubes on, 27
Jewish learning, Rosenzweig on, 191, 200
Jewish people theology, Rosenzweig on, 147–48
Job, 247–58; Abraham and, 118–19; Barth on, 258–67; Maimonides on, 66
Johannine age, 10, 14, 152, 276n4, 277n17, 298n17
Jubilee year, 125, 223–24; announcement of, and Yom Kippur, 131–32; and restoration of Israel, 135–42
Judaism: and anti-idolatry, 50–51; logic of sacrifice and, 29; modern, on law and exceptionalism, 76–98; nonteleological, 201–4; Rosenstock-Huessy on, 12; Schwartz on, 45–49; Spinoza on, 86–89, 93–94; and supersessionism, 303n72; Taubes on, 230–32; and tolerance, 211; and wisdom, 246–47, 251. *See also* Israel
judgment, divine, 131–35; Barth on, 242
justice: Agamben on, 21–23; Spinoza on, 77–85
justification: Barth on, 244–46; of belief, 205–8; in law, 108–19, 187–225; Luther on, 26
Justin Martyr, 216, 307n54

Kavka, Martin, 194–95, 198, 286n66
Kessler, Edward, 308n58
King, Martin Luther Jr., 222
kinship, Schwartz on, 48–49
knowledge: Barth on, 259, 263; Christian, 269; and Jewish-Christian relations, 178–79; Job on, 251–52; Nietzsche on, 166; polemical, ills of, 164–69; recovering, 169–77; Rosenzweig on, 39–40; Schelling on, 38–40; Spinoza on, 80–81. *See also* wisdom
Kreisel, Haim, 66–67

lack, Derrida on, 21
land: Schwartz on, 47–48; Sommer on, 137
language. *See* communication
Lavater, J. C., 308n57
law: Agamben on, 21–26; of atheism, 145–55; Barth on, 226–74; and Christian apologetics, 271–74; freedom and, 187–225; of grace, 198–201; Job and, 247–58; justification in, 108–19, 187–225; Luther on, 109; Maimonides on, 250; modern Judaism on, 76–98; natural, Novak on, 96–98, 182–83; nonrevelatory account of, limits of, 89–94; and pragmatism, 173; Rose on, 94–96; Sabbatical year and, 125–42; Schmitt on, 21; Spinoza on, 77–91; Taubes on, 27; theology of, Bible on,

101–42; wisdom and, 114. *See also* *halakha*; logic of law
learning: community of, 191; Jewish, 191, 200; Jewish-Christian, 216–25; Job on, 257
Lenin, V. I., 106, 291*n*12
Lessing, G. E., 211
Levene, Nancy, 282*n*5
Levenson, Jon, 87, 120–21, 123–24, 129, 291*n*1
Levinas, Emanuel, 250–51
life, divine, aspects of, 32
Lindsay, Mark R., 311*n*38
liturgy: Jewish-Christian learning and, 224–25; Job on, 258; logic of law and, 203–4; Sabbatical year and, 128–31
logic of exceptionalism, 2, 7–98
logic of law, 99–184; Barth on, 263, 268; desire and, 171–77; and election, 179–80; and Judaism, 201–4; philosophical account of, 143–84; Schelling and, 31–39
logic of sacrifice, 9–42; Agamben on, 24–25; alternatives to, 30–42; Barth on, 263; exceptionalism and, 18–19; and Jewish philosophy, 29; Maimonides on, 56; negative effects of, 14; reductionism and, 19; Rosenstock-Huessy on, 10–14
Logos: Barth on, 260, 262; Rosenstock-Huessy on, 11
Lohfink, Norberth, 130
love: Barth on, 242–44, 265; divine command and, 196–97; divine versus human, 198–99; and freedom, 192; Rosenzweig on, 190–91; Schelling on, 36–37; Taubes on, 234, 236–37
loyalty, Agamben on, 22
Luther, Martin, 26, 108–10

Maimonides, Moses, 56–68, 105–6, 284*n*41; Halbertal and Margalit on, 51–54; on intellectual life, 285*n*66; on Job, 247–50; Pines on, 64–68; on Sabbatical year, 125; Seeskin on, 57–64

Mamre, 115–16
Mangina, Joseph, 243–44
Margalit, A., 49–56
Marx, Karl, 17, 106, 291*n*11
materiality: Job on, 250; Jubilee year and, 133; Rose on, 94–96; Rosenzweig on, 191
Mendelssohn, Moses, 305*n*36, 308*n*57
Mendes-Flohr, Paul, 276*n*10
mercy, divine, Maimonides on, 105
messianism: Agamben on, 15–17, 19–23; Ruether on, 139–40; Taubes on, 26, 228, 230–31
Middle Ages, and tolerance, 211
Miller, Patrick, 130
mind, Spinoza on, 80
modernity, and tolerance, 211
monarchy, Spinoza on, 84, 88
monotheism: and exceptionalism, 43–75; Freud on, 281*n*1; Jaffee on, 54; Schwartz on, 45–49
monstrous actuality, Rosenzweig on, 206
Morgan, Michael, 150, 152, 297*n*6
Moses, 229–30
mourning, Rose on, 94–96
multiculturalism, 183
Murphy, Roland E., 293*n*34
Mutakallimūn, 63–64, 285*n*50

natural law, Novak on, 96–98, 182–83
naturalism, Rosenstock-Huessy on, 10–11
nature: Schelling on, 37; Spinoza on, 79
necessity: Maimonides on, 57; Schelling on, 33–35
negative deduction: and persons, 189; Rosenzweig on, 159
negative theology: Maimonides and, 63, 65, 69–70; Schelling and, 70
Negri, Antonio, 277*n*20
neighbor, love of: Rosenzweig on, 193–95; Spinoza on, 92; witness and, 273
Nemo, Phillip, 251
New Thinking, 143–84; term, 145
Nietzsche, Friedrich, 28–29, 166
nonsupersessionism, 178–84

Novak, David, 96–98, 182–83, 215, 217, 219–20; and Barth, 227; on image of God, 105–6, 117–18; on punishment, 134–35; on Spinoza, 287n2; on supersessionism, 303n72

oaths, Agamben on, 22
obedience, Gregory on, 139
Ochs, Peter, 309n70
order: Barth on, 265; and persons, 187–95; Rosenzweig on, 162–64; Sabbatical year and, 125–28; Schelling on, 32; wisdom and, 143–84
Other: God as, Rosenzweig on, 158–62; Schwartz on, 45–46
outbidding, 10–16; Rosenzweig on, 151; Taubes on, 13, 27, 229–30, 232

paganism, 179–80; Rosenstock-Huessy on, 11
pain, Spinoza on, 81–82
particularity, 89–90
passive emotions, Spinoza on, 82
Paul, Saint: Agamben on, 16–30; exceptionalist readings of, 15; Luther on, 109; Taubes on, 26–30, 228–32, 234–35
Pawlikowski, John, 217
peace. *See* rest
persons. *See* human persons
Pharasaic inclusivity, Ruether on, 140
philosopher, Spinoza on, 90–94
Pines, Shlomo, 57, 64–68, 285n50
pistis, 22, 229
Plato, 57–58, 60–61, 284n41
pleasure, Spinoza on, 81–82
pluralism, 181
Pöggeler, Otto, 298n15
polemical knowledge, ills of, 164–69
polemical thinking, 214; drawbacks of, 209–10
power: *versus* control, 176; Foucault on, 169; Geertz on, 177; law and, 175–76; recovering, 169–77; Rosenzweig on, 155–84
pragmatism, lawful, 173

prayer: dialog of, 115–17; Job on, 258
problem solving, parallel, 221–22
proclamation. *See* witness
promissory covenant, 111–12
prophetic sectarianism, Ruether on, 139–40
providence: Maimonides on, 248; Rosenzweig on, 162–64
punishment theology, 109–10, 112, 117, 131–35; Maimonides on, 249

Rashi, 125–27, 132
Rausch, William, 278n28
Rawls, John, 182–83
reason: and apologetics, 206–7; Novak on, 182; Spinoza on, 80, 83, 90–94
redemption, Von Rad on, 103–8
reductionism, Agamben on, 18–20, 23
reflection, Sabbatical year and, 128, 130
relativism, 215–16
religion: Asad on, 176–77; Spinoza on, 85–86
religious materialism, Rosenzweig on, 191
remnant: Agamben on, 18; Ruether on, 140–41. *See also* abiding
rest: Barth on, 244–46; Job on, 251–52, 258; Schelling on, 36, 40, 74; Von Rad on, 106–7. *See also* Sabbath; Sabbatical year
restoration: Gregory on, 137–38; of Israel, 135–42
revelation: Barth on, 270; God and, 188–89; Jaffee on, 55; Judaism and, 251; and law, 199–201; Novak on, 117–18, 182; as orientation, 145–55; and persons, 189–92; Rosenstock-Huessy on, 11–12, 31–32; Rosenzweig on, 40–41, 150, 152–84; Schelling on, 31–32, 35–38, 153; Spinoza on, 77, 282n5
reward. *See* punishment theology
Rose, Gillian, 94–96, 174
Rosenstock-Huessy, Eugene, 9–14, 30, 178
Rosenzweig, Franz, 9–10, 39–41, 178, 188–92; on admission, 209; on apologetic thinking, 205–8; on divine

command, 192–95; on divine freedom, 31–39; on enmity, 212–14; on love, 197; on New Thinking, 143–84; on revelatory law, 199–201; on tolerance, 211–12
Rosh Hashanah, 133
Royal Grant model, 112
Rubenstein, Richard, 109, 131, 292n23
Ruether, Rosemary Radford, 139–41, 217

Sabbath, 106–7
Sabbatical year, 125–42; and liturgy, 128–31; as sign of order, 125–28
sacrifice: of Abraham, 13, 30–31; Rosenzweig on, 146–49; Schelling on, 39–42; Taubes on, 234. *See also* logic of sacrifice
sanctification, Barth on, 245–46
Sanders, E. P., 229
scarcity, metaphysics of, Schwartz on, 46–47
Schelling, F. W. J., 10, 30–39, 69–74, 145, 153, 286n81; influence of, 276n4, 279n51, 297n2, 299n22
Schmitt, Carl, 21, 28, 230, 232, 279n47
Schwartz, Regina, 43, 45–49, 113
Scripture. *See under* Bible
sectarianism, Ruether on, 139–41
secularism: Geertz on, 181; Rosenzweig on, 151–52
Seeskin, Kenneth, 57–64, 69–70, 284n40, 284n41
self-consciousness, 286n81; and apologetics, 42; Christianity and, 272–73; Sabbatical year and, 128; Schelling on, 38–40
sick human understanding, 157, 165–66; Foucault on, 166–67
sin, problem of, 131–35
Sinaitic covenant, 119–25
skepticism, 191, 283n28
Smith, Jonathan Z., 181, 303n74
Snow, Dale E., 297n2
society, Spinoza on, 78
Sodom, punishment of, 110, 117–19
Soloveitchik, Joseph, 217, 219
Sommer, Benjamin, 137

Soulen, Kendall, 180–81, 217–18, 223
sovereignty: Agamben on, 21–26; dialectic of desire and, 143; Schmitt on, 21; Spinoza on, 84, 87
speech. *See* communication
Spinoza, Baruch, 77–89, 106, 289n19; critique of, 89–94; Levene on, 282n5; Novak on, 287n2; Rosenzweig and, 192
spirit, Schelling on, 35, 37
Stahmer, Harold, 275n1, 275n3
state, Spinoza on, 83–86, 91–92
Stendhal, Krister, 229
Strauss, Leo, 282n4, 284n30
substance, Spinoza on, 78
supersessionism, 23, 178, 303n72
syncretism, fear of, 214–15

Taubes, Jacob, 13, 15, 151; on Barth, 227–38, 245; on exceptionalism, 26–30
technology, Foucault on, 169
testimony. *See* witness
theology: Barth on, 227–38; Jewish-Christian learning and, 222–23; term, 207
thought, Spinoza on, 80
Ticciati, Susannah, 254–56
time: Agamben on, 19–20; Rosenstock-Huessy on, 11
tolerance, 211–12; Mendelssohn on, 305n36; Taubes on, 233
tragic self, Rosenzweig on, 189–90
trust, Agamben on, 22–24
truth: and apologetics, 204–25; Barth on, 246–67; holding versus telling, 209; James on, 173; logic of law and, 173–74; recovering, 172–73; Rosenzweig on, 39; Schelling on, 39
truth-claims, defensible, 205

understanding, healthy versus sick, 157, 165–66
unity of God, Maimonides on, 68–75

Von Rad, G., 103–8

war, Foucault on, 169
Wenborn, Neil, 308*n*58
White, Alan, 280*n*55, 280*n*60
will: Maimonides on, 64, 66, 74–75; Schelling on, 73–74
wisdom: Barth on, 259, 263–64; Christian, 269; *halakha* and, 114, 129; Job and, 247–58; Judaism and, 246–47, 251; law and, 114, 175; Maimonides on, 64, 66, 74–75, 250; order and, 143–84; Rosenzweig on, 154, 161–62, 164–84; Sabbatical year and, 125–42; Schelling on, 32, 37–39, 73–74; theology of, 129–30
witness: Agamben on, 25; Barth on, 246–71; history and, 215; justified through law, 204–10; law and, 198–99; and love of neighbor, 273; Rosenzweig on, 154–55
Wolfson, Eliot, 116
Word (Logos): Barth on, 260, 262; Rosenstock-Huessy on, 11
Wright, G. Ernest, 121
Wright, N. T., 23
wrong actions, Halbertal and Margalit on, 53–56
Wyschogrod, Michael, 180–81, 217–18, 222–23, 227

Yom Kippur, 131–32, 134
Yovel, 132–34

Zevi, Sabbatei, 228
Žižek, Slavoj, 15